September 2007

To Helen,

With many thanks for your interest in + support of my work, and with deep admiration for your ability to stand strong + keep singing in the face of tribulation.

Your UU Sister
on The Journey,

Jessamyn Neuhaus

MANLY MEALS

AND

Mom's Home Cooking

THE JOHNS HOPKINS UNIVERSITY PRESS

MANLY MEALS

AND

Mom's Home Cooking

COOKBOOKS
AND GENDER
IN MODERN
AMERICA

Jessamyn
Neuhaus

The Johns Hopkins University Press

Baltimore and London

The Johns Hopkins University Press
2715 North Charles Street
Baltimore, Maryland 21218-4363
www.press.jhu.edu

Library of Congress Cataloging-in-Publication Data
Neuhaus, Jessamyn.
Manly meals and mom's home cooking : cookbooks and gender in
modern America / Jessamyn Neuhaus.
p. cm.
Includes bibliographical references and index.
ISBN 0-8018-7125-5 (hardcover)
1. Cookery. I. Title.
TX714 .N52 2003
641.5—dc21
2002006465

A catalog record for this book is available from the British Library.

Contents

Conclusion
From Julia Child to Cooking.com
261

Acknowledgments

I would like to thank a number of colleagues who provided assistance with this work. Kelly Austin, Elazar Barkan, Kelly Douglass, Erika Endrijonnas, James Gilbert, Barbara Heber, Michelle Ladd, Harvey Levenstein, Jan Bluestein Longone, Kathy Peiss, and Shasta Turner proofread, offered suggestions, listened to paper presentations, and responded to questions, phone calls, and emails with the utmost attention. This project greatly benefited from their insights. Robert Dawidoff's close questioning about my theoretical framework considerably improved the final product. Special thanks to Janet Brodie for her careful reading of early drafts and for her gracious, rigorous, mentoring. I would also like to thank the anonymous reviewer at Johns Hopkins University Press, copyeditor Brian R. MacDonald, and senior acquisitions editor Bob Brugger for their helpful suggestions concerning structure, content, illustrations, and citations.

Kathie Bordelon, the archivist at McNeese State University, provided me with several important documents essential to my work on Maude Reid's World War II scrapbook-cookbook. She also helped me locate an excellent photo of Reid. Dan Nelson and Lisa Buchinger Aldrich shared their family cooking memories with me and substantially enriched my understanding of how individuals use and interpret recipes. Jennie German shared original research and an amazing historical document with me—an act of generosity all too rare in the academic world. I particularly want to thank Peg Bracken, who allowed me access to her fan mail and who is every bit as delightful in person as she is on the page.

I am deeply grateful for the family members who cheered me on during this project, especially my sister and best friend Alison Rash. I am especially indebted to Alison for her meticulous proofreading. I also want to thank my brother-in-law Jason Rash, my aunt Anna Carnathan, and my in-laws Bill and Irene Butdorf and Liz and Rich Mang for assistance with the illustrations, for the words of encouragement, and for the flowers. I could not have completed my research without the hospitality of my grandparents, Phil and Alison Payne. They eased my twelve-hour days at the Library of Congress immensely with their affection, humor, and flattering interest in this project. I owe a special debt to my grandmother, who pampered me with body-and-soul-restoring dinners throughout my stays. My aunt Dana T. Payne made several trips to the Library of Congress in order to help me procure the illustrations for this book: thank you, Tia!

My parents, Dr. John Neuhaus and A. Lori Neuhaus, sent me cookbooks, secondary sources, anecdotes, and newspaper articles and did more proofreading than any parent should ever have to do. They also provided my infant son with a month of outstanding childcare during the final revisions of this project. Their belief in education, their belief in family dinners, and their belief in me have very much shaped my life and this book for the better, and I give them my most heartfelt thanks.

Lastly, I must thank my husband and fellow hang-glider Douglas Butdorf. I could ask for no better cooking, dining, travel, parenting, and life partner than Douglas. Without his support, in more ways than I can name, I could not have completed this work.

I dedicate this book to Solomon William Neuhaus, born January 11, 2001. I hope that by the time he is old enough to wield a frying pan there will be nothing unusual or remarkable about "a man in the kitchen."

MANLY MEALS

AND

Mom's Home Cooking

Introduction
"The Purpose of a Cookery Book"

> *The purpose of a cookery book is one and unmistakable. Its object can conceivably be no other than to increase the happiness of mankind.*
>
> —*Joseph Conrad*

Joseph Conrad's simple faith notwithstanding, cookbooks serve numerous and sometimes obscure purposes. By publishing cookbooks, churches and community groups raise funds; food-processing companies and kitchen appliance manufacturers promote their products; health advocates instruct readers on the nutritional benefits of a particular food regimen; celebrities and chefs foster their personal popularity; and traditionalists help preserve their cultural, ethnic, or family heritage. As historical documents—supplying information about the publishing practices, available ingredients, food fashions, or household technology of the past—cookbooks reveal much about the societies that produce them. Moreover, the purpose of a recipe collection may not be "unmistakable." Cookbooks contain more than directions for food preparation. Authors often infuse their pages with instructions on the best way to live one's life—how to shop, lose weight, feed children, combat depression, protect the environment, expand one's horizons, and make a house a home. Cookbooks thus reveal the recipes for living created by authors, editors, cookery experts, and corporations in the past. They show how foods, food preparation, kitchen labor, gender, class, and race have intersected in the United States.

Cookbooks most vividly demonstrate the way that food preparation and gender seem hopelessly intertwined. Although the majority of married American women with children work outside the home, many continue to assume responsibility for meal planning and preparation. "Mom's home cooking" still holds an important place in American culture and our daily lives.[1] The tenacious link between women and cooking invites close examination of American commercial cookbooks (those published for profit rather than for fund-raising purposes or self-published) from the early through the mid twentieth century. What kind of prescriptive rhetoric, if any, did cookbooks offer? How might they have played a role in creating and maintaining the persistent notion that women must assume responsibility for daily food preparation? What specific responsibilities, according to their authors and editors, did women have in the kitchen? How did cookbooks depict men in relation to food, eating, and food preparation? Did authors and publishers pay attention to the class or ethnicity of their prospective audience? What changed, and how do we explain it?

Not surprisingly, cookbooks in the twentieth century to a considerable degree mirror the history of middle-class life at the time. With roots firmly planted in the scientific cookery tradition of the nineteenth century, the modern commercial cookbook reflected both the widespread move away from employed cooks and servants in the middle-class home and, after about 1920, changes in kitchen technology and food processing. The cookbook industry—and the nation's ideas about domesticity and gender—naturally followed the rise of consumerism and a newly energized domestic ideology aimed at middle-class homemakers.[2] General cookbooks in the 1920s and 1930s increasingly represented cooking as an artistic outlet for dutiful middle-class housewives. Authors sought to redefine cooking as an important and pleasurable part of the modern woman's domestic duties—a signal feature of white middle-class womanhood. Even while social and technological changes dramatically altered the middle-class American home, cookbooks bore evidence of how many Americans continued to believe that a woman's primary responsibility should be her home. Cookbooks echoed a national debate about women's social roles in general and represented particular kinds of food and cooking as gendered. They helped to reinforce the notion that women had inherently domestic natures.

But how did Americans read and interpret cookbooks and their prescriptive messages about gender, domesticity, and the traditional? Unlike many other domestic chores, cooking offers opportunity for creative expression, for experimentation, and public and private appreciation. It can be a heartfelt expression of love and care, a sensual, deeply rewarding experience. Pride in good home cooking and the cooking process itself certainly afforded much pleasure to many Americans throughout the twentieth century. At the same time, cooking the family's daily meals must also be characterized as a time-consuming, repetitive feature of daily home life. Cooking requires constant planning, shopping, and clean up. For those people living in poverty, cooking meals can mean reckoning with deprivation, not creative opportunity. Cooking must be understood as domestic labor as well as a pleasurable activity. Do cookbooks reflect these facts? Does reading cookbooks lead to any meaningful insights about how people really felt about cooking or how they cooked?

There is no simple way to assess the role cookbooks might have played in society. They might demonstrate what people ate; they can as easily portray what people wished they could eat. Community cookbooks, at the least, give recipes that real women (and occasionally men) themselves had created, or at least tried once.[3] Commercial cookbooks, on the other hand, function at a fascinating but murky intersection between the public forces of marketing and publishing and the private lives of those who purchase cookbooks. How can historians know if individual women and men actually *used* the cookbooks that they purchased? Their function in individual homes may differ as much as the individual owners themselves, as the ephemera that one occasionally finds in them (notes recorded in the margins, recipes written on slips of paper, or clippings stuck between pages) testify. Only those in the kitchen can really say how someone read and interpreted a recipe.[4]

This problem of readership faces anyone interested in cookbooks as historical documents. Studying popular texts such as cookbooks, sex manuals, guides to etiquette, women's magazines, and the like may show how various authorities instructed their readership to behave or tried to persuade women and men what to value, but it cannot account for what people actually did. Feminists have criticized such work, sometimes termed the "history of social ideas," for emphasizing gender *norms* rather than the ways individual people might have resisted or complied with those norms. Other historians assert that a study of prescriptive literature can offer only a partial and often misleading view into the society that produced it.

Those studying prescriptive literature address this problem in different ways. Some believe that the advice and instructions found in prescriptive literature such as sex manuals must undoubtedly influence readers' behavior. Many others, however, argue that, although we may not be able to delineate a precise cause-and-effect relationship between readers and prescriptive literature, historical investigations of popular sources such as cookbooks and etiquette manuals reveal important things about American society and culture. Popular texts warrant close examination because they enable us to reconstruct the norms, visual images, and received truths that encased and thus could not help but influence daily lives.[5]

We cannot assume that the authors or editors of cookbooks always directly influenced readers' ideas and behavior, but we can explore in detail how particular books presented images of gender. We can begin to understand the connections that producers of cookbooks in the early to mid twentieth century—a wide range of editors, authors, cooks, consumer analysts, and marketers—made between cooking and gender. As a reflection of publishing policies, advertising needs, and popular demand in a particular era, cookbooks offer evidence about national trends, desires, and anxieties. They tell us less about the real, lived experience of women in the kitchen than about how cookbook producers imagined the ideal, "normal" American home and the roles that men and women would play within it. They tell us less about the diverse number of readers who may have consulted commercial cookbooks than about the homogenized cuisine advocated by publishers and manufacturers—an ideology of culinary assimilation that hearkened back to the nineteenth century.[6] Authors, magazine writers, corporate recipe creators, and advertisers produced cookbooks read by a variety of people for a variety of reasons. But the recipes, language, and illustrations in these books reiterated a powerful set of social norms. Throughout the modern era, cookbooks uniformly advocated very specific gender roles: via the medium of food preparation, they joined a much larger chorus of experts and pundits who insisted that, despite the many changes facing American society in the twentieth century, families could continue to depend on mom's home cooking.

PART ONE
"A Most Enchanting Occupation"

COOKBOOKS

IN EARLY AND

MODERN AMERICA,

1796–1941

1

From Family Receipts to Fannie Farmer

COOKBOOKS IN THE

UNITED STATES, 1796–1920

Recipes reflect the society that produces them. To Patrice Storace, a cookbook collector, "Every cookbook, more or less consciously, is a work of social history."[1] Everything from the discovery of vitamins to the urbanization of the nation to the rise and fall and resurrection of the chafing dish may be traced in their pages. But American cookbooks also have their own history. Their evolution from the earliest colonial cookery manuscripts to today's celebrity "chefbooks" tells an unfolding story of technology, ideology, and necessity. English cooking traditions exercised almost exclusive influence over early American cookbooks, until the rise of domestic ideology in the first half of the nineteenth century began to shape the genre. Both, however, were superseded by the cookery school movement in the post–Civil War era, which was to leave the most indelible mark on American cookbooks in the nineteenth century.

Of course, instructional cooking texts existed long before the publication of the first American cookbook in 1796. Indeed, cookbooks number among the earliest printed texts. Culinary historians cite *De Re Coquinaria*, or *The Art of Cooking*, authored by Marcus Gavius Apicius and dating from the first century C.E., as the West's oldest surviving cookbook. The master cooks for King Richard II compiled the first known cookery manuscript written in English—*Forme of Cury (Art of Cooking)*—around 1390. Written instructions in the fourteenth and fifteenth centuries came from other royal chefs or from noble households.[2] These bore little resemblance to what we know as cookbooks today. Writing them out by hand, professional chefs composed and used such manuals, which include not detailed recipes but rather suggestions that assumed extensive cookery knowledge on the part of the reader. The authors of these rare documents did not in any way intend them for a general reading audience.

The first cookbook printed in English appeared in 1500, and, like earlier handwritten manuscripts, *This Is the Boke of Cokery* addressed the culinary concerns of noble households. Other English household manuals published in the sixteenth and seventeenth centuries, such as *The Good Huswifes Jewell* (1585) and *The English Hus-Wife* (1615), seem also to have been aimed at the gentry or nobility, though claiming to address "the housewife." These early cookbooks offered recipes and a wide variety of other housekeeping information, from medical remedies to instructions on dairy keeping to hints on brewing beer. Professional cooks continued to author instruction manuals addressed to other court cooks during this time as well.[3] In North American colonial society, however, such books remained rare until the 1700s. Women in the American colonies during the seventeenth century may have occasionally exchanged handwritten "receipts" (as in "received rules of cookery"), but they more likely handed down recipes to the girls in the family by word of mouth.[4] A colonial woman would receive instructions in cooking from her mother and other women in the household and later might be advised by friends and neighbors. As Waldo Lincoln, bibliographer of early American cookbooks, writes: "When one considers the numerous almanacs, juveniles and other early imprints of little literary merit which have come down to us in tatters and fragments defying identification, one is forced to the conclusion that few if any books on cookery were imported and that American housewives relied on manuscript recipes and memory."[5] One reason for this absence lies in the nature of cooking itself during this period. Cooking in the very earliest colonial settlements and on the frontier demanded hard, dangerous, and dirty daily work and might accurately be described as a "cuisine of survival." For the first colonists, simply gathering, growing, shooting, and preserving enough food for sustenance, along with collecting enough firewood and water for cooking the food, demanded almost continuous labor—from both men and women—and the niceties of cooking could not be cultivated.[6]

Fireplaces, footed pots and pans, swinging cranes over the fire, and other cooking implements eased some of these earliest difficulties. Fireplaces, though seemingly crude to an observer from the twenty-first century, in fact offered far more flexibility in heat control than open fires. Such cooking facilities, along with access to a variety of vegetables, meats, and seafood and delicacies such as capers and olives in the more settled parts of the colonies, enabled cooks to hone a wider range of culinary skills.[7] The women perfecting these skills did so in the capacity of both servant and mistress. During this period, many households employed some kind of outside assistance for domestic work like cooking. Beginning in 1619, indentured servants and slaves arrived in the colonies, and many assumed cooking duties in individual homes. But most mistresses did more than merely supervise; like their "help," they learned the principles of cooking and food preparation by word of mouth and trial and error.[8]

Few sought out the aid of the written word. But by the turn of the century, cookery texts addressed to gentry—not simply the chefs in royal homes—appeared in Europe. In the 1700s cookbooks began to function less as exclusive manuscripts for the most wealthy or the titled and more as manuals for the rest of the population. In England, printed household advice books by women for other women in the upper middle branches of society—and their servants, including their domestic cooks—began to appear. Titles included Eliza Smith's famous 1727 book *The Compleat Housewife: Or Accomplished Gentlewoman's Companion,* Elizabeth Raffald's *The Experienced English Housekeeper* (1769), and a very popular work by Hannah Glasse entitled *The Art of Cookery Made Plain and Easy,* first published in 1747. French cookbooks followed suit. For instance, the author of *La cuisinière bourgeoise* wrote that he had attempted to "reduce expenses, simplify methods, and go some way toward bringing what has seemed the preserve of opulent kitchens within the range of the bourgeoisie." Published in the early 1700s, *La cuisinière bourgeoise* outsold all other eighteenth-century cookbooks. English recipe collections by the mistress of the house, privately copied in longhand and passed down through generations of women, ceased to be the exclusive domain of nobility. In the late 1600s the wives of the rising merchant class began to compile recipe collections for their own use, carefully indexing and recopying them, as they gathered recipes from their friends, friends of friends, and their own servants.[9]

During most of the 1700s cookery texts that circulated in the American colonies also addressed a readership of upper-middle-class women rather than royal chefs, but those that existed were written and published in England. In 1742 William Parks, a printer in Williamsburg, Virginia, published the first cookbook printed on American soil—a reprint of *The Compleat Housewife* written in London by Eliza Smith. Because Parks eliminated recipes that called for ingredients unavailable in America, the book differed slightly from its English edition. Americans also bought numerous reprints of the English manual *The Art of Cookery Made Plain and Easy* by Hannah Glasse and Susannah Carter's

The Frugal Housewife, first printed in London in 1765 and then reprinted in America in 1772. Smith, Glasse, and others offered far more than advice on cookery. These and other cookbooks in the early 1700s really functioned as general household manuals, offering information on preserving and storing food, instructions for preparing home remedies, advice about domestic economy, and related topics. Cookery, medicine, and household hints equally composed cookbooks well into the nineteenth century.[10]

Not until the 1796 publication of a small cookbook by Amelia Simmons did Americans produce an original cookery text, written and published by a citizen of the "New World." Only six original copies of any edition of the book are still in existence, and historians know virtually nothing about its author, except for her own description of herself as "An American Orphan." She appears to have lived in New England, as the ingredients and recipes in the book demonstrate. The book's publishers, located in Hartford, Albany, and other northeastern towns, also indicate that Simmons probably lived in the same area. A short introduction included in the second and later editions reveal something of Simmons's social location: Simmons asked readers to excuse errors in the first edition and blamed them on the transcriber, as she lacked "an education sufficient to prepare the work for press."[11]

Simmons's text bore the lengthy title *American Cookery, or The Art of Dressing Viands, Fish, Poultry and Vegetables, and the Best Modes of Making Pastes, Puffs, Pies, Tarts, Pudding, Custards and Preserves, and All Kinds of Cakes, From the Imperial Plumb to Plain Cake, Adapted to this Country and All Grades of Life.* It attracted enough buyers to run through four editions, including several revisions.[12] Simmons's cookbook offered the first collection of recipes that focused on American ingredients, written and published by an American. Composed in the flush of new American patriotism, *American Cookery* and its subsequent editions included recipes for "Election cake" (in the second edition only), "Independence cake," and "Washington pie." The emphasis on American-grown ingredients, the descriptive term "American orphan" (anti-British propaganda had long co-opted English characterizations of America as a unruly child), and Simmons's sly reference to American democracy in the title (in the United States every cake from "Imperial Plumb" to "Plain" could find a place at the table) show how this cookbook reflected the political realities of the period.[13]

Simmons gave fairly detailed descriptions of many varieties of fish, meat, and vegetables—salmon, shad, eels, perch, turkey, capons, pigeons, hares, beets, parsnips, asparagus, artichokes, grapes, pears, currants, and seven different kinds of green peas—then a section of "receipts" with advice on how to use such ingredients. *American Cookery* also illustrated the way American cookbooks would, from this point forward, pay a great deal of attention to sweets and baked goods. Simmons's recipes included instructions for making lemon cream, whipped cream, plum cake, "a rich cake," five different kinds of loaf cake, cookies, four different kinds of gingerbread, "soft cakes in little pans," and butter biscuits.

These recipes were a far cry from the orderly list of ingredients and step-by-step cooking instructions found in today's cookbooks. Simmons, like her contemporaries, freely borrowed from other publications and offered only a paragraph of brief instructions, with the ingredients listed as needed. But although cookbook authors, home economists, and culinary historians routinely describe early American cookery texts as completely lacking in precise measurements, Simmons's recipes usually gave fairly specific measurement amounts for most of her ingredients. She offered these instructions for "A Nice Indian Pudding" (the adjective again demonstrated Simmons's patriotism: the English scorned and derided "Indian" corn meal): "3 pints scalded milk, 7 spoons fine Indian meal, stir well together while hot, let stand till cooled; add 7 eggs, half pound raisins, 4 ounces butter, spice and sugar, bake one and half hour."[14]

True, the amount of corn meal a "spoon" held varied from household to household, until standard measuring tools became common in the late nineteenth century. Still, home economists in the nineteenth and twentieth centuries exaggerated the vagueness of early recipes. Other recipes in *American Cookery* even gave specific measurements for spices, although most did not clearly define cookery terms such as "a quick oven" (a very hot oven), a "slow oven" (a smaller fire and cooler cooking temperature), or scalded milk. *American Cookery* did not contain extensive household or medical hints, but it did include a range of preserve recipes and instructions for such activities as making butter, storing potatoes, and judging the freshness of eggs.

Although it was a popular volume, by 1800 *American Cookery* began to look old-fashioned. Due in large part to technological advances, cooking underwent many changes after the turn of the century. The increasing availability of the cooking stove may have been the most significant. Cookstoves first appeared in cities during the 1810s and by the 1850s many households had acquired a wood- or coal-burning range, although until the Civil War cookbooks often offered directions for both stove and open-fire cooking. Keeping a wood-burning stove lit and burning at the right temperature were no simple task, but the advent of stove cooking began to eliminate some of the dangers and complexities of working over an open fire. At the same time, stove cooking called for a whole new set of cooking and cleaning duties.

Stoves had to be kept rust-free and required daily cleaning and black-ing, for example. Some American commentators lamented the loss of the cozy, family-friendly open hearth and fire-roasted meats. In addi-tion, the relative ease of range cooking made the one-dish meal obsolete and seemed to demand a wider variety of cooked foods at each meal. As American historian Jeanne Boydtson writes, "By the end of the century, the transition to multiple-dish dinners had been enshrined in cook-books."[15]

The invention of the ice-cooled refrigerator in 1803 constituted the other major technological advance. Soon it dramatically changed the ability of Americans to store and preserve foods (although mechani-cal refrigeration would not be widely available until the early twen-tieth century). In urban areas, new municipal water systems began to provide water on tap for some prosperous households. In addition, many consumers had access to numerous new and improved kitchen appliances, such as hand-held meat grinders and eggbeaters. Also, in the 1830s and 1840s vegetarianism, diet, and temperance movements spawned their own subgenre of cookbooks.[16] But two distinct socio-economic issues had the greatest impact on cookbook publication in the 1800s: a growing belief in "women's sphere" and the emergence of a distinct middle class during the first half of the century, and cook-ery reform and the cooking school movement in the latter half of the century.

In the early nineteenth century, the postrevolutionary trend of "Re-publican Motherhood" blossomed into a full-blown domestic ideology. American society, in the throes of the dramatic social changes wrought by increasing industrialization and urbanization, sought to redefine the male and female spheres of life and work. No longer linked in mutual struggle against the wilderness to maintain the family farm, men and women increasingly occupied different economies: men joined the mar-ket economy whereas women became linked more closely with house-hold duties. Women's new duty as home consumer, in particular, helped to establish the definition of a middle-class home.[17] Shopping for food and home furnishings helped create the signs of middle-class living.

In the ideal middle-class household, however, the actual labor of cooking fell not to the lady of the home but to servants. For instance, after noting her own compromised social status as an orphan, Simmons described her intended audience in the preface to the book: "As this treatise is calculated for the improvement of the rising generation of *Females* in America, the Lady of fashion and fortune will not be dis-pleased, if many hints are suggested for the more general and universal knowledge of those females in this country, who by the loss of their parents, or other unfortunate circumstances, are reduced to the necessity of going into families in the line of domestics, or taking refuge with their friends or relations, and doing those things which are really essential to the perfecting them as good wives, and useful members of society" (emphasis in original).[18] She aimed her instructions at the woman who had to work to become a "useful member of society," at the woman cooking in domestic service, or the woman who sought to become less burdensome to "friends and relations." Simmons's preface pointed out that, in her view, her cookbook would probably be most useful for such women, although she also seemed certain that "Ladies of fashion" would read her book as well.

At the turn of the century, Simmons's belief that a cookbook would, probably, be used by a woman making her own way in the world illustrated national ideas about cooking. In the early 1800s, Americans began to characterize manual labor in the home, including cooking, as a chore for domestic workers, not the wife and mother of the home. One historian of domesticity describes the changing status of domestic labor during this period as a fundamental change in the social roles of women: "Most dramatically, the housewife's role changed from that of a household manager, who did much of the manual labor required to feed and clothe her family, to that of 'lady in residence,' who cultivated her growing sensitivity to class distinctions, delegated manual work to servants, and concerned herself with the organizational aspects of her ever more elaborate domestic system."[19]

Servant labor—indentured and enslaved—existed in America since the days of the earliest colonies and indeed played a critical role in colonial development. By the time Amelia Simmons composed her cookbook, a significant number of families all over the country expected to engage household "help" in various forms.[20] By that time, the slavery system ensured that African Americans performed virtually all the domestic labor in the financially secure homes of the South, whereas native-born free laborers from the poor and working classes replaced indentured servants in the North. In addition, many immigrant women, in particular Irish women, found ready employment as domestic laborers in private homes. In fact, the Irish "biddy" and cook quickly became a common stereotype. After 1847 many Chinese immigrants served as cooks in California homes. As the standard of living rose for the growing middle class, so did the demand for household servants: as families achieved new social status, they hired domestic laborers as a sign of that status.[21]

Even as a new "lady in residence," however, a woman employing paid labor in the kitchen did not isolate herself entirely from that room in the house. Although Simmons suggested that a general cookbook like hers best fit the needs of women employed as domestic servants, the lady of the house could just as easily have been the one to read a recipe book. This seems likely, in fact, given the low rates of literacy among all women, but especially among the poor and laboring classes. Cookbooks published in the early 1800s did occasionally complain about the shiftlessness and stubbornness of servants, suggesting the presence of servant labor but also assuming that the mistress would read the cookbook.[22] In addition, from the early 1800s to the 1860s, publishing houses in urban centers such New York, Philadelphia, Boston, Baltimore, and Cincinnati most often produced cookbooks. Thus, urban, middle-class Americans had the most access to these publications.[23]

Even in a prosperous home, where a woman had charge of a large kitchen built for servant labor and did not participate in the actual preparation of food, she still expected to preside directly over the kitchen labor of her servants and frequently to be present in the kitchen. She would have understood many of the rudiments of cooking, which she learned by experience, and she consulted written instruction only sporadically, while she planned the meals and gave directions. The recipes she might consult occasionally would be similar to the ones in *American Cookery:* general, with minimal instructions, and a list of basic ingredients. Edith Wharton, for instance, wrote that her mother owned a cookbook and regularly wrote in favorite recipes but added that a family cook did the actual kitchen work. Ladies consulted cookbooks for lessons in how to choose foods, compose menus, and make meal arrangements with the cook, but not necessarily for the practical how-to instructions on home cooking.[24]

Significantly, cookbooks in the first half of the nineteenth century offered recipes designed to appeal to women just beginning to establish themselves firmly as middle-class. Such women sought advice and information to help delineate the newly forming boundaries of middle-class life, which demanded more elaborate meals to reflect rising class status—courses at dinner, table linen and a full set of silverware at every meal, and fancier desserts. Cookbooks responded by including recipes for such food niceties as candied flowers, ice cream, lobster sauce for fish, blanc mange, cucumber soup, and orange sherbet—as well as instructions about entertaining, instructing servants, and paying calls on one's friends. The imitation of European manners and meals, especially French cuisine, also required published instruction.[25]

Of course, the men and women in lower socioeconomic strata and in the rural areas of the country did not participate in many of these new distinctions between men's and women's work, nor did they generally employ recipes for delicacies such as candied flowers. Nonetheless, the *ideal* of such a separation of spheres soon reached a fever pitch in the mid 1800s. This ideal invested a woman's sphere with vast spiritual and emotional value: home as a haven away from the hectic business world, a place where a woman's civilizing influence made her the "angel of the house," became a remarkably widespread norm. As feminist and food historian Laura Shapiro asserts, the new industrial economy created a kind of sentimental backlash whereby prescriptive domestic literature, including cookbooks, emphasized the emotional importance of the domestic work of wives and mothers.[26] Domestic ideology increasingly endowed the home, its mistress, and its meals with new emotional importance, and cookery instruction (as many as 160 cookbooks were published from 1800 to 1850) became part of the new barrage of prescriptive instruction about home life. Mechanized presses and more rapid transportation ensured the dissemination of these instructions.

Catherine Beecher's text of 1846, some of the most influential writing of the nineteenth century, offered a particularly vivid example of such material. *Mrs. Beecher's Domestic Receipt Book* sold briskly during this time and directly linked the activity of cooking to the glorified role of homemaker, insisting that the tedious and wearisome aspects of housekeeping paled in comparison to the rewards reaped by devoted homemakers.[27] As women's historian Nancy Woloch summarizes, "From the 1820s onward, the values of woman's sphere were promoted in a huge barrage of printed matter aimed at a growing female audience. . . . Didactic manuals on housekeeping, marriage, manners, and child rearing confirmed the significance of domesticity."[28]

Cookbooks offered some didactic advice of their own. The American editors of an 1807 English cookbook, *New System of Domestic Cookery*, wrote of American women: "There was a time when ladies knew nothing beyond their own family concerns; but in the present day there are many who know nothing about them."[29] Some authors, in keeping with the new emphasis on motherhood and expressing similar doubts about American women's cooking ability, urged their readers to pay attention to their daughters' kitchen education. Seemingly in response to reform movements that advocated education for women, Lydia Maria Child, in her 1830 *The Frugal Housewife* (renamed *The American Frugal Housewife* in 1835 to differentiate it from the earlier English work), advised mothers to steer their daughters away from frivolous fashion and pointless schooling and toward a more appropriate education in housekeeping: "Education has given a wrong end and aim to their whole existence. They have been taught to look for happiness in the absence of all occupation, or the unsatisfactory and ruinous excitement of fashionable competition."[30] *The Frugal Housewife* proved enormously popular, selling more than 6,000 copies the first year. But Child was only one of several prolific and, sometimes, didactic authors who published cookbooks before the Civil War. Sarah Josepha Hale, Elizabeth Put-

nam, Mrs. A. L. Webster, and Mrs. T. J. Crowen all contributed important and widely selling cookbooks, along with volumes on cookery
penned by professional chefs (virtually always men).[31] Eliza Leslie,
probably the most important of these authors, published her first book,
Seventy-Five Receipts for Pastry, Cakes and Sweetmeats, in Boston in 1828.
From a genteel background and forced by circumstances to make a
living, Leslie went on to write numerous cookbooks, including the 1837
Directions for Cookery, probably the best-selling cookbook of the nineteenth century.[32]

As America became somewhat more urbanized and many families
migrated west, the population became more widely dispersed. Consequently, fewer women could turn to mothers and grandmothers for
advice and instruction about cookery.[33] Cookbook authors like Elizabeth Putnam noted how cookbooks could assist women of moderate
means in their pursuit of knowledge. She offered her 1849 *Mrs. Putnam's Receipt Book; and Young Housekeeper's Assistant* "as an assistant
to the education of young women" and insisted that a reliable cookbook could be "one of the greatest conveniences to a young housekeeper."[34] In their changing society, women perhaps turned with relief
to such published cookery instruction. In addition, private collections
of recipes or "receipt books" during this period, some embellished with
poems, drawings, and essays, show how women may have complied
with the popular "cult of womanhood" while also expressing their
personal creativity.[35]

Authors also often demonstrated a desire to distinguish their books
as "American" (as had Simmons). Some emphasized recipes unique to
certain regions of the United States, especially the South, whereas
others promoted domestic economy, kitchen management, and practical, affordable meals. Authors often stated their intentions to make their
cookbooks available to the woman of moderate means. For instance,
Lydia Maria Child boasted that *The Frugal Housewife* combined "cheap-
ness with great value" and was priced "within the reach of all." Such
rhetoric may have reflected how middle-class women viewed their new
domestic role as being essential to the market economy, emphasizing
the new importance of running an efficient household in order to help
support the business endeavors of the wage-earning husband. Instructions illustrated authors' beliefs that an efficient home, built on the
principles of economy and restraint, contributed to the stability of the
household and, indeed, society. Historian Peter Berg argues that such
cookbooks also "appeared to urge women to take a more prominent role
in finances."[36] By insisting on the importance of good household management, cookbook authors asserted the importance of the "woman's
sphere" to the productivity and stability of the market economy.

By the early 1900s reform movements produced several cookbooks intended for poor and immigrant women, most famously *The Settlement Cookbook, or The Way to a Man's Heart,* by Lizzie Black Kander, published in 1901. But most book authors aimed their instructions not at wealthy society women on the East Coast, southern plantation mistresses, or newly arrived immigrants but toward the growing population of white middle-class housekeepers. The domestic ideology of the early and mid 1800s sought to reassure this growing population of the worth and value of domestic labor. Like Harriet Beecher Stowe's 1864 article, "The Lady Who Does Her Own Work," in the *Atlantic Monthly,* cookbooks spoke to the growing number of middle-class women whose lifestyle demanded a high level of household and kitchen labor but who could not necessarily rely on regular help—and reassured them that household labor had a certain dignity.[37] But although midcentury domestic and cookery writers urged women to embrace a woman's domestic duty as wife and mother and argued that women who hired help shirked the primary responsibility of their sex, many of these white middle-class women still hired live-in domestic servants and cooks.[38] The domestic duties of the "angel of the home" did not, in reality, necessarily include the actual labor of cleaning the home or preparing and serving food.

The decline in cookbook publication after the upheaval of the Civil War did not last long. By the late 1860s and early 1870s, publication rose dramatically, and new periodicals dealing with cooking and culinary issues also appeared. Newspapers began to carry regular cooking columns, as did magazines such as *Ladies' Home Journal* and the *Ladies Home Companion.* Community cookbooks (recipes compiled by local organizations and sold in bound form, usually for fund-raising purposes) first appeared in significant numbers during this time, often to raise money to help rebuild war-ravaged communities. This period also marks the beginning of promotional cookery literature, that is, recipe booklets, pamphlets, and full-length books published to help promote food products and kitchen appliance manufacturers. Advertisers produced thousands of "trade cards," which often included a recipe or household hint. Building on the popularity of these cards, recipe pamphlets featuring name-brand products such as Gold Medal flour, Hershey chocolate, Royal baking powder, and Pillsbury flour appeared in profusion from the late 1800s well into the twentieth century.

Such cookery instruction-advertising reflected how the second half of the nineteenth century experienced nothing short of a food-supply revolution. The Civil War led to new innovations in canning and preserving, and new kinds of food became available to more people. Railways vastly expanded the varieties of foods available to urban populations: railroad cars packed with ice brought out-of-season fruits and vegetables to the major cities, for example. Huge expanses of land in the West offered unprecedented opportunities for cattle ranching. New kinds of marketing promoted more and more canned foods, and home canning also increased with the growing availability of glass "mason jars." Increasingly available processed ingredients, such as refined white sugar, also called for new recipes. At the same time, more and more Americans had the option of dining in a restaurant. Ladies tearooms, cafeterias, and chophouses frequented by men began to proliferate by the last decades of the nineteenth century.[39]

Most important to the development of the cookbook in its twentieth-century form, however, was the rise of the domestic science and cooking school movement in the second half of the nineteenth century. It would be difficult to overestimate the impact of the domestic science movement on cookbooks—and cooking—in the United States. Growing out of the intensifying concern of the middle and upper classes about urbanization and immigration, the cooking school boom began in the 1870s. The Women's Educational and Industrial Society in New York City, one of the earliest examples of a cooking school, first offered cooking classes and domestic service training classes in 1874. The movement really began, though, when Juliet Corson opened the New York Cooking School in 1876.[40] Corson possessed a typical cooking school director's background. She grew up in comfortable economic and social standing (though as a young woman she had to work to earn a living as a librarian), received a good education, participated in women's reform organizations, and had very little experience cooking. One such reform organization urged her to offer lectures for workingmen's wives on food preparation. Her galvanizing interest—food and cooking for the poor—exemplified the movement's philosophies. Charities widely dispensed her 1877 pamphlet, *Fifteen Cent Dinners for Workingmen's Families*, which emphasized economical and plain foods such as suet pudding and boiled mutton.

Thus, while middle-class women consulted cookbooks to assist them with more elaborate meals and attended fashionable cooking classes taught by well-known chefs, they also turned their attention to the food habits of the less privileged classes. Female reformers offered cooking classes at a variety of urban sites: the YWCA, missions, and settlement houses, for example. Temperance workers regularly made links between unappetizing meals prepared by careless wives and the male thirst for alcohol. Pauline Agassiz Shaw's well-known "New England Kitchen" (opened in 1890) sought to "provide cheap, nutritious food to the working class in hope of reducing alcoholism among the poor."[41] But the middle-class interest in reforming the cooking habits of the poor could not be called entirely altruistic. It clearly and blatantly bespoke a desire to "Americanize" recent immigrants and to impose a normative New England–type of cuisine on peoples with very different culinary traditions.

Moreover, many reformers believed their efforts would result in a better-trained pool of servant labor. Rising dining expectations among the middle class meant that a white middle-class woman might be expected to provide multicourse meals, dinner parties, hot lunches for husband and children, and tea parties for her lady friends. These expanded duties made assistance (at the very least) in the kitchen and at table almost a necessity. But women could not always easily obtain such assistance in the second half of the nineteenth century, although the number of private household workers doubled between 1870 and 1910. In fact, during the 1870s and 1880s the United States witnessed a larger proportional increase in the number of household servants than at any other time in U.S. history,[42] but demand far outstripped supply. Opportunities in industry for working-class women lured many away from jobs as cooks and maids, for one thing. Additionally, the higher standards of dining demanded highly trained and highly skilled cooks, schooled in a variety of techniques and able to produce numerous kinds of dishes—and such cooks were not often readily available.[43] Schools such as the Philadelphia Cooking School, founded in 1878, and directed by prolific cookbook author Sarah Tyson Rorer, attempted to produce those cooks. Other organizations, such as the National Household Economics Association, had similar goals and offered similar types of courses.[44]

In the beginning, then, cooking classes and schools offered their instruction to the poor and working classes, intending to groom students for future employment as maids and cooks in New York and Boston. But cooking schools rapidly enrolled far more middle- and upper-class students. The New York Cooking School, for example, offered a popular range of cooking classes, from plain to fancy, for "Ladies." And the most famous of all the cooking schools—the Boston Cooking School—began with a clear imperative to provide cooking instruction to maids and employed cooks. But like other such schools, the Boston Cooking School very quickly became almost exclusively concerned with middle-class home cooks who had to live up to new standards in food and dining.

The Boston Cooking School opened in 1879, proclaiming its desire to be "a force for social betterment" and attracting a good deal of attention as an institute for training working-class girls for domestic service. But, although it eventually began a moderately successful branch in a poor Italian neighborhood, after only a few years the school became primarily a place of instruction for middle-class white women (very similar in background to the ladies who had founded the school). In large part, this shift occurred because the cooking and eating habits of the working class proved quite resistant to reformers' best intentions. Few European immigrants cared to trade their traditional foods for bland New England cuisine. It also proved too expensive for the school to maintain the low-cost courses affordable to working-class girls.[45]

The school's extremely popular cookbook reflected this shift away from "uplifting" cookery for immigrant and working-class women toward practical cooking for middle-class women. Its first director, Mary J. Lincoln, authored the first edition of *The Boston Cooking School Cook Book* in 1884. Like Corson, Lincoln had little cooking experience and came from a well-educated and financially secure family, but her husband's ill health forced her to find a way to earn a living. Along with her most famous cookbook, Lincoln edited the *American Kitchen Magazine*, which included her personal column answering thousands of letters from readers. These letters indicated that many women bought Lincoln's cookbooks and recipe booklets, studied her column, and regularly implemented her advice and used her recipes. *The Boston Cooking School Cook Book* enjoyed tremendous success from its first printing, garnering glowing reviews from newspapers across the country. The *Churchman* raved: "We have at last from Boston something better than Emersonian philosophy or the learning of Harvard—something that will contribute more to human health, and consequently, to human happiness; and that is, a good, practical cook-book."[46]

The reviewer's feeling that the nation needed a "good, practical cook-book" illustrated a widespread concern about home cooking standards. Lincoln herself summarized the situation in her preface, when she asserted that most women in the United States could not call on the assistance of hired help in the kitchen: "Some cook-books presuppose the presence of an assistant; but as three fourths of the women in this country do their own work, these receipts are arranged so as to require the attention of but one person." Moreover, she asserted, many middle-class women simply did not know how to cook: "The statement will appear incredible to most people, and yet it is true, that many women do not know what the simplest things in our daily food are; cannot tell when water boils, or the difference between lamb and veal, lard and drippings. They cannot give the names of kitchen utensils; do not know anything about a stove, or how to pare a potato. This will explain what might otherwise seem an unnecessary minuteness of detail."[47] In just a few decades, assumptions about the prior knowledge of women reading cookery texts had changed significantly. As late as the 1830s, cookbook authors expected their readers to be familiar with the kitchen basics described by Lincoln in her preface. By the last two decades of the nineteenth century, authors felt the need to start at the very beginning, and to offer their readers a "minuteness of detail."

The Boston Cooking School Cook Book did not offer especially groundbreaking recipes, although its description of food (including pen and ink illustrations) and of cooking technique gave readers markedly detailed cooking instructions. The food typified, in many ways, cooking school cuisine. Mrs. Lincoln included numerous kinds of sauces—for everything from main courses to vegetables to desserts—in her book. The ubiquitous white sauce (milk, butter, flour, salt, and pepper) appeared in a variety of guises, complementing or suffocating a range of dishes. Like her cooking school colleagues, Lincoln favored creamed dishes, egg dishes, simply prepared cuts of meat, and straightforward desserts (in moderation) like cake and pie. Whipped desserts and different kinds of puddings, jellies, and custards also found favor. Dishes tended toward the bland and, sometimes, fantastic. Cooking school instructors, though paying strict attention to the digestibility of food combinations and the nutritive value of food, believed in "dainty" dishes and interesting presentation. Salads, according to cookery school dictates, should be tidy, restrained in tomato baskets or frozen or suspended in delicately flavored gelatin. Chicken should be creamed and arranged in a pastry shell. Anything that could be made into a neat ball before serving—fish, cream cheese, potatoes—should be. Leftover chicken, veal, or lamb, according to Mrs. Lincoln, should not be served cold and sliced but as a "Meat Porcupine": a ground beef loaf decorated with bacon "quills," served warm.[48] But although sometimes ludicrous, recipes in most cookery school cookbooks rarely had more than ten ingredients and usually called for only five or six. Some recipes listed ingredients first, along with measurements, while others simply italicized the ingredient and amount within the paragraph of instruction. But all the recipes were easily accessible to middle-class kitchen novices.

The book also emphasized the necessity of science to proper cooking. The idea of "scientific cookery" was critical to the popularity of cooking schools: it directly appealed to middle-class domestic and social ideals. It also tapped into the growing field of nutritional science: in the early 1900s, scientists began to identify vitamins and calories. In her preface, Lincoln called attention to the fact that although many of her well-educated readers may have studied scientific concepts in school, few women utilized basic chemistry skills in homemaking: "Nine tenths of the women who go through a scientific course in seminaries never put any of the knowledge gained into practical use. By the time they have occasion to use such knowledge in their own homes, the Chemistry and Physiology have been relegated to the attic, where they help mice to material for their nests, but help no woman to apply the principles of science upon which the health and welfare of her household largely depend."[49] With her insistence upon the centrality of science to the homemaker's task, Lincoln echoed the call to scientific cookery issued by reformers such as Edward Atkinson. During the last decades of the nineteenth century, Atkinson and other champions of the new nutrition grew ever more confident in the power of new scientific information about eating and food. They sought to alter fundamentally the eating and cooking habits of the lower classes and convert immigrants and the working poor to the morally and physically superior blandness of a cheap, New England–style diet.[50]

In fact, scientific cookery swept the nation during the last decades of the nineteenth century, aided in large part by the growth of the domestic science and domestic education movements. Very much influenced by Catherine Beecher's 1841 *A Treatise on Domestic Economy* and by the development of food science, the growth of domestic science coincided with the expansion of education opportunities for women in the last quarter of the nineteenth century. The land-grant college acts of 1862 and 1890, with their emphasis on education for the "industrial classes," helped create the opportunity for the implementation of domestic science departments at Iowa State College and Kansas Agricultural College, among others. By 1914, as many as 3,500 towns and cities included domestic science courses as part of their public schooling curriculum.[51] A series of conferences held at Lake Placid, New York, from 1899 to 1908 brought together women working in a variety of settings under the broad umbrella of what they finally termed "home economics."

The advocates of scientific cookery and domestic science believed in the ability of scientific rigor and nutritional training to elevate housekeeping and the preparation of food in particular into an exact and perfectible task. The era saw a growing field of expertise in health and nutrition, and cookbooks very much reflected this trend. Homemaking and cooking, argued such advocates, should be as exact and demanding a profession as the study of chemistry or biology. At the turn of the century, women who were college-educated in the sciences but unable to practice professionally instead pursued careers as scientists of the home. As Laura Shapiro rightly points out, it may have been a science but a particularly feminine one, which rendered technology "as ladylike as teatime."[52] It encouraged women to take their brains seriously and to work to apply their hard-won knowledge, but it ultimately bolstered the notion that women's roles should be restricted to home, husband,

and children. Nonetheless, scientific cookery principles had a major impact on cookbooks in the United States.

Fannie Farmer's recipes exemplified how scientific cookery changed cooking instruction in the United States. In 1896, Fannie Farmer, Lincoln's successor at the Boston Cooking School, published a revised and reworked edition of *The Boston Cooking School Cook Book*. It met with so much success that Farmer saw over twenty-one printings before her death. First a pupil, then an instructor at the Boston Cooking School, Farmer became quite a celebrity, and eventually her publishers renamed the cookbook to include "Fannie Farmer" in the title. She worked extremely long hours, lecturing around the country and giving demonstrations, and from 1905 to 1915 she edited a cooking column in the *Woman's Home Companion*.[53] Her text, firmly based on the principles of scientific cookery, utilized exact measurements of ingredients and explicit instructions for cooking. Specifically, she instituted the "level measurement" (making sure the cook filled each standardized measuring receptacle full) and called for the use of standardized measuring cups. Farmer asserted that "Correct measurements are absolutely necessary to insure the best results." She also offered extensive information on the caloric and nutritional aspects of food and cooking and urged her readers again and again to apply scientific principles to cooking.[54]

The popularity of Fannie Farmer's cookbook (the best-selling cookbook in the United States until the publication of *The Joy of Cooking* and *The Better Homes and Gardens Cook Book*) signaled a basic change in the American understanding of cooking. Cookery instruction like Fannie Farmer's assumed that a cookbook would provide women with the primary means of learning how to cook. Fannie Farmer, and her predecessor, understood that for many women *The Boston Cooking School Cook Book* took the place of learned, lived experience in the kitchen. Cookbook authors at the end of the nineteenth century turned away from the most heavy-handed rhetoric about women's sphere and turned toward the rhetoric of scientific direction. Recipes became formulas and anyone could follow a formula, provided she carefully read the directions and followed them all exactly. Baking, the type of cooking that called for the most skill, garnered the most formulas, probably not only because of the difficulty involved in teaching oneself to bake but also because America's insatiable sweet tooth demanded numerous dessert recipes.

But other aspects of late nineteenth-century American culture helped to reshape the role of cookbook as well. Perhaps as a response to the impossible demands required by multicourse meals, the trend at the end of the century toward smaller and simpler meals grew among the middle classes. Nutritionists' warnings against overindulgence and the dangers of dyspepsia fueled that trend. Processed and canned foods made their mark on middle-class cooking at this time also. The advance of new "convenience" foods both reflected and helped cement the changing nature of cooking—from hard-learned skill to reading a formula written by an expert. The first "supermarket," the Great Atlantic and Pacific Tea Company (A&P), had thirty locations by 1869, helping to make packaged and instant foods available to increasing numbers of people. We can, without difficulty, imagine the changes in home cooking made possible when bread became available for purchase, to say nothing of commercial leavening agents, preshelled nuts, and preground spices. Fewer and fewer Americans lived in rural areas, homegrown food became scarcer, and more people utilized processed foods, although most cookbooks in the late 1800s still did not call for many processed or convenience ingredients.

Advertising in particular began to reshape cooking instruction at the turn of the century by spawning an enormous amount of promotional literature, including recipes and recipe booklets. By 1900, in response to the increasing availability of such products, more and more cookbooks and household advice manuals offered information on purchasing processed food brands. In addition, kitchen appliances and cooking equipment appeared in greater numbers in the late 1800s, including new small electric appliances like toasters, chafing dishes, and waffle irons. The gelatin mold reached new heights of popularity in the late 1800s. As the ties between domestic scientists and food, appliance, and utensil manufacturers strengthened, so did the publication of recipes in popular magazines to promote particular products.[55]

The publication of cookbooks sharply increased during and immediately after World War I as well. Public interest in nutrition had been growing since the mid 1800s, and, along with it, the numbers of published cookbooks. As Brander Matthews commented in a 1913 cookbook review for *Munsey's Magazine:* "At last we are awakening to the deficiencies in our food-supply and to the necessity for a better knowledge of the best methods of preparing our food when it is supplied. Both in periodicals and in books the subject is receiving increased attention. . . . And there never was a decade when more American cookbooks were published, or when the general average of those useful treatises was higher."[56] Matthews accurately predicted that Americans would see increasing numbers of cookbooks that paid particular attention to nutrition in the first decade of the 1900s. The First World War created an especially pressing need to establish government standards for food production, as well as good cookbooks that reflected new advances in food science. In 1917 Woodrow Wilson created the Food Administration (FA) and appointed Herbert Hoover to head it. During the war, the FA advocated "wheatless" and "meatless" days, and mounted a "pledge" campaign, asking housewives to sign a pledge that they would follow the food restriction rules outlined by the FA. It also disseminated extensive information on calories, proteins, and the importance of fruits and vegetables and urged canning and preserving. The FA coined the slogan "Food Will Win the War" and advocated the "gospel of the clean plate."[57] It enlisted home economists, who in turn contributed a number of cookbooks to the general public.

Prolific cookbook author Ida C. Bailey Allen published *Mrs. Allen's Book of Wheat Substitutes*, *Mrs. Allen's Book of Meat Substitutes*, and *Mrs. Allen's Book of Sugar Substitutes* during the war. Cookbooks such as Thetta Quay Frank's *Daily Menus for War Service* offered extensive menu suggestions and caloric information on different types of food. Still very much influenced by the principles of scientific cookery, cookbook authors during World War I emphasized the nutritive values of food and careful food preparation. Domestic advice writers, still grappling with the "servant problem," continued to strive toward elevating household duties to a specialized profession and constructing the middle-class woman's domestic work as crucial to the market economy. Cookbooks stressed that as in a time of war, housewives had a patriotic duty to fulfill their domestic duties by utilizing all the tools of nutrition and science.

Authors also began to pay more and more attention to the role of the housewife as consumer.[58] And as the United States moved into the second decade of the twentieth century and became increasingly influenced by consumerism, the role of cookbooks in American homes began to change. Cookery instruction became less and less the province of scientific cookery or cooking school experts, and, as Elizabeth MacDonald wrote in a 1927 column for *House Beautiful* magazine, more the reading material for the average middle-class housewife: "Why is it that the sport of merely reading recipes is so fascinating? On a train journey, several months ago, a passenger directly across the aisle was evidently an addict. She was no starched specialist or didactic demonstrator, but a sensible, stout mother of a family. For two mortal hours, except for an occasional glance out of the window for the name of a station, she fixed her attention on a cookbook."[59] Significantly, MacDonald described this woman as the mother, not the maid or cook, of the family. Between 1896, when Fannie Farmer's first cookbook appeared, and the 1927 edition of the same book, the number of household servants diminished by half.[60] Cookbook authors turned their full attention to the lady of the house and began to regularly depict cooking as a rewarding, fun-filled task—one best suited to the discerning good taste of the mistress of the home.

By 1941 cookbook authors and editors became far less concerned with producing homemaker scientists and far more concerned with constructing cooking as a creative and artistic outlet for intelligent, dainty, middle-class ladies. They insisted that, despite the availability of processed foods, the popularity of smaller, less formal meals, the decline in paid household labor, and the occasional presence of a husband in the kitchen fixing his famous spaghetti sauce, women would continue to retain sole responsibility for the family's daily meals.

2

Recipes for a New Era

FOOD TRENDS, CONSUMERISM,

COOKS, AND COOKBOOKS

In many ways, the end of the First World War saw the beginning of the "modern" era in U.S. society. Changing sexual and social mores, the rapid growth of the automobile industry, the increasing power of mass media and other major elements of post–World War I culture foretold how Americans live today. Numerous aspects of postwar society also directly affected the production of cookbooks and the role cookery instruction played in the home. Flourishing consumerism, key to defining the middle class in the previous century, became absolutely central to American culture during the first decades of the twentieth century. In the 1920s the United States began to engender a true consumer society, a culture in which a great many Americans bought manufactured items not only out of need but also for the pleasure of purchasing. Some business leaders believed that they had a duty to help create this new culture and, to that end, instituted shorter working hours, higher wages, and installment credit. The post–World War I economy roared, fueled by the industrial advances that led to increased wages and allowed for the mass production of new consumer items, including kitchen appliances and food products. Some of those new products, such as the refrigerator, significantly changed food preparation activities, as did the spread of utilities (electricity, gas, water and sewage, garbage removal, and central heating). New kinds of retailing, in particular the growing numbers of supermarkets (15,000 A&Ps in the United States by 1930, for instance), changed the ways people shopped for food.[1]

Cookbook publication also entered the modern age. Cookbooks became more streamlined and standardized yet more detailed than nineteenth-century manuals. Authors and editors had to take into account new kitchen technologies. Recipes increasingly became an advertising tool. Newly available processed foods and simpler menus changed the way middle-class Americans dined and the kinds of recipes they read. Cookbook publication numbers continued to climb throughout the period: as a genre, cookbooks grew in both popularity and availability. They moved away from the rigid dictates of scientific cookery, yet became even more packed with detailed information about cooking and serving food. Back in 1851, Miss Leslie had devoted the vast majority of her book to actual recipes, with a few cookery hints rounding out the volume. By 1884, as the cookery school movement gained ground, Mrs. Lincoln felt it necessary to also include a goodly amount of information about types of food, cuts of meat, and nutritional information along with her recipes. But by 1941 general cookbooks usually contained a wealth of cooking-related advice: recipes, of course, but also cooking times, measuring instructions, descriptions of types of foods, carving directions, menu suggestions, and advice on everything from table service, meal timing, tea-party decorations, and luncheon themes to kitchen decor, kitchen equipment, and kitchen wear (fig. 1). Cookbooks became instruction manuals for every aspect of cooking the meal, from choosing the food at the market to setting the table for dinner. The number of cooking schools had declined drastically (though home eco-

Figure 1 Cookbooks in the 1920s and 1930s often featured photographs or drawings of cooking equipment. Some included photographs of cookery technique as well. From *Anyone Can Bake* (New York: Royal Baking Powder Company, 1927).

M e t h o d   o f   M i x i n g   C a k e

3 Carefully separate the yolks from the whites of six eggs; put the yolks in one bowl and the whites in another; whip the yolks until very thick and "lemon colored."

4 Sift one cup sugar three times and add gradually to the yolks, whipping until mixture is very light and fluffy and the yolks and sugar thoroughly blended.

nomics departments continued to grow), but cookbooks tried to offer the reader an entire cookery school contained between two covers.

Cookery-schools-in-a-book often began with a lesson on the latest kitchen technology. By the end of the 1920s electricity and refrigeration had made an enormous impact on the use of food in the American home. From 1922 to 1929 residential use of electricity increased from four billion to ten billion kilowatts. Increasing numbers of households made the switch from ice box to mechanical refrigeration; although still novel (and quite expensive) in the 1920s and well into the 1930s, the advent of "installment buying" put the refrigerator and other similar appliances within the reach of more consumers. As the gas, electric, and (at least into the early 1920s) ice industries competed over which type of refrigerator would dominate the American market, recipe purveyors seized on the new technology, especially the ability to freeze things at home. Alice Bradley, of cooking school fame and under the umbrella of General Electric, for example, published *Electric Refrigerator Recipes* in 1927. As late as 1928 cookbook authors still gave advice on keeping one's icebox clean and well drained, but Bradley's book marked the wave of the future. In 1932 *Good Housekeeping* offered recipes planned around the advantages of a refrigerator. The title advised "Let Your Refrigerator Do the Work." Electric stoves and cooking ranges also engendered cookbooks. In his 1927 *Adventures in Cooking*, health food advocate Alasker Ramus wrote that he had originally planned his recipes with wood or coal stoves in mind but soon realized that he had to switch his attention to electric stoves.[2]

The New Deal rural electrification project in 1935 helped bring electricity to even more consumers. Electricity in the kitchen fostered the creation of thousands of new household cooking gadgets, along with recipe-filled instructional brochures and advertisements. *Quality Electric Cooking*, focusing on recipes for new electric appliances, appeared in 1936. Home economists at utility companies churned out recipe pamphlets and gave public cooking demonstrations. Recipes requiring waffle irons, toasters, roasters, and coffee makers appeared in cookbooks and in popular magazines. The chafing dish, the darling of late nineteenth-century cooking, enjoyed a strong revival at this time as well.[3]

Advertising became an increasingly important influence on American society, and the volume and sophistication of advertising copy escalated dramatically. Basic food-processing technologies such as meat packing, ice making, beet-sugar refining, and canning grew by leaps and bounds during the 1920s, making advertising a crucial new part of the food business. Advertisers had to create different "images" for different name-brand products, including new frozen and canned foods.

Consumers now had to be convinced to buy one particular brand? of food and to keep on buying it. By the 1920s, food-processing companies such as Kraft-Henix and Kellogg employed hundreds of home economists to develop recipes and to give product testimonials. Other companies—Sears, Roebuck for example—followed suit and hired home economists in their product development, sales, and publicity departments. Although food manufacturers published promotional cookbooks—pamphlets or books published in order to promote a particular kind of processed-food product—as early as 1870, in the post–World War I era this kind of cookery text began to appear in ever increasing numbers. Cooking equipment and kitchen appliance companies began to publish similar recipe pamphlets.[4]

Home economists and cookery instructors deliberately turned their attention to the food-purchasing responsibilities exercised by middle-class women. In the late 1800s, domestic scientists emphasized social and nutritional education and reform, albeit well within properly gendered spheres. But by the 1920s the majority of career home economists worked within the food industry, and their primary duties consisted of marketing and promoting certain products. The new alliance between home economists and industry ensured that many national cooking experts would shift their attention away from the *production* of food out of raw materials to the *purchase* and *assembling* of food products. By 1940 the primary task of home economists and cookery instructors became to train women in consumption rather than production.[5] Home economics courses in public schools began to emphasize the shopping duties of future homemakers. "Most of us are becoming more and more convinced that a principal function of home economics instruction is to train for the wise selection of and utilization of household goods," summarized an editorial in the *Journal of Home Economics*.[6] Similarly, home efficiency experts, who provided detailed directions to the housewife on how to run the home as efficiently as a business, often suggested that consumption constituted the most significant aspect of homemaking. Perhaps most famously, Christine Frederick blended consumerism and efficiency housekeeping in her 1929 *Selling Mrs. Consumer.*

Authors and editors also began to redefine cooking duties in terms of purchases. Cookbooks began to list the ingredients required for a recipe in a separate section on the page. They did so, in part, to ease the shopping tasks of their readers.[7] Publishers underscored the message by selling advertising space in cookbooks to food-processing companies or using the space to advertise other cookbooks. For example, the 1933 edition of Fannie Farmer's *The Boston Cooking School Cook Book* included a series of ads at the end of the book for food products such as vanilla, baking powder, baker's chocolate, and junket. Advertisements in the cookbook for Steero bullion cubes and coffee also included recipe offers. The reader could write away for a free recipe booklet, and thus the reader found a recipe book within an advertisement within a book of recipes. Ads for *Cooking for Two* by Janet McKenzie Hill and *A Book of Hors d'Oeuvres* by Lucy G. Allen found their way into the venerable cookbook's pages, as did an advertisement for *The Candy Cook Book*, by Alice Bradely (principal of "Miss Farmer's School of Cookery," the institution started by Fannie Farmer when she left the Boston Cooking School).

Utility companies, supermarkets, food-processing companies, grain mills, kitchen appliance manufacturers, and canning companies increasingly turned to the cookbook format to hawk their wares (fig. 2). Brand names like Borden, Minute Tapioca, Calumet, Pyrex, Nestle's, Fleischmann, and Del Monte boasted their own recipe pamphlets during the 1920s and 1930s. The *Atlas Flour Cook Book*, published in 1923, contained recipes that all called for Atlas Flour. It also, for good measure, included a line of advertising on each and every page. Sentences such as "Atlas Flour Makes Splendid Cakes and Pastry," "Atlas Flour Is Made

Figure 2 In the 1920s and 1930s, food-processing companies and appliance manufacturers produced thousands of promotional recipes in advertisements, booklets, and cookbooks. The frontispiece of the 1932 *General Foods Cook Book* (New York: General Foods) featured a pantry well stocked with General Foods products.

from Washed Wheat," and "Atlas Flour Makes Wholesome Bread," appeared at the tops of the pages throughout the cookbook.[8] The 1921 *Cupid's Book*—comprised entirely of advertisements for food products such as canned clams and for appliances such as electric stoves—contained recipes and household hints for the new bride. One advertisement addressed "The Bride of Today" who "will be self-reliant in her grocery buying as in other things. She will make a study of food, food brands, and food values—and she will know what she wants!"[9] In contrast to the scientific cookery student of the mid to late 1800s, the cookbook reader of the 1920s made a study of "food brands and food values," not nutrition or the composition of food itself.

As appliance manufacturers churned out more and more recipes and offered them to consumers as part of instructional literature or as free cookery booklets, one technological innovation in particular created a whole new realm for the circulation of recipes and cooking instruction: radio. By the end of 1922, three million Americans owned radios, and the number kept growing. Numerous radio stations, with more airtime than available programs, began to include homemaking experts among their standard featured performers.[10] Many such shows featured local talent, offered simple recipes and homely cooking instruction, and broadcasted to a quite limited audience. But others, through the power of the corporations that created them, reached far more people.

One radio homemaker who got her start during this time, and the one with the most longevity, did not even exist. *The Betty Crocker Show* first aired in 1927, and through this fictionalized spokeswoman, the flour-milling company General Mills found a direct link to consumers. Women wrote in their cooking questions to "Betty Crocker," who answered them on the air. Naturally, she always recommended General Mills products to her devoted listeners. General Mills had discovered one way, through cookery instruction, to hear firsthand and respond to the concerns and questions of their target market.

Another major food conglomerate, General Foods, created the *General Foods Cooking School of the Air* to showcase its version of Betty Crocker—Frances Lee Barton—in the early 1930s. The General Foods Corporation owned the rights to a wide range of name brands, from Swans Down Cake Flour to Birdseye Frozen Foods and Log Cabin Syrup, and the *Cooking School of the Air* featured recipes calling for such General Foods products. Barton went through the recipes step by step, apparently making the dish on the air. Her recipes also focused on using the food products of the sponsoring company. The editors of the *General Foods Cook Book* bragged in 1932 that their radio show provided invaluable assistance to the homemaker, asserting that the "thousands of letters coming to us every week from all parts of the United States tell us that such practical help is what homemakers want."[11] Like General Mills, General Foods offered recipes and cookery instruction to radio audiences across the country—and had discovered a way to both promote their food products and to establish a means of communication between listeners and corporation. The A&P supermarket chain helped initiate the use of radio in this context: it began broadcasting recipes using processed foods in 1931.[12]

Ida Bailey Allen, one of the most prolific cookbook authors in the early twentieth century, made her mark on radio recipes by appearing on national radio programs from 1923 through the 1930s. First a cookery school instructor, then home economics and food editor for a variety of national women's magazines from 1913 to the early 1920s and author of fifty-six cookbooks, Allen did not hesitate to reinvent herself as a radio personality.[13] In keeping with the practices of cookery school instructors and home economics experts of her generation, the line between her recipes and her corporate endorsements frequently blurred. In 1935 she authored a lengthy cookbook entitled *The Budget Cook Book*, a thinly disguised advertisement for "the New Nucoa," a revamped version of a butter-substitute spread. She also served as a spokeswoman for Corn Products Refining Company: her 1927 cookbook *The Modern Method of Preparing Delightful Foods* was entirely devoted to recipes using Mazola.

Several of Allen's cookbooks had covers that featured advertisements for her radio show. Imitating the Betty Crocker and Frances Lee Barton characters, she urged her readers to establish personal contact with her. Through her National Radio Home-Maker's Club, Allen encouraged members to send questions about cooking, which she then answered on the air. In her 1932 *Modern Cook Book* Allen boasted about the "half a million letters" that had "poured in" after she founded the club. To create a feeling of intimacy, she organized her programs and her cooking instruction around the requests and needs of her listeners.[14] First broadcasting from St. Louis, Allen retained a midwestern feel, emphasizing simple home cooking—the kind women produced every day.

In contrast, the popular "Mystery Chef" of the 1930s offered instructions for somewhat more elaborate dishes, from a decidedly masculine viewpoint. John MacPherson, a wealthy immigrant of Scotch descent, adapted the title to save his mother the embarrassment of having a son who gave cooking instruction on the radio. MacPherson's popularity garnered him programs on NBC and CBS in the early 1930s, and he also spent considerable time in his published cooking instruction bragging about the hundreds of thousands of thankful letters he received.[15] On-the-air cooking even seemed important enough for the

U.S. government to get involved. The Bureau of Home Economics at the U.S. Department of Agriculture dreamed up "Aunt Sammy" as a way to disseminate cooking advice in the 1920s and 1930s. Under this fictional character's name, the government published numerous recipe booklets which thousands of consumers received in the mail by request. The booklets emphasized sound nutrition and economical cookery.

Available evidence suggests that the popularity of recipes on the air constituted more than a minor fad. Jan Longone, cookbook historian and curator of several major exhibits on cookbooks in America, believes that Aunt Sammy's popularity in the 1920s and 1930s indicated that Americans incorporated the recipes they received on the airwaves into their daily meal preparation. She points out that people who took the time to write into radio programs requesting instruction (over one million such requests to Aunt Sammy) expressed more than a passing interest in such recipes. Listeners probably drew on at least some of the instruction on the radio when they cooked their own meals.[16] Women in rural areas in particular, with limited access to other kinds of published cookery instruction, might very well have turned to their radios for advice and recipes. For instance, Edna Nelson Jackson, a housewife in Elk Mountain, Wyoming, included recipes from General Foods' *Cooking School of the Air* in her collection of cookery clippings. Her personal recipe collection, stored at the Laramie Plains Museum and spanning the years 1930 to 1970, consists mainly of recipes published in local newspapers but also includes advertisements and cooking brochures that she requested from radio programs.

Jackson's collection includes several of the recipe booklets that General Foods printed for its radio show listeners. These booklets had two holes punched on the left margin, apparently so consumers could easily store a number of such booklets in a binder. Although Jackson stored her recipes in a plastic, spiral bound volume with envelopes for clippings, the booklet from General Foods illustrated a clever marketing ploy. By making them easy to store all together in book form, General Foods encouraged its radio listeners to continue to use the recipe booklets (which called for name-brand ingredients from General Foods) long after the radio program ended. The editors interspersed photos of General Foods products such as Grape Nuts and Sanka in between the recipes to reinforce the message. Jackson's interest in recipes clearly focused on baking (as did many women's): cakes, cookies, and breads comprised the majority of the recipes she collected. The recipes she ordered from the *Cooking School of the Air* consisted of instructions for baked goods such as cinnamon rolls and shortcakes, sometimes accompanied by photo demonstrations of cooking techniques. It is easy to see the attraction of a radio cooking show for a young wife and mother living in the rural West. Elk Mountain, a tiny farming and mining community, had a population of only about 150 people. Moreover, Jackson never learned to drive. Her first and only attempt ended when the car collided with a passing cow. Her somewhat isolated life, then, meant that newspapers, magazines, and the radio provided the recipes that Jackson saved throughout her cooking career.[17]

The inclusion of recipes from the *Cooking School of the Air* in Jackson's collection illustrated the ever increasing importance of food corporations to recipes and cookery instruction in the 1920s and 1930s. In the new modern era, a housewife in rural Wyoming could purchase the same kind of flour—perhaps with recipes included on the packaging or in supplemental literature—as the chic urban working woman in New York City. In some respects, cookbooks in the modern era echoed the call for the homogenized cuisine advocated by cookery school instructors decades earlier. Only now, food conglomerates, rather than zealous reformers, had a vested interest in endorsing the same diet and cookery habits for the entire nation. Many of the trends in food production that began in the late nineteenth century accelerated in the 1920s. Canned, frozen and mass-produced foods on the market continued to proliferate, general stores continued to give way to grocery stores, and transportation advances meant the distribution of processed foods to increasing numbers of people. More urban dwellers meant smaller kitchens and less utilization of home-grown foods. Large corporations controlled the four most important types of food processing: flour milling, sugar refining, baked goods, and meat packing. Giant food-processing companies like General Mills dominated the industry, drawing on their vast resources of advertising talent and money to ensure the introduction of their products into family kitchens. Moreover, they churned out recipes and cooking suggestions to help the transition to different kinds of cooking. The proliferation of corporate-sponsored cookery literature during this period had one overwhelming goal: to ensure that those doing the home cooking would buy the latest kitchen appliances, use the new kinds of processed foods, and favor a specific brand or product.

Advertising, new food products, and new technologies had dramatically changed cookery instruction. But cookbook authors had not by any means left the cooking school entirely behind. Cookbooks in the 1920s and 1930s demonstrated the continuing importance of cookery school cuisine to twentieth-century cookbooks. However, they also revealed a growing backlash against "old-fashioned" cooking school instructors and their recipes. Mary Stevens began her 1934 *Primer of Modern Cooking* (a typical title during a time when authors stressed the contemporary appeal of their recipes) with a discussion of the fundamental changes in cooking that processed foods had wrought: "True, it still takes heat to boil coffee—but the coffee comes in vacuum-packed cans, the heat may be electric, and the finished product instead of serving merely the hot breakfast cup, is likely to emerge from an automatic refrigerator as a coffee mousse, and drift into a late supper party."[18] Stevens's comments expressed her ideas about the changing nature of basic cookery—the availability of electric heat, for example—as well as her attitude about cooking and eating. The transformation of a breakfast beverage into a dessert at supper exemplified 1920s and 1930s food and cooking trends.

Amusing, relatively simple, "different," and probably heartily endorsed by coffee manufacturers, coffee mousse was part of a new kind of cuisine in the United States that called for a minimum of cooking skill and a maximum of original presentation using processed foods. Cookbooks throughout the 1920s and 1930s offered tips and tricks for doctoring canned soup: adding cream, mixing different kinds of soup, adding chopped fresh herbs. Canapés and appetizers comprising different packaged and canned foods appeared in many cookbooks. Like their cookery school predecessors, many authors called for clever presentation and prettified dishes, although, unlike their predecessors, these authors relied quite heavily on packaged and processed foods.

Mary D. Chambers, author of *One-Piece Dinners* and associate editor of *American Cookery* magazine (first published by the Boston Cooking School), revealed her cookery school background on the frontispiece of her 1924 cookbook. It displayed two photographs of finished recipes, both of which could have been found in a cookbook published ten years earlier: a salad of cream cheese balls and a shepherd's pie with a marshmallow crust. In a typical passage, she described how to present potatoes fit for company: "If, instead of plain sliced or cut-up potatoes, you scoop them into balls before cooking, toss them in a little tarragon or chervil vinegar, mix them with mushrooms, and garnish the salad after dressing with stuffed olives, or beets cut into fancy shapes, or shreds of sweet pepper, you will have a potato salad good enough for the most critical-minded guest."[19] Fussy salads such as this, often with sweet ingredients, remained popular in the 1920s, especially early in the decade. Gelatin salads, frozen salads, jellied soup, and tiny crustless sandwiches with an amazing variety of fillings also made routine appearances. Authors sometimes included timbales, croquettes, and creamed dishes—recipes dear to the hearts of cookery school instructors. One 1922 cookbook published by *McCall's* magazine recommended stuffed baked cucumbers as a "special luncheon dish" and numerous cookbooks advocated sweet, creamy, inoffensive, cooking school desserts such as prune whip and junket.[20]

Recipes for pineapple fluff and jellied chicken salad proliferated, and *The Boston Cooking School Cookbook,* with its vast selection of such dishes, remained a best seller. But other authors called for a change. The cookery school backlash focused on salads. Throughout the 1920s and 1930s, cookbooks continued to include a disproportionate number of recipes for desserts, cakes, pies, cookies, candy, and other sweets, but many authors scorned sweet salads. In the late 1920s and 1930s, the simple green salad became the mark of a truly knowledgeable home cook. In her chatty 1939 volume *Much Depends on Dinner,* Mary Grosvenor Ellsworth, food editor of *House Beautiful* magazine, railed that too often, Americans made salads that looked "more like boudoir ornaments instead of food." She saw signs of improvement, however, and asserted, "Almost any well-equipped kitchen today boasts at least one well-anointed wooden salad bowl—and you can't put a pineapple marshmallow whip in one of those." Lucy Allen warned in her 1935 *Modern Menus and Recipes,* "Little fussiness, such as paper frills, too much sprinkling of chopped nuts, or dashes of whipped cream, as well as elaborately decorated salads, are distasteful to the epicure." She offered this advice notwithstanding her own recipes for molded salmon with frozen horseradish sauce and for "Cheese Cherries" (maraschino cherries cut into petal shapes, surrounding a ball of cream cheese, with parsley as a stem).[21] Even cookbooks with whole sections of jellied salads, some replete with whipped cream and chopped nuts, often explained how to prepare a green salad with French dressing (not the contemporary reddish, sweet dressing, but a simple oil and vinegar mixture, sometimes with a few herbs or flavored vinegar).

"Foreign cookery" marked another way that food fashion moved away from cooking school cuisine. Most authors and editors, when they included recipes "from other lands," gave instructions for extremely mild and Americanized versions of dishes from Europe and, sometimes, Mexico. But these recipes did reflect a growing interest in international cuisine. Regional cookery, especially southern cooking, also enjoyed the attention of a number of authors in the 1920s and 1930s (and authors of these volumes sometimes pointed out that mass-produced food threatened traditional regional cuisine). Many authors offered bland curry recipes and a few Chinese-influenced dishes during this time, as well. A wide range of dishes came under the title "Chop Suey" in 1920s and 1930s American cookbooks. Usually these recipes called for some kind of sliced meat accompanied by rice. But while some asked the reader to procure "souy sauce," others added tomatoes, green peppers, Worcestershire sauce, and other stewlike ingredients to the mixture.

These "foreign" and regional recipes revealed how virtually all cookbook authors assumed a white readership. For example, authors often utilized a stereotypical "Mammy" or "Juanita" figure to introduce a regional recipe or describe an ethnic dish. Some contained stereotypical Negro dialect. Others seemed to equate the days of slavery with the heyday of southern cuisine, something the producers of "Aunt Jemima" syrup had done in the late 1800s.[22] All presumed that their readers would have no culinary traditions or culturally specific cookery habits of their own. And in an era of virulent nativism, authors could not imply that their readers might already have family or cultural connections to "foreign" cuisine. Cookery books presented versions of polenta, Spanish rice, goulash, chili con carne, oyster loaf, grits, German baked goods, tamale pie, and spaghetti to mainstream U.S. audiences—and never suggested that the reader might already be familiar with such dishes. Spaghetti made perhaps the biggest inroads into mainstream cookery. Pizza may still have been an exotic dish, but during the 1920s, many housewives became familiar with at least one spaghetti recipe. These recipes called for well-cooked noodles, tomatoes, and cheese, at a minimum. Some used a clove or two of garlic, and others, fresh spices. In addition, during the 1920s canned spaghetti began to assume its long-lived popularity, although cookbooks rarely reflected this fact.[23]

At the end of the 1930s, then, a cookbook might easily include a recipe for both *arroz con pollo* and Grape-nut custard. A spread made with crushed potato chips, sweet pickles, and mayonnaise resided comfortably in the same book as an elaborate cheese soufflé.[24] As contradictory food trends jostled for recipe space in cookbooks, meals themselves changed shape. Many cookbooks contained a clarion call for simpler, less elaborate meals. More and more Americans forwent heavy, hot breakfasts in favor of cold cereal and milk, and ate a hasty lunch at a cafeteria or lunch counter during the day. Whereas some authors gave extensive instruction for formal teas and dinners, others urged their readers to forgo formality and throw a buffet supper or a curry feast. The editors of *America's Cookbook*, published by the Home Institute of the *New York Herald Tribune*, assured their readers in 1938 that "There is no reason why a simple dinner at which guests are to be present should start with fruit cocktail and trail through soup, entrée, roast, salad and dessert." The editors urged an alternative menu comprised only of beef stew, mixed green salad, fruit, and coffee.[25]

Although meals got smaller and less formal in the post–World War I era, many cookbooks provided full and detailed menus, sometimes for an entire calendar year. Along with such menus, the inclusion of nutritional information charts and graphs in many cookbooks showed the continuing influence of domestic science on food preparation in the 1920s and 1930s. Publishers took particular care to discuss vitamins and "balanced meals" in the prefaces and introductions of their books, and food-processing corporations constantly advocated the healthfulness and nutritional value of processed and canned foods. A few health gurus, such as Bernarr Macfadden of *Physical Culture* magazine fame, published cookbooks expounding on the importance of whole-wheat bread, moderation at meal times, and limiting one's intake of refined sugar. Macfadden's extensive, though hardly illustrious, publishing career included numerous treatises on the connection between food and health. The recipes in his 1924 *Physical Culture Cook Book* did not call for an especially radical diet, although it did include instructions for making dandelion puree. Many of the recipes—timbales, stuffed tomatoes, jellied chicken, and grapefruit jelly with marshmallow garnish— fit nicely into the cooking school tradition.[26] George Conforth, leader of a Christian health food movement, echoed the health gurus of the previous century by eliminating meat from the diet and offering recipes such as "Roast Protose with Dressing," "Pea Cutlets," "Lentil Headcheese," and "Gluten Mush" in his cookbooks. He included a recipe for the ever popular timbale, but his called for lentils.[27] Macfadden and Conforth and others like them constituted a distinct minority by the end of the 1930s, but many authors included at least some discussion of nutritional meal planning in their cookbooks.

Contemporary cookbooks document the significant food fashions in the 1920s and 1930s, but how well do they reflect the way people really cooked? A study of general cookbooks cannot, for example, account very well for regional differences. Cookbooks in the post–World War I era—influenced in large part by food corporations—both reflected and encouraged a homogenization of eating habits in the United States. But, of course, differences in location, class, and cultural background influenced daily home meals around the country. Creole cooking, for instance, flourished among Americans living in Louisiana. And it seems unlikely that the daily meals of an African American sharecropper in rural Mississippi would be much affected by the popularity of chafing dish recipes and frozen salads in the 1920s. However, cookbooks published during this time can tell us, at a minimum, what kinds of recipes interested many mostly middle-class consumers. Does interest equal use? Maybe not, but as Harvey Levenstein points out in his social history of food and eating in the United States in the 1920s and 1930s, giant food corporations like General Mills offered recipes and cookery instruction on the radio, at grocery stores, in magazines, and on product labels because women "seemed practically starved for it."[28]

In other words, although General Mills may have been exaggerating when it claimed thousands of letters from every part of the nation poured in to its radio Betty Crocker each week, consumers, especially women, *did* write in for recipe booklets. They *did* snatch up recipe instructions as fast as the A&P could print them. They *did* write to the home economics departments in popular magazines with their questions about cooking. And they *did* buy cookbooks. I am leery of drawing a direct link between cooking instruction and cooking habits, but the proliferation of recipes at a variety of sites in the 1920s and 1930s—and their eager consumption by radio listeners, magazine readers, and shoppers—indicates that printed cooking instruction did have a place in many American kitchens.

Moreover, sales patterns in the 1920s and 1930s demonstrated that cookbooks offered consumers more than simple cooking instruction: as commodities, cookbooks also created an idealized world where everyone always had more than enough to eat and anybody could learn how to cook. During this time, people purchased cookbooks in increasing quantities throughout two events that did not seem likely to create a demand for recipes: Prohibition and the Great Depression. French cuisine, the epitome of fine dining, had gained a footing in urban restaurants at the beginning of the century. But when the Eighteenth Amendment took effect in January 1920, such restaurants lost both their financial and culinary base.[29] Tearooms and cafeterias—with considerably lower standards for eating—took their place. Prohibition brought about the introduction of "cooking wines" and artificially flavored alcohol substitutes for cooking in home kitchens, as well as a boom in highly sweetened cocktails to disguise the taste of low-grade alcohol.[30] Only a few temperance cookbooks, such as Mary L. Kuhlmann's *The White Ribbon Recipe Book*, dedicated to those who chose not to use "ardent spirits" in their cooking, graced the shelves of bookstores during the 1920s.[31]

Yet cookbook publication continued to climb. Many authors simply did not include recipes that called for any kind of alcoholic ingredients, while a few joked lightly about the situation. One contributor to *The Stag Cookbook*, published in 1922, gave a recipe for bouillabaisse that called for wine. In the paragraph of instructions, he quipped: "Now have the Eighteenth Amendment repealed and add to the mixture one cup of white wine, the juice of half a lemon, two large tomatoes, pepper, salt, and one or two bay leaves."[32] When the government did repeal the highly unpopular Eighteenth Amendment on December 5, 1933, several cookbook authors rushed into the void with advice on selecting wine and stocking a liquor cabinet. Prohibition had not slowed growing American interest in the "cocktail party." Throughout the 1920s, cookbooks gave extensive recipes for canapés and hors d'oeuvres to serve at such parties and cocktail parties became, according to cookbooks at least, not only an acceptable but also a chic way to entertain.

But how practical were elaborate cocktail parties—with a vast array of canapés served by a maid and mixed drinks made by a bartender—for the average middle-class family during the dark days of the Great Depression? A review of cookery books from the 1930s reveals one of the most interesting phenomena in the history of cookbook publishing in the United States: while annual incomes plunged, while the Depression tested the boundaries of "middle-class," while many families went hungry or even starved, cookbooks continued to sell well during the 1930s. And not only those cookbooks emphasizing economical cookery sold well. In fact, only a few cookbooks made cheap but healthful eating a focal point. An author might make a passing comment about keeping an eye on economy, but all handled the issue as lightly as possible. In 1930s cookbooks, the housewife always faced a budget that had been merely "curtailed" or perhaps she might be "watching her pennies." About the abundance of recipes and published cookery instruction during the 1930s, Levenstein writes: "The most striking thing about this outpouring of information about food is the dearth of material on economizing."[33] But perhaps the continued demand was not so surprising, considering the idealized world of cookbooks that seemed to provide a fantasy retreat of culinary possibilities. Not so surprising really, considering that, as Elizabeth MacDonald observed in 1927, women seemed to read cookbooks like novels, turning the pages as "eagerly as a detective story."[34] Some cookbooks must have been read more for diversion and relaxation, as escapism (like a detective story), than for their practical culinary advice. In this sense, some consumers probably bought cookbooks more for their entertainment value than for hard-core advice about the harsh realities of cooking and eating during an economic depression. As a recent article in *Publishers' Weekly* noted, "cookbooks are as much about reading and fantasizing and experiencing how other people do things in the kitchen as they about cooking per se."[35]

In fact, cookbooks sold even more briskly in the 1930s than the previous decade. A 1933 article in *Publishers' Weekly* asserted that "Of all the staple stock shelves in bookstores the country over, the most active seem to be those which hold the cook books, and the related cocktail and diet books." Middle-class Americans possibly may have read cookbooks for advice on eating within a budget, but buying fewer cookbooks did not seem to be a common way to trim the food bills. The *Publishers' Weekly* statement also pointed to another, somewhat paradoxical, food trend of the 1930s: the rise of dieting, "slimming," and "slenderizing" cookbooks.[36] Women read much advice about obtaining thinner figures, even as other women struggled to find enough to eat. Cookbooks remained a steady seller, but not necessarily those emphasizing limited food supplies. The authors of this article went on to name Fannie Farmer's *Boston Cooking School Cook Book* as a best seller, noting that in 1930 total sales of the cookbook had reached 1,436,000 and had increased to 1,531,043 by April 1933.[37] Although no spendthrift cookery text, Fannie's Farmer's book did not by any means focus exclusively on frugal recipes.

Helmut Ripperger, the regular cookbook reviewer for *Publishers' Weekly* from 1934 through the 1960s and a cookbook author himself, wrote an article in 1934 on the growing popularity of "regional and specialty cookbooks," noting the public's interest in new and interesting—not economical—recipes.[38] Ripperger mentioned only one economy cookbook, *Short Cuts and Leftovers*, in his 1939 article "More of the World's Fare," and he dwelt not on the book's recipes but on its novelty cover. In 1938 he advised booksellers to stock up not on pennywise recipe books but on regional cookbooks and novelty books such as a reprint of Amelia Simmons's *American Cookery*.[39] Ripperger's background as an art historian and seasoned traveler (he had been the American viceroy in Bremen during the early 1900s) gave him a more worldly attitude toward cooking than many other Americans, and he expressed a great deal of impatience with badly written cookbooks throughout his long career at *Publishers' Weekly*.[40] Ripperger may not have been the typical American consumer, but he was not alone in his assertions that cookbook authors should not be overly concerned with issues of economy. In marked contrast to the home economists and home demonstration agents who strongly emphasized economical cooking and provided practical hints on the subject during the Great Depression, most cookbook authors offered little in the way of truly thrifty recipes or kitchen advice.[41]

In a 1935 cookbook review, Ripperger took one author to task for her discussion of economical housekeeping techniques. To be sure, *Alice Foote MacDougall's Cook Book*, a fairly popular volume, did offer a two-faced view of economizing. MacDougall herself ran a very successful chain of tearooms and did not need to employ the money-saving tips she gave readers. In his usual acerbic style, Ripperger demolished Mac-Dougall's ill-conceived penny-pinching hints, in particular her suggestion that "in clear dry weather, you can make fairly good shoes by using carefully cut and shaped cardboard made from cereal cartons." Ripperger scoffed: "Come, come, Mrs. MacDougall. What to do when the weather is wet, and it is sometimes. Am I to ruthlessly cut up the mickey mice [*sic*] on my Supersuds cartons (not a cereal, I admit) to make soles? Your soles should be 'fillets of.' "[42] MacDougall's advice *did* seem rather ridiculous, given that people who may have been forced to eke a few more weeks out of their children's shoes with cardboard probably did not often consult cookbooks filled with exquisite little tearoom dishes. In reality, families facing severe economic hardship might dine on bread and coffee for breakfast, bread and watery soup for dinner. But

Ripperger's admonition that the only soles in a cookbooks should be "fillets of" illustrated the pervasive notion that cookbooks did not necessarily have to reflect the realities of food shortages and hard times experienced by many American families in the 1930s. Ripperger often emphasized that cookbooks should be a high-quality genre—nicely bound and printed, with recipes calling for the best ingredients and replete with a sense of style and almost sensual satisfaction. He also implied that cookbooks, as a whole, should be the province of the upper and middle classes; of people who did not have to worry about the children's shoes or simply getting enough to eat. Ripperger intended only to give MacDougall's cookbook a poor review, but he also ably demonstrated the fairly widespread understanding that commercial cookery instruction need not be concerned with the cooking problems of those who might be truly struggling to make ends meet. He seemed to articulate the feeling of many consumers, perhaps even those who could not always afford to actually concoct the rich and dainty recipes found in popular cookbooks.

The continued popularity of cookbooks during the Depression speaks to their complexity as a genre. Seemingly intended for practical, everyday use, might not have people also read cookbooks as a kind of escape, just as they attended Hollywood films in record numbers throughout the 1930s? Could cookbooks have served as a kind of vicarious look into luxury and abundance? Addressed to middle-class readers, who experienced neither extreme deprivation nor extreme wealth, cookbooks might possibly have also been purchased and read by those who aspired to that class. However, the brisk sales of general, commercial cookbooks during the Great Depression did quite clearly and inarguably demonstrate one thing: the modern cookbook had come to stay. Both in times of great economic prosperity and in times of widespread unemployment, recession, and hardship, cookbook sales remained steady.

In 1937 Ripperger wrote that he never had so many new cookbooks to review as he did that year. He also noticed that the popular press gave an "ever increasing amount of attention" to cookbooks. Even as severe economic depression gripped the nation, advertisers, domestic advisors, and periodicals continued to offer recipes and cooking advice. *The Reader's Guide to Periodical Literature* shows a marked increase in citations under "Cookery" during the 1930s. Popular magazines bulged with cooking advice and cookery columns, and many instituted home economics departments (second to food companies, women's magazines employed more home economists than any other industry). In the preface to *America's Cook Book*, published in 1938, Emily Post described the way housewives around the nation had begun to amass recipe collections: "The present craze of testing new recipes, and collecting approved ones, is said to be rivaling stamp-collecting, and even threatening the supremacy of bridge," she wrote wryly.[43]

The proliferation of recipes in magazines and periodicals seemed to bear out Post's assertion. Virtually all newspapers in both small towns and metropolitan areas, including African American presses, included recipes and cooking hints. *Woman's Home Companion* ran a regular feature entitled "Prize Recipes of the Month," selected from readers' submissions, as did the *Delineator*. Food manufacturers also ran recipe contests. Swift's "Silverleaf" Brand Pure Lard, for instance, offered $1,000 for the best recipe using its product. Sometimes food-processing companies and magazines teamed up, as when the *Pictorial Review* ran a contest in 1935 for the best recipe using one of the food products advertised in that month's issue. *Better Homes and Gardens* published cooking tips from its readers in a regular feature called "Confessions of Good Cooks." *Ladies' Home Journal* held a regular "Cookery Clinic" in its pages, with information on topics such as storing cream sauce and making mayonnaise.[44] *Ladies' Home Journal* and *Good Housekeeping* both utilized black and white instructional photographs of cooking techniques and of finished recipes. And most of the women who edited these columns went on to author their own cookbooks in the 1930s, 1940s, and early 1950s.

The inclusion of recipes in women's popular magazines and in advertising literature did not begin in the 1920s. But with the increase in cookbook publication and advertising campaigns involving cookery instruction, it seemed like recipes flooded the country in the 1920s and 1930s. Cookbooks themselves grew to encyclopedic portions, containing thousands of recipes and extensive information about cookery technique, nutrition, and table settings. More and more cookbooks utilized photographs, sometimes zooming in on a pair of hands at work to illustrate a specific technique or type of kitchen appliance. They also began to include short introductory paragraphs before each recipe, as well as lengthier chapters on nutrition, stocking one's kitchen, budgeting, and cooking technique. Cookbooks in general became more "chatty," and although the recipe form became increasingly rigid and prescriptive, cookbooks began to take on more personality.

Of all the big "kitchen bibles" that appeared in the 1920s and 1930s, none so marked the future of cookbook publication as *The Joy of Cooking* by Irma Rombauer (who collaborated with her daughter Marion in later editions). Rombauer self-published the first edition of *The Joy of Cooking* in 1931. After Bobbs-Merrill acquired the rights in 1935, it published the second, mass-market edition in 1936. Anne Mendelson argues in *Stand Facing the Stove*, her definitive history of *The Joy of*

Cooking, that this cookbook assumed the prominent place it still holds in American kitchens due to Rombauer's unique ability to establish a special rapport with her readers. She points out that Bobbs-Merrill naturally desired to publish a book that could compete with the other popular cookbooks at that time—*The Boston Cooking School Cook Book*, *The Mystery Chef's Own Cook Book*, and *The Settlement Cook Book*. Mendelson argues that *The Joy of Cooking* differed markedly from these other "kitchen bibles." Unlike Fannie Farmer's book and *The Settlement Cook Book*, *The Joy of Cooking* used a pleasantly conversational tone and gave recipes shaped by Rombauer's own very limited cooking experience. This provided a marked contrast to the almost militaristic voice of authority in other cookbooks. And unlike some of the popular corporate efforts to produce all-encompassing, encyclopedic cookbooks in the 1930s—*The General Foods Cook Book* for instance, or the large cookbooks published by the editors of popular magazines—*The Joy of Cooking* had an individual author with an unmistakable voice. Corporately produced cookbooks could not help but seem more distant and more intent on marketing their products.[45]

The Joy of Cooking received favorable reviews from newspapers and from *American Cookery* magazine when the commercial edition came out in 1936 and it sold briskly. But it was not until 1943, when sales of *The Joy of Cooking* surpassed Wendell Willkies's *One World* (a story covered by *Time* magazine), that Americans began to truly embrace the cookbook as a classic.[46] *Publishers' Weekly* mentioned the privately published 1931 edition only in passing: the editors thought only Rombauer's cover (which depicted Saint Martha taming a monster with food) worth describing.[47] Although Rombauer and her editors stumbled onto a distinctive printing format for her recipes, in the 1930s her recipe style would not have been totally astonishing. Recipes in *The Joy of Cooking* interspersed the ingredients for a recipe, printed in bold, into the instructions. The two-column format of the pages did mark a departure from standard recipe form and distinguished the book, but the technique of forgoing a list of ingredients at the beginning of the recipe did not originate with Rombauer.

In the 1920s and 1930s authors and editors tried out a variety of different recipe formats, searching for the same kind of distinctiveness *The Joy of Cooking* eventually enjoyed. Some listed all the ingredients first, then proceeded with the directions. Directions almost always appeared in simple paragraph form well into the 1920s; in fact, numbered step-by-step directions did not become common until the 1950s. Some cookbooks listed ingredients within the paragraph of instructions, sometimes in bold, although none used quite the same clear spacing as Rombauer; Mary Lincoln, for example, had italicized her

Frizzled Beef on Toast

Figure 3 Several lengthy cookbooks for young girls appeared in the 1920s and 1930s. Pictured here is the frontispiece from Louise Bennett Weaver and Helen Cowles Le Cron's *When Sue Began to Cook with Bettina's Best Recipes: A Beginning Cook Book for Girls from Eight to Fifteen* (New York: A. L. Burt, 1924).

ingredients as the recipe proceeded. Others had recipe titles in the far right margin so that a reader flipping through the book might easily find a certain recipe. Some recipes, especially those for extremely simple canapés or desserts, did not list exact measurements at all but were just a short paragraph, more suggestion than instruction. Also during this time, more cookbooks began to leave blank pages for the reader to write in her own recipes or recipes copied from others. Publishers experimented with covers, bindings, photographs, and illustrations throughout the 1920s and 1930s.

As the *Publishers' Weekly* articles in the 1930s indicated, more and more booksellers saw cookbooks as reliable money-makers, and publishers and authors scrambled to make an impression on the market. One increasingly popular kind of cookbook—recipe books for children—reflected the changing cookbook market (fig. 3). The "juvenilization" of cookery that had begun during the previous century, when cooking instructors assumed the role of all-knowing kitchen authority and when processed foods had ensured the growing deskilling of cookery, helped create a demand for children's recipes.[48] Americans wrote and published cookbooks for children since at least the late 1800s, but during the 1920s and 1930s such books became even more popular and widely published. Numerous cookbooks for children came out on the market during that period, including *Kitchen Magic, Young People's Cookbook, When Sue Began to Cook with Bettina's Best Recipes: A Beginning Cookbook for Girls from Eight to Fifteen* and *Polly Put the Kettle On: A Story for Girls*.[49] These cookbooks illustrated the increasing importance of published cooking instruction in American kitchens. Although they usually featured a loving mother character that gave her children close and careful lessons in cooking, the authors clearly believed that their books actually took the place of such a figure. A child who really did learn how to cook by mother's side would have little need for commercially published cookery instruction. Cookbooks for the juvenile reader demonstrated the assumption that cooking probably did *not* have a part in a child's regular education. They demonstrated the assumption that cooking skills had to be taught by an authority—an authority increasingly found in printed form. Despite the steady increase in the numbers of home economics departments in public schools, cookbook authors seemed convinced that learning how to cook required a cookbook.

In contrast to similar books published in the 1950s, these cookbooks gave a truly thorough course in cooking rather than a few simplistic recipes for pigs-in-a-blanket and ice cream sundaes. Constance Wagner, author of *Kitchen Magic*, offered recipes for fried chicken, cheese fondue, cakes, biscuits, pork chops, coffee, creamed dried beef, French dressing, veal cutlets, spaghetti, and the still-popular white sauce. Sue, in Louise Bennet Weaver and Helen Cowless LeCron's *When Sue Began to Cook*, learned how to make such substantial dishes as meat loaf, veal birds, doughnuts, salmon loaf, baked ham with browned potatoes, tuna timbales, corn bread, and deviled eggs. In *Polly Put the Kettle On*, by Jane Abbott and Henrietta Wilcox Penny, Polly made entire meals. One menu consisted of panned beefsteak, hashed brown potatoes, escarole salad with French dressing, asparagus in cream, and pineapple. Another menu boasted whole-wheat biscuits, green peas in butter, sliced tomatoes on lettuce, mayonnaise, fricassée [*sic*] chicken, watermelon, and coffee. These cookbooks did not offer cooking as a game for a child on a rainy day. The authors intended their instruction to lay the groundwork for a lifetime of practical cooking.

Polly's cooking adventures also illustrated the way cookbook authors in the 1920s and 1930s had begun to depict the role of the paid servant in the kitchen. The story of *Polly Put the Kettle On* begins with the departure of the family cook, Hannah, who needs to tend to her ailing sister (the sister does not have a disturbing illness, merely a broken leg). Polly's mother is away visiting family and Polly's brothers are spending the summer away from home working at a "mining camp," and so Polly and her busy physician father are left alone. Polly, age fourteen, begs her father for permission to cook the daily meals, and a kindly neighbor, Mrs. Wood, steps in with her daughter Peg to assist with Polly's kitchen education. Before long, it is clear that Polly, armed with the latest information on cooking technique and nutrition, will surpass the cooking ability of the vaguely ethnic, perhaps African American, Hannah. Polly has, in fact, wanted to learn how to cook before, but, as she explains to her father: "I never get a chance to cook anything because mother's always afraid I'll upset Hannah and send her [Hannah] into one of her tantrums."

Throughout the book, the author contrasts Polly's meals, made with love for father, to Hannah's old-fashioned and, frankly, slipshod ways. Of her very first attempt at cooking breakfast, Polly notes: "I coddled the egg, which Hannah never does, and the toast was peachy golden. I nearly burst with pride." When she takes stock of the cooking utensils, she realizes Hannah has been neglecting them: "She sighed a little because they were not shiny like Mrs. Wood's and were all smudgy on the bottom, and she made a mental note against Hannah, but Peg cheered her by promising to help scour them to a bright finish." When Mrs. Wood intones that "Nearly all vegetables should be steamed," Polly wonders if Hannah has ever used a vegetable steamer. Then Polly finds the steamer "far back in a corner of the cupboard where Hannah relegated the things she considered too 'new-fangled' to bother with."

When Hannah returns, Polly is so bold as to assert, "I shouldn't wonder if Dad wanted us to teach you a few things," to which Hannah responds indignantly: "Me! Well, I swum! . . . Teaching me when I've cooked good enough for the Mays for twenty years come February." The situation comes to a head before long, and here the author briefly switched to Hannah's point of view: "First it was Polly saying 'Oh, Hannah, steam the peas! They are ever so much better that way, Dad *prefers* to have his vegetables steamed,' or it was the Doctor himself saying, persuasively, 'That bread is perfect, Hannah, but next time bake whole-wheat. Polly will tell you how.' (She had broken a plate directly after that!). . . . When Polly suggested that they have more fruit for dessert and less pie she *did* give notice." Polly restores harmony by reminding Hannah of how much the two brothers love Hannah's fruit-cake at Christmas and, in the end, succeeds in reforming Hannah's cooking technique: "So [Hannah] steamed the vegetables and baked whole-wheat bread and tolerated Polly and Peg in her kitchen; if she grumbled over her work no one minded. Her temper was leavened with loyalty to the family she had served so long."[50]

Polly's story vividly illustrated a tension common to cookbooks in the 1920s and 1930s: as authors reassured their readers that middle-class women (even girls of fourteen) could excel at and deeply enjoy cooking ("I nearly burst with pride"), they also knew that middle-class readers still wanted to relegate cooking duties to servants. Authors still acknowledged that some Americans continued to associate cook-ery chores with immigrant labor or African American servants, even as they preached about the joy of cooking. The authors of this cookbook resolved the tension by imbuing Hannah with abiding "loyalty to the family she had served so long," making her part of the family—a truly fairy tale ending. The possibility of Hannah quitting would have con-cerned the family much. As Polly herself noted, "You know help's as scarce as violets in January in Leesville [their hometown]."[51] Indeed, by 1925, the publication date of *Polly Put the Kettle On*, "help" had become as scarce as violets in January in many towns and cities, and cookbooks vividly reflected this fact.

Well into the 1930s the advertisements for cleansers, food products, and kitchen appliances that appeared in women's periodicals and in popular magazines often depicted a maid in attendance as the lady of the house demonstrated the efficacy of Draino or the gentleness of Ivory soap flakes. In a 1939 advertisement for Pyrex dishes in *Ladies' Home Journal*, an African American woman in a maid's cap grinned at a pie being held aloft by a fashionably dressed white woman (fig. 4). "Lawsy[,] how you make such chicken pie?" draws the response "It's your recipe, Bessie . . . and my Pyrex dish!"[52] In the advertisement, the mistress of this fictional household incidentally underscored her ownership of the home's cookware and the home itself. It also rather vividly portrayed the history of white recipe cooption. But, more significant, the ad emphasized the white homemaker's ability to produce a chicken pie so appetizing that "Bessie"'s eyes just about pop out of her head. Like this advertisement, cooking columnists, food department editors, and cookbook authors in the 1920 and 1930s aimed their advice and expertise at middle-class white female consumers. And they stressed that such women were or could become wonderful cooks.

Cookbooks constantly discussed how the lack or presence of a maid

Figure 4 A 1939 advertisement for Pyrex cookware illustrated how recipe purveyors in the 1920s and 1930s began to emphasize that only the mistress of the home, not a paid cook, could produce truly artistic food. From *Woman's Home Companion*, February 1939.

shaped the cooking duties of these women. They showed that even a newly "cookless" woman with little kitchen experience could—by following a recipe correctly, buying the right ingredients and cookware, and using the right kitchen technology—bake herself a chicken pie. As literary scholar Alice Deck notes, in twentieth-century advertising and popular texts "the white housewife gradually [became] as capable a cook as her Mammy."[53] But authors made it clear that many of these housewives could not necessarily whip up chicken pies without the recipes of more experienced cooks. As the nature of servant labor changed in the United States, cookbooks assumed or implied that many of their readers might be doing "their own cooking" for the first time and offered advice accordingly.

In one respect the Pyrex advertisement reflected an important shift in household "help" in the 1920s: by the second decade of the twentieth century, a domestic laborer was most likely to be an African American woman (45.8 percent of all "domestics" by 1920). Industrialization in the nineteenth century had already helped to create the so-called servant problem by offering less demeaning work for untrained laborers, often for better pay. The growth of public schooling in the early twentieth century created more education opportunities for young, poor women. And the First World War expanded the opportunities for nonservant types of employment, especially for the Irish, German, and Scandinavian immigrants who had comprised much of the servant labor pool in the Northeast and Midwest since the 1850s. As Daniel Sutherland writes in his history of American domestic service: "Wartime labor demands had drawn many girls from service, into factories and offices. Less than a dozen occupations had accounted for female labor opportunities before 1870, and most women worked in half of those job categories. By 1920, though, women were working in dozens of occupations. Workers who might have been forced into service by economic necessity ten or twenty years earlier had new alternatives; they no longer needed to sacrifice their freedom to feudal notions of master-servant relationships."[54] African Americans still held the majority of household service jobs in the South and in increasing numbers in the northern states. Households in the West and Southwest mainly employed Chinese immigrants (especially as cooks), Mexicans, and Native Americans. The total number of all women employed in domestic labor decreased in the first decades of the twentieth century, although the actual number of household servants increased from 1,509,000 in 1900 to 2,025,000 in 1930. Of these, cooks increased the least, from 240,000 in 1900 to 274,000 in 1930, and overall the ratio of servants to private families decreased. By the early 1930s, only a very small percentage of American homes employed full-time servants, and even fewer employed live-in servants.[55]

Immigrant restrictions, in particular, contributed to the diminishing numbers of American homes with servants. The National Origins Acts of 1921, a response to widespread nativism and anti-immigration sentiment, severely curtailed the number of immigrants allowed into the country each year. The declining numbers of immigrant women caused considerable consternation among those who wished to employ household servants. In 1925 Henry H. Curran, the U.S. Commissioner of Immigration, tried to soothe such worries by publishing an article entitled "The Cooks are Coming" in *Ladies' Home Journal.* He reassured readers that despite the new immigration restrictions, "the cooks" would still be coming from Europe: "From Ireland the lassies are coming here to be servants. . . . There are servants who are coming from England and Scotland as well, in excellent numbers. From England they come trained and ready, as a rule. . . . From Norway and Sweden there come servants in increasing numbers, and many of them are especially trained in advance by attendance at post-high-school courses in domestic science in their native lands." He assured readers that "while the cooks who have already come since July, 1924, from far countries are studying, cooking and playing here in America, there are more following in their steps every day at Ellis Island," and added: "May you get one of them—and good luck to you."[56] We cannot know if Curran's comforting descriptions soothed his readers. But popular publications and cookbooks did often articulate the concerns he addressed—namely, would middle- and upper-class Americans be able to procure reliable "help" in the twentieth century?

Even if Curran had been right about abundant new populations of cooks, the Great Depression would have made it a moot point for many families. Although many did not, some quite wealthy and financially comfortable families felt economic pressure during the 1930s, and in such cases, the cook's salary would have been one of the necessary sacrifices. In her regular column for *Women's Home Companion*, Eleanor Roosevelt described shifting American expectations about servant labor in 1935 and offered some reasons for the changes: "It is perfectly obvious that more and more people in this country are doing their own work or engaging only part-time help and the great majority have no servant at all. This is partly due to the fact that labor-saving devices make it more possible for housework to be done by one person expeditiously and thoroughly, and partly due to the fact that in many cases there is no money for household help."[57] Roosevelt went on to urge women employing maids to recognize the dignity of their employees' labor. She also declared that maids deserved clean and spacious living quarters if they "lived in," but in the 1920s the percentage of maids who did so declined rapidly. Finally, she argued that the United States needed to establish schools for domestic work to help make servant labor a skilled profession. Other household advisers and columnists echoed Roosevelt's assertions about the impact of "labor-saving devices" and of the Depression on expectations about household "help." They also noted the growing popularity of smaller apartment dwellings for the upper and middle classes and increasingly informal ways of socializing.

Indeed, the growing availability of processed food, the popularity of smaller, simpler meals, and the availability of utilities such as gas, electricity, and water had cut down on mealtime preparation, from an average of about forty-four hours a week to under thirty.[58] Yet statistics showed that middle-class women spent about the same amount of time overall doing domestic work, with shopping chores taking up the time saved by easier meal preparation.[59] Moreover, even thirty hours of kitchen work a week still took a significant amount of time and effort. Authors often assumed that their readers would, at the very least, aspire to have a paid servant in the kitchen, and large, encyclopedic cookbooks typically included a short section on table setting and proper service, giving directions for service with a maid *and* without a maid. A humorous little 1940 cookbook for the new bride entitled *Don't Phone Mother* included a whole chapter on cooks and maids in the home. But the author noted that many women would not be able to afford servants: "Of course, you want a helper, and as soon as you can really afford one. Until then save your longings for bath tub reveries, and dream of them along with mink coats."[60]

Many authors, therefore, tried to convey the idea that cooking itself had never been a loathsome task or menial labor, asserting that their readers would take readily to cooking and, in fact, get much pleasure out of food preparation. June Platt, who went on to author several cookbooks, wrote two articles for *House and Garden* on the topic of "cooking without a cook." She offered bracing and breezy advice for the newly cookless or "helpless" reader: "What a lark! The cook's fired, most of the furniture has gone to the auction rooms, and we're installed in restrained economy in two-rooms-and-a-kitchenette," she wrote cheerfully in her 1935 article "No Cook and a Kitchenette." She advised readers in a similar position to make very simple meals, with few courses: soup, "a wonderful main dish," and fruit or cheese for dessert. Try economical one-dish meals—tripe en casserole, chicken stew, lobster-and-salmon pie, baked chicken custard, spinach ring with mushrooms—she counseled.[61]

Four years later, Platt's finances seemed to have improved, and her article "How to Cook without a Cook" referred not to being cookless but instead offered advice on how to cope with "cook's day off" (perhaps simply a polite way of allowing readers without a cook—and there would have been many—to enjoy her recipes). She suggested dishes such as onion soup, baked beans, *petits pots de crème au fromage*, and cucumbers in sour cream for cookless cooks: "We [Platt and her husband] occasionally, suddenly, have an uncontrollable desire to have a perfect orgy of cooking. We love to cook, and we do it with a vengeance." Their love did not extend to cleaning up the kitchen: "Do we cook a good dinner? We do. Do we use too many pots and pans and dishes, and do we make a mess of the kitchen? We do. Do we leave it all for cook to clean up? No indeed, I should say not. We wouldn't dare, besides it really wouldn't be fair. But what about the dishes? We solve that problem neatly by having an extra maid who comes in by the hour, after dinner, and cleans up the mess."[62] Many cookbook authors gave similar versions of Platt's advice on the benefits of very part-time or occasional labor in the kitchen. In the 1920s and 1930s, in cookery instruction, more and more middle-class women ventured into the kitchen, although many did not stay around to clean up afterward. Washing dishes simply could not be described as fun and creative.

Most authors seemed to assume their readers needed assurances that living without a cook or maid need not impinge on one's dinner parties or compromise the family dinner table. Helen Hilles in her 1937 *To the Queen's Taste: A Cook Book for Moderns*, gave a typical description of modern hostesses (including herself), who entertained casually and stylishly, with or without "help": "We may or may not have a maid. But, even with an extra in for the evening, we can't serve more than eight with traditional pomp. So we have buffet suppers, evening parties, cocktail parties, or a noon meal on Sunday and call it breakfast. . . . We live with a certain amount of style."[63] Hilles's cookbook reflected the way cookbooks insisted that changing types of meals did not equate a less stylish way of life. It also exemplified the lighthearted way numerous cookbooks in the 1920s and 1930s described the "servant problem."

In fact, no "problem" really existed, cookery books exclaimed. "There are plenty of clever American wives of today who do not find their lack of a maid a handicap to entertaining their friends, even to giving formal dinners in which every worth while tradition of proper service is followed," wrote the author of a popular 1932 cookbook called *Macy's Cook Book for the Busy Woman*. Busy, clever American wives could, with a little planning and attention to new styles of entertaining, achieve a dinner party all by themselves. As Dorothy Myerson asserted in the 1939 edition of the *Homemaker's Handbook*, "The lack of a waitress certainly should not curtail one's hospitality, since it is not impossible for the hostess to cook and serve a good dinner gracefully. Intelligent planning is the secret of success."[64] Although middle-class white women might have been forced into cooking for themselves and their families, cookbooks in the post–World War I era reminded their readers again and again that cooking would come naturally to them.

Alice Foote MacDougall described her first cooking experience as an act of desperation: "The cook had walked out, leaving me in the dark, as far as cooking was concerned, and face to face with a problem in the shape of a 5-pound fowl in the ice box. Limited means made the bird a luxury. It must be used. It must be cooked, and since no one else was there, I, filled with fear, assaulted the situation." Despite her fear and inexperience, she supposedly achieved a scrumptious chicken fricassee: "No chef ever achieved such a masterpiece, so the children said, and I modestly agreed. Truth forces me to admit, that maybe appetites, whetted by the unusual experience, had something to do with the ultimate glory of this my first experiment."[65] The "unusual experience" of preparing food for the family, MacDougall and others explained, should not strike fear into the hearts of their readers. In fact, the reader might experience a heady sense of achievement—and cook a delicious dinner as well.

The changing nature of paid, household labor helped to change the nature of cookery instruction itself. Cookbooks and recipes began to portray cookery as a suitably enjoyable activity for a refined middle-class woman. A 1933 article in *Collier's* magazine entitled "The Cook's Day In" vividly illustrated this trend. It described a modern-day cooking school where middle-class girls, and even wealthy students, embraced the joy of cooking. "Cooking has become the hobby of girls in all branches of society," explained the author, Betty Thornley Stuart. She went on to relate a conversation between two privileged girls at one of the cooking schools she visited. One, a "pretty brunette with a million-dollar figure" comments: "I made that chocolate cream roll on Thursday, and *did* we eat it up! I hoped there'd be some left to show my cook Helga when she got in, but there wasn't a crumb. I don't think she really believes yet I can make what I say I do. When I went to roll it up, I had palpitations. It looks so easy when it's done in class, but when I was the roller—well, it reminded me of the first time I soloed." Another girl responds: " 'I never flew,' said the little blonde at the next table, 'but I took up high-diving last summer. I flavored mine with almonds and put in chopped nuts. What about you?' " "Grand Marnier," the brunette replies. The expensive hobbies (flying a plane, high-diving), the exotic liqueurs, the girls' beauty and fitness (quite literally, a "million-dollar figure"), the maid-in-residence (Helga): the obvious signs of a pampered, wealthy existence highlighted the fact that these two women did not cook because they had to, but because they found it as exciting as any other costly, thrilling pastime. Undoubtedly a doctored or fabricated conversation, this exchange nonetheless illustrated the way published cookery instruction had begun to portray the activity of cooking as a lark, as a fun and enjoyable hobby suitable for even a woman of means. Even the young women in this class who "had at least two servants, some a lot more . . . were just as interested in their cooking class as the girls who'd married on the slimmest of white-collar hopes, or the settlement children who headed families of four," wrote Stuart.

Stuart included recipes in the article—the aforementioned chocolate roll, pecan pie, plain muffins, and a pan-fried salmon recipe with onions, green pepper, and tomato. "Even women who never cooked before are doing it now—and liking it," asserted Stuart. "You'll be taking over the cooking and compliments yourself," she assured the reader.[66] Such emphasis in cookery instruction on the middle-class woman's role in the kitchen did not begin in the 1920s. The success of the Boston Cooking School and Fannie Farmer's cookbooks in the late nineteenth century had been rooted in the interest of middle-class white women in recipes and cooking instruction. In fact, Stuart's reference to the "settlement children" taking cooking classes alongside high-society beauties echoed the divided interests of nineteenth-century cooking schools. By the 1920s Americans had been bemoaning "the servant problem" for over a century, and cookbooks aimed not at the paid professional but the married middle-class woman "doing her own work" had circulated since at least the early 1800s.

But beginning in the 1920s, the emphasis on *cooking* in actually helping to define the domestic role of the middle-class wife and mother increased exponentially. Domestic ideology certainly had a long history in the United States by the 1920s, but only in the second decade of the twentieth century did cookbooks begin to uniformly insist that cooking—and the pleasure of providing good food for one's family—could be a *fun* and creative task in and of itself. Rombauer chose her title well. It perfectly reflected the growing zeitgeist around kitchen work in the twentieth century: as a title, *The Joy of Cooking* neatly captured the message that so many cookbook authors attempted to convey in the 1920s and 1930s. They did not rely on the stern spiritual overtones of domestic ideology so common to nineteenth-century household manuals in order to convince middle-class women to do "their own cooking."[67] Cookbooks in the 1920s and 1930s aimed to give cooking an image overhaul and to reinvent it as an amusing and delightful occupation; an occupation suitable to the artistic, creative sensibilities of white middle-class ladies and not a laborious task best relegated to "Biddy'"s uninspired efforts in the kitchen. Every kind of food-processing company seized upon the medium as well. In an effort to sell more cake flour, more refrigerators, more Mazola—and more cookbooks—authors and editors spoke directly to white, married, middle-class housewives with children. No longer a chore, cooking was the fulfilling, artistic, and joyful occupation of a loving mother and wife. The notion that making a chocolate roll could be as exciting as flying a plane for the first time epitomized the way cookery instructors reconstructed cooking in the 1920s and 1930s as far more than merely enjoyable: they depicted cooking as downright thrilling. As Stuart wrote in the conclusion to her article, "Cooking is fun!"[68]

3

"Cooking Is Fun"

WOMEN'S HOME COOKERY
AS ART, SCIENCE, AND NECESSITY

 When cookbook authors, food corporations, and popular magazines put their efforts into reconfiguring cooking as a joy that middle-class white women would gladly embrace, they responded to the pressing need to sell their wares and to the changing nature of both servant labor and food preparation. American eating habits had entered the modern age, and Americans wondered how changes in kitchen work would impact the family and the nation. Food preparation required less and less actual cooking skill, as giant food-processing companies took over many time-consuming kitchen tasks. With the assistance of delis, automats, and a whole slew of packaged, canned, and premade goods, a woman would never need to learn the cooking skills perfected in the kitchens of previous generations—or so believed many Americans. Partly in response to this concern, cookbook authors and editors wanted to show American women that home cooking could be incorporated into their modern role. Specifically, they emphasized that cooking could be a fun, fulfilling part of modern life. Recipe purveyors increasingly portrayed cookery as an artistic pursuit, best undertaken by refined and intelligent middle-class ladies. As American culture grappled with the appearance of "The New Woman," cookery books began to reflect the nation's concern with how the modern era would shape women's domestic role: authors and editors began to emphasize the art, the science, and the necessity of home cooking done by the mistress of the house. They began to construct the twentieth-century version of a domestic ideology.

What would the American home be, worried some, without an apron-clad woman kneading bread and canning fruit? For not only cooking but also all of women's "traditional" roles seemed up for debate during the 1920s and into the 1930s. Women's education rapidly increased after the turn of the century, and in the early twentieth century, college women made their mark on both the private world of home and the public world of work. "Women's professions," such as teaching, library work, and the settlement house movement, provided many college graduates outlets for their new skills, and a few women ventured into less accessible professions, such as law and medicine. Women's clubs and temperance unions offered white middle-class women a means of influencing civic affairs. And many scientifically trained women had worked for decades in the domestic science movement.

World War I also challenged the divide between "women's sphere" and the public world. Factories employed record numbers of women workers, and although many of those women came from lower-income groups, some social reformers believed women's wartime employment could be interpreted as the harbinger of increased equality.[1] Meanwhile, suffrage created widespread debates and discussions about the question of equality. Decades of activism and organization, beginning with the antebellum women's rights movement, culminated in the 29 August 1920 ratification of the Nineteenth Amendment granting women the right to vote. For many Americans, the passage of the Nineteenth marked the beginning of a brand new era in U.S. society, one in which women participated as equals with men. Not that suffrage affected all American women equally: making the suffrage movement the focal point for women's issues best fit the needs of middle- and upper-class white women. But without a doubt, 1920 did mark a new period of questioning and debate in American popular culture about the role of women in its society.

Besides women's suffrage, a number of factors helped fuel the anxieties and debates about women's roles. In the 1920s America seemed unsure if it would embrace a new era of modernism or retreat to "old fashioned" values and way of life. Many decried the dirt and chaos of the city, yet eagerly embraced the new conveniences and utilities of urban life. Prohibition demonstrated the continuing power of moralistic and temperance movements, yet at the same time young college women gleefully stashed "hooch" in specially made garters. Many citizens continued to believe that America offered unlimited opportunity for all, yet nativism and racial discrimination continued unabated. Racial tensions rose, and a shocking number of lynchings occurred throughout the country, especially in the South. Meanwhile, the National Association for the Advancement of Colored People and the dynamic black separatist Marcus Garvey galvanized African Americans to resist discrimination and oppression, while black poets and writers created a "Harlem Renaissance."

Perhaps most significantly, from 1890 through the 1920s Americans experienced the emergence of the modern sensibility in sex. "Sex o'clock" in the United States announced its arrival at a variety of sites: advertising which drew on sexy images, pulp fiction, sexy jazz music, and Hollywood stars like Clara Bow and Rudolph Valentino, who capitalized on their attractiveness. A growing youth subculture, especially the girls, worried their elders by forgoing porch-swing courting and instead "petting" in the backseats of cars. The bobbed hair, makeup, and short skirts flaunted by young women seemed deeply shocking to their mothers. The arrival of Freudian thought on American shores and Margaret Sanger's active campaign for birth control only made these parents more nervous. A flood of marital sex advice—including the work of the influential Havelock Ellis—began to stress the importance of regular, pleasurable, nonreproductive sexual intercourse to a happy marriage. But clergy, physicians, newspapermen, and cultural commentators fretted over the state of marriage itself. Certain social changes seemed to bode ill for the institution of marriage: increasing numbers of college-educated women; the fact that more married middle-class women assumed paid employment during the 1920s; and a rising divorce rate. A full 25 percent increase in the number of female wage earners caused much comment on—and several cookbooks for—"the working girl."[2] Naturally much of the handwringing over women's place in the work force failed to take into account that for women of color and poor white women, paid (and underpaid) employment did not exactly represent a new frontier.

In the 1930s discussion about women's employment took on a harsher tone. Women's employment came under increased fire during the economic calamities of the 1930s, and family life in general seemed dangerously threatened by the era's hardships.[3] The Depression shattered America's optimism about the new modern era and also put into question the "old-fashioned" way of doing things. Many men, ashamed by their inability to provide for their families, deserted them. The marriage and birth rates fell, and commentators expressed concern about how these changes would impact the morality of young men and women. Unemployment was endemic, and calls for women to "stop taking jobs away" from men abounded. Female employment did increase slightly during the 1930s, from 22 percent of workers in 1930 to 25 percent by 1940. But widespread condemnation of this trend ignored the fact that low-paying, dead-end jobs such as typist and secretary accounted for most of the increases in women's paid employment. Still, the perception that men's livelihood could be threatened by the changing nature of women's role in society added another dimension to the emergence of a reinvigorated domestic ideology in the 1920s and 1930s. Women, according to this familiar but newly energized twentieth-century version of gender norms, belonged at home and not in the marketplace. Women should be content at home, not working frivolous jobs to earn a little "pin money" and taking employment away from men with families to support. The backlash against the gains of feminism surely and swiftly helped to spread such ideas. Commentators in women's magazines and other popular media, bolstered by the growing cultural cachet of psychology and the authority of "the expert" in U.S. society, disseminated the idea in increasingly strident tones that only marriage and childbearing could provide a truly fulfilled womanhood.[4] A woman's real job, according to much popular rhetoric in the 1920s and 1930s, consisted of getting married and raising a family—and cooking for her husband and her children.

In fact, for some Americans cookery became the most important symbol of a woman's devotion to home and family. According to some cultural commentators, the United States needed middle-class white women to assume home cookery duties in order to maintain a stable society. Now that fewer and fewer middle- and upper-class families employed a cook, *someone* would have to assume food preparation duties. At that moment of possibility, Americans could have decided that cooking the family's daily meals need not take place in the home, under the care of the woman of the house. Refrigeration, utilities, kitchen technology, and food-processing corporations had already taken much of the hard labor out of food preparation. Couldn't anyone in the house put together a meal out of boxes and cans? Or why not move all meal preparation processes to an efficient factory-like setting? But in keeping with a long-standing American antagonism toward communal social structures and, more significantly, the abiding power of gender norms in U.S. society, the only real option lay in reconfiguring cookery as a middle-class white woman's joy. As historian Katherine Parkin points out in her work on Campbell's soup advertising, processed-food companies *could* have marketed their goods with the message that ease of preparation allowed anyone in the home to make the family's meal. Instead, they continued to "promote the belief that food preparation was a gender-specific activity."[5] Cookbooks did the same.

In the past, when housekeeping reformers suggested alternatives to the gendered, domestic work of a private household, they received very little support from ordinary Americans, although cooperative housekeeping enjoyed a brief vogue in the late 1800s. Melusina Fay Peirce, wife of philosopher Charles Sanders Peirce, envisioned a system of communal baking, cleaning, and shopping in a series of five articles for the *Atlantic Monthly* in 1869, and the popular press paid considerable attention. When she published *Cooperative Housekeeping* in 1884, the idea again received the attention of the press, especially in *Good Housekeeping* magazine.[6] Feminist socialists Marie Stevens Howland and Alice Constance Austin created extensive architectural plans between 1874 and 1917 for utopian cities that included communal kitchens and dining rooms.[7] Perhaps most famously, Charlotte Perkins Gilman's socialist attacks on household drudgery in the late nineteenth and early twentieth centuries called for drastic changes in family, sex, and society's structures. In her 1898 book *Women and Economics*, she advocated the professionalization of cooking and communal eating arrangements. "While we treat cooking as a sex-function common to all women and eating as a family function not otherwise rightly accomplished, we can develop no further," she wrote.[8] Martha Bensely Bruère, another domestic reformer, also called for cooperative housekeeping and cooperative marketing in her 1916 *Increasing Home Efficiency.*

Americans could have turned toward commercial services or other types of cooperative housekeeping to provide meals and perform other household labor, but they did not. For one thing, appliance manufacturers naturally had a vested interest in making sure this work remained in the home. Additionally, the post–World War I "Red Scare" ensured that many Americans looked askance at anything remotely communal. Some asserted that removing household labor from the home would create social mayhem, and cultural commentators pointedly rejected the idea of restructuring American cooking and eating habits to incorporate ideas about communal or cooperative housework. In the 1920s and 1930s, magazine writers and newspaper columnists decried such ideas as undermining the foundation of American society. Authors of marriage and sex manuals, for example, frequently commented upon the importance of home cooking to marriage, family, and a democratic society. Mary Borden's 1933 sex manual *The Technique of Marriage* drew on fears about modern living, political systems, race, and gender norms to paint a sinister picture of a disintegrating nation eating in communal dining rooms. The title of one chapter, "Cookery Book or Communism," made a direct link between women's acceptance of home cookery duties and social stability. Borden lambasted "the modern women" for not taking up household cooking duties:

> The modern woman must choose (she seems to have chosen already), but let her choose with her eyes open. Quick-lunch counters, cafeterias, and drug stores are multiplying like weeds, and they are phases of the new communal American state. If the women of America accept them

and abandon their kitchens in favor of them, the rest will follow, and with it, eventually, the whole of our individualistic system. Is there an oven in any house in any state of the forty-nine that bakes bread for a family? Is there a wife or mother of Anglo-Saxon stock anywhere between the Pacific and Atlantic seaboard who knows how to knead the dough and takes time to make the bread? If there is, the young women of New York, Chicago, Cleveland, Buffalo, and San Francisco don't know of her existence.

Borden clearly outlined the choice facing white ("of Anglo-Saxon stock") women: the homemade bread of solid, dependable American homes or the "quick-lunch counters" of the socially degenerate cities—cities teeming with foreign immigrants and radicals.

Feckless young women, warned Borden, should consider the alternative to traditional home cooking, that is, communism of the vilest sort:

> No one will have kitchens, all the cooking will be done in communal kitchens, and all the communal food you eat will be eaten very much as now in communal dining rooms. You will never have to order a meal or wonder what on earth to have for dinner by way of a change. You won't even have to pay for it. You and your husband will sally out three times a day with your food tickets and sit down in the communal dining hall of your district and be fed. I say you and your husband, but I should correct that and say, you and your comrade of the moment; for you will not be married in any sense worth considering; since the family as a social unit will be long since abandoned.[9]

In this particular diatribe, cooking stood for the "American way of life." That is to say, *home cooking* produced by *white middle-class women* stood for the American way of life. "Cookery Book or Communism" dealt not simply with the importance of home-cooked meals, but with the importance of women cooking at home.

Cookbooks then, were part of a larger body of prescriptive literature concerned with women's obligations to hearth and home. Not all cookbooks, by any means, emphasized the domestic responsibilities of the woman in the kitchen. But, in their introductions or prefaces, cookbook authors did often draw on the prevalent notion that cooking duties made up an essential portion of a woman's role in the home—if not the most important. They reinforced the new domestic ideal: the modern woman happily cooking all the family's meals at home. In this typical passage from a 1928 cookbook by Cammille Dooven, *The Modern Cook Book*, the author linked not only the health of the family but also the health of the nation to a woman's home cooking: "The backbone of a nation is the good housekeeper, and the homemakers' greatest asset is the ability to prepare good food. The future happiness of children depends on their health, and health is obtained only through well prepared foods, fresh air, and exercise. The future of your husband and his ability to provide for the home that which is necessary in life, depend on good health and energy, and in order to have a reserve amount of energy and health one must be properly fed."[10] Similarly, Ida Bailey Allen's lengthy blank verse poem entitled "Home" (included in the introduction to her 1939 *New Modern Cook Book*) described a woman's cooking duties as the bedrock of society. A woman's homemaking, she asserted, created "the center of industry," "The center for which civilization exists."[11] Again, such rhetoric did not first appear in the twentieth century, but it took on a new, heated vehemence in the 1920s, shaped by a cultural backlash against feminism, and more widely disseminated by improved publishing and advertising techniques.

George Frederick's 1930 *Cooking as Men Like It* offered perhaps the most obvious example of a cookbook that harangued its readers on the critical role of cooking in modern America and criticized modern women for failing to take up their God-given job as family cook. Though not a best seller, Frederick's book probably reached quite a few readers. His wife Christine Frederick, well known as a home efficiency expert, authored several popular cookbooks herself and wrote numerous magazine articles and newspaper columns. So her husband's cookbook may well have generated considerable interest. Frederick grew apoplectic when he discussed the way women's failure to realize the importance of preparing good meals for the family contributed to the widespread masculine ailment of dyspepsia. He began his book by pointing out that higher education had ill-prepared women for their most important job: "The fact is that the great majority of young women of the past two generations have spurned any knowledge of cookery and preferred going into businesses. On the day such young women set up housekeeping they probably knew less about food preparation than they did about Greek poetry or astronomy." Unlike Mary J. Lincoln, who urged her readers to apply college learning to cooking duties, Frederick dismissed women's education outright as harmful to home and family.

Calling attention to the way feminism, as well as higher education, discouraged many women from a proper study of the domestic arts, he asserted that the most intelligent women eventually gave up outside interests to focus on the home. These able and successful women, according to Frederick, realized that true feminine satisfaction could be achieved only by homemaking—and cooking: "Such women instinctively know that is a false ideal for so many women today to 'come out of the kitchen' and slur all interest in food in favor of chimerical pursuits of one kind and another which so often come to naught." He added that "this exodus from the hearth is a condition particularly dangerous to women's basic happiness and fundamental status in life." He assured the reader that "It is today socially smart and normal for a wealthy bride to don an apron and cook." Moreover, he continued, a woman put not only her happiness but also her attractiveness at stake when she did not hone her cooking skills (even if her financial resources stretched to servants in the kitchen): "Rich or poor, we must eat, and rich or poor, a woman cannot evade the responsibility of serving good food (which means knowing what good food is, which in turn means being at least a good amateur cook)—just as a man cannot evade special family financial responsibilities. A man can no more help thinking less of a woman who cannot prepare a simple meal than a woman can help thinking less of a man who is undependable financially." Frederick then went on to claim, "I do not care how fair or wealthy or famous she be (to paraphrase an old saying), she is not 'fair' to me or to most other men if she cannot prepare me an appetizing meal!" A woman who did not personally cook and serve food in her own home, he insisted, "is robbing herself of the most subtle, instinctive attraction to man, is depriving herself of her most deep-rooted basis of appeal and charm, and is tampering with the very foundations of human happiness, both for herself, her family, and society as a whole." Frederick summarized his views by stating: "There is no more severe indictment of our age than the decline of the dinner at home."[12] And, by extension, no more severe indictment of the modern woman.

current standard

Although in a vitriolic class of its own, Frederick's ranting did articulate themes addressed by other cookbook authors. Preachy Alice Foote MacDougall came close to Frederick when she concluded her 1935 cookbook with a long tirade against women who willfully gave up their blessed place at the hearth. "It is no exaggeration to say that much of the evil of war and the horrors of the amoral society in which we live might have been avoided had the woman not abandoned the home for desk and telephone," she asserted.[13] Many authors assumed that their readers might very well know nothing about the kitchen (having pursued a business career or a college degree) and lamented the resulting deterioration of home and society. Even Hazel Young, whose 1938 cookbook *The Working Girl Must Eat* wholeheartedly embraced the notion of women working outside the home, spoke out in her 1940 cookbook *Better Meals for Less Money* against the flighty woman who refused to give her full attention to planning and preparing meals: "It's the little woman down your street—and ours—who doesn't let her housekeeping or her husband's small salary bother her too much. She is so busy with her bridge club and seeing every movie! She never takes the time to get a good old-fashioned dinner with a meat pie or a beef loaf or a thrifty stew. She runs to the delicatessen at the last minute for some chops, and potato salad, and cream puffs for dessert. It's strange, but she is always behind on her housekeeping allowance."[14] Authors like Young cautioned that the modern young woman, with processed and take-out foods increasingly available to her, must still pay close attention to cultivating her cooking skills. Women must not let outside interests or employment interfere with one of their most important roles in the home—food preparation.

In *Feeding Peter*, a cookbook published in 1924, "Judith" (the fictional protagonist) exemplifies the flighty young woman who has never given much thought to homemaking. Judith marries a man who has been injured in World War I and thus cannot keep Judith in the style to which she's become accustomed. Judith cannot, in short, hire a cook, and so she seeks the culinary assistance of her friend "Caroline." At the beginning of the book, Caroline gently scolds Judith on her widely traveled friend's lack of preparation for this, a woman's most important job: "To most women marriage means meals—three of them per day, seven days in the week. But you have studied railroad guides instead of cook-books. Judith dear, you can read a train schedule in four languages, but I defy you to tell me the difference between 1 tsp and 1 Tbs."[15] Caroline may have addressed her remarks to Judith, but the author probably meant her humorous chiding for the reader. Cookbook authors noted again and again that their readers may have never stepped foot in the kitchen. But they also emphasized that as modern young women and wives, their readers could easily learn how to cook, and should enjoy it.

Learning how to cook, though, required precise measurements, standardized cooking equipment, and up-to-date knowledge about cooking methods. In the 1920s and 1930s, authors continued to emphasize the importance of correct measurements and strict adherence to the recipe—both legacies of the cooking school movement. Fannie Farmer's innovation, the level measurement, had clearly come to stay. Admonitions to employ careful cooking technique abounded in cookbooks, and authors urged their readers to use standard measuring cups, to learn food values, to keep up on the latest kitchen equipment, and to follow every recipe exactly. According to numerous cookbooks in the 1920s and 1930s, if the reader employed proper technique and precise measurements, she could not help but cook every recipe perfectly. Some authors stated bluntly that "bad luck" simply did not exist in the kitchen. For example, the editors of the 1921 *Cupid's Book* gave this typical advice: "Don't just 'trust to luck' in cake making. It is far better to use a tested recipe, handy utensils, good materials, accurate measurements, a carefully regulated oven, and enjoy cake success every time."[16] As Ida Bailey Allen preached in her 1935 *Modern Menus,* "There is no such thing as 'good luck' or 'bad luck' in cooking, if the recipe measurements are absolutely accurate and the homemaker understands the range."[17]

Many authors included numerous charts, diagrams, and descriptions at the beginning of their books to educate the reader about the kitchen utensils and correct technique, which would supposedly guard against "luck" in cooking. Photos and drawings of different kinds of kitchen implements, and instructions for their use, often appeared. Although cookbooks avoided much of the stiffly instructional tone of earlier domestic science cookbooks, authors often issued a call for careful and accurate measurements. Jessie DeBoth, a prolific cookbook writer, asserted in her 1925 *Home Maker's Cooking School Cook Book* that "cooking by 'guess work' is now a thing of the past" and that "recipes have been so well standardized that no one need have failures if they start with good materials, follow directions, and use adequate equipment."[18]

General Foods Cook Book, published to promote the numerous processed-food products made by General Foods, emphasized that modern cooking required careful measurements and exact recipes. The section on basic cooking technique titled "Doing the Job—The Modern Way" began by describing the twentieth-century kitchen: "Aeroplanes—skyscrapers—metal furniture! All tell of swift-changing ways of doing things. But so, too, do kitchens! Science has come into the kitchen and changed our way of cooking, has set about bringing materials and processes under control. We begin to know, instead of guess."[19] Authors in the 1920s and 1930s, like their foremothers in the scientific cookery field, often contrasted careful measuring, mixing, and recipe following with what they imagined as the sloppy cooking techniques plaguing the nation. They pointed out that modern advances in food technology made bad cooking a thing of the past, asserting that such advances, paired with knowledge about strict measurement and cooking technique, created a perfectible science. In her *Primer of Modern Cooking,* for example, Mary Stevens pointed out that the modern young woman would be more likely to turn out better pies and pastry than her mother would, with far less difficulty: "The bride still may adore her mother's old-fashioned chicken dumplings, because some of these good things haven't changed a whit, but she is apt to be a bit critical of mother's pies. It has become so much simpler, with modern conveniences, for even a bride to turn out a pie with its crust as flaky as new-fallen snow, and its modern 'chiffon' filling as gossamer as its name." Scientific advances, processed foods, and proper technique—not learned skills— would enable women to enjoy the joy of cooking.

Stevens, like many other authors, depicted modern cooking as a *fun-filled* activity that *also* produced better food than the kitchens of previous years: "Happily, modern cooking is not a work-a-day job at all, but a most enchanting occupation. Scientists have taken the drudgery out of cooking, and left the joy of it. Food packers have provided intriguing products to play with, the very names of which were unfamiliar to our mothers. Things like gelatin soups, sandwich pastes, puréed vegetables, ready-to-use fruit juices and ready-mixed biscuits. Why, if a roast chicken, gravy and all, compactly sealed in a can, had ever shown up in our childhood kitchens, the cook would have quit—then and there."[20] Paid household cooks, suggested this author, were simply a thing of the past. Because cookery could no longer be considered hard labor but "a most enchanting occupation," cooking could much more easily be incorporated into the middle-class white woman's domestic duties.

The modern cook of the 1920s and 1930s carefully measured all ingredients level while following a recipe to the letter and understood that perfect food would always result with correct technique. But she also infused her cookery with artistic flair and creative touches that mere servants simply could not create. As "a most enchanting occupation," home cooking demanded not arduous hours at the stove but creative touches and artistic devotion. *Macy's Cook Book for the Busy Woman* asserted that "the preparation of properly balanced meals . . . is a science as exact as the compounding of drugs," but that cooking also required "the vision of an artist."[21] Many authors echoed such statements.

"Although, personally, we have the greatest respect for the ladies of the Boston Cooking School," wrote Jean Aaberg, "they continue to fill us with a sort of antiseptic horror. The whole thing is on the basis of a chemistry experiment; and leavening is all that matters in life, they seem to infer."[22] Aaberg's dismissal of the "antiseptic" Boston Cooking School ladies exemplified the rise of a new kind of rhetoric about cookery: home cooking as art. Although the previous century's dictums on the exact scientific nature of cooking still shaped cookery instruction in the 1920s, most authors took care to note that cooking should be viewed as an art (fig. 5). Earlier cookery instruction sometimes compared cookery to an art, but in the 1920s and 1930s such comparisons occurred at an unprecedented pace.[23] In the modern era, cooking advisers and authors frowned upon cooking as a "chemistry experiment." Cooking must be understood, they asserted, as artistic expression—and an expression of love and devotion to the home.

As Ramus Alasker wrote in the 1927 *Adventures in Cooking:* "Those who develop the art and the science of cooking will not find it drudgery."[24] Numerous authors made the same kind of claim: they described their intelligent, well-bred, white, middle-class, female readers as

Figure 5 In the 1920s, cookbook authors stressed that cookery was an artistic and creative pursuit, well suited to middle-class white women. The original caption to this photo from a 1930 cookbook read "The Queen of the Kitchen Plying Her Art." From George Conforth, *Better Meals for Less* (Washington, DC: Review and Herald Publishing, 1930).

entirely capable of developing the art and the science of cooking and thus able to avoid the "drudgery" of cooking. In fact, these women had the best qualifications for "developing the art and science of cooking." When cookbook authors Margaret Allen and Ida Hutton described the art and science of cooking in 1928, they took pains to show that a woman acting as both cook and hostess could best provide the meals for her family: "Physicians preach that our outlook on life, our capacity for work, even the quality of our work, depends on what we put into our stomachs and how. Then it seems obvious that whoever lays a foundation for vigorous mental and physical health through good food, well cooked and attractively served, is doing as important a job as any that falls to the lot of all but the most talented women. A careless servant can't plan and cook and serve such meals. It takes knowledge—of food values, and individual needs; executive ability—to plan, direct, organize, cut costs; creative imagination—to give variety and attractiveness."[25]

The title of Hannah Dutaud's 1935 cookbook—*The Glorious Art of Home Cooking*—illustrated the growing emphasis on cooking as the creative pursuit of the middle-class woman. Dutaud asserted, as did numerous other cookbook authors in the late 1920s and 1930s, that "cooking is recognized as an art and a science."[26] Another cookbook bearing a revealing title—*The Romantic and Practical Side of Cookery* ("romantic" referred to the creative and exciting part of cookery)—began with a poem on the creative inspiration of the kitchen entitled "My Domain": "Here I am an artist, / Creating as I measure, sift, beat and bake, / With busy brain, light hand and joyous heart; / My kitchen is a happy place to dream and bake a cake." In the domain of one's kitchen, sifting, beating, and baking took on the mantle of creation, not drudgery. The author went on to assert: "How many beautiful pictures we can execute, not with brush and canvas, but with food and implements." Ida Bailey Allen offered a blank-verse poem, "The Landscape Cook," that made a similar claim about the "beautiful pictures" women could render with food. It described how a woman stood gazing at a sunset, then recreated the beautiful image with foods she was preparing for dinner, using a blue plate as the sky, sliced tomatoes and yellow dressing for the sunset, and lettuce and parsley for the background of trees and shrubs.[27]

Many authors drew a direct comparison between home cooking and the desire to paint or write. "Never let anyone tell you that cooking is not an art," counseled Mable Claire in *Macy's Cook Book for the Busy Woman*. "A good cook feels the same urge that makes an artist want to paint a picture or a writer write a story."[28] A promotional cook book for the Royal Baking Powder Company drew a similar parallel: "To one person it is given to take brushes and colors and so combine them that there is produced a work of art. To another is given the ability to set down the melody lying in his imagination so that when it is played there comes forth music which is called a masterpiece. Just as paints and oil and musical notes are all about us, so there are, at every hand, wide varieties of food products which one may fashion into dishes which, too, are works of art."[29] Popular magazines echoed these comparisons. For example, Ann Batchelder, the food editor for *Ladies' Home Journal*, titled an article on steak recipes "Still Life, by Mother."[30]

John MacPherson, "The Mystery Chef," went so far as to argue that cooking actually made a more lasting impression on the world than other kinds of artwork. First he compared a biscuit recipe with an enormous steel ocean liner: "Now long before that ship was even thought of, or before man dreamed of building ships from steel, some housewife who wanted to escape the slow process of making raised bread created a recipe for hot biscuits; and as long as man inhabits the earth hot biscuits will be enjoyed in millions of homes." He pointed out that some artworks could be destroyed—fire or neglect may ruin the work of a great painter—and that others may be inaccessible to all but a few people. "How different with your work as an artist at the stove!" he wrote. Recipes live on and on, each touched by the creative interpretation of the cook.[31] MacPherson's fervent depiction of recipes as more capable of longevity than a painting—but as a similar kind of creation—exemplified how authors drew on the imagery of the artist at his easel or the composer at his piano to drive home their assertions about the art of cooking.

Bristow Adams, in his preface to Phoebe Dane's 1931 *333 New Ways to a Man's Heart*, called forth the image of French culinary masters to make his point about the artistry of food preparation. He began: "To the French, cooking is an art, which means that all who practice cooking in that land of delicious food are artists, wielding pots and pans and working in meats and vegetables with much the same gusto as the inspired sculptor attacks a block of marble with hammer and chisel." French women in the kitchen, he claimed, had the same kind of standards: "Watch a French homemaker at work and compare her to the sculptor with his block of marble or the painter with his canvas. She is constantly tasting, adding a bit of this or that seasoning. Watch her eyes, how they light up when she achieves just the right flavor. It is a perfect reproduction of the eyes of the painter when he has achieved the right line or color. And the French husband gives his artist housewife-cook the same fulsome appreciation of a good dish as he would give a poet for a well turned sonnet or a composer for a beautiful melody."[32] Cookbooks for children utilized the same imagery of an artist bent on creation. As her mother explains to Ann in *Kitchen Magic,* "Don't think that cooking is all science, either. It's just as much of an art. The kitchen is a studio, as well as a laboratory, and a fine cook is really an artist." She continued: "When you get so your tools are as dear and familiar to your hands as a painter's brushes are to his, and when everything you make, no matter how simple, has a light touch that is all your own, then you will know what a real joy cookery can be. I can't think why some people call it drudgery."[33] Again, the home cook escaped drudgery when she perceived her kitchen implements as artist's tools and food as a palate. In *Polly Put the Kettle On*, after a conversation with her father, Polly mused to herself about the artistry of the kitchen (and how their servant Hannah seemed unable to enact that kind of art): "And Dad says that to be able to cook well is as important a gift as Cousin Emily's painting. I'd never thought of cooking that way—it just seemed like work the way Hannah did it."[34] Once again, only a well-bred, middle-class, white girl can achieve art in the kitchen. Cooking was only work when servants did it. An Irish "Biddy" might not have been able to achieve artistry at the stove, but a well-bred Polly could.

Although many encyclopedic cookbooks in the 1920s and 1930s dealt with nutrition information at length, cookbook authors could frankly admit that, in contrast to the laboratory-like instructions found in earlier cookbooks, their cookery instruction had far more to do with the art and fun of food than with kitchen science. Wrote Mary Ellsworth, author of the popular 1939 *Much Depends on Dinner:* "I can't and don't pretend to domestic science. My ambition is domestic art. If I can develop the cunning, the perception necessary to produce a perfectly balanced sauce, I shall never care about its calories, vitamins, or mineral content." Similarly, in *Of Cabbages and Kings*, William Rhode called for an outright rejection of domestic science concerns about nutrition: "Eating is fun, and cooking is fun, and to hell with all the calories and balanced meals! Let us again sit around big, comfortable tables and enjoy our meals. It does not require any more money. It merely requires a little more relaxation and a little more attention to the fundamental artistry of cooking." Hazel Young made the same plea in *Better Meals for Less Money:* "The last few years, everything has been so serious—even Food [*sic*]! Everyone has gone scientific and has been so busy tracking down vitamins, and what-have-you, that no one has really enjoyed a square meal. That's all wrong. Food is Fun [*sic*] and it's fun to cook and to learn to cook," she asserted.[35]

Food might be fun and cooking might be a creative joy for those who truly cared about their art, but another reason might compel a woman to hasten to the kitchen: her marriage. George Conforth, the health food advocate whose cookbooks emphasized restraint and moderation at the table, urged readers to consider cooking a sacred art entrusted to the woman of the house and good meals an essential element in marital happiness. "Every housewife and mother should be an artist in preparing food for her family. She should indeed regard cooking as one of the finer arts, to which she can afford to give nothing less than the best that is in her," he counseled. After all, a woman's marriage might well depend upon good home cooking: "While thus enthusiastically putting herself into her work, she will gain pleasure and satisfaction from it which will well repay her for the effort. Then, far from finding housework a drudgery, her life will be a pleasure not only to herself but to her family. While it is frequently true that 'those persons whom God hath joined together in matrimony, ill-cooked joints and badly boiled potatoes have put asunder,' the exact opposite of this may and should be true."[36]

Similarly, Hazel Young characterized the recipes in her book for the married working woman as "home insurance": "We don't guarantee that reading this book will get you a husband in six weeks, but we do claim that it will help you to keep the one you already have. Learning how to mix flavors as well as colors in your foods is a grand form of home insurance. Just try it for awhile, you married girls!"[37] Phoebe

Dane made the connection absolutely clear in *333 New Ways to a Man's Heart*. In her introduction, Dane asked readers if they ever "smiled over a little paragraph called, 'The Way for Any Woman to Regain Her Husband's Love.' It begins like this: 'Go to the butcher's and select a thick, juicy steak,' and continues with directions for cooking that steak and serving it most invitingly." Dane went on to argue that such articles were right on the money: "It's become a habit of mine, when one of my younger married friends comes to me with a tale of this quarrel or that misunderstanding, to say, 'Let's see, what are you going to have for dinner tonight?' The usual mournful reply is, 'What does it matter?' Well, it matters a lot, and I tell her so. Then, if she really hasn't any special ideas on the subject, I jot down a couple of recipes that I know from experience produce a peaceful and contented mood, and say, 'Serve these for dinner and talk the thing over with him afterwards.' It would surprise you how successful such a simple idea can be!" She ended by assuring her reader that the recipes in this book would "produce the sort of food that makes men hurry home from work."[38] Dane's readers would have instantly recognized, in 1931, the kind of articles to which Dane referred. Whereas many cookbooks emphasized the art and science of food prepared by the mistress of the house, popular magazines and other cookery books often noted the important role of home cooking in making a home—and a husband—happy.

Moreover, they also discussed at length the differences between men and women in the kitchen and at the table. Dane's fictional article suggested serving steak to "regain a husband's love," and numerous articles in popular magazines repeated that same advice. The idea that steak might magically restore a man's love began with certain assumptions about the kinds of food men liked. In the 1920s and 1930s, cookbooks contained a vast amount of information on men's food preferences. At the same time, cookbook authors, food editors, and columnists exerted a major effort to define "the male cook." Men not only liked certain kinds of food, but cookbooks depicted them as fundamentally different kinds of cooks—simply by the virtue of being male. Cookbooks consistently drew and redrew the lines between the male appetite and the female appetite, the male approach to cooking and the female. With some variations on the theme, and in a very different tone, authors and editors of cookery instruction for men, however, made the same basic assertion: in the modern era of processed foods and servantless kitchens, the white middle-class woman would assume responsibility for the family's daily meals and she should learn to enjoy it.

4

Ladylike Lunches and Manly Meals

THE GENDERING OF FOOD AND COOKING

From 1929 through 1937 Byron MacFadyen contributed a semiregular column to *Good Housekeeping* on cooking from the male point of view. (A similar commentator, Leo Nejelski, also appeared in *Good Housekeeping* occasionally.) MacFadyen covered a variety of topics, from grilling food in the backyard ("Picnics for Men Who Hate to Leave Home"), the versatility of French dressing ("A Man Cooks with French Dressing"), and the male desire for simple food ("Courses—Courses—Courses! They Are All Right in Their Place, But Usually a Man Wants a Simple Meal"). In his articles, MacFadyen emphasized that men possessed the ability to cook well and, in fact, to cook extremely well. He often pointed out that men did not enjoy the same kind of fussy food that women liked but preferred simple dishes (fig. 6). MacFadyen offered recipes, cooking tips, and advice for women who sought to make "Dishes Fit for Gods—And Men!"[1] His column offers only one example of how numerous magazine writers and cookbook authors distinguished the ways that men and women cooked, and ate.

Authors writing commercial cookery instruction for men generated a markedly different kind of cookbook than similar instruction for women. For one thing, cookbooks for men often seemed created to be read as much as novels as manuals of instruction, containing commentary on men in the kitchen, earthy humor, cartoon illustrations, travel anecdotes, and hints on choosing a fine wine to complement one's

Figure 6 Byron MacFadyen's recipes for men appeared semiregularly in *Good Housekeeping* during the 1920s and 1930s. From "When a Man Goes Culinary," *Good Housekeeping*, January 1930.

meal. As a whole, they almost always lacked the basic introduction to the kitchen and detailed discussions about recipe following and level measurements so common to general cookbooks. Publishers marketed cookbooks for men as a novelty, as just-for-fun books, rather than practical everyday manuals. Moreover, virtually all cookery instruction for men contained similar messages about gender and food.

Most obviously, authors invariably contrasted the hearty, simple appetites of men with the more finicky but less refined palates of women. Cooking instructors and magazine writers had discussed that contrast for decades, but in the 1920s authors constantly explained the differences between male and female appetites.[2] Many authors also dwelled, at length, on masculine superiority in the kitchen. In all cases, if the article or the cookbook dealt specifically with male cooks, they clearly stated so. At the same time that cookbooks urged women to consider cooking an art, they depicted men as already aware of this happy fact— and thus reiterated the idea that white middle-class women needed to learn how to enjoy cookery as an imaginative and creative pursuit. Numerous cookbooks aimed at middle-class women emphasized the culinary ignorance of their readers. But cookery instruction aimed at the middle-class male reader emphasized his natural skill in the kitchen and his natural artistry with food. And they all provided reassurance to the man at the stove that his work in the kitchen differed decidedly from the day-to-day cooking done by women. They portrayed men's interest in cooking as a hobby, as an occasional event, in contrast to women's three-times-a-day job, 365 days a year. By defining male cookery as a special event, authors and editors also defined everyday cookery as women's work. In this way, much of the instruction ostensibly written for men in fact offered considerable commentary on women's duties in the modern era.

Perhaps the simplest explanation for the depiction of men as only occasional home cooks rested with social expectations about paid employment. Although cookbooks provided more than a few recipes for the woman working outside the home (indeed, whole cookbooks devoted to the subject enjoyed moderate success in the 1920s and 1930s), and although a growing percentage of white married women worked outside the home, the domestic ideology of the era insisted that homemaking—including preparing the daily meals—constituted a woman's most important job. As the sole wage earner in the family, a man could hardly be expected to do the daily cooking. His job ended when he returned home from work. As numerous historians point out, the Industrial Revolution created a sharp divide between the home and the market: production shifted to the factory, while the private sphere became a space of consumption. Moreover, those spheres became rigidly gendered, with women assuming the role of consumer and men of producer.[3] Despite the real labor that cooking daily meals demanded, Americans measured work value in terms of wage earnings, and thus cooking the daily meals could not be considered work suitable for the man (the wage earner) of the home. Any cooking he might do in the home would have to be considered supplemental to the daily task of providing three meals a day.

And, after all, "tradition" bound a woman to the kitchen. Even before the Industrial Revolution, even when the growing, harvesting, and production of food required the labor of both men and women in the family, it was the woman of the family—or her female helper—who concocted the stew in a pot and put it over the fire.[4] Yet this powerful tradition cannot fully explain why 1920s and 1930s periodicals and cookbooks so consistently depicted men as hobby cooks or why it seemed vitally important in cookery instruction to delineate so clearly, so uniformly, and so vehemently the difference between male and female cookery. Such depictions must also be recognized as part of a broader discourse that helped define middle-class women's role in the home. With the modern kitchen conveniences of the twentieth century, even a man with a full-time job outside the home could conceivably take responsibility for a significant amount of the home cooking. But instead, cookbooks for men almost universally depicted cooking the family's daily meals as the province of women. The attention given to what the man of the house did in the kitchen and what he enjoyed eating underscored the woman's pursuits and preferences. If men only entered the kitchen as a hobby or to exercise their natural ability to employ the artistry needed for really fine cooking, their presence would not undermine the prescriptions that constructed women as essentially domestic creatures. In fact, it strengthened them. If men confined their cooking to flights of fancy with spaghetti or scrambled egg recipes, they only reinforced the increasingly powerful idea that a middle-class white woman—and not her servant or the community or anyone else in the household with the aid of canned and premade foods—would be responsible for the practical, daily, home cooking. Each representation helped reinforce the other. Just as Western society requires a racialized "Other" in order to define white subjectivity, Americans needed the man in the kitchen to help define the white middle-class woman's daily, domestic role in the twentieth century.

masculinity

Moreover, authors and editors took pains to depict men as essentially different kinds of culinary creatures than women in order to safeguard the masculinity of the male hobby cook. Instructors urged the modern woman to take up the joy of cooking and in various ways depicted home cookery as an essential part of women's domestic duties. They therefore had to make sure that male cookery did not in any way overlap those duties; to do so would be to blur the line between both masculine and domestic feminine identities. Many Americans, even today, seem to assume that women just "naturally" take responsibility for the family's meals. But in cookery instruction, the "natural" distinctions between female day-to-day cooking and male occasional cooking required constant explanation, definition, and reiteration. Authors confidently, a little too confidently, described the many ways men and women differed when it came to food and cooking. If such natural and obvious differences existed, they would not have required such concerted, detailed descriptions. The advance of food and cooking technology (the availability of processed foods in particular) and the decline in paid kitchen help in the 1920s, however, put into question the "natural" link between food preparation and gender. The authors and editors of cookery instruction during the 1920s and 1930s, then, could not let a man enter the kitchen without scrupulously showing that male hobby cooking would not undermine the long-standing connection between women and food preparation and would not threaten masculine identity.

Authors utilized elaborate rhetorical devices that assured their readers that hobby cooking could be a suitably masculine activity. Most obviously, the authors of cookery instruction for both women and men took care to differentiate between male and female appetites. Some cookbooks made merely a glancing reference to men's different kinds of eating habits. The 1933 edition of Fannie Farmer's cookbook, for example, suggested a menu briefly described as "A Luncheon Men Will Like," comprised of mixed grill, hard rolls, "Club Indian pudding," and coffee.[5] Others, such as Eleanor Howe's 1939 *Feeding Father*, focused entirely on meals and dishes men supposedly liked. But all cookbooks, whether they merely touched on the subject or dwelt on it at length, described men as hearty eaters fond of meat, strong flavors, and coffee, very much disinclined to tuck into a frilly salad plate. Howe spoke for many authors when she summarized: "Just how does [*sic*] a man's food preferences differ from those of women? Well, for one thing, a man wants more substantial, plainer food. He likes a meal to be composed of only a few dishes, but he wants those to be tasty, full of flavor and perfectly cooked. He likes, also, to know what he is eating, he wants to be able to recognize each main ingredient in its familiar form. In a word, fancy cooking is wasted on the average man but good cooking is appreciated to the limit!"[6] In his 1934 article for *House and Garden*, Leone B. Moats chastised the women of America for refusing to come to terms with the fact that men despised fussy foods: "You can't appease a man's appetite with a fruit salad or a bit of fluff like marshmallow-date whip, and yet women continue to overlook this fact and go right on serving dishes that have no relation to muscle and brawn," he scolded. He advised women to "Keep your dainties for women's luncheons but remember that where such delicacies as squab leave a man cold, the very mention of corned beef hash with a poached egg on top will bring a gleam to his eye." If "fancy cooking" did not appeal to men, other specific kinds of dishes, such as corned beef hash, did. Moats went on to recommend oyster stew, planked steak (a way of cooking and serving meat and fish, popular in the 1920s and 1930s, on a seasoned plank of wood), onion soup, French fried potatoes and deep-dish apple pie.[7]

Authors never hesitated to make sweeping, universal generalizations about male food preferences. "Men love oyster stew," asserted Mary Stevens in *A Primer of Modern Cooking*. In *New Dishes from Left-overs*, Coral Smith urged the reader to disguise leftovers with cheese, as "Men, particularly, are fond of cheese dishes." In Edith Key Haines's self-titled 1937 cookbook, her list of "Dishes Men Like" included onion soup, curried eggs, meat cakes, hamburger hash, baked chicken, pork chops, corn pancakes, curried carrots, kidney bean salad, blueberry loaf, and chocolate cake. A 1940 cookbook entitled *Formal Dinners* included a menu for a "Men's Dinner": celery au jus, fish borscht, beefsteak, St.

Louis jockey club sauce, spoon bread, macaroni and mushrooms, southern stewed tomatoes, salad with Roquefort dressing, and café brulot
[*sic*]. Steak, stewed tomatoes, and Roquefort dressing often appeared
in such menus (spoon bread less frequently so). An entire chapter in
Sunset's Host and Hostess Book, edited by Helen Muhs, offered recipes
"With, for, and by Men." The suggested recipes included baked sirloin
steak, chicken stew, stuffed shoulder of veal, rice-beef casserole, spaghetti (enough to serve "4 enthusiastic men"), fried shrimp, fried oysters, waffles, kidney stew, and curried eggs.[8]

When Hazel Young turned her attention to meals for men in *The
Working Girl Must Eat*, she recommended a menu of fresh pineapple
cup, broiled tenderloin steak, French fried potatoes, buttered new peas,
stuffed celery, ice cream puff, and butterscotch sauce. On the important
topic of steak, and a few other key dishes, she instructed her reader to
be sure to "learn how to cook a steak properly as 'He' likes it. The girl
who can broil a steak well, make good coffee and light fluffy biscuits,
will be forgiven many sins and omissions." In contrast, her recommended menu for an all-girl bridge party included fresh fruit salad,
creamy dressing, strawberry jam, hot clover leaf rolls, Danbury tarts
with savory cheese (a cheese ball flavored with salt and paprika), salted
almonds, and crystallized ginger.[9]

Another cookbook aimed at the woman living alone, Marjorie Hillis
and Bertina Foltz's *Corned Beef and Caviar*, actually divided men into
different categories, with very specific menu suggestions depending on
which kind of man the reader planned to entertain. For example, according to Hillis and Foltz, a teetotaler would enjoy a bland menu of
cream of mushroom soup, Maryland chicken, scalloped sweet potatoes,
string beans, hot rolls, currant jelly, lemon chiffon pie, and coffee. For a
young beau or the friend of a younger brother, they recommended that
the reader be prepared to offer beer and steak. "Steak is, incidentally,
sure-fire with most men. It is preferred by practically all young men
and unsophisticated men of any age, and by at least half of the rest of the
sex," they wrote. In contrast, an "older man" needed a more sedate
menu: tomato juice or sherry, sherry biscuits, clam broth, poached filet
of sole, anchovy sauce, potato balls, peas, compote of stewed fruits, and
Sanka. Finally, a potential Mr. Right required especially careful menu
planning: "He is, really, more than the perfect guest—he is the perfect
beau, and he may be the perfect husband. In fact, he's such a valuable
property that you'd better plan his meal with care, if not with prayer."
Hillis and Foltz offered two dinner menus for feeding this paragon: a
highball, hot bacon rolls, split pea soup, sautéed croutons, roast duck-
ling, small browned potatoes, lima beans, bananas in rum, and coffee, or

chicken curry soup, veal cutlet, peas, honey dew melon, baked potato, and coffee.

Hillis and Foltz explicitly warned against presenting a potential beau with frilly, fussy food. They offered a fictional "case study" to illustrate their point that men required fundamentally different kinds of food than that women enjoyed. They described how "Miss S." drove away a potential beau by inviting him to a sickeningly feminine "Pink Cocktail Party." "Miss S." added grenadine to the cocktails and served dainty little canapés of smoked salmon on crackers and circles of toast spread with a mixture of cream cheese and strawberry jam, but the man in question seemed unimpressed: "Miss S. feels that it was a lovely party and can't understand why the young man who was the secret reason for her giving it has never been able to get around since—even when she invited him."[10] Poor "Miss S.!" She obviously failed to learn that men only went for simple, hearty fare, heavy on the oysters, meat, and green salads. A pink cocktail virtually guaranteed male revulsion.

The male preference for hearty, spicy dishes began early, as Sue, the protagonist in the children's cookbook *When Sue Began to Cook,* learned. When she and her friend Ruth Ann prepare a luncheon one day, they revel in the lovely food and decorations: " 'I do like a "lady-like" lunch, Aunt Bettina,' said Ruth Ann today, when we sat down with Mother and Robin to our Escalloped Corn, cocoa, orange salad and bread and butter. 'When everything is dainty and pretty like this, I always feel hungrier. . . . I like to set the table, too,' Ruth Ann went on, 'and have a dear little fern in the center, like this one, and a clean table-cloth, and pretty china, and everything.' " But Sue's brother Robin protests this feminine frippery and loudly asserts that his favorite kind of lunch is the kind that "Uncle John" likes best: meat and potatoes and lots of them. A few days later Uncle John himself makes an appearance as Sue finishes up dessert preparations. Just as Sue is "piling the whipped cream" onto fruit gelatin (which "does make the prettiest, daintiest dessert"), John walks in. His presence causes much mirth since Ruth Ann and Sue "had just told each other that we could think of only one person who might not like such a lady-like dish, the person referred to being Uncle John, and here he was." But Mother saves the day: "Luckily, Mother had meat and potatoes for him."

Sue summarizes her observations on masculine appetites while she and her mother make stuffed green peppers: "Today we made another fussy dish that Uncle John wouldn't like, but fortunately, he didn't happen in today at lunch-time. I told that to Mother and she thought it sounded crickle [*sic*] of dear old Uncle John, but I didn't mean it that way. I just meant, as I have said before, that he likes plain food best.

Many people on farms seem to—particularly men." Sue concludes that her brother Robin shows every sign of developing an appetite as masculine as Uncle John's: "I'm afraid Robin is going to grow up to be like Uncle John, for he didn't seem to like our green peppers much,—but Ruth Ann and Mother and I appreciated them enough to make up for Robin's finikiness, if that's the way to spell it."[11] However, Robin's prerogative as a male, not his "finikiness," dictated his tastes, as Sue herself pointed out when she told her mother that men (especially hardworking farm men) liked plain food best. Just as Ruth Anne's female appetite accounted for why she felt hungrier when "everything is dainty and pretty," so Robin's male appetite explained his dislike for fussy stuffed peppers.

Cookbooks that made the male eater a focal point made similar assumptions about the kinds of dishes that men liked. Margaret Allen and Ida Hutton's *Man-Sized Meals from the Kitchenette*, Phoebe Dane's *333 New Ways to a Man's Heart*, Eleanor Howe's *Feeding Father*, Iris Prouty's *Feeding Peter*, and Louise Weaver and Helen LeCron's revised 1932 edition of their popular 1917 cookbook *A Thousand Ways to Please a Husband with Bettina's Best Recipes* (*When Sue Began to Cook* picks up Bettina's story with her daughter, Sue, learning to cook) all made it a point to describe the differences between male and female food preferences. In Howe's cookbook, for instance, men's food preferences seemed carved in stone—inflexible and eternal. Her recipes invoked the male appetite as a proven, absolute fact: from salads to cakes to breads, Howe knew what types of food men would always choose. "Father is a natural potato 'hound'—all men are—that's all the more reason for serving them to him in the form he really does like and for seeing that they are perfectly cooked," she lectured; she then gave recipes for French fries, glazed sweet potatoes, potatoes au gratin, and hash browns. On the topic of desserts, Howe informed the reader that "men undoubtedly have a penchant for such substantial items as pie, ice cream and chocolate cake. But they appear to like the homey, less spectacular desserts almost as much." She also scolded that "we women are apt to forget that a sharp, tangy, aged cheese with some good plain crackers is gratefully received as a dessert substitute by almost every man, once in a while." Women, apt to be on a diet might easily feed their men the wrong kind of dessert, according to Howe.

Howe's recipes not only described the male appetite at length but also urged the woman cooking meals to plan around that appetite. She prefaced her pudding recipes, for example, this way: "The men—bless 'em—ask for nothing better, from time to time, than some simple homemade dessert of pudding to complete the perfect meal. The suggestions offered here may not all be *your* favorites, but they will be favorites of the man of the house, so that makes them worth while, doesn't it?" (emphasis in original). Howe explained that "first consideration has frankly been given to the 'men' rather than 'u,'" in her menus, and emphasized that "there is no denying that men's tastes in foods do vary from those of women, and it is definitely the intention of this book to cater to their preferences."[12] Other authors also made the connection between a husband's happiness and a wife's ability to put aside her own preferences in meal planning. Cookbooks regularly depicted men—and the need for pleasing men at the table—as the driving force behind women's daily cooking. In her budget-minded cookbook *Better Meals for Less Money*, Hazel Young noted that "Today women may be making the headlines in every field, but in most households the men still have plenty to do with setting the meal patterns." Marjorie Swift and Christine Herrick echoed that sentiment in their introduction to *Feed the Brute*: "The 'brute,' who in most cases has to work very hard to provide for his family, is rightly considered, in connection with culinary affairs at least, the most important member of the household."[13]

But although authors like Swift and Herrick insisted that women should plan their meals around "the most important member of the household," cookery instruction for men frequently criticized women's home cooking. *Esquire* magazine, for instance, featured the "the woman who is doing everything wrong" in nearly all its cookery articles published in the 1930s and early 1940s.[14] George Frederick, among many other authors, expressed outrage at the incompetent cooking that women forced on men. In *Cooking as Men Like It*, Frederick did not hesitate to associate overly sweet, overly processed, and ill-prepared foods with women's tastes and women's cooking: "The male of the human species likes strong flavors. He hates the pallid, pasty, insipid dishes which so many American and English women serve." Divided into chapters with titles such as "Food Crimes: What Men Object to in Cookery," "Steak and Chops as Men Like Them," "Vegetables Cooked So That Men Won't Hate Them," "Salads That Men Can Endure," and "Meat Substitutes Men Won't Damn," Frederick's cookbook made it clear that men in America had for too long been subject to vastly inferior food prepared by the woman of the house. In his introduction, he pinned the blame directly on women's lack of cooking skill.

Men, he explained, often enjoyed excellent lunches at restaurants or at good hotels when business took them traveling, but the trouble began when such a man returned home to "a dinner of overdone meat, badly prepared, and vegetables as soggy and tasteless as so much paper pulp. Not even the coffee is as good as he is accustomed to having." Frederick felt it necessary to "speak bluntly" about the impact of such terrible cooking on matrimony. He asserted that "one of the reasons why fewer men brave matrimony today is because home no longer offers them the comforts of good cookery." "Just why a man should be thrilled at the idea of setting up housekeeping in order to suffer incompetent cookery, canned goods and delicatessen, and put up with a wife whose brightest idea about meals is to go out for dinner, has not yet been satisfactorily explained," he griped. He went on to critique women's weakness for fussy food and overly scientific methods: "The first thing a wife should realize is that she is catering to her husband's appetite, not to his curiosity. What the inner man craves is food—not puzzles, tricks, new inventions, or chemical experiments." "Few things move men to manslaughter more than does poor cookery," he joked, adding that "A woman should remember that she is trying to produce a palatable dinner out of an oven, not a surprise package out of a silk hat."

Apparently, because she penned a laudatory introduction to the book, Frederick's wife Christine Frederick agreed wholeheartedly with her husband's take on women's cooking. Yet as a busy, well-known home efficiency expert, magazine columnist, and author herself, did she still make time to cook dinners every night that pleased her husband's demanding palate? At any rate, she seemed to agree with Frederick that women did not enjoy the same natural abilities as men. His scorching condemnation of women's skills focused on the female inability to raise cooking to the level of fine gastronomic art: "Food, as such, does not 'lift' or inspire most women; it has to them no psychological values, no romance, allusion or imaginative appeal. It is all a stark, dreary business, a necessary evil; sometimes a stale routine that, they assert, infinitely bores and even nauseates them. In this one can feel some sympathy for them, if they must cook constantly and have no imagination and no sense of pride and skill in the art. But why do they not develop more such pride and skill?"[15] Although in an overblown class of his own, Frederick was not alone in calling attention to women's inability to embrace fully the artistry of cooking. In fact, his advice fit in well with the gentler (and less misogynistic) cookbooks that urged *women* to recognize that cooking must be undertaken as an art. And he was certainly not the only author to insist that *men* just naturally had the imagination and artistry required for good cooking.

Cookery instruction for men stressed the culinary accomplishments of the masculine members of the family, but it also occasionally portrayed the man in the kitchen as the object of gentle self-mockery. However, these humorous depictions reinforced the idea that male cookery should be viewed as a lighthearted game, not an important three-times-a-day, undertaking. For instance, in 1935 the *Delineator* ran a series of cartoons by Will Danch featuring two gentlemen in aprons,

WILL DANCH

"Very well. If this is the ice cream,
what did you do with the meat?"

Figure 7 Although most recipes for men stressed male culinary skill and imagination, cartoonists occasionally made the man in the kitchen an object of humor. From *Delineator*, October 1935.

one mustached and rotund and the other clean shaven and slim. Both rolled up their shirtsleeves every month and tackled a new recipe. In the September cartoon, the two men compare the completely flat bundt cake they have made with the photo of a towering cake that accompanies a magazine recipe. "It doesn't look much like the picture, does it?" they say, puzzled. In October, Clean Shaven frowns at a baffled Mustached while he peers into the oven: "Very well. If this is the ice cream, what did you do with the meat?" asks Clean Shaven (fig. 7). In keeping with the Thanksgiving season, our heroes produce a roasted turkey in the November issue, but then gaze mournfully at the dish saying "And the way he said 'gobble, gobble!'" December saw them attempt a traditional Christmas dish, but they have to rush into a smoking kitchen bearing water while Clean Shaven scolds "You would light the plum-pudding!"[16] The humor in the trials and tribulations of these gentlemen rested with the simple fact of their gender. Their inability to produce a cake more than a half inch high could be the subject of fun—and not the tragedy so often depicted in cookery instruction when the young bride baked an inedible cake (fig. 8). Their scamper to put out a kitchen fire would have been funny to the reader because male incompetence in the kitchen did not present a really serious matter. A woman burning up the plum pudding represented a more grave transgression because cooking composed a good portion of her real job: homemaking.

Figure 8 In contrast to articles which sometimes poked fun at male cookery failures, when a woman ruined a cake it meant tears and recrimination. From "Measure and You're a Better Cook," *Good Housekeeping*, April 1943.

But even though authors frequently injected a note of humor into their instruction for men, few admitted bungling their cookery as badly as the characters in the Danch cartoons. In "What to Cook When the Wife Is Away," authored by Bozeman Bulger and published in *Ladies' Home Journal* in 1921, the author described how he and a buddy made a sad mess of their corned beef and cabbage (a dish often cited as suitable to masculine appetites) until another man rescued them. This pal also gave them recipes for good coffee and for several egg dishes. By the time his wife returned, Bulger had the cooking skills necessary to serve her a beautiful breakfast of baked eggs and bacon.[17] Many authors utilized this particular literary device: when their wives left them alone, they consulted cookbooks, called up friends, and easily taught themselves how to cook. In 1939 George Rector, cookbook author and famous New York restaurateur, published one such article called "When the Wife's Away" in the *Saturday Evening Post*. Funny, eye-catching drawings by Wyncie King accompanied the article: a complacent man in a chef's hat drives fierce-looking lions and tigers in the shape of pots and pans through a hoop much to the astonishment of his wife; a tuxedo clad gentleman waltzes with a demure potato-head woman, while he pointedly ignores a sad salad-head woman bearing the label "Salads and Do-Dad Foods" (fig. 9). Rector offered a variety of recipes and cooking tips, ostensibly for the man left to his own cooking devices. Beginning with steak—nearly always mentioned in such articles—Rector took the reader through simple recipes for baked potatoes, scrambled eggs, potato cakes, and a few tricks for fancying up canned vegetables. At the end of the article, however, Rector admitted to using a ruse to attract the attention of male readers: "As a matter of fact, though, this when-the-wife's-away business is just a gag to persuade more men to dive in among the pots and pans and come up with a hankering after the greatest and oldest of indoor sports. Anything to convince the American man of the great truth that a stove is as promising an item of sporting goods as a bagful of matched irons."[18]

Other authors also utilized such sports metaphors. When Byron MacFadyen urged his readers to encourage their young boys to learn to cook, he asserted that "Your boy may be just as proud of the white, mealy potatoes he has baked as when he strikes out three boys in a row in a ball game."[19] Authors took pains to equate cooking with such highly masculine activities. For instance, the anonymous author of "Men, Meet the Kitchen" published in the *American Home* in 1933, described men taking up cooking as a hobby "like golf, bowling, and collecting arrowheads." One of the contributors to that article described his cooking hobby as a way of "letting off steam," the same way other men do "with a mashie, at chess, or perhaps at cards." This author made a point of

Figure 9 This drawing illustrated the supposed male preference for simple, hearty foods like potatoes: the ignored salad-headed lady wore a label reading "Salads and Do-Dad Foods." This drawing accompanied an article by George Rector entitled "When the Wife's Away" in the *Saturday Evening Post*, 1 December 1934.

detailing his own manly character: "Sissy? Not at all! I'm a newspaper editor and a lot of loafers around the office say I'm 'hard boiled.' But I'd trade a chance to scoop the competition on the murder of the mayor to get home and tackle some new concoction I'd just run across." Like the authors of similar articles, he emphasized that women simply lacked (or had not developed) the panache, the imagination, and the flair that men exhibited in the kitchen: "A woman will take a recipe, follow it faithfully and religiously to the dot, and set out a dish which, albeit appetizing, is exactly the same dish a thousand other women are setting out at the moment."

In contrast, he asserted, men always exercised creativity in the kitchen: "When you get on intimate terms with the kitchen, however, you as a man will never be content to let it stop at that. What woman would have thought of adding a cupful of chili to that old standard salmon soufflé recipe above, as I did, and thereby achieve a most delicious and novel dish?" The author concluded that men's cooking allowed for more creativity and flair because they were not required to do it every day (again drawing on the sports metaphor):

> Women have no imagination in the kitchen. Bless their hearts, why should they? This business of getting together three squares a day; of including something filling for a healthy husband and enough calories and vitamins for the babies and few enough fattening effects for herself; and all the time staying within a budget that possibly isn't what it used to be—there's little time left for imagination.
>
> With a man it's different. He can experiment and enjoy it, like trying out a different golf stance or a new kind of gadget on the car.[20]

[handwritten margin note: "well rounded diet"]

Not all authors so generously accredited women's lack of imagination in cooking to the monotony of being forced to provide meals every day for the family, though some noted it. But most did describe women as being wedded to their cookbooks, unable to venture out into new culinary realms. The numerous articles in popular publications that featured these imaginative and artistic amateur male chefs reinforced the message of numerous cookbooks in 1920s and 1930s: women needed to shed the shackles of the cooking school, loosen up, and joyfully embark on their careers as kitchen virtuosos. At the same time that cookery instruction for men reassured readers about the masculinity of the man in the kitchen, it also reinforced the gender ideology in general cookery instruction.

"Men, Meet the Kitchen!" offered male cookery instruction typical for the 1920s and 1930s in several ways: it used sports metaphors, it included commentary on women's cookery, and it defined male cookery as a fun and creative hobby. But its inclusion of recipes by real-life male cooks made it especially typical. Articles and cookbooks often featured recipes attributed to their masculine creators, perhaps to reassure the reader that *real* men *did* cook. In particular, editors of magazines whose readership consisted of both men and women—*American Home, Better Homes and Gardens, House and Garden,* and *Sunset*—relied on this technique. Three months after the publication of "Men, Meet the Kitchen!" *American Home* followed up by publishing winning recipes submitted to a contest for the best male-created recipes. Drawings of a man holding aloft a cake, a man bearing a steaming tea kettle, and another man seated on a stool peeling potatoes illustrated the resulting article, entitled "And We Learned about Cooking from Men!" Recipes included fried oysters, a cream cheese-caviar-paprika spread, "Italian Spaghetti" (a dish regularly deemed appropriate for male cooks), baked beans, and "Scrambled Eggs à la Morning After." *Better Homes and Gardens* sponsored a similar contest in 1937, and published the results in an article entitled "Mere Men . . . But Can They Cook!" Jean Guthrie, author of the article, described the "fine young mountain of letters" the magazine received from "hundreds" of contestants. The magazine did not print all the prize-winning recipes, which included "A Man's Boiled Dinner," "Salmon Loaf," and "Dad's Chowder," but they did include recipes for "Strawberry Pie De Luxe" and "Spanish Omelet."[21]

Cookbooks used recipes created by real-life men, as well. A 1922 cookbook comprised entirely of recipes contributed by well-known male figures in entertainment and business contained self-descriptions of male cooks ranging from the hopelessly incompetent to the inspired. However, the editor of *The Stag Cookbook,* Mac C. Sheridan, went to great lengths to emphasize that men, given some room in the kitchen, could be wonderful cooks. He dedicated the volume to "That great host of bachelors and benedicts alike who have at one time or another tried to 'cook something'; and who, in the attempt, have weakened under a fire of feminine raillery and sarcasm, only to spoil what, under more favorable circumstances, would have proved to be a chef-d'oeuvre." And the poem that opened the book conveyed, lightheartedly, Sheridan's belief that the recipes in his collection provided evidence of the superiority of male cooks. It read, in part:

> *At range and at oven, at (whisper it!) still,*
> *A man is undoubtedly master;*
> *His cooking is done with an air and a skill,*
> *He's sure as a woman—and faster!*
> *He may break the dishes and clutter the floor,*
> *And if he is praised—he deserves it—*
> *He may flaunt his prowess until he's a bore . . .*
> *But, Boy, what he serves—when he serves it!*

Although done somewhat jokingly, Sheridan made sure that the reader understood, from the very first pages of the book, that the recipes he had collected demonstrated the ability of men to produce awe-inspiring meals. He stressed that men could make dishes that bore traces of an indefinable "air" as well as skill, and make such dishes faster and better than a woman could. The recipes themselves did not, however, prove especially unique. The usual masculine favorites appeared (steak, clam chowder, waffles, bouillabaisse, rice pudding, several spaghetti recipes, and oysters) along with a few unusual and regional dishes (hog jowls, turnip greens, and fried elderberry blossoms). Although *The Stag Cookbook* was not a best seller, the edition I examined had clearly been read, and used, by its owner. The reader-cook added stewed tomatoes and celery to the list of ingredients for a round steak recipe, for example.[22]

Masculine food, according to cookbook authors, often required a masculine touch. Montague Glass, in his 1931 *Good Housekeeping* article "Amateur Cooking for Husbands," depicted himself as good, if infrequent, cook. He explained how he sometimes cooked spaghetti for his family and insisted upon using garlic and onion in the recipe. The female members of his family complained loudly, and Glass quoted the remarks made by his wife and daughter:

> *Important Member of the Family* (formerly president of three suffrage organizations, *count* them, and a charming lady when she wants to be, but now she doesn't *want* to be): "Now, listen, I'm not going to have you smell this entire house up with onions and garlic."
> *Her Daughter* (pleadingly): "Don't *let* him, Mummy!"[23]

Glass treated their feminine resistance to strong smells and tastes with a light hand in this article and subjected himself to a certain amount of parody, but in the end he produced a mouthwatering platter of spaghetti (recipe included) that could only have been made with the daring and imagination of a male cook. Similarly, Edward W. Bock lamented in *The Stag Cookbook* that he could not eat the food he really craved— lobster with mayonnaise, filet mignon panned in brown butter, veal loaf, fried eels, hot fresh doughnuts, strong black coffee—because his wife would not let him.[24] Recipe writers like these men directly contrasted masculine preferences for strong flavors and rich foods with women's pallid palates.

Cookery instruction aimed at women also often lauded male culinary imagination. In 1934 Nell B. Nichols, home economics editor for *Woman's Home Companion*, praised creative masculine twists on traditional dishes. In "When He Cooks," she wrote: "He is not satisfied to broil steak and to fry potatoes in the traditional way—not if he has a hunch he can improve upon it. In other words, he experiments." With what kinds of food did "he" experiment? The usual assortment of masculine favorites: sausage cups with eggs, fried oysters, pork chops, steak with melted cheese, waffles, kidneys and lamb chops, and Roquefort cheese salad dressing.[25] Other female authors also wrote admiringly of men's talent for cooking certain masculine kinds of food. Mary Ellsworth advised her readers that when it came to cooking wild game, women needed to learn from men. According to her, even "that stupid Jones man" transformed himself into a chef during hunting trips: "Yes, let's admit it, any patronizing feminine laughter you may have indulged in over the plight of a couple of helpless males reduced to their own cooking in the wilds had better be hushed. It's probably the best cooking in the world. No, I don't mean guides, I mean that stuffy-looking, bald, stupid Jones man. You can't imagine what Harry sees in him. Well, among other things he's a demon of skill and finesse when faced with a string of partridge, three grubby utensils, and a bed of birch embers."[26] Men's cooking expertise, then, applied especially to the certain kinds of food that men supposedly preferred to eat, and in certain kinds of manly situations, such as hunting trips. Even old Jones could achieve culinary masterpieces in the forest that women could not.

Both cookery instruction for women and recipe writers for men seemed to assume that men would just naturally want to cook different kinds of food than women did and could do so better than women. The author of "Men, Meet the Kitchen," described how a man's first foray into a kitchen, and into a cookbook, would lead that man to a recipe previously ignored by the woman of the house. The author recommended that when a man had the house to himself, he should "walk boldly into the kitchen and look around," "sit down and smoke a cigarette and turn idly through a cookbook." Reading that cookbook, "the first thing you'll notice is that some sturdy, man-size but seemingly complicated recipe in the book sounds awfully darned appetizing. You vaguely wonder why the wife or the cook (if other than the wife, which is getting to be rare, times what they are) has never run across that particular recipe, has never made a stab at it."[27] The male reader, however, would do more than "make a stab at it." In fact, in contrast to the woman of the house or the cook, he would be able to read that recipe, improvise creatively, and finish up with a dish perfectly suited to male appetites. In such cookery instruction, some authors assumed that households employed a cook, and, in fact, cookery instruction to male readers continued to mention paid "help" in the kitchen after most such references had disappeared from instruction for women. But, in the majority of the cases, when an author compared male and female cooking, he aimed his remarks toward the mistress of the home, not a paid laborer.

Authors suggested again and again that while the woman of the house might need detailed recipes and explicit cookery instruction, men did not. They depicted men as freer and more imaginative in the kitchen, and the recipes themselves reflected that fact. In sharp contrast to the instruction published for female readers, virtually all recipes written for men had a decidedly looser approach (notwithstanding advice to women to employ creativity in the kitchen). Many eschewed the lists of ingredients, precise measurements, and detailed directions that other cookbooks in the 1920s and 1930s had begun to emphasize. Recipes written by or intended for men gave breezy, often funny, and often rather vague directions for putting together dishes. For example, Walt Louderback's recipe in *The Stag Cook Book* for corn chowder began with this introduction: "The appetite for this dish must be approached from the windy side of a promontory in early spring with a sixty pound pack between the shoulder blades, aforementioned pack to contain for a couple of congenial souls a pound of bacon, a pound of dry onions, two cans of corn and one large tin of condensed milk." His directions included a boisterous order to "Now throw the bacon and onions into the corn pot and wait as long as you are able so that the ingredients become thoroughly familiar with one another."

Stewart Edward White offered another campfire recipe (mulligan stew), noting that "This is a camp dish to be cooked over an open fire. I guarantee nothing on a stove. I know nothing of stoves, and have a dark suspicion of them." His recipe concluded: "Cook slowly until you can't stand it any longer, and fly to it." And William Johnson's recipe for oysters called for similar macho ingredients: "one keg of freshly dredged oysters put on the deck of the schooner not later than eight p.m." and "one hundred pounds of ice put on top of the oysters." His "recipe" read: "Shell and eat at 5:00 a.m. on the way to the fishing grounds with salt to taste, and occasional draughts of hot coffee."[28] According to authors such as these, men not only preferred different kinds of food, but required an entirely different approach to cookery and cookery instruction: less restrictive recipes, for instance, with vague, macho directions, for food eaten around a campfire or on a fishing boat.

According to cookery instruction for men in the 1920s and 1930s, the feminine approach to food quite simply fell short of men's natural culinary prowess. In fact, the criticism of women cooks as unimaginative and, at the same time, prone to fussy, frilly food, did not occur solely in food-related publications. A 1939 article in *Collier's* magazine, for example, presented both sides of the "debate." "Women Can't Cook" by Ted Shane and "Men Can't Cook" by Mary Dunham, published on facing pages, engaged in sharply worded criticism of how the opposite gender behaved in the kitchen. Ted Shane's article opened with the statement "Meet the little woman, happily juggling calories, cookbooks and can-openers in her mechanized kitchen in the innocent belief that she's getting a meal. Well, she isn't." No, continued Shane, "the little woman" did not produce meals but rather, indigestible concoctions bearing no resemblance to the kind of real food men enjoyed: "She refuses to learn that men like food—simple food looking like food, and not like one of Queen Mary's hats." He directly condemned cookbook cookery as the prison of the female cook: "For when a woman becomes a slave of the cookbook, heaven help her family." In Shane's opinion, men, not women, possessed the qualities needed for creating truly delicious meals. When men cook, he asserted, "they prove the old adage that a man can do anything better than a woman can. Yes, they cook rings around their wives. Dinners are served piping hot, accompanied by piquant sauces, tasty green salads."[29] Cookbooks for men, however, rarely included practical instructions on how to produce a piping hot dinner or choose tasty salad greens at the market—men did not seem to require the step-by-step direction on food shopping, cooking technique, and serving that women did.

Mary Dunham, on the other hand, attacked Shane's assertions about male superiority in the kitchen. The beginning of her article assumed the sarcastic tone she maintained throughout: "Meet the lord and master, blandly making an ass of himself as he concocts one of those culinary atrocities that make normal women shudder. He's going to expect you to eat it, too. And praise him for it." Her crisp description of the male cooking craze suggested that the popular media bombarded Americans in the 1920s and 1930s with cookery instruction by and for men: "You couldn't pick up a magazine without seeing some actor, prize fighter or sandhog with his favorite pot, giving you his original little recipe for frying eggs or ham or both. . . . From the looks of things, man's delusion that he's a natural-born cook and the little woman, at best, is to be pitied, is here to stay." Dunham attempted to deflate the egos of men who believed they could cook, but who relied on outdoor cookery, "when the eater is ravenous from air and exercise." "Half raw potatoes, charred bacon and canned peaches have been known to build up a reputation as a master chef for men I've known who have had the audacity to take over the commissary department at the end of a hard trail," she wrote bitterly. She concluded: "Despite the current fashion to belittle women as cooks and lovers of good food, they will go on producing and eating the same with the distinction that has marked their efforts along these lines for centuries."[30]

Although she may have exaggerated to give her article punch, Dunham's reference at the end of the 1930s to the fashion of "belittling women as cooks and lovers of good food" speaks to an important trend

[handwritten margin note: When men cook must praise]

in popular literature and in cookery instruction during that decade: the representation of men, often famous and always very manly, as original and artistic cooks whose natural abilities outstripped women's feeble culinary efforts.[31] In articles and cookbooks intended for male readers, authors asserted that men, by virtue of their gender alone, instinctively created better salads, better meats, and better meals. And these authors implied or stated outright that women needed to pay more attention to the all-important topic of cooking. Even in *A Thousand Ways to Please a Husband*, Bettina's husband trumped her in cooking. A popular storybook-like cookbook published in 1917 and substantially revised in 1932, *A Thousand Ways* tracked the first year of meals in the marriage of "Bettina" to "Bob" and gave ample evidence of Bettina's skill and good sense in the kitchen. Bettina enjoys much praise from Bob for that skill, yet in one of the earlier chapters, Bob's ingenuity in the kitchen flummoxes Bettina. In a chapter called "Bob Helps to Get Dinner," Bettina asks him to make the French dressing:

> "Will you make the French dressing for the salad? See, I'll measure it out, and you can stir it this way with a fork until it's well mixed and a little thick."
>
> "I know a much better way than that. Just watch your Uncle Bob; see? I'll put it in this mason jar and shake it. It's a lot easier—and there you are! We'll use what we need tonight, put the jar away in the icebox, and the next time we can give it another good shaking before we use it."
>
> "Why, Bob, what an ingenious boy you are! I never would have thought of that!"

Shaking the French dressing constituted the extent of Bob's contribution when he "helped get dinner," but he did so with creative flair and intelligence. When it was time to mash potatoes, Bob's manly strength and sporting ability, somewhat pent up from sitting at a desk all day, ensured smooth potatoes: "'Here, Bettina, let me mash those potatoes! It's fine exercise after a day at the office!' And Bob seized the potato masher with the same vigor that he used to handle a tennis racquet. 'Good for you, Bob! They can't have a single lump in them after that!'" Bob's natural affinity for cooking also helped him make "splendid popovers" the very first time he tried.[32] Good-natured Bob, though lacking the misogynistic edge of a George Frederick, managed to convey that he could easily produce wonderful dishes, and come up with ways of doing things in the kitchen that Bettina "never would have thought of" doing.

Examples such as Bob's wizardry with the potato masher illustrate the way numerous cookbooks and popular cookery instruction in the

1920s and 1930s depicted men and women as, at best, different in appetite and in kitchen habits. At worst, they depicted men as possessing vast amounts of natural, fun-loving, cooking ability while women labored over silly salads and burned the meat. Authors built on the theme of "artistic" cooking to point out the many ways women's cooking lacked that elusive quality. Their diatribes about women's lack of creativity in the kitchen and the dogged female reliance on boring recipes, had a definite undercurrent: an urgent message to the women of America to follow in their husbands' footsteps and shore up their cooking ability. Cookbooks for men reinforced the definition of humdrum everyday meals as women's work, specifically, the work of wife and mother; in contrast, male culinary prowess could only be exercised as a hobby or as an occasional event. But, by defining male cookery as a special occurrence, these recipe collections and magazine articles actually helped to define the opposite kind of cooking—routine cookery for family meals—as the province of their wives, that is, middle-class, white, married women. They helped to reinforce the growing domestic ideology of the twentieth century.

The authors of cookbooks and popular cookery instruction also had to be sure that their readers could not possibly doubt the masculinity of the man in the kitchen. They had to be sure any cooking a man might do would not overlap or intersect with the domestic responsibilities of women. Cookbook authors, editors, and contributors took care to ensure that a man's foray into the kitchen could not possibly suggest that a man would eat or cook like a fussy, overly scientific domestic scientist or a careless, uninspired housewife. In short, they had to show that a man would never, ever cook like a woman. In one of the most obvious examples of the anxious way cookbook authors asserted the masculinity of the man in the kitchen, James Montgomery Flagg quickly defended the dessert dish he contributed to *The Stag Cookbook* (wine jelly with eggs and oranges) as a suitably male and heterosexual dessert: "It sounds rather punk and ladieshomejournalish but it is a perfectly good dessert."[33] Ladylike cooking could render a man "punk" and ladylike himself if he was not careful to explain that his recipe did in fact satisfy real he-man appetites. Authors and editors insisted that their female readers should, could, and would assume responsibility for the household's meals. Consequently they had to demonstrate that if a man entered the kitchen, he did so with a very different set of recipes and cookery goals.

General cookbooks in the 1920s and 1930s constructed cooking as a fun, creative outlet for white middle-class housewives in order to encourage women to happily take up the kitchen duties left by departing cooks. Cookbooks made it clear that ready-made foods and processed foods would not change gender-specific food preparation duties. Cookery instruction for men contained many of the same messages about women's cookery duties, as defined in opposition to men's hobby cooking. They had to be sure to classify male cookery as a hobby like woodworking or golf because they could not suggest that men might take any further responsibility for the family's daily meals. They could not suggest that the availability of processed and premade foods or the increasing numbers of white, married, middle-class women in the work force would, in any way, challenge traditional gender norms. They had to police diligently the boundaries between kitchen as women's space and kitchen as male hobby space. They had to emphasize men's natural flair and ability with food because that would locate man-made meals outside the realm of everyday home cooking.

Cookbooks for men had to depict male cookery as fundamentally different from female cookery for the same kinds of reasons that General Foods and Irma Rombauer depicted cooking as a joy and an art: the importance of redefining women's social and domestic role in the new, modern era. With more women attending college, driving cars, smoking, using birth control, flashing their knees in the flapper fashions, and voting, the reemergence of a domestic ideology that placed woman at the center of the home and in the kitchen, providing comfort in a busy world, made sense. As Americans grappled with the rapid pace of social and technological change in the twentieth-century kitchen and society itself, it made sense for authors to reassert the basics. Men like corned beef; women like gelatin salads. Men enjoy occasional cooking; women should learn to enjoy everyday cooking.

But for historians, cookery instruction begs the question of just how such rhetoric about male and female appetites might have shaped real men and women's understanding of gender roles. Short of detailed oral histories, we cannot really know exactly how individual consumers interacted with specific texts. We cannot forget that American citizens did not read cookbooks as a collected group of artifacts from a particular era, the way historians now can. The patterns discernible in this literature after reading hundreds of cookbooks and popular magazines may or may not have been discernible to average readers in the 1920s and 1930s. Evidence like Mary Dunham's reference to other articles on the topic of men and women cooking does suggest that at least some people perceived a growth in gendered rhetoric about cooking. The fact that popular magazines and cookbooks often ascribed masculine recipes to real men—and held contests in which men entered their own recipes—also suggests that publishers felt that such recipes and contests might appeal to their readers. In addition, it demonstrates the interest of some men in cooking and reading about cooking in the

1920s and 1930s, just as recipe contests in women's magazines seem to indicate that a goodly number of readers expressed enough of an interest in cookery instruction to submit their own recipes.

Cookbooks also present a slightly different problem for historians of prescription literature. After all, recipes are by their very nature prescriptive: they demand a certain set of actions, performed in a certain sequence, to produce a certain product.[34] We can assume, at the very least, that *some* people in the 1920s and 1930s followed *some* of the recipes in the cookbooks. The ever rising sales figures of cookbooks and the popularity of recipes and cookery instruction in magazines demonstrate some level of engagement with the recipes offered by instructors. The continuing popularity of *The Boston Cooking School Cook Book* showed consumers' continued interest in straightforward cookery instruction, with clear and concise directions, while the popularity of *The Joy of Cooking* demonstrated a widespread desire for a less lecturing presence in the kitchen. We must also remember that for many men and some women cooking was indeed a joy. We eat to stay alive but also to celebrate our communities, to mark important events in our lives, and for the simple pleasure of the senses. Preparing good food surely gave many people during the 1920s and 1930s real pleasure.

We also cannot forget how women (and men) use cookbooks in ways their creators never intended. For example, one of the people who enjoyed preparing food during this era used her cookbook, *The Household Searchlight Recipe Book* (first published in 1931, and revised in 1937 and 1939), less as kitchen manual and more as a filing place for her vast recipe collection. Born in 1917, Sadie Lenore Winterstein moved to a small, rural Michigan town after spending the early years of her marriage in San Francisco working as a nurse in the Red Cross. After the arrival of the first of three children, she and her husband moved to the Midwest. *The Household Searchlight Recipe Book* was one of the encyclopedic cookbooks coming out on the market in the 1920s and 1930s. Published by the *Household Magazine*, and group-authored by the residents of "The Searchlight" (a seven-room house populated by "a family of specialists whose entire time is spent in working out the problems of homemaking common to every woman who finds herself responsible for the management of a home and the care of children"), this cookbook had hundreds of recipes and dictionary-like tabs for easy reference.[35] The *Household Magazine* never enjoyed the kind of cultural and publishing power of similar magazines such as *Good Housekeeping*, but it sold enough editions of this cookbook to issue two revisions. For Winterstein, however, the recipes in this cookbook represented not strict formulas but simply suggestions. She rarely followed a recipe exactly, although she collected cookbooks all her life. Winterstein loved to cook, and in her family, women took a great deal of pride in that ability. But they relied on their own experience and learned cooking ability rather than written recipes in a book.[36]

The recipes stored within the pages of Winterstein's cookbook tell a story of a cooking career that spanned four decades. Included are two clippings from the early nineteenth century, given to Winterstein by her mother or mother-in-law. One, dated 12 October 1912 from *People's Popular Monthly*, gave tips on keeping food fresh in an ice box, a description of the properties of buttermilk, and recipes for, among other things, hot ham sandwiches, layer cake, peanut drop cookies, and cooked vegetable salad. The other, an article from *Farm and Fireside* published 1 November 1916 offered hints on canning and readers' recipes for veal birds, baked peaches, fried cucumbers, and oatmeal cookies. Winterstein's recipe collection also contains clippings from magazines, advertising literature that included recipes, a page from a calendar printed with recipes, and recipes in her own writing for cucumber relish and coconut cookies. The recipes she copied down, both in the blank pages of the cookbook and on separate slips of paper, follow the pattern often used by practiced cooks: they usually listed the recipes with minimal directions and/or measurements. Her cucumber relish recipe, for instance, is to the point: "Peel cucumbers and take seeds out. Put salt over all. Let stand overnight. Drain in the morning." After a brief list of ingredients for the dressing, the recipe concludes "Boil good. Put in chopped stuff. Boil and seal." She also tucked the instructional card for her new Maytag washer into the pages of this cookbook. Like Winterstein, many women used their cookbooks as a kitchen filing cabinet and as a place to store appliance warranties or purchase receipts.

Winterstein seldom followed a recipe, and the pages of her cookbook bear no markings whatsoever, but the fact that she wrote in recipes on the blank pages provided for that purpose and that she used the cookbook as a place to store recipes she had cut out or copied shows that she obviously interacted with this book. As it happens, this particular cookbook did not dwell on gender roles or the food preferences of men and women. But even if it had, Winterstein may have never even read such passages, skipping instead to the "meat" of the recipe—the ingredients and the instructions—and making her own improvements on the recipe in her kitchen. In exploring the ways that gender norms appeared in cookery instruction, I do not mean to imply that numerous and different kinds of readings did not occur. Winterstein, for one, probably cared little about any superfluous writing a cookbook contained and preferred to look only for recipes she might use to feed her husband and family. But other less experienced cooks may have pored over the menus, marketing tips, and discussions about cookery technique found in this cookbook. Also, like Winterstein's family, women in the 1920s and 1930s might have bonded around the issue of cooking as a shared female skill, not a duty imposed by food corporations, *Good Housekeeping*, and cookbook authors.

But the messages in 1920s and 1930s cookbooks about the role of white middle-class women—and men—in the kitchen, as scattered and perhaps ineffectual at the individual level as they were, did set the stage for the next important phase in cookbook publication. They did help to help to define, amid the national debate about women's and men's social roles in the modern era, the domestic duties of the white middle-class woman. They reinforced her role as an important consumer. They suggested that she was more and more likely to be "cookless" in the kitchen, but that she could experience cookery as both science and art. And by depicting male cookery as strictly limited to the special occasion or as a fun-filled hobby, and men in the kitchen as bolder and more creative than women, cookbooks intended for male readers reinforced the messages in general cookbooks about women's domestic roles.

When World War II began, cookery instruction became increasingly the province of food corporations and huge magazine publishers, but it also became even more pointedly concerned about the role of women in the home and in the kitchen. The widespread rhetoric about a woman's job as the provider of home meals during the war played into long-standing notions about patriotism and the home, but it also built on the foundation laid by the cookbooks of the previous twenty years. It helped cement the idea, which proliferated in the 1920s and 1930s, that the preparation of the daily meals should fall to the mistress of the home.

PART TWO
"You Are First and Foremost Homemakers"

COOKBOOKS

AND THE

SECOND

WORLD WAR

5

Lima Loaf and Butter Stretchers

After Japanese warplanes bombed the U.S. naval base at Pearl Harbor on 7 December 1941, and after President Roosevelt declared war on 11 December, patriotic fervor swept the nation, reversing years of isolationist sentiment in a matter of weeks. Many Americans felt suddenly united in a shared patriotic purpose when the country went to war. But historians have ably demonstrated that racial tension, economic inequity, and other social conflicts in the United States continued to shape American society during the war.[1] The prejudice and injustice that Americans faced before the war continued during the war: race riots in urban areas, the forced internment of Japanese Americans in the West, the institutional racism facing enlisted men of color, the combination of sexism and racism facing women of color at home on the job front. On the other hand, men and women all over the country truly put their best into the war effort and believed fervently that their sacrifices would help build a better world. The difficulties of sorting out propaganda, inflamed rhetoric, editorial comment, and heartfelt patriotism in America during this period present a complicated puzzle for the social historian.

A study of wartime prescriptive literature and cookery instruction presents puzzles of its own. Just as cookbooks in the 1920s and 1930s cannot, by themselves, give us incontrovertible evidence about how Americans actually cooked and ate during that time, cookbooks published during the war years may tell us more about what food manufacturers and book publishers *believed* women should cook than how women actually cooked. But the prescriptive rhetoric concerning women's cooking duties that characterized so much cookery instruction from 1941 through 1945 does show how cookbook authors and editors continued to be greatly concerned about women's domestic role. Just as cookbooks in the 1920s and 1930s emphasized that middle-class women should think of home cooking as an art and a joy, cookbooks published during the war years depicted food preparation in the home as a woman's most important wartime job—indeed, a job critical to the defense of the nation and to victory. World War II cookbooks demonstrated the continuing growth of a twentieth-century domestic ideology.

The barrage of recipes and cookbooks that hit America in the 1920s and 1930s continued unabated in the 1940s, even as paper rationing somewhat restricted publishing during the war. By the 1940s, few periodicals, newspapers, and food-processing corporations lacked a resident recipe purveyor. Almost every women's magazine featured monthly recipes and cooking tips, and, often, cookbook reviews and bibliographies. Florence Richardson, writing under the name "Prudence Penny" for the *Mirror*, offered standard home recipes, as did many of the home economics directors for women's magazines, such as *Good Housekeeping*'s Dorothy Marsh and Dorothy Kirk at *Woman's Home Companion*. Mary Grosvenor Ellsworth contributed a regular column to *House Beautiful*, as did Edith Key Haines to *Town and Country*. And all these women edited or authored general cookbooks as well. Radio shows, especially local shows, continued to feature cooking programs: the cookbook *Victory Vittles* featured recipes for rationing contributed by listeners of the Polly Patterson radio show in California, for example. Billie Burke, best known for her portrayal of the Good Witch of the North in *The Wizard of Oz*, hosted a show called *Fashions in Rations*.[2] Specialty cookbooks, such as Helmut Ripperger's volume on mushroom cookery and several books on cooking with fresh herbs, appeared more frequently on the market. A few cookbooks devoted entirely to Italian, Mexican, or Chinese cookery also appeared, as did volumes on how to cook with wine and how to cook with a chafing dish or a gas ring.

In terms of sheer popularity (numbers of copies sold), however, the big "kitchen bible" cookbooks and glossy corporate-sponsored cookbooks, fat with product placements, far outpaced smaller and more specialized kinds of cookbooks. Such large, encyclopedic cookbooks contained a vast number of recipes and advice on everything from kitchen design to china patterns to shopping for food. As publishing technology advanced, these cookbooks began to add numerous photographs of completed dishes or other kinds of illustrations to their pages.

Some offered photographs or drawings of the latest kinds of kitchen equipment, and others featured elaborately arranged shots of carefully garnished completed dishes. They almost invariably gave menu suggestions, often covering a week or a month. "Special event" menus for holidays often appeared. Publishers continued to experiment with formats, fonts, and covers. Some included blank spaces for comments or the reader's notes, and others boasted extensive indexes and cross-references. In short, publishers, editors, and authors tried to create the one enormous, general, cookbook that every housewife would want on her kitchen shelf; a cookbook that answered every cooking and cooking-related question a housewife might have and that she could consult as religiously as a bible.

During the war, food-processing companies and appliance manufacturers continued to make recipes an important part of their marketing strategies and attempted to produce "kitchen bibles" of their own. For example, the Culinary Arts Institute, a food product clearinghouse, churned out a myriad of committee-authored pamphlets in the 1940s and 1950s promoting a wide range of foods from corn to frankfurters. In 1938 the institute also produced an extensive general cookbook, *The American Woman's Cook Book*, which contained hundreds of recipes and numerous vivid full-color illustrations provided by different food producers, and had tabs like a dictionary. Its popularity ensured a new edition every year throughout the 1940s. Ruth Berolzheimer, the book's editor and director of the Culinary Arts Institute, went on to edit numerous other books and pamphlets (which often re-presented and recycled recipes from previous books, in order to pack in more advertising), including one specifically aimed at wartime cookery.

Popular women's periodicals also sought a piece of the cookbook market by publishing all-encompassing cookery books. *Good Housekeeping* magazine published its version of a massive, comprehensive kitchen bible in 1942, and it enjoyed the same success that had seen their 1922 volume on cookery and household tips—*Good Housekeeping's Book of Menus, Recipes, and Household Discoveries*—through decades of reprints. Helmut Ripperger heralded the publication of *The Good Housekeeping Cook Book* as a new high standard in cookery instruction.[3] Another domestic magazine aimed at female readers, *Woman's Home Companion*, threw its weight behind a comprehensive cooking book the same year as *Good Housekeeping*. Meta Givens, trained in home economics and employed by several food corporations, worked as food editor of the *Chicago Tribune* and wrote a syndicated newspaper column. She also authored a very popular "everything you need to know about cooking" volume entitled *The Modern Family Cook Book*, first published in 1942. This best-selling cookbook underwent several revisions and sold thousands of reprints, well into the 1950s. A reviewer for *Consumers' Research Bulletin*, however, gave only tepid praise for Givens's books, writing in 1943 that the cookbook offered "nothing particularly original or exciting, but contains the basic rules for preparation."[4]

This reviewer also mentioned *The Joy of Cooking* without much enthusiasm, but the 1943 edition of Irma Rombauer's extensive cookery book did in fact offer some "original and exciting" kinds of recipes. When Rombauer's 1939 cookbook, *Streamlined Cooking*, failed to make much of an impact on the cookbook market, the author incorporated many of those recipes into the 1943 edition of *The Joy of Cooking*.[5] Such recipes gave *The Joy of Cooking* an even greater advantage against other long-selling classics such as the *Settlement Cookbook*. Rombauer's book now offered advice on the latest appliances and food products, and sales of *The Joy of Cooking* surpassed *The Boston Cooking School Cook Book* in 1944. On the other hand, Rombauer also included recipes using fennel, broccoli, and kale.[6] Her ability to create different recipes for ingredients as disparate as fresh dandelion greens and canned soup helped ensure the success of *The Joy of Cooking* and illustrated the different directions American food trends took in the early 1940s. Specifically, Rombauer struck a balance between American delight in new convenience food and the growing influence of the gourmet movement in the United States.

One of the leading voices of the new gourmet movement created the single most famous recipe published during the war. Mary Frances Kennedy Fisher's recipe for "Sludge, Or How to Keep Alive," appeared in her third book, the 1942 *How to Cook a Wolf*. This recipe directed the reader to grind together carrots, onions, celery, cabbage, other assorted vegetables as the budget permitted, a small amount of beef and a large amount of whole-grain cereal, stew the ingredients, and eat the results cold or reheated (if the reader could afford the fuel for reheating).[7] Destined to become a classic, *How to Cook a Wolf* attained enough popularity to run through numerous reprintings and a substantial revision in the 1950s. But Fisher's work appealed to a limited audience. Since the publication in 1937 of her first book, *Serve It Forth*, Fisher's unique writing style—part cookery instruction, part travel memoir, part autobiography, part philosophical reflection—captured not a mass market but a more literary group of readers. She also produced well-respected translations of work by Jean Anthelme (Brill-Savarin).

Fisher advocated fresh ingredients, simplicity, and, above all, reverence for food and for eating. In this she embodied some of the most important elements of the new gourmet movement that, somewhat paradoxically, emerged full force in the United States during the 1940s. The magazine bearing the title of the movement—*Gourmet*—began publication in 1941. The publishers of the magazine drew on a tradition of "high living" and dining that never really died in the United States—though Prohibition, the Depression, the dearth of fine restaurants, and changing eating patterns (including fewer household servants) had undermined it to a great extent. *Gourmet* sought to uphold the notion of dining for dining's sake and its aficionados resisted what they perceived as the prevailing attitude about cooking and eating in the United States, that is, a dry emphasis on vitamins, balanced meals, and a Puritan-like approach to food in general. *Gourmet* founder and publisher Earle Mac-Ausland anticipated and exploited a trend toward "food writing," not simply cookery instruction but elaborate travel and food-related essays.[8] *Gourmet*, and its readers, believed that the pleasure of rich, tasty, and exotic food should be embraced.

Understandably, many Americans found such an approach to eating downright unpatriotic during wartime, but *Gourmet* persisted and throughout the war published articles about and lavish photographs of such food. Perhaps gourmet recipes during the war served the same kind of purpose that some cookbooks may have during the Great Depression: a way of escaping daily anxieties and uncertainties. Not every reader of *Gourmet* could afford to maintain the kind of life-style the magazine advocated. For these readers, *Gourmet* might well have provided a fantasy world of fulfillment, a glimpse into an exotic universe of luxuriant food and drink. At the end of the war, *Gourmet* congratulated itself on having kept alive a tradition of high living. When Lucius Beebe, society observer, began a new column for the magazine in 1945, he looked back on the war years and remarked blithely, "The torch which set the cherries jubilee in flames was never wholly extinguished."[9]

Gourmet may have had limited appeal during the war, but it marked the way of the future for cooking and eating in the United States. The move toward the kinds of eating advocated by the magazine—an appreciation for "ethnic" cuisine with authentic ingredients, the emphasis on fresh rather than processed foods, and attention to restaurant dining—foretold many of the factors that most influence cookery today. Other cookbook authors in the late 1930s, most notably James Beard, advocated similar kinds of cooking and eating. Strong flavors, fresh ingredients, and a pointed rejection of fussy, pallid foods marked the recipes in Beard's debut cookbook of 1940, *Hors d'Oeuvre and Canapés*, and all his following cookbooks. His books sold briskly, and culinary historians regard him as one of the most important pioneers of contemporary cuisine. During the 1940s other cookery instructors echoed Beard's approach to cookery. Many shared his disdain for marshmallow encrusted dishes and elaborate gelatin salads, for example. Others urged their readers not to forget the delicious superiority of home-cooked soups to soup from a can. And some advocated growing one's own herbs to flavor meals better. Moreover, the number of restaurants, at least in urban areas, increased during the 1940s. As employment shot up, so did the numbers of people eating in cafeterias and luncheonettes, and refugees from Europe swelled the ranks of professional chefs.[10]

When James Beard asked "four famous gourmets," in a 1942 *House Beautiful* article, to name their favorite cookbooks, their answers reflected both the popularity of gourmet authors and the abiding influence of old standbys. Sheila Hibben, cookbook author and contributor to the *New Yorker*, cited Fannie Farmer and *The Settlement Cookbook*. Gaynor Maddox, a syndicated food columnist, also recommended *The Boston Cooking School Cookbook*. But Crosby Gaige, cookbook author and food writer for *Country Life*, lamented Fannie Farmer's contribution to "the mediocrity in our native meals" and claimed that the hundreds of meals he had eaten that had been "prepared by Fannie's formula" had made him "prematurely bitter." He went on to praise M. F. K. Fisher's work, as did Louise Andrews Kent, author of the respected "Mrs. Appleyard" cookbook series. *House and Garden* published an article on a similar theme that same year. In "Seven Cooks in Search of a Gourmet," the anonymous author reprinted recipes such as lobster mousse and roast pheasant from "gourmet" cookbooks like June Platt's *Plain and Fancy Cookbook*, Shelia Hibben's *A Kitchen Manual*, Helmut Ripperger's *Cheese Cookery*, and *Cooking à la Ritz* by Louis Diat, head chef at that famous hotel.[11]

Cookbook reviews in the 1940s acknowledged the growing importance of such gourmet and specialty volumes, but at the same time praised new editions of dependable old kitchen bibles. After the United States declared war, however, reviewers began to pay special attention to how cookbooks could help Americans face rationing, food shortages, and other wartime food-related problems. From the end of 1941 through 1945, wartime concerns had an enormous impact on both food and cookbook publishing trends—and on food advertising. When General Mills hawked its flour, it could point out that with new enriching ingredients, bread had "extra vigor" and was "the official extender during wartime rationing." A General Foods recipe for piecrust that called for very little shortening took on new importance as "Victory Pie Crust."[12] Everything from cake flour to tomato juice became loaded with nutritious and patriotic goodness, at least according to advertisements. And cookbooks began to feature extensive sections on war-related issues such as rationing and nutrition.

In 1943 Harriet Anderson reviewed a number of new cookbooks for *Woman's Home Companion*. She briefly mentioned a new diet cookbook and Fannie Farmer's new cookbook for children. But she emphasized sugar-saving cookbooks, herb cookbooks (to add flavor to a restricted diet), and general cookbooks written specifically for wartime cookery.[13] In 1941 Helmut Ripperger reviewed more than sixty-one books for his article on the year's new cookbooks, and in 1942, more than fifty, and he included a section on "war cookery" in both. His 1941 review, published in July before the entry of the United States into the war, cited several English cookbooks on the subject. Ripperger urged bookshops to stock up on *Old and New British Recipes*, the sale of which benefited British War Relief (though he had his doubts about the book's "potato wine" recipe). He later devoted an entire article to cookbooks that raised funds for various war relief agencies.[14]

In 1942 Ripperger did not add his voice to the chorus of critical praise for *How to Cook a Wolf*. But he offered favorable comments about other wartime cookbooks, namely *Wartime Meals* by Margot Murphy (who wrote about food for the *New York Times* under the name Jane Holt), Harriet Hester's *300 Sugar Saving Recipes* and a volume entitled *What Do We Eat Now*, coauthored by home economics experts Helen Robertson, Sarah MacLeod, and Frances Preston. Ripperger cautioned that wartime cookery should not be viewed as an emergency measure. He argued that American cooks should learn how to embrace economy and restraint (along with simple, classic, European-type foods) for their own sake. "So many people seem to think that war cookery is a sort of *faut de mieux*," he complained. "And so it is, but so much more too," he continued. "I am suspicious of our sudden conversion to 'saving' and 'rationing' and 'substitution,' three qualities that have been apparent in European kitchens for centuries."[15]

Ripperger's dubiousness was well founded. The vast majority of cookery instruction during the war urged saving, rationing, and substitution in the kitchen, but only "for the duration." Ripperger's apt comparison to European kitchens highlighted the fact that food limitations seemed practically un-American—something to be considered only during a national emergency. Moreover, even though Americans as a whole supported the war cause, even though they had embraced many New Deal "big government" programs, they retained a deep suspicion about federal involvement with food supplies. When the Office of Price Administration (established in 1941 and granted authority to ration goods and regulate prices in 1942) rationed sugar in 1942, Americans met the first steps toward rationing with skepticism. Although the government asserted that the war cut off several major sugar importing sources, that sugar-beet farmers faced labor shortages, and that the military needed sugar for munitions, many Americans seemed dubious.[16] In November, coffee became a rationed food product, followed in 1943 by certain canned foods, meats, fish, butter, and cheese, and again some Americans expressed frustration with the new limitations at the grocer's and the butcher's. The government intended rationing to help prevent inflation and to distribute staples more equally during uncertain times, and to a certain extent it accomplished this. But food prices continued to rise throughout the war, and many Americans never became reconciled to the rationing system.

The rationing system itself presented complications that added to the frustrations. The local government distributed a ration coupon book for each individual man, woman, and child, with blue coupons for canned foods and red for fresh and canned meat, and dairy foods. The federal government assigned a particular point value to each coupon— which varied among the different regions of the country—and those point values changed every month, when the old coupon books expired. In order to purchase a stick of butter, then, the shopper had not only to pay for the butter but also to hand over the set amount of coupons with the correct number of points for that butter—and the retailer had to keep track of the number of points each food item cost. Women's magazines, newspapers, and cookbooks attempted to assist the consumer with ration point charts and hints on meal planning.[17] But citizens chafed against the restrictions, even as they rallied around the war cause. Expensive black markets, or simple favoritism on the part of retailers and wholesalers, ensured that some citizens would always have more access to certain products. And as James Beard recollected later "It was considered chic to circumvent rationing. The attitude was like that towards prohibition."[18] The Office of Price Administration itself came under considerable fire, from both private citizens and food companies. General Mills, for example, protested to the agency that rationed shortening created less demand for flour.[19] Many Americans seemed unsure if food shortages, often caused in certain locations due to transportation problems, truly existed.

The rationing of fresh meat, in particular, annoyed Americans. Associated with hearty appetites and bountiful meals, fresh meat had long played the starring role in American meals. A federal campaign for voluntary meat reduction called "Share the Meat" failed in 1942 to create sufficient changes in American diets. But the rationed amount of fresh meat allowed each individual—two and a half pounds per week, not including poultry—meant America still ate far more meat than almost any other nation in wartime or in peace. Of course, Americans supported feeding "our boys in the army" a goodly helping of meat every day—they just did not want to have to make too many changes in their daily diet to do so. (In fact, given better nutritional knowledge, better-trained cooks, and a higher quality of canning and preserving technology, the U.S. armed forces in World War II probably ate better than any other military in any previous war.) Cookbook authors and editors paid particular attention to the problem of meat shortages. The adjustment to meat rationing spawned literally thousands of recipes and pages of rhetoric in cookbooks.

A European refugee or an English citizen facing severe food shortages would have been shocked by America's consternation over the "meat problem." After all, numerous other kinds of food remained readily available to Americans, including many different kinds of meat. A 1943 cookbook by Florence Richardson ("Prudence Penny") began a chapter called "Meeting the Meat Problem" with a cartoon depicting a housewife hiding a cleaver and beckoning the family cat to come closer. The accompanying poem read: "Your husband used to criticize / If you cooked the roast too tough / And turned on you a bitter frown / At steak not done enough. / Today it's not so hard to please / The master of the house / He eats his portion meekly / Be it elephant or mouse!"[20] Probably few people anywhere in the world turned to elephant to "meet the meat the problem," but in a war-torn world rife with shortages and starvation, not a few rats probably found their way into people's stomachs. The readers of this cookbook, however, did not face those kinds of deprivations—the humor of the cartoon and the poem depended upon that fact. But a feeling of deprivation rapidly spread among the middle classes after the federal government rationed meat, at least judging by the fevered response to "the meat problem" found in wartime cookery instruction.

Many authors suggested using meat substitutes, such as eggs and cheese, in main dishes to help fill the gap left by dwindling red-meat supplies. Ann Robbins addressed the issue in her cookbook *100 Meat-Saving Recipes*, published in 1943, a year many publishers produced volumes on wartime cookery. Her recipes utilized frankfurters, fish, baked and stuffed vegetables, eggs, cheese, and pork, all slightly easier and less expensive to obtain than fresh red meat.[21] The Culinary Arts Institute produced a version of its popular *The American Woman's Cook Book* to address the issue directly. In *The American Woman's Meals without Meat Cook Book*, recipes for egg dishes, macaroni, and fish dinners all provided answers to the question "How will we cook without meat?" Its editor, Ruth Berolzheimer, also recommended foods in gelatin molds and vegetables stuffed with other kinds of food. The copy of this book that I examined seemed to have been used, and its owner favored dishes that might have appeared twenty years before at a ladies' luncheon: cheese and rice croquettes, peppers stuffed with cheese, and asparagus loaf.[22] Indeed, authors often called upon the old favorites such as croquettes, hash, jellies, assorted sauces, and "escalloped" dishes to use up every bit of the increasingly precious meat in the home.

A promotional booklet for Knox Gelatin—*Mrs. Knox's Meatless Main Dishes and Leftover Hints*—offered recipes in 1942 for ham mousse, meat loaf, and stuffed green peppers.[23]

Whatever strategy cookbook authors advocated for "solving the meat problem," they nearly always did so with hearty can-do cheer. They never lamented the restrictions imposed by wartime necessity. In fact, they reassured readers again and again that new recipes and astute cookery advice would help Americans continue to enjoy mouthwatering meals throughout the war. While citizens may have complained to each other about meat supplies and the rationing system, cookery instruction and food advertising remained relentlessly cheerful and upbeat about the necessary sacrifices of the war. Individuals may have privately bemoaned rationing, but cookbooks maintained a determinedly buoyant tone about the necessary diet limitations facing Americans during wartime. In fact, they emphasized the importance of "sharing the food" and adhering to the rationing system. Authors constantly suggested that with their assistance—in the form of recipes and cooking suggestions—Americans could easily meet the challenges of wartime cooking without sacrificing nutrition or, indeed, gustatory pleasures. In a typical passage, Arthur Deute enthused in his 1944 *200 Dishes for Men to Cook* that his recipe for "Super Steak, War Style" would transform sirloin fans into rump roast lovers: "Come Victory, it is safe to prophesy that the aristocratic strip sirloin, just to name one cut, will have to sell itself all over again and have a hard time doing it to families who have learned how to make an ordinary rump steak or a bit of the round turn handsprings, as it were." A good recipe, he asserted, could make the most humdrum meat more tempting than even sirloin.

Deute also commented that "One thing that this war is teaching us is the deliciousness of veal kidneys," reiterating the assertions of many authors who insisted that "variety meats" could be made into tasty, meaty main dishes.[24] Although recipes for brain, heart, liver, and kidneys appeared in 1920s cookbooks, Americans definitely consumed these organs less frequently by 1942. But the war, asserted some authors, would force Americans to rethink their reluctance to cook with the less-than-choicest cuts of meat. Betty Watson, in her 1943 *Cooking without Cans*, commented that "Wartime rationing focuses attention on those ends and bits and hindquarters of meat that in other days were tossed to the dog—if not first thrown away in the butcher's refuse can." She added a warning: "Those women who have been depending on steaks and chops and roasts all these years may suddenly find themselves 'out on a limb,' unless they are adventurous enough to plunge into new and strange recipes." Marjorie Mills, author of a 1937 cookbook for single women, produced a wartime cookbook bravely entitled *Cooking on a Ration: Food Is Still Fun,* and in her chapter on meats, she noted that "you can really cook delectable stews and casseroles from all points of the compass on an animal. Heads, tails, shins, knuckles, and other oddments you hadn't even a bowing acquaintance with a few months ago are making the culinary Blue Book because of their low ration point value."[25]

Authors also touted variety meats as highly nutritious. References to the vitamins and minerals found in kidneys, hearts, and livers did not come amiss at a time when many around the nation seemed more concerned than ever about nutrition. Statistically, the numbers of malnourished people in the United States declined with the wartime boom in employment, the dissemination of information about vitamins and nutrition, and the institution of the welfare system. However, concern about the health of the nation increased after 1941. Earlier cookbooks also focused on the importance of balanced meals and good nutrition, but during the war they upped the ante considerably and consistently linked the health of the family with the defense of the United States against annihilation. The scandalous news that 40 percent of the first one million men called in for induction into the armed forces had been rejected as physically unsound ignited a national panic.[26] When cookbook author Margot Murphy urged her readers to educate themselves about the most healthful kinds of foods, she alluded to this disturbing fact, then went on to lament the general ill health of most Americans: "I think that today's American may for the most part be fairly described as bespectacled and subject to long and painful sessions in the dentist's chair. We have a terrific number of nervous breakdowns, and our newspapers are liberally sprinkled with obituaries of people who, in their early sixties, fifties, and even forties, have dropped dead from a sudden heart attack."[27] She went to provide an extensive section on vitamin values and nutrition.

Murphy's description of the bespectacled and nervous citizens of America helped to bolster her message about the critical role of good nutrition to winning the victory. Murphy, and many other authors and editors, did not hesitate to make a direct connection between war defense and nutritious meals. The federal government made the same connection. The National Research Council formed the Committee on Food Habits and enlisted Margaret Mead and other anthropologists to study the eating habits of the nation and report their findings. In 1941 the government issued a Recommended Daily Allowances (RDA) of nutrients: one or more leafy green or yellow vegetable servings; two servings of citrus fruit, tomatoes, or raw cabbage; three of potatoes and all other vegetables and fruits; four servings of dairy; five of meat, poultry, fish, eggs, or dried peas or beans; six of bread, flour, and cereals; and seven of butter or fortified margarine.[28] The experts had spoken: the best diet consisted of fairly enormous amounts of food, with much emphasis on newly discovered nutrients such as thiamin and riboflavin. These recommendations, along with wartime concern about the health and fitness of its citizens, helped fuel the government's campaign to educate Americans about proper diet. As had been the case in World War I, experts from the government, food-processing companies, and cookbook authors urged Americans to take steps toward a healthier diet, but now they utilized even more advanced advertising and media techniques.[29] Cookbooks seized upon the new government-endorsed nutrition standards, and charts depicting "The Seven Food Groups" appeared often in wartime cookbooks, as did the RDA recommendations and other federal information about nutrition.

Cookbook authors and editors, responding in part to both meat rationing and a wave of highly publicized, detailed information about nutrition, began to offer recipes using vegetable proteins and soy products. Such recipes appeared regularly in cookbooks published after 1941 until the end of the war. Cookbook advice to housewives about how to cook with these meat substitutes reiterated similar campaigns by the Office of War Information and the War Food Administration. They urged consumers to cook and eat protein and meat substitutes—inexpensive and highly nutritious—throughout the war. Arguably the most successful cookbook of the period, the 1943 edition of *The Joy of Cooking* included recipes using both soybeans and other kinds of vegetable proteins. *American Cookery* magazine published an enthusiastic article about soybeans, calling them the "Star on the Food-for-Defense Stage" and the 1944 periodical *Meal Planning Guide* offered recipes using soy flour in everything from meat loaf to candy, pastry, and ice cream.[30] The authors of *Kitchen Strategy* suggested lima bean loaf as a good meat substitute. Katherine Fisher, in a 1943 article for *Good Housekeeping*, managed to use both variety meats *and* soy products in her recipe for ground liver and soy flour dumplings.[31]

The unflappable Ida Bailey Allen easily repackaged her recipes to meet wartime cookery needs, and her 1943 *Double-Quick Cooking for Part-Time Homemakers* included recipes for soy and oat cookies, cheese soy rabbit, soy biscuits, and peanut flour loaf. *Your Share*, a promotional cookbook from General Mills and its popular fictional spokeswoman Betty Crocker, offered only one entirely meatless main dish (nutburgers), focusing instead on meat "stretchers." Betty Crocker did recommend the lavish use of beans as a source of protein, however:

Are you looking for proteins with point value low?
If so, the legumes you'll enjoy,
All the Navy Beans, Lima and Kidney, you know,
And don't forget Pinto and Soy!
They're plentiful, popular "Victory" fare
Don't ask for the canned—they're at war,
These recipes give you real treats to prepare
Serve once—and they'll all ask for more!

Other authors offered less jovial advice on using protein substitutes. In *Cook's Away*, published in 1943, Elizabeth Case and Martha Wyman somberly admitted that their recipes for lima bean loaf and soybeans were "more nutritious and filling than epicurean."[32]

Some cookbooks published in 1943, 1944, and 1945 made no reference to the problems of wartime cookery, but most did, and authors and editors invariably focused on the scarcity of meat and the importance of protein in the diet. But solutions to sugar rationing came in a close second. That a rationed amount of eight, then twelve, ounces of sugar per person per week might seem scanty made sense, given America's propensity for highly sweetened foods. Since the nineteenth century, cookbooks consistently devoted the majority of their recipes to desserts and baked goods. Food studies scholar Amy Bentley makes the compelling argument that the long-standing associations of men with meat and women with sugar intensified during the Second World War, and that sweet home-baked desserts, cookies, and cakes remained an intensely feminine skill, helping to bolster gender norms during wartime.[33] In cookbooks, meat eating and cake baking did often mention the gender of the person eating the meat or baking the cake. But they also depicted both meat and sugary desserts, especially cake and pie, as something men, women, and children all enjoyed eating and, in fact, needed to keep their morale high. The numerous recipes in commercial cookbooks published during World War II that utilized sugar substitutes or smaller amounts of refined sugar also emphasized the patriotic necessity of sugar rationing (referring to the use of sugar in weapon production).

Sugar rationing, asserted authors and editors, served an important wartime purpose, and low-sugar recipes offered a significant way for women and families to contribute to the war effort. Case and Wyman, for instance, included recipes using corn syrup in a chapter called "Victory Aids," as well as recipes for sugarless chocolate cake and sugarless frosting. Harriet Hester's no-nonsense *300 Sugar Saving Recipes*, published in 1942, suggested plainer kinds of baked goods to help win victory. Her recipes included coffee gingerbread, mincemeat fruitcake, prune pie filling, honey frosting, and low-sugar piecrust. Ruth Berolzheimer suggested making candy at home with refined sugar substitutes, and she infused this activity with patriotic importance: "Make candies at home and encourage the children to spend their dimes for war stamps," she advised. And in her 1942 recipe booklet, *Sugarless Recipes,* Ruth Odell offered tips for saving the precious commodity, such as adding a pinch of salt instead of sugar to vegetables for flavoring. She reminded readers that "Every bit of sugar wasted may mean fewer cartridges for the boys who are fighting."[34]

Cookbooks also emphasized that the armed forces required fats for military purposes, because glycerin could be made into gunpowder and shells. Editors, authors, and magazine writers urged women to return any leftover fat to the butcher for wartime recycling. As Betty Crocker instructed her readers in *Your Share:* "To help your country, save every bit of FAT [*sic*] that comes into your kitchen!" The wartime recipes in *Your Share* also offered readers advice on sparing another rationed fat: butter. One page depicted a family, heads bent in prayer, under the pious heading "Spread the Butter [*sic*] thin that we may have butter on our bread." Betty Crocker's butter-extending tips included a recipe for a mixture of gelatin, milk, salt, and yellow food coloring, which, when mixed into a pound of butter, would extend the amount and shelf life of the butter. Ida Bailey Allen offered a similar recipe extending both butter and meat spreads. Women's magazines, cookbooks, and newspaper columns printed recipes for butter extenders made with gelatin, cream, or unsweetened custard. And during the war, margarine became far more widely used than in the prewar era. A butter-flavored spread recipe in *Coupon Cookery* called for mayonnaise, evaporated milk, gelatin, salt, and margarine.[35]

Butter, sugar, and meat garnered innumerable hints, tips, and recipes in World War II cookbooks, and nutritional information about fats and proteins received the most marked attention in wartime cookery instruction. But authors and editors also discussed, at length, the nutritional value of all foods. Some authors expressed the belief that American housewives were too dependent upon processed and canned foods, both of which would be more difficult to obtain during the war. They argued that American women needed to learn more healthful kinds of cooking—in marked contrast to the cookbooks in the 1920s and 1930s, which blithely recommended the liberal use of processed foods. The title of Betty Watson's 1943 cookbook—*Cooking without Cans*—showed her interest in weaning readers from processed foods. In the introduction, Watson chided "Are you dismayed because wartime rationing restricts canned goods to a minimum? Has your culinary world tumbled because you can no longer pick up the telephone and tell the butcher to send a specified cut of roast, or a particular thickness of steak?" And at the end of her book, she concluded: "American women may be forced by these new conditions to alter their marketing habits. Necessity has moved us to stir ingenuity into the stews of yesterday. By force of circumstances, daring and skill must be substituted for those 'quick' dinners which used to come out of a can."[36] Similarly, Harriet Hester gave recipes for soups, baked beans, and chili con carne, remarking "Many of us who have grown accustomed to cooking with a can-opener will feel at a loss during this war period. Some of our most tried and true friends will be missing from the canned goods shelves."[37]

The proper cooking of fresh vegetables, in particular, seemed to require numerous hints and recipes in World War II cookbooks. Since the advent of the cooking school movement in the nineteenth century, cookery instruction virtually always emphasized the proper cooking of vegetables. And contrary to popular assumptions today, as early as 1900 cookery instruction advised readers to cook vegetables in as little water as possible, for as short a time as possible, in order to retain nutrients and vitamins. Although many Americans preferred their vegetables to be very well cooked, authors stood unanimous on the subject: vegetables should not be soggy but fairly crisp and never overcooked. Many of the lengthy vegetable cooking times recommended by cookbooks in the early twentieth century seem to suggest that water-logged, overcooked vegetables were the inevitable result, but we in the age of genetically engineered food have to remember that these authors dealt with fresh ingredients of vastly different quality. Peas purchased in the supermarket may well have required longer boiling in 1942 than today. Wartime concerns about nutrition only increased cookbook attention to the proper way of cooking vegetables. Marjorie Mills, for example, spoke for many cookbook authors when she wrote: "We're urged to grow and eat as many more vegetables, but if the same limp and dejected vegetables trail across the dinner table, it will be a sawdust path of duty. (Sorry to scold, but the way some people cook vegetables is scandalous. It's no wonder families rebel.)"[38]

Mills's comment refers to wartime government campaigns that urged Americans to grow and eat their own vegetables. Beginning in 1942, the U.S. Department of Agriculture made a determined effort to encourage citizens to plant "victory gardens" and to educate them about the benefits of such gardens. Although evidence shows that the country did not embrace gardening as wholeheartedly and with as much goodwill as the media sometimes suggested, in 1943 Americans grew a significant percentage (40 percent) of the fresh produce they consumed that year.[39] A few cookbooks, like other media sources, heralded the American return to gardening and encouraged readers to utilize fresh grown vegetables in their kitchens. For example, Alice Winn-Smith wrote confidently in her 1942 *Thrifty Cooking for Wartime:* "We shall be planning on our Victory gardens and foods we can grow at home during the war period, so that salads will fill a more important place than ever on our tables."[40]

Many cookbooks also offered instructions on canning foods. But, like victory gardening, home canning probably received more attention in the media than it actually warranted, in terms of how many home-canned jars of vegetables housewives produced. In terms of morale building, however, home canning perhaps deserved the publicity. Home canning seemed a deeply patriotic thing to do. If she could afford the initial expense of canning equipment, a woman who canned her own vegetables preserved precious food and stockpiled against an uncertain future, and she did so without hoarding. *The Modern Hostess Cookbook*, a wartime periodical of recipes and home hints, summarized this feeling about home canning: "Canning is a contribution to the war effort because more foods are needed than have been needed in the past. By canning at home, you will be the means of saving some of the surplus food that might otherwise go to waste. Then too, home canned foods require no transportation, which relieves the load on our transportation system and clears the tracks for the uninterrupted flow of war material and foods to our armed forces."[41] Home canning fulfilled patriotic and nutritional ideals nicely, and numerous cookbooks, like the 1943 edition of *The Joy of Cooking*, devoted long sections to the process of canning and making jam and jelly. Similar canning and preserving sections in wartime cookbooks revised a trend from the early part of the century, when most cookbooks contained information on the topic.

Wartime cookbooks gave the homely skill of vegetable canning new attention, but other food trends found in 1920s and 1930s cookery instruction continued. Authors encouraged their readers to try recipes for "foreign food," for example. In fact, as Ripperger suggested, much European cuisine lent itself to the thrifty stews and sturdy casseroles that many cookbooks advocated. Pasta, cheap and filling, also appeared regularly. In her 1944 *Mother Hubbard's Cookbook*, Marion White featured a section called "From the Strangers in Our Midst," which included hearty recipes for Hungarian goulash, Cuban *arroz con pollo*, and Chinese cabbage soup with meat balls.[42] Curries continued to be popular, as well as a wide variety of "chop suey" dishes, along with the more new-fangled "chow mein." Frank Shay, in his 1941 *The Best Men Are Cooks*, included recipes for such exotic fare as paella, polenta, *frijoles refritos*, frogs' legs, pizza, and blintzes.[43] But Shay wrote and published his book before American entry into the war. Somber stews with a thrifty European flavor were one thing, but rich paella quite another.

During the war, cookery instruction changed its tone. No longer did most authors trill about the fun and artistry of home cooking. They reconfigured food as a serious matter: "Food will win the war," they asserted again and again. They described the cooking duties of middle-class women as an act of patriotism; the defense of the family's health, and thus the nation, began in women's kitchens. And women took this challenge very seriously. A combination of propaganda and marketing barraged the nation with messages about the more-important-than-ever cooking duties of women, but some women sifted through the rhetoric to arrive at the conclusion that what they did in the kitchen during this national crisis *did* matter. One woman—Maude Reid of Lake Charles, Louisiana—kept a diary and scrapbook about cooking during the war, realizing that food preparation in the years 1942 through 1945 had taken on historical significance. Maude Reid created her own version of wartime cookery instruction, and it reveals much about the recipes she read and used during those years.

6

"Ways and Means for War Days"

THE COOKBOOK-SCRAPBOOK

COMPILED BY MAUDE REID

When General Mills set out to convince women in 1943 that the purchase of a certain brand of cake flour had important patriotic repercussions, it did not aim its advertisements at women like Maude Reid. First of all, she was a little too old: born in 1882, she was almost sixty when the United States entered the war (fig. 10). Furthermore, she had never married and never had children. Instead, she enjoyed a long and highly successful career as a nurse for the parish school system in Lake Charles, Louisiana. She attended Bellevue Hospital's School of Nursing in New York City, and received degrees in social work and public health from the University of Virginia. She had been the first public school nurse in Calcasieu Parish. Finally, Reid, a southerner, failed to fit the profile of the prospective Betty Crocker reader. General cookbooks, especially cookbooks published by food-processing companies, ignored potential regional differences among their readers and encouraged a homogenized diet.

Maude Reid also possessed an unusual hobby. As a nonprofessional historian and avid newspaper reader, she collected thousands of clippings over the years and gathered them into scrapbooks, sometimes adding her own comments and insights to the pages. A descendent of one of the first white settlers in Lake Charles, she had an abiding interest in the history of the county, its families, and its important events. Many of her papers are now stored in the Maude Reid collection at McNeese State University in Lake Charles. But one of Reid's

Figure 10 Maude Reid, author of the
cookbook-scrapbook "Ways and Means for
War Days." Published courtesy of McNeese
State University Library, Lake Charles,
Louisiana.

scrapbooks—a small spiral notebook with a paper cover and a clipped
headline reading "Ways and Means for War Days" pasted on the
front—has not been included in the collection. Reid undoubtedly authored the book: her name, street address, and a date—August 1943—
are inscribed on the first page under the title "Cookery in Our Town
During the Global War"; the handwriting in the book matches other
documents she wrote; and her family sold this document at an estate
sale after Maude Reid's death.[1]

In some respects, "Ways and Means for War Days," fits into the
tradition of women's "receipt books," that is, hand-copied recipes collected by middle- and upper-class women into book form. But Maude
Reid's book cannot be described solely as a "receipt book" for several
important reasons. First, it does not appear that Reid actually used this
book to do her own cooking. Her writing instead suggests that she used
this scrapbook to preserve wartime recipes for the edification of others.
Second, she obviously collected these recipes and clippings with the
intention of recording a historical event, that is, cooking during war
conditions. In other words, she self-consciously created a historical
document to help future readers better understand how the war af-

fected eating and cooking in Lake Charles, Louisiana. Nor, I believe, did Maude Reid intend to seek a professional publisher for this book or to use it as a fund-raising book. The inclusion of personal notes on some of the issues of wartime living, the casual organization of the book, and the numerous clippings taped into its pages seem to preclude those possibilities. Instead, Reid set out to create a kind of scrapbook of the historical events she saw taking place around her, with her own commentary on those events, via the medium of cookery instruction. Her book, then, offers a double-layered source for helping us understand how women read and utilized published recipes during the war years: both her commentary and the scrapbook itself give historians a view into a wartime kitchen.

Maude Reid had an abiding interest in cookery and recipes that did not begin with the onset of World War II. In 1918 she had painstakingly copied an entire cookbook into a black, imitation leather notebook. On the front page of the notebook, Reid recorded the title and publication information of the copied book: *An English Butler's Canapés, Salads, Sandwiches, Drinks*, by Samuel E. Daris, published in 1916, Hirshler Books, New York. She also recorded the circumstances of how she came to copy the book: "Copied by me from a book in the possession of Mrs. A. Lery, Lake Charles, who in turn secured it from the butler in the household of her brother, Henri Bendel, New York City." Reid worked as a nurse at this time: she noted that she made this copy "during the long night hours while on night duty, and signed her book "Maude Reid, R.N."[2] This notebook revealed Reid's social status as a trained professional and as a woman sharing recipe books with other upper- and middle-class women.

But a few years before she copied this book, Maude Reid undertook the far more demanding task of creating a cookbook of her own recipes. This undated and lengthy document consists mostly of recipes written in Reid's longhand, a few clippings and photographs of food cut out of newspapers and magazines, and a fairly substantial section on household tips.[3] Although undated on the first page (which also lacks a title), the newspaper clippings and the recipes themselves (including pre-Prohibition punch recipes) suggest that Reid put most of this collection together sometime between 1911 and 1914 but continued to add to it for several years. In contrast to "Ways and Means," this cookery book may have been intended for some kind of publication or for use as a comprehensive cookbook. Reid did not offer extraneous comments on the recipes, and she organized the recipes into an order very similar to commercially published cookbooks. For example, on the first page in the book, she taped in a table of weights and measures, then listed "Must Haves" for the kitchen. She began her recipes with a section on appetizers and canapés, then moved on to soups, and so on. This structure simulated that of a general, commercially published cookbook. Most of these recipes seem to be Reid's own, but she credited a few to friends and family and to women's magazines such as *Good Housekeeping* and *Ladies' Home Journal*. Reid does not mention the First World War in this document, but she did include a clipping published during the war of "War-Time Dinner Menus," which emphasized using leftovers and complying with "wheatless and meatless" days.

The recipes in this earlier cookbook demonstrated Reid's own cooking proficiency and her interest in regional foods such as okra, crayfish, sweet potato pone, and jambalaya. Fannie Farmer and the cookery school movement also shaped Reid's book: she included an article by Farmer on formal dinners, and her menu suggestions follow the pattern established by the cookery school movement. In addition, the cookbook gave some evidence of Reid's financial and social status. In an entry dated August 1911, she described in detail "My Sunflower Party," including the elaborate floral decorations all over the house. She also listed the menu, which featured a fruit salad with mayonnaise and decorative pickles cut into star shapes and a fancy ice cream dessert: yellow ice cream, with chocolate shavings, made to resemble a black-eyed Susan, accompanied by "little gold cakes." Like many other middle-class ladies throwing afternoon parties, Reid's menu emphasized delicacy and prettiness. Similarly, the elaborate Christmas dinner menu, dated 1910, described a truly sumptuous meal and reflected Reid's southern cooking tradition: gumbo filé and rice, stuffed celery, olives, court bouillon a la Creole, roast turkey, rice and oyster dressing, individual cranberry molds, mashed potatoes, macaroni au gratin, winter squash, onions in butter sauce, hot buttered rolls, corn pone, stuffed Virginia ham, white asparagus salad, mayonnaise, fruit cake, ice cream, white grapes, nuts, raisins, dates, St. Julien claret, and black coffee. Also, "baskets of apples and chestnuts to be roasted," a buffet of eggnog, cider, nuts, and candies, and "Christmas cakes of all descriptions."

Reid's menus—for teas, luncheons, Sunday suppers, and parties—revealed a comfortable life-style, and indicate that she and her family had the time and resources for elaborate meals and decorations. At more than six hundred pages, this earlier cookbook of Reid represents a far more time-consuming and formalized effort at writing cookery instruction than "Ways and Means." And in its own way, it is as instructive about cooking and recipes in the early twentieth century as "Ways and Means" is for the years 1942 to 1947. But the more casual collection of recipes, and the far more detailed, dated, commentary in Reid's World War II cookbook allows the historian a clearer view of how Reid and women like her operated in the kitchen on a daily basis.

"Ways and Means" does not progress in a strictly linear manner. Reid did not make daily or weekly entries like she might have in a diary. She dated the book 1943 on the first page but also included clippings from 1942, as well as her own thoughts about events that happened in 1942. Some comments she obviously wrote in later. Often, her tenses move back and forth from the past to the present. And although she included some personal comments, she did intend her book to serve as a historical record. The first line of the book reads: "So many interesting problems have arisen since we entered into this terrible war in December 1941, in regard to our daily food that I began writing in this book about them." She then immediately began to summarize the situation: "Common, every-day things quickly became scarce early in 1942 and then disappeared altogether. For more than a year now we have not seen in any grocer's, canned pineapple, canned pork and beans (that we once relied upon for a quick pick-up meal) or corned beef."

Like commercial cookbooks of the time, Reid focused her main attention on food shortages, especially meat, but she spoke far more frankly about those shortages and the difficulties of the rationing system than upbeat commercial cookbook authors and corporately produced cookery instruction. For instance, instead of discussing their nutritional value, she flatly refused to eat "variety meats." In 1943 she wrote "Most of the meat—except at rare intervals—found at the butcher's is pork, ham, and, not infrequently, liver," adding "Of course, there is a display of other glandular organs—sweet breads, kidney, heart, etc. But I can't eat these. At least, not unless I was *very* hungry." A coffee lover, she took a similar stand against herb tea. She pasted in an article on sassafras tea published in the *Beaumont Enterprise* on 19 November 1942, and next to it she wrote: "Some of our townswomen are drinking mint tea, so the clipping below is suggestive. Mrs. Rudolph Krause, Sr., tells me that she drinks mint tea and finds it delicious but somehow these herb and root teas leave me cold. I can't help but associate them with the dreadful Webber's Tea that my mother used to dose us with in the spring of the year and I can yet shudder at the memory of the nauseous dose!" She also remained dubious about clipped suggestions for using raccoon, rabbit, alligator tails, shark steaks, and muskrat meat and scoffed at the suggestion from a 25 April 1942 article in the *Lake Charles American Press* to eat rice polish as a source of vitamin B1. "The fad for vitamins has brought us to this—Rice polish is fed to pigs to make them fat," she wrote. "Since I have no desire to look like a pig, I pass up rice polish!" She also expressed deep shock that butchers in Lake Charles had horsemeat for sale. She remained unconvinced by the grocer's explanation that people bought it to feed their pets. Reid pasted in a cartoon that depicted a line of dogs waiting at the butcher shop for horsemeat. One dog comments to another "I never thought I'd live to see this." Next to the cartoon, Reid wrote:

> I never thought I would live to see it, either, but horsemeat is being sold here. Bride's grocery carries it regularly in frozen cartons. When I asked if people bought it, he said-"Sure, they buy it for dogs and other pets."
>
> I have not tried it on my Joe Palooka—my cat. He still eats liver, beef and pork liver. He sometimes uses up my red points and I am forced to fall back on eggs or cheese for my protein needs.

Reid mentioned Joe Palooka several times in her book, and she must have been very fond of him to use up her red points to keep him in liver.

Joe Palooka's liver consumption was only one of Maude Reid's worries when it came to her red points and to food rationing in general. The point and ration system, as Reid described it, had a dramatic effect on her daily life. Many of the recipes have notes about point values: "Takes four points for a can" or "6 slices in a can—6 points," for example. She sometimes described how long it took her to find certain rationed food items, such as how far she had to drive to look for a can of condensed milk. She taped several of the round red cardboard points into the book, most likely after rationing had ended. Under one, she wrote: "Here is one of the precious points we used to get meat, cooking fats, salad oil, and butter." Next to a *Good Housekeeping* article about meals that required no ration points (many food items, such as chicken, cottage cheese, and fresh fruits and vegetables were not rationed), Reid taped another of the "precious points." Reid clipped a 1944 Christmas poem that humorously expressed women's frustrations about food shortages. Reid gave the title and the author, but did not tell from which periodical she procured "Santa Claus, Please Listen," by Virginia Scott Miner:

Who was that woman who used to say
"Give me a giddy gift any day
Give me things that sparkle and shine
With a uselessness almost divine;
Give me things that I'd like to try
But never, never would just go buy?"
Who was she? Well, I might remember.
But Santa, this is a new December.
The things I want are brand-new tires
And sun-porch screens made of copper wires;
I could use rib roasts or the yawning roaster,
And how I'd love a pop-up toaster.
I'd almost settle (oh, change must utter)
For some country eggs and a pound of butter!

Reid did not comment specifically about this poem, but it articulated some of the same feelings she did, particularly when discussing the meat shortage: frustration, irritation, a sense of deprivation, but also a wry sense of humor about the situation.

Reid often mentioned her frustration at being unable to obtain red meat for her meals. As many commercial cookbooks suggested, women felt a real sense of being stymied in the kitchen, especially concerning meat shortages.[4] The plethora of recipes for meat substitutes and meat extenders in "Ways and Means" indicates Reid's concern about "the meat problem." Reid resorted to eggs and cheese for her protein needs numerous times, not only when Joe Palooka's appetite used up her red points. The very first recipe in the book gives instructions for a kidney bean loaf consisting of beans, grated cheese, bread crumbs, onion, shortening, egg, salt, and pepper. She enthused "Here is a recipe for [a] meat substitute that almost defies detection. You would be willing to bet that there is meat in it so clearly is the meat flavor duplicated. It is just as good sliced cold as served hot, and it makes a nice sandwich." She billed her meatballs and spaghetti dish as "a good meat extender." A clipped recipe for "War Beef Patties" from Gulf States Utilities extended the beef with white potatoes—Reid described the finished product as "very good."

By Reid's definition, meat meant beef. Pork, though more easily available, did not count as the best kind of meat. Along with her recipe for "Pork Chops, Victory Style," Reid explained: "While beef is scarce, we still have pork obtainable at the meat counters, and while I was brought up to believe that pork is too heating for summer eating, we are sometimes forced to eat it for lack of any other meat. It also takes fewer coupons—and that counts in rationing." She also comforted herself by noting "Pork = Rich in Vitamin B-1, so important to steady nerves and proper utilization of starchy and sweet foods." By 1945, she wrote, ham proved more difficult to obtain, forcing Reid to create a new recipe for "Okra Gumbo in Wartime":

> Because ham is very difficult to get—and red point value high—during the war my okra gumbo which usually has a base of raw sliced, cubed ham, has been changed to get its meat flavor by using canned chicken soup.
>
> But by May, 1945, chicken soup had disappeared from grocer's shelves, so I substituted strained vegetable soup and tomato soup. This with my seasoned okra and shrimp make a really delicious gumbo.

Reid did not include a recipe with this tip, perhaps because she assumed that her readers would have their own gumbo recipes.

Reid's comments on canned pork meat, an ingredient which virtually never appeared in commercial cookbooks, illustrated the way that meat shortages "forced" Americans to turn to pork. She clipped several color photographs from advertisements for this canned meat, and recipes for dishes such as "creamed Treet and eggs," and "macaroni and Prem." Reid noted that "Because of meat scarcity and high ration points we have learned to use canned pork shoulder such as 'Spam,' 'Treet,' 'Prem.'" On another page, she gave a recipe for "Baked Spam," but noted that it did not require a particular brand: "Use any canned pork shoulder. I like Morrell's best when I can get it." As she did for several recipes, she gave menu suggestions with this recipe: "Serve with baked potato and limas or, peas and baked squash, greens and spaghetti casserole," and she reminded the reader that "it can be broiled in thick slices as it comes from the can. Serve sizzling with squares of crusty, buttered hot corn-bread and apple sauce."

Reid's use of this advertising material tells us something that commercial cookbooks cannot: women did read, clip, and utilize the recipes offered in popular advertisements for processed foods such as Treet—especially when meat shortages left them grasping for a meat main dish. But that did not mean Reid took all suggestions equally. When *Life* magazine printed a wry article, with photographs, by an English man who sent in recipes for "Spam à la Grecque" (mixed with garlic, bread crumbs and herbs, then fried in oil), "Spam Chop Suey" (fried and added to mixed vegetables, cooked five minutes), and "Spam Réformé" (sliced and served in Algerian wine sauce with green vegetables) in 1944, Reid conscientiously labeled the article "Ways of Serving Canned Pork Shoulder that we know as 'Spam,' 'Prem,' and other trade names." But she went on to remark briskly: "Dress it up and give it a fancy name—it is still canned meat—best just simply plain boiled and served with appropriate vegetables. We pay 6 red points a can for this meat."

Reid also recorded several wartime recipes for butter extenders—while noting that she herself had not actually tried them. She preferred to use margarine or oleo products. She specifically preferred "Nucoa," the product hyped by Ida Bailey Allen a few years earlier. Moreover, Reid knew that extended butter did not keep as well: "Suggestions for extending butter have been given too. That is, adding milk and gelatine [*sic*] to a pound of butter to make 2 pounds. This does not keep as well as the oleo products—so I have not tried it." She dutifully recorded the recipe for a butter stretcher using cream and egg that, according to her notes, had been "Given by 'The Mystery Chef' over the radio—June 1944." But she candidly added: "(Incidentally, I never tried this formula, although many of my friends did. I continued to use margarine, but carefully, because even this is hard to get)." On the facing page, labeled "Butter Extender for use in making sandwiches," Reid pasted in a clipped Knox gelatin advertisement. The ad had a series of black-and-white instructional photographs showing how to make a butter-extender sandwich spread. She also wrote down her own "Butter Saving Tricks," such as letting the butter soften before spreading and using bacon fat as a butter substitute in biscuit recipes. Reid preferred margarine, but felt it necessary to include these recipes for extending butter because they represented an important example of cookery in her town during the war.

She did not, however, feel a need to include many recipes for getting around sugar rationing. Perhaps her personal preferences overwhelmed her duty as a historical observer: Reid did not care much for sweet desserts, as she explained at the beginning of the book: "The sugar rationing did not greatly inconvenience me because I seldom make puddings, etc., relying more on fresh or canned fruits for my dessert." Nor did she give instructions for home canning or preserving. She did, however, note that many citizens in her town took up victory gardening with a vengeance—although she never mentions doing any gardening herself. Next to a clipping depicting a huge anthropomorphized carrot with hoe and rake in its hand and the slogans "Vegetables for Victory / America Needs More Food / Plant a Victory Garden," Reid wrote: "And many of our townspeople were doing this very thing. Those who had any land at all, if no larger than a handkerchief, began plowing, or perhaps turning the soil by hand if they had no horse. Every afternoon after 5 o'clock, these workers descend on their garden plots and work until darkness falls."

Sugar shortages and victory gardens merited only a brief mention by Reid, but she wrote a considerable amount on the importance of saving fats and turning them over to the butcher for wartime recycling. For example, she clipped this poem entitled "Out of the Frying Pan" by Margaret Fishback, from the 30 September 1944 edition of *Collier's* magazine:

> *Fat that once went down the drain*
> *Saves our soldiers scars and pain.*
> *Fat we used to throw away*
> *Lives to fry another day.*
> *What a joy to fry a Jap!*
> *Save that grease and set your cap*
> *For a Nazi on the side.*
> *He'll be nicer too, when fried.*

That clipping also noted that "One tablespoonful of waste fat supplies the nitroglycerin for five bullets, or the glycerin needed for seventy-

three small-pox inoculations, or two applications of sulpha ointment."
This poem illustrates the well-documented proliferation of racist war
propaganda (in this case, not "Germans" but "Nazis" are destined for
the frying pan, whereas all "Japs" must be fried), but for Reid it probably articulated an important kitchen directive. Under the poem, she
wrote: "We all have a can for waste fat in our kitchens. When the can is
filled, we take it to the grocer's who gives us 2 red points and 2 cents a
pound. Every drop of fat in my house is saved religiously."

Reid saved quite a number of clippings and articles dealing with the
conservation of fats. One such article, called "Cook to Save Fat" and
clipped from the September 1945 edition of *Better Homes and Gardens*,
offered tips like baking croquettes in the oven, restuffing potatoes,
broiling fish fillets, using drippings for cooking and so on. Under the
article, Reid wrote in a description of the fat shortage in her town: "All
fats have been very scarce within the past year of 1944 and well into
1945. Of course, much has been taken for munitions, but—we at home
can't get along without fat altogether. We need it for heat and energy—
for meals that satisfy. Therefore, we resort to every sort of device to
save fat in our kitchens and to make what we have go as far as possible."
And on the next page she taped a newspaper headline from the 24
October 1945 edition of the *Lake Charles American Press* that reads "Up
Goes Point Reward! Now You Get 4 Points Instead of 2 for Each Pound
of Used Fats."[5]

The fact that Reid often cooked with fat ensured that saving fats and
making the fat go as far as possible would get attention in her cookbooks. Similarly, her love for coffee induced her to frequently write
about coffee rationing and coffee extenders. For instance, she clipped a
7 February 1943 article from the *New Orleans Times-Picayune* about
coffee substitute—a mixture of burnt corn bran and sweet potato peel-
ings—recommended by "Uncle" Charlie Bell, an "86-year-old Negro,
who as a young boy knew at first-hand something of the travail of the
War Between the States period." Reid offered no further comment here,
but in other places she argued sharply against the use of coffee substitutes and extenders. In an entry dated November 1942, she wrote:
"Coffee rationed—1 pound every 6 weeks. Only those persons over 15
years old may purchase a pound of coffee. All sorts of 'extenders' suggested. My sister—who really drinks brown water—pours all excess
coffee from the pot, bottles it, places it in the refrigerator and re-heats it
next day. I refuse to drink such stuff. I shall use my coffee—1 tablespoon
for the cup and 1 for the pot—and when the coffee gives out, shall drink
tea or cocoa." In 1943, she happily heralded the removal of coffee from
the rationed lists:

Due to our efforts to combat the sub-marine menace of our enemies we were able to secure coffee in sufficient quantity this summer to take it off the rationing list. Three cheers!

However, while rationing was on we heard over the radio and read in papers and magazines how we might extend coffee. From President Roosevelt on down. But I paid no attention to this sort of thing. There is only one way to make coffee and that is the right way. I would rather have a week's supply of good coffee, than six weeks of brown slop water.

Here, Reid's comments tell us two important things about cookery instruction during the war. First, we can assume that Reid was not the only woman to disregard some of the cookery advice that came from popular sources like women's magazines, newspapers, or even FDR himself. According to their tastes, or their family's preferences, some things must have been more important to stretch and extend than others. Second Reid's perception that she heard and read a great deal of advice on this issue speaks to the proliferation of cooking instruction during the war.

Reid's diary reflects how recipes deluged the nation during the war years. For instance, she included an article in her scrapbook that discussed how cookbooks and published cookery instruction continued to sell well during the war. Reid clipped an article from the *Beaumont Enterprise*, a Texas paper, on the increase in cookbook sales during the war. The article, dated 10 March 1943, described how cookbooks continued to sell steadily that year. It also compared the rise of cookbook publication with the number of cookbooks published during World War I. The article bore the headline: "With food rationing already in operation, the cookbook is becoming a best-seller." The anonymous author wrote:

A survey of the family economics bureau of the Northwestern National Life Insurance company shows that in many book stores the cook books are outselling the popular novels as housewives seek the aid of experts in solving their wartime food problems. The company reports that the meatless and wheatless days of the first World war [*sic*] brought out 18 new cookery books in 1918, but in 1942 a total of 41 new works on cookery were published and this year many more are on the way. The survey showed that most large city book stores now carry from 15 to more than 100 different titles on cookery, as compared with a dozen or so such books only a few years ago.

A variety of factors contributed to this increase in cookbook publication. Culinary books served in part as a kind of escape from wartime fears, just as they had during the anxious days of the Depression. They facilitated daydreams about times of peace and plenty. And, since the 1920s, as women began to rely less and less on learning cookery skills at home or hiring a domestic cook, recipe books became more and more popular. Perhaps most significantly, women facing food restrictions and rationing felt a real sense of bewilderment, as Reid's scrapbook emphasized.

Reid did not mention, at any other point in "Ways and Means," commercially published cookbooks, but she did effectively document the numerous other sources that "housewives seeking the aid of experts in solving their wartime food problems" might have used. Inside of the front cover of "Ways and Means," for example, Reid taped a brochure entitled "You Can Shorten the War with Food," published by the War Food Administration and the Office of Price Administration. She included other such pamphlets as well: a brochure of recipes and food saving tips from the Gulf States Utility Company (which featured a recipe for sausage substitute made out of beans) and a mimeographed sheet of muskrat, or "marsh hare," recipes printed by the United States Department of the Interior, Fish and Wildlife Service.

The recipes she clipped and saved ranged from advertisements for canned meat to readers' recipes published in local newspapers to recipes created by home economics experts at popular magazines. Although she had not tried his recipe for a butter stretcher, Reid must have listened to *The Mystery Chef* on the radio at least occasionally. Although perhaps not a typical media consumer, her recipe collection does give us an idea of the numerous sources offering recipes and cooking instruction to women during the war. And as Maude Reid's comments about these recipes illustrate, we find that women seized on some as practical and rejected others as not very useful. Their own preferences for sweet desserts or strong coffee might very well have influenced women's use of wartime cookery instruction, as did regional differences in diet. Although she rejected muskrat recipes and retained doubts about butter stretchers, Reid found some suggestions helpful and must have used them in her own kitchen: in Maude Reid's diary, we have a rare account of one woman's real, lived experiences planning, cooking, and eating meals during the war. Such insights are far harder to glean from general, commercially published cookbooks.

We know from her previous cookbook that Maude Reid had a long-standing interest in food and cooking, and in "Ways and Means" she frequently notes her own food favorites and the way to cook them. Her menus are especially suggestive on this point. When Maude Reid recommended certain accompaniments to a recipe, she wrote out of her own experiences with creating meals. After a recipe for "Kraut and Speck" (sauerkraut and pork or bacon) she wrote: "Baked or browned potatoes belong with this dish. Then add a deep dish berry pie to complete a hearty meal. Delicious on a crisp winter day." She described sauerkraut as "Appetizing, quick and unusual," adding "I have it twice a week—it is a good scrubbing brush for your stomach." Her deep-fried bacon recipe included several suggestions for serving. "With it serve mustard sauce," she wrote. "Or, you might serve Major Gray's chutney if you can find any. Or, plain sliced tomatoes may be used, or pickled beets. Since this is a rich meat dish, cabbage will fit in nicely. Or omit these, and serve sliced tomatoes, potato salad, baked apple, bottled beer for the beverage for your Victory Dinner," she advised. Her menus regularly demonstrated such firsthand knowledge of cookery technique and meal preparation. When a clipped recipe for "Fish Loaf" called for one large can of salmon, Reid had no difficulty reworking the recipe, explaining "We can rarely get a can of salmon, and for a substitute I use canned pollock—a fish that comes from Massachusetts." Maude Reid had clearly cooked many of the things she recommended in her book, including some of the dishes suggested by magazine and newspaper writers. Her scrapbook demonstrates that women must have used at least some of the wartime recipes published in popular magazines; they must have taken published cookery instructions into their own kitchens.

Reid had not always, however, relied on her own kitchen labor. As a middle-class southern woman, Reid had employed maids in the past, but the war changed that. Under a clipped drawing of a woman stuffing a turkey while a cat sits on a kitchen chair watching, she wrote, as a statement, not a question: "No maid since the war started, I prepare my own holiday meals. Does this suggest me and my devoted 'Joe Palooka' who waits patiently, and like the gentleman he is, on a stool nearby?" The drawing *had* suggested a vision of herself to Reid, at least. And although she gives no more information about employing household help, this short note does imply that part of the challenge of wartime cookery lay in the exodus of paid household servants out of the home and into war production jobs. Certainly many of the suggested menus in her earlier cookbook would have required servants. And her earlier cookbook credited several recipes to "Aunt Susan," an African American woman who worked for Reid's family. But budget concerns were not unknown to Reid. During the years immediately following the war, surging food prices forced her to rethink her budget constantly, as she explained: "I try to balance my budget. But you have to be a trained seal to balance a budget these days. Prunes that used to sell for 10¢ a pound are now 32¢.

Peppers that were 3 for [a] dime are now 15¢ apiece. Black-eyed peas at 10¢ a pound are now 23¢ a pound and of inferior quality at that." And as a working woman, Reid had learned the value of a paycheck. The meat stretchers and bacon-fat biscuit recipes she marked as especially good and an especially good value in her cookbook have the ring of truth. Unlike most commercial cookery instruction, we can easily conclude that at least one woman used some the recipes, economy hints, and wartime cooking instruction found in "Ways and Means."

Reid understood the historical import of daily life events such as coffee rationing and fat recycling. More important, Reid took the time to record her thoughts on these events. Also, as a nonprofessional historian and as a southerner, Reid brought a certain perspective to the difficulties of food shortages and food rationing. In one section of "Ways and Means" she quotes extensively from an unexplained source of "private letters" written during the Civil War. She introduced this section with a comment on the relative comfort she and other Lake Charles citizens enjoyed during World War II: "We think we are enduring hardships at home now because it is difficult, or impossible, to get many commonplace things that we have learned to depend upon to make life easier, but we can get by without them we have learned and there was a time not so very long ago when what we think are necessities would have been luxuries only for the rich." She went on to quote from these desperate letters, dated 1862 and 1863, in which women make coffee out of corn and find only mule and rat meat for sale in the market. Reid also made a list of the pathetic kinds of substitutions Louisiana women made during the Civil War, such as coffee from sweet potato squares and tea from blackberry leaves. And she suggested that having to stretch ground beef with oatmeal during World War II rationing might not be such an enormous sacrifice. In one of her last entries, dated 12 June 1947, she described rationing as a bother but not a real calamity:

> It was a great nuisance and a certain amount of hardship, but we realized it was a small sacrifice to make in comparison with that of those who served in the armed forces during these long war years.
>   Let's hope it will never be necessary again.

And in her final words, a sentence dated 1952, she expressed a similar sentiment: "Looking back over these notes I am aware that while we were inconvenienced during the war period, we actually did not suffer, and compared to the invaded countries of Europe and their people—we were in Paradise."

An atypical woman in many ways, Reid's wartime cookery book revealed feelings shared by many. Along with other Americans, Reid felt frustration and annoyance on a daily basis with food rationing, the point system, and significant shortages of food products and food on which they had grown to depend the previous two decades. But as illustrated by Reid's document, Americans also possessed an under-current of conviction that cookery during this war did not present insurmountable difficulties. Although not packed with "we can do it" rhetoric, Reid's realistic cookery instruction did exhibit a quiet sense of capability. Her deftness with gumbo or a revised fish loaf recipe could only come from practical kitchen experience. As a professional nurse and accomplished cook, Reid faced the food crises with some irritation, especially when coffee was in short supply. She also demonstrated some impatience, especially with "impudent" store clerks, who knew they would not be fired because of wartime labor shortages. And finally, she expressed patriotic pride, in her salvaging of fats, for example, and in the townspeople's victory gardens, and also her thankfulness for the foods that did stay available during the war. But she did not panic. She knew she could cook and she knew that she could handle the "interest-ing problems in regard to daily food" that began when the government first rationed sugar in 1942.

But Reid's status as a single woman *did* make her atypical, as far as the publishers of many commercial cookbooks and numerous recipe purveyors were concerned. When cookbook and recipe publishers hit their wartime production peak, they did not aim most of the instruction at women like Reid, but at middle-class, white, married women with children—just as they had for the two previous decades. Maude Reid clearly believed that cookery during World War II deserved the atten-tion of a historically minded private citizen like herself, who could record how the war affected daily meals in her home. And she very clearly believed that adherence to food rationing, salvaging fats, and eating lima bean loaf could help win a U.S. victory: she saw the connec-tion between home cooking and the national emergency. But she did not, anywhere in her cookbook, suggest that, as a woman, her most important wartime job lay with the cooking of nourishing and satisfy-ing home meals. General Mills and a whole host of other recipe makers set out to popularize precisely that idea during the war, but it seems likely that their message would have fallen on deaf ears in the case of Maude Reid. That kind of rhetoric was not meant for the women around the country who had already been accustomed to both working a job and cooking in the home, and who fed only themselves and per-haps their cats every evening. Judging by her record of cookery during the war, Maude Reid appears to have remained unmoved by the pleas of cookbook authors and food editors to view kitchen work as the most urgent wartime duty for women. But the amount and the intensity of that rhetoric cannot be ignored in a study of general cookbooks during the war years; indeed, it comes through as a prevailing theme.

7

"The Hand That Cuts the Ration Coupon
May Win the War"

WOMEN'S HOME-COOKED PATRIOTISM

Maude Reid clipped a cartoon from the 21 July 1942 *Beaumont Enterprise* that summed up the feeling among many Americans that no food could compete with home-cooked food from the United States. Under the title "Home Cooking on the Foreign Front," three burly, red-cheeked men with "U.S.A." on their army cook hats dish up meals at three different locations: Ireland, China, and Germany (fig. 11). The cartoon illustrated the continuing popularity of chop suey in the early 1940s and inadvertently admitted that such a dish had little to do with Chinese cookery. But more importantly it also showed how Americans utilized the symbolic importance of home cooking during the war. According to this cartoonist, Americans could not only produce better food than our allies, but on the German front an American hamburger could even be a valuable war weapon.

On the home front, according to numerous cookbook authors and recipe producers, food also constituted a valuable war weapon—the *most* valuable war weapon. But unlike this cartoon, cookery instruction always placed a white, middle-class, apron-clad woman—not a tough military man—at the stove. After the United States entered the war, discussions about male culinary prowess in cookbooks and popular magazines virtually disappeared, at least in comparison to the multitude of such references in the 1920s, 1930s, and in the post–World War II years. A man might occasionally appear in a Swan's Down cake flour advertisement, demonstrating that the flour made cake baking so

Figure 11 A cartoon clipped by Maude Reid showed how Americans viewed food as an important war weapon. Attributed by Reid to the *Beaumont (Texas) Enterprise*, 21 July 1942.

easy that even men could do it. Or Dad might step into an article on low-ration-point recipes in order to toss an onion, spinach, and egg salad. But the men who had boasted about their bread sticks, barbecues, and beef stews in 1941 fell silent in 1942. Dad did not have time during the war to help his daughter learn how to cook chicken paprika, as he had in a 1941 article in *Parents' Magazine*.[1] Cookery instructors turned their full attention to women, to the cooking responsibilities of married women with children, and presented home cooking as the key to victory.

The numbers of general, commercial cookbooks published in the

United States continued to grow during the war. Although not every such cookbook dealt at length with wartime cookery concerns, most authors and editors seemed to believe that the war demanded new kinds of recipes and new types of cookery instruction. First and foremost, cookbooks during the war offered extensive advice—some practical, some not so practical—on how to cope with rationed foods and food shortages. They also stressed the patriotic import of eating economically and strictly within rationing limits. Second, they emphasized the importance of sound nutrition and healthfulness during this particular national emergency. Virtually all authors and editors expressed utter confidence in the ability of Americans to change their diets to comply with rationing without sacrificing taste and nutrition. General, commercial cookbooks, like other kinds of popular literature, conveyed total support for the war effort. Most reiterated the heartily cheerful and patriotic sentiment articulated by the famous "Rosie the Riveter" poster: "We can do it." The outpouring of commercial cookery instruction during the war directly responded to American concerns about changing food supplies and availability, with a markedly patriotic emphasis on keeping health and spirits high with mom's home cooking.

What accounts for this outpouring on the centrality of a woman's home cooking to the safety of the nation? In short, the same kinds of factors that shaped cookery advice in the 1920s and 1930s: decreasing numbers of paid cooks in middle-class homes and the need to sell cookbooks to and promote home cooking among middle-class white consumers. Perhaps most important, anxiety about gender norms at a time when "traditional" gender roles seemed threatened created the need for such messages, though now that threat came from wartime upheavals and uncertainties rather than "the new woman" and processed foods. The war only intensified America's need for a domestic ideology in the modern era. I do not mean to dismiss the real patriotic longing to help win the war that women may have brought with them to the kitchen. But as prescriptive literature, loaded with rhetoric about domesticity, cookbooks demanded far more of their readers than simple patriotism. Cookbooks published during the war years urged women to use a fair share of rationed foods and to ensure their family's good health and sound nutrition. But they also insisted that a woman's wartime duties included creating a relaxing atmosphere at the dinner table, where war-weary families could rest and enjoy delicious, satisfying meals. They insisted, in short, that women belonged in the kitchen.

Cookbook authors in the 1920s and 1930s had often stated outright that their middle-class readers might be facing the kitchen without the assistance of paid laborers. But by the 1940s, far fewer cookbooks dealt at length with "the servant problem." Nor did many bother to give serving directions for both hostesses with and without maids. Rather, cookbooks usually just assumed that the reader was a woman (mistress of the home) who would do the cooking for her husband and children. Authors had good reason to make that assumption. The war offered an unprecedented number of alternatives to working as a cook or a maid, and many women did not hesitate to leave such jobs in private homes for better paying and less stigmatized work. African American women in particular found better employment opportunities, although they faced discrimination and racism on the job front. By 1944 domestic workers made up only 9.5 percent of all women workers. A great many women lost those industry jobs at the end of the war, but despite the efforts made by employment agencies to "call back" domestic servants at the war's conclusion, the percentage of middle-class homes with a paid cook continued to decrease after 1945. Fewer and fewer women had kitchen "help," and cookery instruction reflected that reality.[2]

Wartime opened up employment opportunities not only for women previously employed as servants but for all women. During 1942, 1943, and 1944, thousands of white married women, many with children, entered the paid work force for the first time. The government urged women to fill the labor shortages left by enlisted men. But federal propaganda also made it clear that, like butter extenders, women's wartime employment would be needed only "for the duration," and not a moment more—an expectation shared by millions of Americans, male and female. And though factories desperately needed women's labor, few made any changes to accommodate female workers. Lack of adequate day care for the children of working women, for example, illustrated the way that the American business world and American society refused to alter workplace structures to incorporate women workers. Even as federal advertising campaigns urged women to take up employment for the war cause, they also made sure to emphasize that only in a world crisis would women take time away from their *real* jobs as wives and mothers. Although Americans heard and read about more women (meaning middle-class white women) working outside the home, they also heard and read a great deal about the temporary status of this employment and how the true, fundamental vocation of women remained homemaking.[3]

During the war, cookery instruction helped reinforce traditional gender norms by presenting cooking as the most important wartime employment of women. Like other kinds of prescriptive literature that mentioned women's employment, cookbooks often acknowledged that women might be working outside the home, or perhaps volunteering for the local Red Cross, but they treated this work as a temporary measure in an emergency situation. During the previous two decades, authors had sometimes assumed that a young wife (without children) might continue to work outside the home, perhaps for financial reasons. Domestic magazines occasionally included articles such as "6 O-clock Steak Dinner for an Office Wife," which gave tips and hints on how working girls with husbands to feed should manage their time.[4] In wartime, however, a "working woman" most often meant a woman helping the war effort by taking on the unusual task of outside employment. Hazel Young's wartime edition of *The Working Girl Must Eat* included a new introduction that repositioned "the working girl" as a war worker, and underscored the increased importance of good home cooking during wartime: " 'Out of the kitchen' and 'in the defense plant' are taken for granted these days and young girls and old, from Sister Sue to Grandma, are working from morning till night and even from night till morning. That makes meal getting a bit incidental and certainly rather haphazard. This we know is a pity, for 'food must fight for Freedom,' and good meals, well planned and cooked with care, play no small part in keeping the family fit and efficient."[5] Young, and many other authors, briefly mentioned women working outside the home, and offered quick and easy meals for "Rosie the Riviter." But writers never failed to emphasize that employment must not interfere with preparing "food that fought for freedom." They emphasized that family fitness required good home cooking, done by the woman of the house. And like almost all Americans, cookbook authors assumed that only within the nuclear American family could freedom-fighting food be produced and that only mother could produce it.

Susan B. Anthony, niece of the famous suffragette, attempted to offer an alternative in her book *Out of the Kitchen—Into the War.* Unlike Young, when Anthony used the phrase "out of the kitchen," she meant out the kitchen altogether. Anthony criticized what she perceived as an onslaught of advice to women during the war about food preparation—advice that actually called for more effort and more time spent in the kitchen. She advocated communal kitchens and other kinds of support for the working woman.[6] Anthony echoed the kitchen reform supporters of the early twentieth century and the few women who, during World War I, had called for similar radical changes in the structures of domesticity and food preparation. But Anthony and her ideas could not hope to compete with the increasingly entrenched notion that only a woman's home-cooked meals could provide food fit for war duty. Food corporations, appliance manufacturers, and all kinds of advertisers had, of course, a vested interest in ensuring that the private home meal, prepared by mother, continued to be the norm. But in addition, few Americans seemed to have ever seriously considered possible long-term alternatives—communal meal preparation, for example—to women preparing daily meals in the middle-class home, particularly during the anxious days of wartime.[7]

Authors had been writing for decades about the artistic and creative opportunities home cooking afforded the middle-class housewife and asserting, moreover, that only the mistress of the house could provide really nutritious and well-cooked meals. A paid cook could, at best, be taught how to incorporate some of the nutritional knowledge possessed by middle-class white women—as in the case of Polly's Hannah. Wartime cookbooks elaborated on those assertions. Authors of cookbooks published in 1942, 1943, and 1944 depicted cooking as an almost sacred task, and most definitely a patriotic necessity—and one that could only be undertaken by the mistress of the home. For example, Florence Brobeck described how easily homemakers could take over the cooking when "Maimie" left the kitchen for wartime employment:

> For economic, sociological, and a great many other reasons, household help of all kinds is scarce, and will continue to be scarce in the coming years. As time goes by, "Maimie Doesn't Work Here Any More," is going to be the slogan above more and more kitchen doors. Maimie will be stewarding on an airliner and week-ending on the other side of the Atlantic—when she isn't making a Pacific hop. That leaves us right where we were before Grandma and Granddad could afford a hired girl—we'll be doing the housework ourselves and liking it much more than Grandma liked it, because we'll have a whole new world of satisfyingly easy and beautiful wares and tools with which to do our job.[8]

Brobeck exaggerated when she assumed that her readers had not had to do their own housework since "Grandma's" time, because increasing numbers of middle-class white women had done their own home cooking since at least 1920. But her perception that many "Maimies" had quit their work as domestic servants corresponded with statistical reality. And Brobeck's confidence that women would happily take up "satisfyingly easy" housework illustrated how cookery instruction continued to depict home cooking as an enjoyable new job and a necessary task for the modern, middle-class woman.

By calling forth an image of "Grandma" engaged in household labor, Brobeck used a common rhetorical device of wartime cookbooks. Numerous authors made reference to the brave pioneer women who helped colonize America and to those women's hearty, satisfying cooking. Ida Bailey Allen, for instance, described a statue she saw in Kansas of a pioneer woman, and drew a parallel between this early American's many responsibilities (preserving food, tending chickens, milking cows, smoking hams, churning butter, dipping candles) and women's multiple domestic tasks during World War II. Mary Taylor rallied the wartime housekeeper with the image of pioneer women in her 1943 *Economy for Epicures.* She wrote: "Each new limitation, or possible elimination, of a familiar staple causes a slight restriction of our usual pleasant, easy way of life. This is a challenge to the ingenuity of housekeepers, perhaps not comparable to, but at least reminiscent of, the challenge met by the pioneer women."[9]

In her 1943 *Ration Cook Book,* Demetria Taylor's rousing introduction called for women to meet wartime cooking challenges with as much courage as "our great-grandmothers" showed. She also criticized the lazy cooking done by modern women. "Those were *not* the good old days," she scoffed. "The good days are *now.* Time to prove that our great-grandmother's blood still runs in our veins. She fought along with her men. No sacrifice was too great for victory. We fight, too, on the home front. We battle to assure our families a healthful diet, restrictions or no. *And we win the fight.* We are already becoming a healthier, hardier, less pampered race" (emphasis in original).[10] Many authors pointed out that women had faced other wars with determined optimism and clever recipes. The authors of *What Do We Eat Now? A Guide to Wartime Housekeeping,* used the image of "our forebears" to depict women's home cooking and homemaking as the essential female wartime task. They wrote: "Our responsibility is a grave one. It compares with that which confronted our forebears. We, too, face the unknown and drastic changes in our way of living. We must be able to meet the changes, to adapt ourselves and our homes to them, to make the best of them, as did the early settlers—in ways that will promote the welfare and happiness of the family and therefore the Nation."[11] Every loyal homemaker, according to cookbooks, would take up the "grave responsibility" of managing the home front and, in particular, the home front kitchen. By doing so, they asserted, homemakers would be able to safeguard the welfare and happiness of the entire nation.

Advice about "the kitchen front" offered the same kinds of cultural messages about gender roles found in other popular publications. Domestic magazines, newsmagazines, government propaganda, movies, novels, and newspapers all helped to reinforce the idea that, despite wartime social upheaval, a woman's true job as wife and mother remained unchanged. Of all the wartime commentary, advertising, and propagandizing that depicted women as essentially domestic creatures, cookbooks most actively made the connections between home cooking, patriotism, and the female role in family and society. As the author of *Thrifty Cooking for Wartime* stated: "Yes, American women are willing to scrub, work in defense plants, drive ambulances, and do hundreds of other things for victory. But with it all, not one of us will neglect the home, to preserve which all this fighting is done."[12]

Homemaking and home cooking had to be the first and most important duties of American women, according to many cookbooks. When "Betty Crocker" addressed the women of wartime America, there could be no mistaking the role she expected women to play. "Hail to the women of America!" began the introduction to *Your Share*. It continued:

> You have taken up your heritage from the brave women of the past. Just as did the women of other wars, you have taken your positions as soldiers on the Home Front. You have been strengthening your country's defenses—as plane watchers—as flyers—as members of the armed forces—as producers, in war plants and homes—and in Red Cross and Civilian Defense Activities. The efforts and accomplishments of women today are boundless!
>
> But whatever else you do—you are, first and foremost, homemakers—women with the welfare of your families deepest in your hearts.[13]

Wartime cookbooks, more pointedly than any other popular source, urged women to take up their duty as home cook—a job no longer considered the menial task of a paid laborer (at least according to these authors). Plane watching, plane flying, service in the military, war production work, Red Cross and Civilian Defense—none of these could compete with the job that came first and foremost: cooking.

According to the authors and editors, no single female wartime task could so affect the outcome of the war as good home cooking and adherence to rationing regulations. The wartime edition of *America's Cookbook* underscored that point:

> The kitchens of America have gone to War. Today every homemaker is drafted and the kitchen apron is her uniform. In small towns, in big cities and on farms, American women are standing up to daily battles as momentous as those on the military fronts—the battle of supply and demand, of food values against food shortage, of flavor versus monotony. And, like our boys in blue and brown, housewives must expect much hardship and little glory. Yet their smallest decisions have tremendous results. The struggle in the kitchen will decide not only the health and morale of the home front but the conservation of our nation's food supply. Women are hastening or retarding our final Victory. The hand that cuts the ration coupon may win the war.[14]

Like the federal government's "Home Front Pledge" campaign, which urged women to vow to forgo black markets and always pay for rationed food with points, cookbooks during the war placed a woman's marketing and cooking duties well above any other defense activity in which she might participate.

The authors of *Thrifty Cooking for Wartime* did not hesitate to compare the battlefront to the kitchen front. Everyone has to play a part in winning the war, they wrote, "and the one to be played by American housewives in their own kitchens is no less important than that of the worker in the munitions plant or the soldier advancing with the tanks."[15] *The Authentic Victory Cook Book* linked food preparation and President Roosevelt's famous "Four Freedoms": "Food will win the war. Yes, if we are to preserve our way of life, if we are to secure for ourselves and our children freedom from want, freedom from fear, freedom of speech and freedom of religion, homemakers have a job to do right here at home."[16] Cookbooks in the 1920s and 1930s had encouraged middle-class women to think of home cooking as a creative and fulfilling task, and as a necessary task even in the new era of processed foods and changing kitchen technology. But when the United States entered the war, cookbooks began to depict home cooking as vital wartime defense work. As Ruth Berolzhiemer wrote: "What we, the homemakers of America, do in the kitchen to prepare good food economically and serve it attractively will be a significant part of our country's war effort."[17]

Wartime cookbooks underlined the two most essential aspects of the homemaker's defense: maintaining the health of the family and keeping the family's spirits high, with plentiful, well-cooked, and palate-pleasing meals. Women had to accomplish these tasks, moreover, with food supplies rationed to ensure enough food for all. Cookbooks emphasized vitamins and nutritious meals, but they placed the responsibility for those meals solely on homemakers. The editors of *What's New in Food and Nutrition* summarized: "We cannot win the war or the peace without adequate food for our armed forces. We cannot have adequate food without adjustments and sacrifices in every home. Our Nation must depend upon homemakers if sacrifices and adjustments are to be made without loss of health and strength on the home front. This is the homemaker's opportunity to serve not only her family but the Nation by planning and preparing the basic foods needed to provide health protection for herself and members of her family."[18] Working against the "loss of health and strength on the home front" demanded even more care and attention to vitamins and food values than had been necessary previously—and the whole nation depended on women to "plan and prepare the basic foods needed to provide health protection." The health of the nation depended on the health of its individual citizens, cookbook authors and editors explained, which, in turn, depended on home cooking. As the author of *Square Meals on Short Rations* wrote: "Poor health is an insidious saboteur that works havoc with the total war effort. Every healthy American Family [*sic*] is a fighting unit on

the side of the United Nations. Furthermore, every such family is helping to build a strong America that can face the future unafraid."[19] At all
times, cookbooks counseled, the health of the family must be maintained through careful meal planning, careful marketing, and careful
cooking.[20]

In wartime cookbooks, women's contributions to the war effort encompassed meal planning, marketing, and cooking for the family—but
often nothing else. When the editors of *The Good Housekeeping Cook
Book* asserted, "Because manpower has become a pressing war need, it
is even more important than ever to serve nutritious meals that will
keep the family in fight trim," they seemed to assume that women's
work lay not with fulfilling the desperate need for more "manpower"
but with making the family fit to fight.[21] Similarly, *The Authentic Victory
Cook Book* assumed that a homemaker would never give up her all-
important work of meal preparation, especially when other members of
her family might be employed in war production and require balanced,
nutritious meals: "The homemaker has a special war task if members of
her family are engaged in defense work. The meals that these defense
workers eat will mean the difference between their keeping in the front
line of production and having efficiency, energy, and endurance on the
job or becoming fatigued, irritable, weak, and careless and cutting
down production by absenteeism."[22] Defense workers required wholesome and nutritious food, obtained with the family's fair share of ration
points and carefully prepared by the wife and mother in the home.
Wartime cookbooks constantly depicted a woman's home cooking as "a
special war task" with important repercussions in the battle for Victory
(fig. 12).

As historian Mary Drake McFeely writes, "To make kitchen work
not just an everyday necessity, but a patriotic duty, an integral part of
the war effort, the United States government and the media wrapped
the job in the language of the battlefield. Military imagery made home
cooking part of meeting the challenge of the war, summoning women
to play a special role in the war effort."[23] For example, Ruth Berolzheimer's *Military Meals at Home* gave every recipe a military twist,
encouraging women to think of their cooking duties as wartime defense
work. "SOS needn't mean 'Same Old Stew' when served these ways,"
the book boasted. Other recipes received a similar cheery militariza-
tion: "Your doughboy will think he landed in officers' mess when this
ham is on the menu." "Roast pork garnished with orange slices for
Sunday dinner certainly deserves a twenty-one gun salute." "French
fried eggplant from your galley will bring your whole regiment to
attention." "The toughest top sergeant will sniff sweetly when macaroni and cheese appears at chow." "Well-blended gravy or sauce adds

Figure 12 Cookbooks published during World War II encouraged women to think of cooking duties as wartime defense work. Here a homemaker leads refined sugar substitutes toward victory. From Eleanor M. Lynch, ed., *The Modern Hostess Cook Book* (New York: Dell, 1942).

firepower to any chow." "America's favorite dough-puncher is really mother with her luscious apple pies."[24] Cookbooks like these depicted mom's work as "dough-puncher" and her meals for the "whole regiment" (the family), as well as "the top sergeant" (the husband), as the real wartime labor of women.

Did "America's favorite dough-puncher" also cultivate a victory garden? When cookbook authors discussed women's wartime domestic duties, victory gardening received far less attention than kitchen work. Despite the enormous amount of publicity the popular press gave victory gardens, few cookbooks offered much comment or instruction about planting and harvesting vegetables. But they did offer advice and instructions about other food-related duties. Many wartime-edition cookbooks included a new section on canning foods, for instance. And when authors urged women to rally around and take up pots and pans for the war cause, they paid special attention to the lunch box. *Coupon Cookery* offered an especially illustrative example of how cookbooks depicted a hearty, tasty, vitamin-packed lunch box meal as essential to victory. Entitled, "A Lunch That Packs a Punch," the chapter on lunch box meals included a striking illustration of a lunch box helping to win the war: a huge lunch box with legs and muscled arms stands on a vanquished Japanese caricature, grips a loopy Mussolini by the throat, and punches out Hitler (fig. 13). The accompanying poem reads: "If Uncle Sam can get food / To all our fighting men / It's not too much

Figure 13 Wartime cookbooks emphasized the importance of hearty, nutritious lunch box meals prepared by the mistress of the home. From Penny
Prudence [pseud.], *Coupon Cookery* (Hollywood, CA: Marray and Gee, 1943).

for us to pack / A lunchbox now and then. / The mid-day meal must
fight fatigue / That's always somewhere lurkin' / It takes a tasty,
hearty lunch / To keep our workers workin'."[25] Cookbook authors and
editors were not the only ones to instruct Americans on lunch box
meals. Some schoolteachers, for instance, encouraged children to learn
and sing at home songs about the importance of the lunch box. One
song, to the tune of "The Battle Hymn of the Republic," went: "In the
lunch box you must put a hot and creamy soup, not tea, / Make the
sandwiches of whole wheat bread with meatloaf, cheese, poultry, / You
must sometimes add an egg and always fruit or celery / In all our
factories, / Pack a lunch a man can work on."[26]

But magazine writers and cookbook authors and editors, in particular, emphasized the importance of hearty, homemade lunch to the war
cause. The chapters and sections on lunch box cookery in wartime
cookbooks almost always exhorted women to prepare meals for boxed
lunches with particular care. "America is at work, but at work produc-
tively only if those lunch boxes contain nourishing meals, made up of
food as ample and well balanced as a substantial lunch served on the
home table," warned Ida Bailey Allen. "It is because many of these
packed lunches are not sufficiently nourishing to meet the needs of
the day's strain, that many colds and illnesses develop among workers, contributing directly to the unnecessary loss of time from work
through illness, which totals about 460,000,000 hours of lost manpower a year," she admonished. Margot Murphy described the lunch

box as "a part of the war program, and an important part. It carries
sustenance and mealtime enjoyment that promotes good spirits, good
health, and good work."[27] Marjorie Mills warned her readers to avoid
dainty ladylike sandwiches when it came time to pack a lunch box: "No
unsatisfying trifles these days! A sandwich must 'pack a wallop' in the
way of nutrition and flavor and satisfying nourishment."[28] At the same
time, cookery instruction made sure to note that women should cheerfully shoulder this duty and look upon it as a challenge. As the author of
Ration Cook Book wrote in a chapter entitled "The Lunchbox Goes to
War," a homemaker had to use "originality, imagination, and ingenuity"
when packing a lunch box. "The lunchbox is a challenge to the homemaker," she wrote, adding that women had to be sure to make lunch box
food "interesting and attractive as well as nutritious."[29]

Thus cookery instructions for lunch box meals incorporated the
two most important elements of wartime cookery (according to cookbooks): making sure the family received proper nutrition, and cooking
attractive tasty meals that satisfied all the senses and used only a fair
share of available foods. Indeed, many cookbooks argued that the attractive presentation of dishes and relaxing, satisfying repasts was as
necessary to kitchen front defense as nutritious meals. The authors of
What Do We Eat Now introduced their book by describing how home
cooking meant more than putting meals on the table: it meant creating
a home. Home cooking, they explained, helped create a "haven" where
defense workers, schoolchildren, and the war work volunteer could
"return for rest, relaxation, and recreation." Prescriptive literature for
women had, since at least the mid 1800s, described the home as a
woman-created haven from the rest of the world. But during the war,
that haven had new patriotic import. The homemaker had an obligation
to assume the "generalship of the home forces" and maintain the "calm-
ness and serenity that is needed in times such as these."[30] In her 1943
cookbook of meat-saving recipes, Ann Robins asserted that women
needed to take an extra few minutes in the kitchen, even in the rush
of wartime work, in order to ensure that sense of serenity at the dinner table: "With so much to worry us these days, with the strain so
constant, it is more important than ever to have meals well prepared,
hot and varied. Monotony must be avoided."[31] Marjorie Mills also
evoked the idea of meals as a retreat from the confusion, disruption,
and fear of wartime: "In this troubled universe it's more than ever
important to make meal time loom up as a little island of serenity and
contentment."[32]

In cookbooks, women's kitchen duties did not stop with nutritionally
sound meals but extended to preparing meals that provided "islands of
serenity." As Florence Richardson counseled, a woman had to ensure

that her family got not only meals loaded with vitamins and nutrients but also food that just plain tasted good. Moreover, a woman had to be careful not to make meals an unappealing lesson in balanced eating: " 'Nutrition' has to be sold to the family, but not by strong-arm methods. Men and children will not eat food because it is 'good for them'— unless they like it! The way to sell nutrition, then, is to prepare wholesome foods in a way that they will not only like, but ask for more! And above all—don't talk about it! Let the food be so delicious that it speaks for itself." According to Richardson, delicious meals should be a woman's job and, furthermore, during the war a woman had to do this job with a smile and without hesitating to assume full responsibility for the family's food. Similarly, the recipes in *Coupon Cookery* began with a drawing of a woman pulling a rabbit out a hat at the dinner table, while her family happily anticipates the meal. The accompanying poem encouraged the reader to cheerfully take up cooking duties: "It may not be convenient / But we don't admit defeat / For in spite of War and Rationing / America must eat! / It may take a deal of cunning / And a bit of laughter, too / To keep the meal-time pleasant / When the coupons are too few!" Cookbook writers and editors, like the author of this poem, suggested that women's ability to "keep the meal-time pleasant" ranked as highly on the list of female wartime duties as keeping the meal nutritious and making sure the family adhered to rationing. Florence Richardson's cookbook included a list of "Seven Golden Rules for Victory which Mrs. America must follow." Rule number six dictated that: "Thou shalt smile! The fine old American tradition of a happy mealtime depends upon cheerful preparation and service of the food."[33] Ruth Berolzheimer took a similar stand in the introduction to *The Wartime Cook Book* when she wrote that women needed to take total responsibility for creating wholesome and relaxing meals in times of rationing and worry: "Above all, the intelligent homemaker will absorb most of the strain of constant adjustment herself—presenting her family always with well-prepared nourishing food served most attractively."[34]

In fact, the vast majority of wartime cookbooks made the preparation of nourishing and attractively served foods entirely women's responsibility. Ida Bailey Allen, in *Double-Quick Cooking for Part-Time Homemakers*, stands out as one of the few authors who advised employed women to enlist the assistance of all members in the family when it came to household chores and daily cooking. A few articles in women's domestic magazines also suggested that the man of the house might, on occasion, *help* with the cooking if the woman worked outside the home, but the authors assumed that primary responsibility for meal preparation rested on women's shoulders. One 1943 article in *Good*

Housekeeping suggested that the working wife should allow her husband to help with breakfast, but only if he expressed a willingness to do so: "If your husband offers to help with breakfast, fine!" And the title of the article revealed who really did the cooking: "I've Got My First Job—And I Still Get the Meals."[35] As the plethora of magazine articles in the 1920s and 1930s on male cooks had reiterated, the duty of daily meal preparation belonged only to the woman of the house. Men might cook as a hobby, or because it afforded a little relaxation, but the actual *work* of preparing meals every day belonged to women. The entry of the United States into World War II only reinforced this idea: now warriors in a world conflict, men had even less time for hobbies or leisure activities and women had an even greater responsibility to provide good meals for their families.

Interestingly, in one article from a popular domestic magazine that described a real-life household during the war years, the husband and father of the family did prepare meals on a regular basis. *Ladies' Home Journal* ran a series of articles under the title "How America Lives" that profiled a real family every month. In October 1942 the magazine interviewed Mary and Fred Berkman, of Hartford, Connecticut, for the series. Irish, Catholic, and working-class, both Berkmans spent long hours at factory jobs. The article made it clear that Mary had only taken a job when Fred's ill health, and then the war, had made it necessary for her to do so (although Mary herself emphasized that she enjoyed working outside the home and earning her own paycheck). During his illness, according to the author of the article, Fred "cooked, washed, ironed, cleaned," and even when he had recovered enough to get another job, he prepared "a first rate Sunday dinner" every week while Mary worked. He also came home at lunchtime to meet his children and "fix them hot soup and sandwiches."[36] If accurate, the case of Fred Berkman shows that we cannot assume that simply because popular cookery books and magazines very rarely depicted men cooking Sunday dinner or feeding the children lunch that men never did so. But as the article makes clear, Fred Beckman's financial status had forced him to "cooperate" with Mary's work schedule. Cookbooks almost never, and magazines rarely, depicted any family as less than middle-class. In an *ideal* household, that is, securely middle-class, Mother never needed to work outside the home. And certainly, a woman's home-cooked meal remained the ideal, even when reality might not match up.

From 1942 through 1945 magazines rarely depicted men doing any kind of cooking, especially compared to the boomlet of articles on the topic in the prewar era. But at least four cookbooks for and by men appeared during the war years: the aforementioned 1941 *The Best Men Are Cooks* by Frank Shay; George Martin's 1942 *Come and Get It! The*

Compleat Outdoor Chef; Arthur H. Deute's *200 Dishes for Men to Cook*, published in 1944; and *Men in Aprons: If He Could Only Cook*, by Lawrence Keating, also published in 1944. Both Martin's and Shay's books received favorable reviews in *Publishers' Weekly*, and fairly well known publishers produced the books by Keating and Deute. Again, though not best sellers, these books reached more than a few readers. Deute's book, for example, attained enough popularity for the publisher to issue a revised edition in 1952. Cookbooks by and for men published during the war years shared numerous similarities with those published in the 1920s and 1930s. These chatty books read almost like a novel. They contained little of the basic kitchen instructions such as measuring or stocking the pantry found in general cookbooks. As in earlier cookbooks for men, the authors described at length the kinds of dishes that would appeal to masculine appetites—strongly flavored, meaty, and hearty. And they asserted that men in the kitchen could produce such dishes more ably than women could, though such assertions became markedly more subdued during wartime.

In a 1942 review, Helmut Ripperger praised *The Best Men Are Cooks* and hesitantly agreed with Shay's statement that "women have reduced cooking to a science while men cooks are working to restore it to its former high estate as one of the finer arts." Ripperger wrote primly that this idea "is worth thinking about."[37] Shay's book, published in 1941, cannot really be considered a wartime cookbook, given that the United States did not enter the war until December 1941. Indeed, Shay's vehemence about male cookery and the male appetite sounds more like prewar rhetoric than the subdued writing about men in the kitchen that emerged during the war. His more lavish recipes also reflect prewar plenty and interest in foreign cookery. Shay offered recipes for clam chowder, smoked poultry, chili, corned beef and cabbage, paella, and polenta, and he assured the reader that all of his recipes were fit for masculine consumption. Shay took care, for example, to explain that crown roast of lamb "looks a bit feminine, but if we leave the paper frills off the spikes, no one will suspect," and that mushrooms [cooked] under glass "looks a bit effeminate and takes some fussing, but many a gourmet insists that it is the only way to keep the delicious flavor of the mushroom."

In some cases he argued that certain dishes, such as mayonnaise, had to be wrested away from feminine influence: "In a cookbook designed for men, mayonnaise seems a bit out of place. This may be due to the treatment this delightful sauce has taken at the hands of the ladies and the canners," he observed. But good mayonnaise, he argued, "takes downright masculine patience to prepare it properly." He reserved especial scorn for feminine curry recipes, though his own curry called for nothing more potent than a little curry powder, lemon, and chicken stock. "The traditional curry, even the best stab we Americans can make at it, is so emphatically masculine that only a woman who has taken leave of her senses will attempt it," he wrote. "Feminine *manuels de cuisine* are full of delightful but pale little luncheon curries, served in the inevitable rice mold." He also blamed feminine cookbooks for crimes against sandwiches. Women's sandwiches, according to Shay, were insubstantial and downright silly: "One lovely example calls for the hostess to place upon the table an innocent-looking loaf of bread wrapped in cellophane and tied with ribbons. When goggle-eyed desperation overtakes her guests and they are beginning to estimate the time and distance to the nearest beer-drop, the hostess dramatically unties the ribbons, lifts the top as the sides fall revealing dainty little nothings designed only to surprise the eye and further aggravate the guests' appetites." He went on to describe real, masculine sandwiches such as corned beef on rye or hot roast beef with gravy: "Men, let's make our own sandwiches. Let's make them thick with plenty of meat hanging over the edges and slathered with sauces and condiments." Shays argued that the feminization of cookery instruction had also ruined the concept of a buffet supper: "This distinctively masculine institution has been adopted by the ladies, who, if pressed, will very likely insist they have only refined it, which means in anybody's language that they have dolled it up. Their magazines feature the proper layouts of flatware and napery, loading the old sideboard up with so many gadgets and other impediments to good eating that only the most intrepid male can sustain his appetite."[38] Shay's diatribes against the "dolled up" buffets and insubstantial sandwiches created by women referred directly to the kinds of recipes and cookery advice aimed at women—middle-class women "doing their own cooking"—that appeared in prewar magazines and newspapers and cookbooks. But by 1944, when these sources had for the most part infused women's cooking with patriotic meaning, cookery instruction for men had also eased up on its rants against the woman in the kitchen.

Only in the introduction to his 1944 *Men in Aprons* did Lawrence Keating indulge in a lengthy, though tongue in cheek, denunciation of women's cooking. *Men in Aprons* presented each chapter as a letter from "Al" to "Bill." Al's first letter begins by pointing out that women, not men, bore the responsibility for most poor meals throughout history: "Friends, who was it got up all those meals, so many of which brought no happiness, but only acute gastritis? Was it Man? Nope! Bet your sweet life it wasn't. Was it Woman? *Yes!* So by George, it's high time men stuck their heads through the neck-loops of aprons and got busy having fun around the larder." Al then says that he is looking for a hobby and cooking seems a practical one. "I've needed a hobby as you say you have too, and I wanted one making things," explains Al. "But not useless gadgets like tie racks and wobbly tables." He agrees to exchange recipes with Bill, but "only recipes with masculine appeal. He-man stuff."

Al goes on to relate a story he supposedly read in the newspaper, about a wife who appeared in court with a black eye, charging her husband with assault. When the judge angrily inquired into the nature of the dispute that had resulted in the woman's black eye, the husband, a man "emaciated as if badly in need of a square meal," explained that "his Mrs. had been feeding him nothing but codfish cakes. It was codfish cakes every blessed night at their house, except occasionally it was codfish balls." One night, he snapped: "Last evening at 7:04, he said, everything went black and he up and socked the Little Woman." The Mrs. admitted that yes, she served codfish every night: "She adored codfish." The Judge sympathized deeply with the man and fined him only one dollar. Al used this story as a warning and a call for men to learn their way around the kitchen. Why must men, he complained, rely on women for their dinners? After all, a woman might see nothing wrong with serving one bland and unappetizing kind of food for months! Men knew better. For the most part, however, Keating refrained throughout the rest of his book from long discussions about the inadequacy of women's cooking. Unlike, say, Frederick's 1920 heated diatribes about women's failures in the kitchen, Keating's book strove for a somewhat lighthearted tone. He aimed not to spill pages of ink on denouncing women's cooking but to encourage men to enjoy cooking.

For instance, Keating claimed that catering one's own poker game or being the hunting trip cook would earn much praise (even a thank-you gift of a bottle of whiskey) from the participants. He reveals to Bill: "There is surely a heap of satisfaction, Bill, in watching things you prepare with your own little hannies disappear into hungry mouths." A home-cooked meal could also, he asserted, be an asset to the bachelor. A neatly aproned bachelor bearing a golden-brown cheese soufflé, served "amid snowy napery and gleaming silverware," was sure to win the heart of the "Only Girl": "Does such culinary prowess overwhelm the maiden? Does it visit upon her visions of lying comfortably abed on cold mornings? You said it. Thus, gentlemen, can deftly be torpedoed feminine insistence on a career." The pleasure of food preparation, and its usefulness in securing both masculine and feminine admiration, takes up far more space in Keating's book than misogynistic complaints about women's cooking failures—excepting his anecdote about codfish.

Keating did not swerve from the established wisdom about male taste preferences and female taste preferences. *Men in Aprons* consistently depicted men as hearty eaters, fond of meat and powerfully flavored dishes. Like cookbook authors in the 1920s and 1930s, Keating did not hesitate to make sweeping generalizations about all men's appetites. "Men like undainty things, dishes they can sink their fangs into," he wrote. When he compared masculine and feminine appetites, he ascribed salads to ladies and beef to men: "Women like light salads and creamy dishes, dainty things, colorful things. Men prefer heartier dishes—for example they like French fried potatoes but look upon shoestring potatoes as a nuisance. They like a dish such as short ribs of beef, but feel cumbersome toying with a dainty salad." Keating also assumed the hearty, more casual tone in his recipes that instruction for men had taken since 1920 (although his was one of the first cookbooks for men to give specific, numbered steps of instruction in each recipe). In addition, he recommended masculine cooking garb, such as "a big coverall apron with a print on it of George Rector waving a cleaver as he chases a fat pig and some chickens."[39]

Both Martin's *Come and Get It!* and Deute's *200 Dishes for Men to Cook* concentrated on recipes, not extraneous discussions about male and female cooks or the most masculine kind of apron. For example, Martin explained in his introduction that, although he wrote many recipes with the male outdoor chef in mind, he hoped that ladies, as well as "masculine wielders of the skillet," used his cookbook.[40] Deute noted, in passing, that men loved beef stew and apple pie, but most of his recipes did not detail the appeal of such dishes to masculine appetites. He did point out that many a young bride presented her husband with "such a delightful little affair as a dinner course of broiled whitefish [reminiscent of the Codfish Lady], boiled potatoes and a chilled tomato topped with mayonnaise," and that such a dinner could only result in "a man's putting on his coat and going out to see what the boys are doing. And the bride in tears." He went on to suggest gently the alternative of broiled fish and potatoes baked in their jackets and sprinkled with parsley for color, but that tip comprised the total of his remarks on feminine cooking.[41] In an era when women's home cooking had taken up the defense of the nation, fewer authors felt inclined to attack women's fundamental lack of cookery ability. In a time when soldiers really and truly went into battle "for Mom and apple pie," cookery authorities could hardly criticize mom's piecrust.

But cookbooks did continue to reinforce the notion that men enjoyed eating particular kinds of food. When men appeared in wartime cookbooks and recipe articles, they most often appeared eating certain kinds of food—meats, stews, sandwiches, plain vegetables, pie, cake—and not as cooking experts tooling around in the kitchen.[42] In wartime, men appeared in cookery instruction as soldiers far from home, dreaming about the cookies their mothers used to make, or as hardworking employees at a munitions factory, in need of substantial lunches and comforting dinners (fig. 14). As a 1942 article in the *American Home* recommended, a woman should strive to give her solider sons on leave "the food they've dreamed and boasted of for months." The article included recipes for apple pie, fried chicken, popovers, and chocolate cake. For the bride unsure of her husband's favorites, the author advised: "Give him food that every man likes. Fried chicken, steak, roast beef, apple pie, lemon meringue pie, chocolate cake, hot breads—all are men's favorites." For those more versed in their husband's, son's, or sweetheart's favorites, the article made it clear that serving such foods meant the world to a man: "Remember when he came home from school and ate three breaded pork chops, creamed potatoes, and escalloped corn? Try the same dishes and see his eyes sparkle. 'Mom remembered,' and you couldn't have a higher tribute."[43] In wartime cookery instruction, women's home cooking assumed new patriotic meaning and male appetites assumed new importance as well: as soldiers and war workers, they deserved dishes that best fit their masculine tastes.

Marion White evoked the image of fighting men dreaming of home-cooked food when she encouraged women to retain an interest in cooking despite rationing and food shortages: "It is good to learn that cookbooks are becoming as popular as novels, for that means that American women are not losing their interest in cooking, no matter

Figure 14 During World War II, recipes for the man in the kitchen virtually disappeared from popular magazines. Magazine illustrators were far more likely to depict men as soldiers or war workers, consuming meals cooked by mothers and wives. These photos accompanied an article in the April 1942 edition of *American Home*.

how restricted their purchasing may be. American men are scattered around the world, but where they are—in the windswept Aleutians or the African desert or the jungles of Asia—they are still dreaming of apple pie the way Mother used to bake it."[44] White and other cookbook authors presented men's favorite dishes as more than just masculine favorites. Now, these dishes took on vast sentimental importance. In the 1920s and 1930s, serving masculine favorites symbolized a woman's commitment to her marriage and to fulfilling her own domestic duties. During the war, serving masculine favorites symbolized a woman's commitment to supporting and nurturing the men who would fight for freedom. In February 1941 Ethel McCall Head cautioned her readers in an *American Home* article that "Rosebud cakes may be fine for us girls—but it takes something hearty, supremely seasoned, to please the men!"[45] In wartime, it became even more important to skip the rosebud cake (sugar being scarce anyway), and serve the man of the house more filling food. He needed sturdy meals to accomplish his work in war production or civil defense.

When cookbooks offered instructions for satisfying lunch box meals, recipes for stews that stood up to reheating, and suggestions for the most nutritious and filling kinds of breakfast foods, they often noted the importance of feeding the war production worker well. And despite the numbers of women working in factories and at shipyards, many cookbooks depicted the wartime worker as male. In *Victory Vitamin Cook Book for Wartime Meals*, for example, Florence Harris dedicated an entire chapter to "Food for the Men on the Night-Shift." Her recipes and advice in this section combined ideas about masculine appetites and assumptions about men's limited culinary interest. The man coming home from the night shift could be encouraged to get his own meals, she advised, provided that the wife stocked the right kind of food and left very explicit directions for reheating. "You might clip colored illustrations of food which he is to prepare and put them out where he can see them," she advised. "Their very attractive coloring may induce him to prepare a really adequate meal." Also, according to Harris, "Few men will bother to cook meat for themselves, but they do not object to frying eggs." And a man will fry hamburgers if a wife formed ground meat into patties and left them ready to fry, she asserted. Be careful, cautioned Harris, not to leave unsuitably feminine food for the war worker: "Don't expect a tired man to enjoy foods which are hard to eat: for example, dripping wilted salads. Loaf cake is generally liked by men. They don't find it as hard to eat as a layer cake with sticky icing. And few men object to pie any hour of the day or night."[46] Harris's description of women providing simple but substantial food for men, who would cook hamburgers but eschewed preparing anything much more elaborate, illus-

trated the continuing entanglement of gender norms and food preparation advice found in earlier cookbooks—but with a twist. In wartime
cookbooks, both mom's apple pie and dad's love of apple pie bore new
significance as expressions of loyalty to the American way of life. Masculine preference for hearty food signaled more than simple likes and
dislikes: it meant keeping the home front strong for wartime labor and
civil defense. Providing loaf cake for a war worker meant more than
meeting the masculine preference for simple foods—it meant protecting
the health of the man on the war production line.

Many of the same issues that had shaped cookbooks in the 1920s and
1930s continued to shape them in the 1940s. Publishers, corporations,
and women's magazines continued to search for ways to sell cookery
instruction and food products to middle-class women. During the war,
the numbers of households employing cooks fell drastically, continuing
a prewar trend, and commercial cookbooks aimed virtually all their
directions at the middle-class housewife who cooked meals for her
husband and children. More and more of those women did turn to
written cookery direction. Although food rationing and shortages of
certain foods never truly constituted a crisis, women expressed real
frustration and confusion—not surprising given that many of them had
learned to cook not by experimenting with foods but by following
written directions. Maude Reid and others like her who felt confident
about their cooking abilities might not have felt so panicked. But those
who had been "doing their own cooking" for only a few years might
well have needed expert advice on how to cope with the changing
availability of staples such as refined white sugar, beef, and butter.

Such advice could be readily located at the bookshop: cookbook sales
continued to climb during the war, and consumers had more cookbooks
from which to choose than ever before. During the early 1940s, this
cookery instruction, like most other kinds of domestic prescription
literature, endowed homemaking and cooking with patriotic importance. Often depicted as an artistic and creative pursuit in the 1920s and
1930s, home cooking became a more serious matter in wartime cookbooks. Authors and editors invested a woman's home cooking with
wartime symbolism, and at the same time gave renewed attention to the
kinds of food men—war workers and soldiers—preferred. Cookbooks
depicted food preparation as both a means to keep those on the home
front healthy through the judicious use of vitamin-rich and nutritious
food, and as a way to keep spirits high and to provide a soothing respite
from the stress of wartime. Moreover, they reinforced the message that
cookery instruction in the 1920s and 1930s had begun to spread with a
vengeance: middle-class wives and mothers needed to devote themselves to providing the daily meals for their families. They needed to

learn—by reading cookbooks and studying recipes and utilizing exact measurements and following directions—how to cook attractive and nutritious meals. Cookbooks published in 1942, 1943, 1944, and 1945 rarely addressed the fact that many women in this demographic held jobs outside the home during the war and had often been forced to manage family and home duties on their own while husbands and fathers served in the military. They virtually ignored the fact that some women had joined the military themselves; during World War II, for the first time, women had engaged in all military activities except combat. With the world in a state of upheaval, with women donning overalls and taking up blowtorches (albeit in smaller numbers than women who entered into office and professional work), with girls going off to serve in the Women's Army Corps (WACs) or in the special Navy unit for women (Women Accepted for Volunteer Emergency Service or WAVES), cookery instruction evoked the comfortably familiar image of mom baking in the kitchen and serving at table.

Familiar, but factual? Without a doubt, much of the cookery instruction that utilized the rhetoric of mom and apple pie drew more on nostalgia than reality. After all, many of those same publishers and authors had spent the previous two decades convincing the middle-class white woman to try her hand at cooking. Moreover, many of those women had eagerly turned to canned, packaged, and prebaked foods to assist them with the chore of daily food preparation. If she lived in an urban area and especially if she held a job outside the home, mom's apple pie, in the 1920s and 1930s, might have just as easily been purchased at a bakery as made by loving hands at home. (I'm exaggerating somewhat, because, of all the things that women still seemed to make at home and "from scratch," baked goods topped the list.)[47] When cookery instruction evoked the image of a woman as soldier of the kitchen front, battling the war on her own turf, it drew more on the *ideal* of women's home cooking than actuality. When they depicted soldiers rushing home for a taste of mom's fried chicken, they reinforced the same kind of gender and domestic ideology that had been shaping cookbooks since 1920: the *ideal* of a wife and mother who provided all the daily meals for her middle-class nuclear family, and who enjoyed doing so. In wartime, that idealized woman gladly shouldered the burden of food rationing, for the family's and the nation's sake, and she relied on expert cookery advice to help guide her.

Only twenty years earlier, cookbooks had been helping to invent this ideal, by explaining to middle-class women that cooking should be viewed not as a chore but a creative challenge. Wartime cookery asserted much the same thing about learning how to cook when the government had rationed butter, beef, and other staples. The women who appeared in ruffled aprons in wartime cookery instruction taking "The Home Front Pledge," studying the government's RDA chart, preserving the harvest of a victory garden, salvaging fats, and smilingly coping with the upheavals of food availability during wartime were a twentieth-century invention. Before the modern era (and after the Industrial Revolution), the mistress of a middle-class or upper-class home did not aim to do the cooking (or canning, fat salvaging, and pledging) herself: that woman aimed instead for the savvy instruction, supervision, and management of a cook and/or a maid. The war created circumstances that encouraged entrenchment of a modern domestic ideal—the idea that middle-class white women would gladly "do their own work" while keeping house—that had still seemed somewhat shaky in 1920s and 1930s cookbooks. Drastically reduced numbers of household servants virtually ensured that middle-class homes would be left "cookless"—and cookery instruction rushed in to assure its readers that this was as it should be. The all-important task of safeguarding the health of the home front and keeping up the spirits of the family at mealtime belonged only to the mistress of the home.

When Japan formally surrendered on 2 September 1945, Americans as a whole desired nothing more than to "get back to normal," but as Maude Reid's complaints about continued food shortages showed, at least another year would pass before Americans had easy access to the kinds of food they wanted. Reid wrote with obvious frustration about food shortages and high prices that continued even after rationing ended. She complained about price-gouging grocers and also about the behavior of women fighting for limited food. She described one shocking incident:

> In July, 1946, the A. and P. store got in a case of butter and the women pushed the front screen off hinges [*sic*] to get in the store and once in battled so furiously to reach the butter that the store manager feared they would break the glass section in the meat department, so he announced there was no more butter.
>
> Thereafter (until the O.P.A. ceased to exist) a quarter of a pound was rationed out at the checkers stand where shoppers pay for their groceries. I never dreamed that Lake Charles women would behave like this.

America and its allies had won the victory, but for the ladies of Lake Charles, the war was not quite over: on the kitchen front, obtaining butter meant braving the near riot conditions down at the A&P. But the Lake Charles ladies fought the price gouging at the grocery store. Reid also devoted several pages to a discussion of how women had forced grocers to lower their prices during the postwar period. She illustrated her discussion with a cartoon dated 28 July 1946 that depicted a grocer saying "Would you like some butter?" in musical tones, and a stout woman in a flowered hat haughtily answering "NO THANK YOU!" A sign on the counter indicates butter first priced at $1, then 95¢, then 85¢. The caption reads: "Ah, sweet revenge!" Reid commented: "This is a picture of 'buyer's resistance'—our effort to bring down prices. We really did use these tactics in Lake Charles and did succeed in bringing down the prices of butter, but we did not do so well with meat."

By the time the 1950s began, however, America had entered a whole new era of abundance. Beef and butter were back on the shelves, and a robust economy enabled more women than ever to attain middle-class social and financial status. Cookbooks once again had to reconfigure the cooking duties of middle-class white women. By 1950 three decades of cookbooks had been urging women to take their place at the stove and discover for themselves the joy of cooking. For three decades, cookbooks had depicted daily food preparation as a learnable skill and had been assuring these women that cooking itself was too important and too much fun to leave in the hands of servants. The wartime infusion of patriotic symbolism only strengthened the ideal of home-cooked meals made with love by wife and mother. For three decades, certain kinds of food and cooking had been gendered in cookbooks. In the 1950s such cookbook rhetoric reached a crescendo, adding to the onslaught of postwar prescriptions concerning gender and domesticity. In the 1950s cookery instruction helped create a kitchen-based version of the feminine mystique that we might aptly call "the cooking mystique."

PART THREE
The Cooking Mystique

COOKBOOKS
AND GENDER,
1945–1963

8

The Betty Crocker Era

On 1 November 1945 the United States government removed ration restrictions from all foods except refined white sugar. Butter and meat shortages persisted, however, for at least another year, and inflation kept prices high. Sugar rationing did not end until June 1947. Maude Reid grumbled that although the rationing of butter and other fats had ended, "we did not find any in the stores so we were not any better off." But Americans *were* better off, far better off, than much of the world in 1946. Wartime destruction created famine conditions from China to England and starvation threatened millions of people. President Truman and Herbert Hoover, head of the hastily created Famine Emergency Committee, mounted a wheat conservation campaign, among other strategies, to enable the United States to send surpluses to needy nations. Reid described the beginning of the campaign in an entry dated 1 March 1946: "Today begins the sale of dark flour—no more white flour to be milled for the present—in order to share our wheat supply with hungry Europe. Millers are prohibited from producing any flour after March 1, 1946, that consists of less than 80 percent, by weight, of the cleaned wheat." Recipes for using "the new emergency-type flour" in cookies and cakes soon appeared in women's magazines and in flour advertisements. And polls indicated that Americans seemed quite willing to comply with a voluntary reduction in butter, fat, and wheat consumption.[1]

But in sharp contrast to such statistics, most Americans bought as much of the previously rationed food as they could obtain in the years immediately following the war. The ladies in Lake Charles who fought each other for butter in July 1946 more accurately depicted the general American response to the end of rationing than the polls that asserted Americans truly wished to share their food supply with the rest of the world. America's love of meat, in particular, threatened the government's wheat conservation plan. The Office of Price Administration imposed controls on meat in July 1946, but the relentless demand continued to drive up prices, and political pressure forced Truman to remove the controls in October.[2] Numerous Americans complained about food rationing during the war, and concern about famine conditions elsewhere in the world could simply not provide enough impetus to change eating habits after the war. In fact, not until the Marshall Plan took effect in 1948 did the United States offer truly systematic food aid to Europe.

Maude Reid succinctly dismissed the idea of Americans voluntarily eating less as a naive one. In one entry, Reid responded to a 26 April 1946 article from the *Lake Charles American Press* that described the wives of senators and congressmen following President Truman's call for European-sized portions at the dinner table. She wrote: "These recipes for menus to conserve food for the hungry of Europe and Asia were given publicity in the hope that women in the U.S. would adopt them. How naïve!" The U.S. government had, perhaps naively, asked Americans to voluntarily reduce their caloric intake and to cut back on precisely the same kinds of food that had been scarce or unavailable during the war. Some cookbooks published in 1946 and 1947 cautioned readers about conserving these food supplies, but cookery instruction never advocated a real change in American diet. Just as Helmut Ripperger feared, America's "sudden conversion" to saving, rationing, and substitution did not last. Authors who recommended lima bean loaf and organ meat recipes during the war eagerly cast aside their somber rhetoric about "the kitchen front" and shook off concerns about postwar shortages.

Consumers seemed more than ready to stock up on cookbooks in anticipation of the new era of abundance. Cookbook publication in the postwar era soared. As a 1947 cookbook review in *Publishers' Weekly* put it, America in the postwar years experienced "a cook book boom."[3] It chose an apt phrase: in the late 1940s and 1950s, both the economy and birthrate boomed. But Americans also lived under the shadow of the deadly explosion that ended World War II—the atomic bomb. The postwar era, a time of both prosperity and paranoia, encompassed many such contradictions. More Americans than ever before—with the help of the GI Bill, inexpensive suburban housing, and rising salaries—achieved middle-class status and enjoyed a sense of prosperity. Yet poverty spread throughout the inner cities and in rural areas. Many felt that the Allies decisively won the battle for freedom, but legal segregation denied some Americans their most basic rights. Citizens and politicians proclaimed it an era of peace and unity, but fears of subversion and dissidence ran rampant, and the Cold War increasingly shaped national and international policy. Americans gladly embraced a consumer lifestyle, snapping up new appliances, automobiles, and houses, while beat poets composed tirades against materialism. Little Richard, singing to integrated audiences of frenzied teenagers, turned the phrase "tutti fruitti" into a blatant sexual come-on, while Pat Boone made the same phrase sound utterly innocuous.

Contradictions also shaped food trends during the 1950s. Today, many Americans associate 1950s food solely with garish Jell-O salad and canned soup casserole recipes produced by food corporations. Yet the gourmet movement continued to gain ground in the 1950s, and cookbooks reflected both the influence of convenience food cooking and growing gourmet culinary sensibilities in the United States. Cookbook authors as a whole told Americans to go ahead and enjoy the new era of abundance, easy-to-make foods, and fun dining. Authors and editors rushed to furnish the growing middle class with cookbooks for suburban living and the "new casual" kind of dining for a new mobile, modern age—the age of push-button kitchens, televisions, and the automobile. They also offered a vast new array of specialty cookbooks for the suburban homemaker and for the growing numbers of Americans interested in "foreign" cookery. In the 1950s specialty cookbooks began to make significant inroads into the cookbook market and seriously challenged the market share held by a select few "kitchen bibles" first published in the early twentieth century and revised and reissued over the years. And processed foods and processed-food companies achieved the final conquest of American diets and cooking habits: many recipes in postwar cookbooks became even simpler—a matter of combining and garnishing premade foods.

As a brief postwar recession gave way to a revived and strengthened economy, more cookbooks—replete with photographs, detailed recipes and all manner of kitchen instruction, and padded with corporate advertising—poured onto the market than at any previous time in U.S. history. In 1946 and 1947 a few familiar titles still dominated the cookbook best-seller list. For example, by 1947 the *Good Housekeeping Cook Book* sold over a million copies. *Better Homes and Gardens Cook Book* also sold steadily, as did a small book with easy, general recipes called *Pocket Cook Book*, by Elizabeth Woody. In 1946 *Publishers' Weekly* assured its readers that most cookbooks sold reliably and asserted that bookshops would do well to keep them in stock. They pointed out the long-standing popularity of *The Boston Cooking School Cook Book*, *The Better Homes and Gardens Cook Book*, and *The Settlement Cook Book*. They also noted that after 1943 *The Joy of Cooking* averaged 20,000 copies a month in sales. Indeed, after its 1952 revision Rombauer's book attained more sales and more long-lived fame than any other privately authored cookbook. *The Joy of Cooking*'s sales vastly exceeded those of any other cookbook, excluding those sponsored by magazines or food-processing companies.[4]

But soon these familiar titles would face a slew of challengers for cookbook market dollars. The authors of a 1946 *Publishers' Weekly* cookbook review listed numerous cookbooks promoted by publishers, which they believed would sell well: *The Mystery Chef's Own Cook Book*, James Beard's *Cook It Outdoors*, Malcolm La Prade's *That Man in the Kitchen*, *Men in Aprons* by Lawrence Keating, *Casserole Cookery* by Nino and Marian Tracy, Marguerite McCarthy's *The Cook Is in the Parlor*, and *American Regional Cookery* by *New Yorker* food writer Shelia Hibben. In the 1950s publishers promoted, reissued, and sold more cookbooks than ever before, and expanded the cookbook market by producing more specialized and novelty cookbooks. By the end of the 1940s and in the early 1950s cookbook reviewers often referred to the enormous numbers of cookbooks on the market and the increasing variety of topics that cookbooks addressed. Although general cookbooks sold briskly during the 1950s, in some ways the postwar era saw the beginning of the end for all-purpose cookbooks. The market simply became too huge for any but the most familiar, classic, general cookbooks to generate a substantial number of sales.

A cookbook reviewer in 1955 described how publishers found it increasingly difficult to make a general book successful: "In the usual frantic pattern of the publishing business, since cookbooks have become popular and profitable, everybody has started publishing them, and the market has become highly competitive. Editors say that it is increasingly risky to launch a general cookbook, and increasingly expensive to launch any kind."[5] The expense was due not only to marketing costs but also to the production of the book itself. In the 1950s cookbook readers demanded color photographs, elaborate page layouts, and unique cover designs. During this time, women's domestic magazines and other popular periodicals began to offer even more full-color photographs of food, along with expanded home economics departments, and extensive monthly recipe columns. Cookbooks, in turn, became splashier, bigger, more vividly and elaborately illustrated. They continued to cover a wide range of topics, from marketing to menus. Prefaces, introductions, and commentary on specific recipes expanded. But cookbooks themselves, as a whole, became more specialized.

Cookbooks covered every imaginable topic in the 1950s: low-sodium cooking, cooking for the home freezer, cooking for company, cooking for the dieter, cooking for cocktail parties, cooking like a Californian, cooking like a peasant, economy cooking, cooking for two, cooking for one, cooking for children, cooking like Alice B. Toklas, cooking with a blender, cooking for buffets, cooking on a hot plate, cooking with a chafing dish, and cooking with a pressure cooker. There appeared cookbooks devoted entirely to pies, cheese, chicken, salad, sour cream, wild game, herbs, mushrooms, hamburger, casseroles, omelets, macaroni, or oysters. Cookbooks with international, "ethnic," and regional recipes proliferated as well: Chinese, Italian, Texan, Indian, German, Swedish, French, Greek, Russian, Viennese, Jewish, Shaker, and Mennonite cookbooks all appeared during the 1950s. Publishers revised nearly all the "kitchen bibles" that had been best sellers in the past in order to keep pace with the onslaught. *Fannie Farmer's Cook Book, Good Housekeeping's Cook Book, The Joy of Cooking*, and *Better Homes and Gardens Cook Book* all underwent substantial revisions in the postwar period. Bookshops struggled to keep up, and many created special cookbook promotions, displays, and sales during the 1950s to keep customers informed about the ever increasing numbers of new cookbooks on the market.[6]

In 1952 Elinor Parker, of the Scribner Book Store in New York City, wrote an article for *Publishers' Weekly* on the cookbook boom. As a bookseller, she offered her perspective on the expanding cookbook market. Only a few decades before, she noted, bookstores regularly stocked only one or two cookbooks: "Our senior salesman at the Scribner Book Store tells me that when he first started to work here in 1919 there was exactly one cook book in stock—Fannie Farmer. When I began to sell books in 1928 I remember only three or four—Fannie Farmer, the *Settlement Cook Book*, and a couple of specialty books." In contrast to those earlier years, in the spring of 1952 her bookstore had to contend with forty new titles and four new and revised editions, by her count. Parker asserted that "the rise of amateur cooks" in the 1930s and the disappearance of the professional cook during World War II directly accounted for the steadily growing popularity of published cookery instruction. She observed that "Whatever else the depression depressed it certainly had the opposite effect on the cook book industry." Other commentators in the 1950s regularly pondered the rise in cookbook publication. In an article entitled "Too Many Cookbooks," *Newsweek* magazine echoed Parker's concerns and worried that forty new titles would simply overwhelm Americans. As one cookbook reviewer for *Saturday Review* wrote in 1954, "Recently I have been forced to wonder if perhaps the preparation of food, as detailed in the seemingly endless stream of cookery book coming off the presses, wasn't fixing to edge into the infinity class."[7]

As Parker made clear, the cookbook boom of the 1950s built on an earlier surge in cookbook publication in the 1930s. But cookbook publication and the publication of recipes in newspapers and popular periodicals escalated in the 1950s for several other important reasons. After initial shortages and price hikes in the mid 1940s, postwar American society experienced a period of economic prosperity and consumer abundance the likes of which had never been seen before. Americans sought, with a vengeance, to redress the physical deprivations and emotional anxieties of the Great Depression and the war years: many wanted more than anything else for life to "get back to normal." They wanted to enjoy the fruits of their labor. For many families, wartime employment and the postwar GI Bill increased the possibility of moving up the class ladder, and rich and hearty foods seemed an essential marker of the good life. Weary from the strain of wartime separations, economy, and anxieties, Americans happily enjoyed hearty, satisfying meals. In an essay on her mother's cookbook, magazine writer Sydney Flynn remembers how the recipes her mother used in the late 1940s reflected the American delight that greeted the end of rationing and the return of abundance. "Melt six tablespoons of BUTTER," gloated one recipe, for example.[8] The American appetite for meat, butter, and other rich foods, formidable at any time, increased exponentially in the 1950s.

And food companies ensured that America's appetite would be met by an increasing amount of processed food. The dramatic increase in the availability, variety, and use of processed and packaged foods—more widely obtainable than ever as supermarkets spread throughout the country—constituted one of the most significant aspects of postwar cooking. In a 1947 cookbook review for *Parents' Magazine*, Juanita Wittenborn ascribed the cookbook boom to changing ideas about food and food products, asserting that "There are new foods, new methods, new ideas, new food combinations."[9] Most of the "new foods" and "new ideas" came courtesy of processed, boxed, frozen, instant, and canned food companies, who perfected many new techniques during the war and rushed to take advantage of Americans' increased buying power after the war. And these companies found Americans ready to buy. Sociologists Margaret Cussler and Mary de Give, in a 1952 study of southern rural eating patterns, summarized their subjects' enthusiastic response to the availability of processed foods: "Why shell peas or squeeze oranges, asks the housewife in increasing numbers, when prepared frozen peas, orange juice—practically anything you can name—

are so readily available? Cook Boston baked beans for six hours when you can buy a can for fifteen cents?"[10] Many Americans shared the opinion of the author of a 1951 cookbook who avowed: "Frozen vegetables are God's own gift to the busy housewife."[11]

And just as they had in the prewar era, frozen vegetable, orange juice, and baked bean companies relied heavily on recipes and cookery instruction to help sell their products. Everyone from potato chip companies and dairy councils to the makers of "infra-red broilers" and electric mixer manufacturers utilized free recipe booklets, recipes in magazine advertisements, and recipe contests to sell their products. The most famous of these contests, the Pillsbury Bake-Off, began in 1949. It enjoyed tremendous success and convinced hundreds of women (only occasionally did a man compete) to devise recipes using Pillsbury products.[12] It would be difficult to even estimate how many Americans read and used recipes off labels or from printed advertisements or in promotional cookbooks. But such marketing techniques did, without a doubt, produce results for corporate advertisers. Consumers snatched up promotional recipe booklets as fast as companies could print them, and privately authored cookbooks recommended that housewives collect promotional cooking pamphlets and learn from them.[13] Companies saw remarkable success with their cookery promotionals. The Pillsbury Bake-Off alone attracted thousands of contestants over the years and garnered considerable publicity in the popular press.

But no promotional cookbook came close to General Mills's cookbook coup in 1950: *Betty Crocker's Picture Cook Book.* The Washburn Crosby milling company, a Minneapolis mill founded in 1866, introduced radio listeners to their fictional spokeswoman Betty Crocker in 1927. But the company had employed a fictional female named "Betty Crocker" since 1921. That year, Washburn Crosby created an advertising campaign—those who solved a puzzle received a pincushion shaped like a miniature sack of flour—that generated stacks of mail from consumers. When women sent in the solved puzzle, many of them also asked the company for advice about certain perplexing baking and cooking questions. The bemused advertising department turned over the letters to the company's female test kitchen employees and home economics experts: Agnes White and Janette Kelly. Washburn Crosby quickly recognized a potential gold mine and created a fictional spokeswoman (whose work would be done by White, Kelly, and others) to answer these letters. Company executives thought "Betty" sounded friendly and wholesome, and they chose the surname "Crocker" to honor the retired director of Washburn Crosby, William G. Crocker.

In 1928 several regional grain mills, including Washburn Crosby, merged into General Mills, but Betty Crocker remained one of the company's most valuable employees. When Marjorie Child Husted assumed directorship of the company's home economics department in 1926, Betty Crocker already had a well-established bond with the American public that grew with the popularity of *The Betty Crocker Show*, a radio program. When other food companies began to question the legality of misleading the public about the existence of a woman named Betty Crocker, General Mills executives hastily made Husted assume the role of "the real Betty Crocker." She continued to play the role into the early 1950s, when she appeared as "Betty Crocker" on *The World Is Yours* (the first program CBS broadcast in color) and demonstrated how to bake an apple roll. Later, radio personality Adelaide Hawley Cumming took over the role, and hosted *The Betty Crocker TV Show* on CBS from 1950 to 1952. Cumming also appeared regularly on *The Burns and Allen Show* from 1954 through 1959. Although she reportedly often told fans that she was "merely the manifestation of a corporate image," Cumming became fairly well known as "the real Betty Crocker."[14] Despite subsequent in-house bickering over the origin of Betty Crocker and various contradictory publicity releases about her history, few American housewives seemed troubled about the question of Betty Crocker's existence. They even accepted the "portraits" of Betty Crocker that General Mills produced at regular intervals. The most recent portrait was a "composite" Betty Crocker created in 1996 out of photographs of women from different ethnic backgrounds. Today, in a twenty-first-century version of the letters answered by White and Kelley, those who send email queries to the Betty Crocker web site receive reply emails signed "Betty Crocker."[15]

The cookbook, more than any other single factor, made Betty Crocker a lasting success. Publishers even nicknamed the wildly successful book, with its distinctive red and white cover, "Big Red." In the 1920s company officials believed that Betty helped put a friendly, motherly face on their corporation and that she encouraged young women to reach out and ask for kitchen advice—and product advice. But Betty's pleasing countenance did not fully explain the popularity of *Betty Crocker's Picture Cook Book*. Indeed, Betty Crocker's portrait did not appear anywhere in the cookbook, although her signature and her personal notes to the reader did. Published in 1950, this cookbook sold more copies than any other nonfiction book that year and remained the fastest-selling cookbook for years. Savvy marketing on the part of General Mills accounted for much of the book's success. General Mills, maker of Gold Medal Flour, was greatly concerned about keeping the flour market strong in an era of prepackaged foods and did an enormous amount of test marketing before the publication of *Betty Crocker's*

Picture Cook Book. And the company had decades of letters from consumers from which to draw information. It also utilized the financial and marketing resources of a major publishing firm by publishing the book jointly with McGraw-Hill. One other feature stood out in *Betty Crocker's Picture Cook Book:* the photographs. Though not by any means the first cookbook to use instructional photographs of cooking procedures and techniques, the *Picture Cook Book* very effectively incorporated hundreds of step-by-step black and white photos, along with a few vivid color photos of completed dishes. The book used photos that captured the baking process as if on a television show, and thus tapped into the growth of a TV-influenced culture in the United States.[16] It also jammed each page full of graphics, different kinds of type, and assorted cooking hints.

The recipes themselves supported the book's parent company in every way: baked goods which used General Mills products (usually referred to by brand name) constituted the vast majority of the recipes. Helmut Ripperger's 1951 review of *Betty Crocker's Picture Cook Book* took particular issue with this imbalance and with the kinds of recipes in the book: "Even the most casual inspection will show that the book is completely out of balance and the reasons are obvious: of its 449 pages but *twenty-eight* are devoted to meat *and* fish, with fish covered in all of four pages! Many of the receipts are capricious, unoriginal or, contrariwise, so original as to make the classic cook shudder. What say you to a *Potage St. Germaine* which is a pea soup garnished with 'thin slices of Bologna sausage'—and what would the French say?" (emphasis in original). Why would anyone, he asked, be tempted to make something called "Emergency Steak," which was ground beef extended with crushed Wheaties flakes and decorated with strips of carrot to resemble the bone in a real steak. "No, I do not make these things up," he wrote wonderingly of this particular recipe. Ripperger also critiqued the blatantly promotional nature of the book, as well as the type of recipes it contained. He objected, and strongly, "to being asked to pay nearly five dollars for a book which is nothing but a glorified piece of advertising." He complained that brand names like Gold Medal flour, Softasilk, and Wheaties appeared in bold print and upper case Roman type on virtually every page. "I'll give a shiny new penny to each and every reader who does not find one, or two, or even three on every page," he wrote.[17] Ripperger's caustic—and well- founded—comments did not, however, represent the majority viewpoint. The cookbook garnered complimentary reviews in the *New York Times, Saturday Review,* and the *Chicago Sunday Tribune* and by 1951 had gone through seven printings, selling over 2 million copies (far exceeding sales of General Mills's other cookbook efforts). It eventually achieved more sales than any other published cookbook: over 40 million copies sold by 1996. (*Better Homes and Gardens Cook Book,* first published in 1930 and with more than 30 million copies sold by the late 1990s, comes in second.)[18] For recipe readers long used to the combination of product promotion and recipes, the use of brand names in recipes did not trouble many. Although Ripperger seemed shocked by the disproportionate number of dessert recipes in *Betty Crocker's Picture Cook Book,* twentieth-century cookbooks often gave far more recipes for baked goods than any other kind of food, seemingly in response to consumer demand. Women who rarely used other kinds of recipes apparently turned more readily to cake, pie, and pastry recipes.

Many Americans also did not share Ripperger's outrage about the bologna soup and the "Emergency Steak" type of food found in Betty Crocker recipes. In the 1950s these kinds of mock dishes, and recipes that combined canned ingredients under fancy names, appeared in a great many cookbooks. In 1957 the French philosopher Roland Barthes described such recipes as "ornamental cookery." He lamented the kind of food that fled "from nature thanks to a kind of frenzied baroque (sticking shrimps in a lemon, making a chicken look pink, serving grapefruit hot)." He asserted that in ornamental cookery "there is an obvious endeavor to glaze surfaces, round them off, to bury the food under the even sediment of sauces, creams, icing and jellies." He argued that this bourgeois exercise in obfuscation created a cookery "based on coatings and alibis" which tried to "extenuate and even to disguise the primary nature of foodstuffs, the brutality of meat or the abruptness of sea-food."[19] Barthes critiqued popular French cuisine, but his descriptions readily evoked American postwar food fashions.

Barthes failed to mention that numerous other kinds of cookery at different historical periods also utilized "coatings and alibis." Indeed, the scientific cookery of the late 1800s depended on a "sediment of sauces, creams, icing and jellies." Still, Barthes accurately described how postwar society rushed to embrace the plastic and the mass-produced—even in the kitchen. He also spoke to the impact of processed foods on cookery. Americans depended more and more on processed foods for the basic ingredients of their recipes, moving the cooking process well away from "the primary nature of foodstuffs." Betty Crocker may have devoted most of her cookbook to baking "from scratch," but General Mills flourished primarily by introducing numerous kinds of packaged mixes to the market. Recipes in the 1950s moved further away from cookery that required real kitchen skill and toward directions for heating, combining, and augmenting canned and frozen foods. Although not unique to the 1950s, "ornamental cookery" such as hot grapefruit and pink chicken did appear regularly in postwar cooking instruction. Like the photographs in the cookbooks themselves, many 1950s recipes relied on Technicolor shades. And they called for a startling range of "sauces, creams, icing and jellies."

Historians of popular culture and of food, however, have sometimes overstated the extent to which strange Jell-O salads, Velveeta cheese sauce, and other "coatings and alibis" constituted everyday food in the 1950s.[20] These scholars rarely mention, for example, that many cookbooks authors took the same kind of stand against sweet, marshmallow-encrusted salads that their 1920s and 1930s counterparts had. In the 1950s numerous authors advocated simple green salads, served in garlic-rubbed wooden salad bowls, and dressed with flavorful dressings like Roquefort cheese or olive oil and tarragon vinaigrette. But, without a doubt, some of the trends that shaped food fashions in the 1950s deserve their reputation. Tuna noodle casserole with crushed potato chip topping, Jell-O rings, casseroles of every imaginable kind, and sandwich loaves all regularly appeared in 1950s cookbooks. The food-shaped-to-look-like-other-kinds-of-food recipes (such as Betty Crocker's "Emergency Steak"), which made limited appearances at the beginning of the twentieth century, came back with a vengeance. For instance, Beth McLean, author of the 1950 *Modern Homemaker's Cookbook*, recommended an appetizer she called "The New Pineapple Look" that consisted of liver sausage molded to look like a pineapple, with sliced olives simulating pineapple skin and a real green pineapple top to complete the "good-tasting fake."[21]

The prolific Ruth Berolzheimer and the Culinary Arts Institute included a recipe for "Carrot Croquettes"—pureed carrots fried into the shape of whole carrots and topped with parsley—in *500 Delicious Dishes from Leftovers*, published in 1952. Berolzheimer also published a recipe for "Mock Duck"—lamb shoulder in the shape of a duck—in her 1949 *The Body Building Dishes for Children Cookbook*, another recipe booklet from the Culinary Arts Institute. "For a really hilarious dinner," she assured the reader, "nothing equals this schoolmate of Donald Duck." Authors routinely suggested that children, especially, would enjoy foods made to look like other food or something other than food. Many seemed convinced that all children loved pear halves made to look like bunnies with the help of almonds and pimentos. The editor of the *Parents' Magazine Family Cookbook* stretched the concept to its limit when they published a recipe for a cottage cheese mound garnished with carrot sticks and called it "Golden Porcupine."[22] With the birth rate at an all time high, cookbooks turned renewed attention on the child eater—and advocated new food disguises and assorted "fun food" for children's meals.

The baby boom contributed also to the continuing popularity of cookbooks for children and young adults. Even many cookbooks meant for adult readers included a section for "Junior Cooks." In contrast to prewar books, however, the recipes in 1950s children's cookbooks presented more novelty foods than real meals. In keeping with the overall trend in cookbook publishing, juvenile cookery instruction tended to focus on combining or heating up canned, processed, and frozen ingredients. The recipe for "Hot Dogs" in the 1955 *Better Homes and Gardens Junior Cook Book* called for "6 frankfurters, 6 Coney buns, butter or margarine." A biscuit recipe instructed the child on how to bake biscuits from a packaged mix. Cookbooks aimed at teenagers—a new consumer and social category in the 1950s—also contained exceedingly simple recipes that often focused more on entertaining or dessert cookery than practical home cooking. These too emphasized cooking out of cans and with packaged mixes. Margaret Gosset and Mary Elting's cookbook for teenagers, *Now You're Cookin'*, advised the teenage cook to seek out the best processed foods and to use promotional recipes for foods. They noted that "prepared foods, canned and packaged, often have basic recipes and a few variations right on the labels," but cautioned the teenage consumer that "some brands are better than others." Find the best brand, they counseled, and "use it steadily so that your flapjacks will be predictable," adding that "booklets from flour mills, cheese manufacturers, refrigerator and other companies usually have excellent recipes, tested in their kitchens."[23] Most cookbooks for children, such as *Betty Crocker's Cookbook for Boys and Girls*, consisted primarily of this kind of "predictable" cooking from a mix, a box, or a can.[24] Most cookbooks, but not all: Irma Rombauer's effort in this area, *A Cookbook for Girls and Boys*, published in 1946, and Helen Evans and Philip S. Brown's 1959 *The Boy's Cook Book* offered more complex recipes and menus. But a child experimenting in the kitchen would be far more likely to encounter a menu suggestion like the one found in *General Foods Kitchen Cookbook* for "Her Very First Meal": hamburger patties, canned spaghetti, frozen peas and carrots, lettuce with bottled dressing, packaged rolls, and lemon instant pudding.[25]

Menus consisting entirely of heated canned foods, frozen vegetables with butter, and instant desserts proliferated in 1950s cookery books (fig. 15). They often appeared in cookbooks for adults as well as teenagers, especially in cookbooks addressed "to the bride." Indeed, sometimes the lines between cookbooks for teenagers and cookbooks for brides blurred. Like the birthrate, the marriage rate in the 1950s soared, and the age of first marriage dropped. Many authors assumed that the new wife had never before set foot in the kitchen and so required the most basic of instruction. Although cookbooks in the 1920s and 1930s also often made this assumption, in the postwar period packaged and

Figure 15 Beginning in 1920, commercial cookbooks increasingly recommended using canned and processed foods. Here, the 1959 menu for "Her First
Meal" included canned spaghetti, packaged rolls, frozen peas and carrots, and
instant lemon pudding. From *The General Foods Kitchens Cookbook* (New York:
Random House, 1959).

processed foods increasingly appeared as the solution to cookery ignorance. In Dorothy Malone's 1947 *Cookbook for Brides*, the "recipe" for
"How to Make Good Cocoa" consisted of nothing more than advice on
getting a good packaged variety.[26] Several cookbooks offered timetables, even minute-by-minute timetables, for preparing dinner and
for entertaining. Some authors felt the need to include steps such as
"Set table," "Get dressed," "Make coffee," and so on. Mary Welch's
Your First Hundred Meals gave a schedule for making a simple dinner
that included steps for lighting candles, carrying the salad dressing
to the table, and announcing dinner. In addition, Welch's menu suggestions emphasized frozen and prepared foods such as pudding mix,
frozen asparagus, cake mix, and especially canned soup. In one strange
recipe, she asserted that "Mint jelly gives a different flavor to canned
tomato soup."[27]

Numerous other authors also recommended combining canned soups with other canned soups or other prepared ingredients for an unusual and easy to prepare dish. *The Parents' Magazine Cook Book*, for example, recommended making "Peanut Butter Bisque" by adding processed peanut butter to a can of tomato soup.[28] Although cookbooks utilized canned soups since 1920, in the 1950s this particular kind of premade, processed food became even more popular. Some cookbooks published in the 1950s confined *all* their soup recipes to mixing and doctoring canned soups. "Aren't you lucky," Beth McLean asserted in her 1950 *Modern Homemaker's Cookbook*, "to live in an age when a whole array of fine-flavored soups are all made for you?"[29] Mildred Knopf made a similar comment in her 1959 cookbook *Cook, My Darling Daughter:* "As your generation replaces mine, you will have advantages never enjoyed by mine. The short-cut advantages of the frozen soups, of the improved canned soups, will challenge you to combine them, using your imagination to invent and discover."[30]

Cookbooks in the 1950s often described the cooking process as combining packaged ingredients in inventive and imaginative ways, or fussing over processed foods to arrive at new and fun dishes. Although cookbooks themselves grew bigger and flashier, cookery instruction offered simpler recipes, relying more and more upon processed foods. For example, onion dip, one of the most famous recipes of the 1950s, called for no real cooking but instead simply instructed the reader on how to combine premade foods. In 1954 Lipton introduced the onion dip recipe—a combination of a package of their dry onion soup mix and sour cream—and it met with instant and widespread success.[31] This dip epitomized many aspects of postwar cuisine: the recipe came from a processed-foods company that wanted to sell more of its product; it called for a bare minimum of cooking skills; and the dip fit right into the new kinds of entertaining and eating that Americans began to do in large numbers in the 1950s—at least, in suburbia.

Only about 20 percent of Americans lived in the suburbs during the postwar era, although that minority garnered a remarkable amount of attention both in the 1950s and in later historical analyses of the period.[32] The growth of the suburbs most markedly shaped American society by creating a new idealized life-style. Away from the crowded, dirty cities but not removed to the isolated country, suburbs offered Americans a new definition of middle-class living. Mainstream cookbooks certainly presumed a suburban reading audience. Not that chic urban dwellers as well as country farm wives did not also serve Lipton dried onion soup mix dip, for with the continued improvement of shipping and the spread of supermarkets Americans increasingly shared in a homogenized diet. But the suburbs offered an especially conducive setting for very casual dining and entertaining, such as cocktail parties, buffet suppers, or backyard barbecues. Authors raved about the new suburban dining and the demise of formal entertaining. "A revolution is taking place in home cooking!" declared Ida Bailey Allen in the 1957 revision of a cookbook published ten years before. She then enthused about the way cookery had become "movable": "Sometimes in the kitchen or kitchenette; in chafing dishes on a buffet table; with electrical equipment on the terrace or piazza; on a barbecue or grill in the garden or back yard; at the fireplace."[33] Numerous authors agreed with Allen and declared the dawn of a whole new kind of casual, fun-loving entertaining. And they provided recipes to match the spirit of this kind of entertaining. The aforementioned onion soup dip, for instance, could be easily whipped together and served poolside or at a patio party—along with some of the new ruffled potato chips for dipping.

But at the same time that cookbooks advocated less formal dining and entertaining, they also encouraged their readers to throw theme parties complete with elaborately decorated and fancied up party food. *The General Food's Kitchens Cookbook* had complete menus for parties with themes such as "Come to the Mardi Gras," "Old South Open House," and "Alpine Fondue Party."[34] In particular, parties with a Hawaiian theme spread like wildfire through the pages of commercial cookbooks, and bland Polynesian style recipes also enjoyed much popularity. Perhaps pineapple cannery owners played a part in this: recipes using canned pineapple proliferated in 1950s domestic magazines and in promotional literature. However, while the ladies of suburbia concocted pineapple kebabs and cookbooks gave instructions for making things like "appetizer loaf" (a combination of sweet pickles, ripe olives, stuffed olives, parsley, cracker crumbs, cottage cheese, and green peppers, shaped into loaf), gourmands also made their mark on American postwar cuisine.

The gourmet movement in the United States grew along with the increasing mobility of Americans in the 1950s. Pan Am's first round-the-world-flight in 1947 helped facilitate America's move toward the incorporation of different "ethnic" foods, but especially French cuisine, into our national diet. Back in the late 1800s, scientific cookery and cooking school experts urged immigrant families to give up the dishes of their homeland in favor of a uniformly New England–style diet. But by the 1950s, Hungarian goulash and Italian pizza seemed perfectly suited to new more adventurous eating and entertaining. Although cookbooks in the 1920s and 1930s often included a bland version of spaghetti and "Chinese" chop suey, not until the 1950s did "foreign" cookery really gain a foothold in mainstream American kitchens. General cookbooks increasingly contained dishes for exotic dishes from

Europe, Mexico, and Asia. The author of the 1955 *Cocktail-Supper Cookbook*, for example, recommended a menu called "Spanish Fandango" for a festive meal. It included Madeira, fried shrimp, paella, and flan. *The Complete American Cookbook* included recipes for chow mein, Javanese rice, tamale pie, egg foo young, Italian sausage in cabbage leaves, chicken risotto, and garbonzo beans with sausage.[35] The authors of *Simple Cooking for the Epicure*, published in 1949, even asserted that a woman who harbored suspicion of foreign foods was sure to retain old-fashioned and outdated ideas about culinary matters in general: "Fifty years ago 'foreign foods' were viewed with suspicion and horror. Our forebears were solidly behind the opinion that all foods with foreign names were simultaneously too greasy and too hot—whether they were Chinese vegetable dishes or French soups. This is ridiculous, we realize now, and when mother isn't present we admit that either the Turkish or Mexican way of preparing rice has her mushy product backed off the map."[36] "Mother" apparently had a lot to learn from modern daughter and modern daughter's cookbooks, especially when it came to "foreign" cookery. True, many of theses recipes called for considerably toned down versions of more authentic dishes. But on the other hand, mainstream cookbooks such as *The General Foods Kitchens Cookbook* called for saffron, oysters, mussels, olive oil, and long-grain rice in their paella recipes and turmeric, coriander, and garlic in their Indian lamb curry recipes.[37]

The 1950s also saw gourmet restaurants make a concerted comeback, at least in major cities. Restaurant reviewing became a much more influential profession, almost entirely due to the efforts of Craig Claiborne. Claiborne joined the *New York Times* in 1957 as food editor and instituted the star rating system (four stars for a superb restaurant, three for a good restaurant, and so on). His avid interest in the work of individual chefs helped create a new standard for fine dining and food writing. He published his first cookbook, *The New York Times Cookbook*, in 1961, and it became one of the few general cookbooks of the postwar era to achieve substantial sales (nearly three million copies). Claiborne, like others in the growing gourmet movement, asserted that the key to a gourmet approach to cuisine lay not with food snobbery but with appreciating "different" kinds of dishes in the spirit of culinary adventure. Gourmets, according to this definition cooked with attention to flavor, freshness, and the sensual experience of fine dining. The enormous (over 800 pages) and popular cookbook published by *Gourmet* magazine in 1950 emphasized that the editors believed in the simple pleasure of eating. The editors asserted that "the mere satisfaction of hunger is a satisfaction which man shares with the animals," but that gourmets took pleasure in their food, "artistically, emotionally, imaginatively." All the recipes in *The Gourmet Cookbook* came from the magazine and most focused on French and American dishes, each introduced by a short paragraph sprinkled with literary references or lyrical descriptions of food.[38]

When *Time* magazine published its popular, oversize, photo-laden cookbook in 1958, the editors stated their hope that the book's numerous foreign recipes would appeal to gourmet readers: "It is designed in part for armchair gourmets who, far from the kitchen, may want to tempt themselves with culinary delights." Their recipes for bouillabaisse, halibut soufflé, goose with garlic sauce, and a curry packed with authentic Indian spices bore out that claim. Fondue and flaming food—two mainstays of 1950s gourmet cuisine—got their own chapter. But the editors also included a menu for a gourmet dinner (illustrated by a woman in evening dress lighting candles at an elegant table) that relied heavily on foods that would hardly strike today's readers as gourmet. "The soup was bought dehydrated, the trout and potato puffs [commonly known as tater tots] on the table frozen and the bread semibaked," wrote the editors.[39] While some recipes demanded home-made chutney and real risotto, other recipes blithely called for tater tots and dehydrated soup—all under the umbrella of "gourmet." Cookbooks embraced the concept of gourmet eating but also strongly emphasized ease of preparation, and authors freely recommended premade ingredients. Gourmet cookery, asserted many authors, did not necessarily require advanced cooking skills or complicated recipes.

For example, it would be difficult to imagine a less "gourmet" organization than the Culinary Arts Institute—which emphasized processed and packaged foods and very simple recipes. Yet in 1955 its booklet *The Gourmet Foods Cookbook* offered recipes for oysters Rockefeller, cherry soup, black mushroom wine soup, brioches and croissants, beef stroganoff, ham mousse, chicken Kiev, roast pheasant, and Caesar and green goddess salads. The editors clarified that "gourmet" meant cooking with a little flair, not cooking with impossibly exotic ingredients: "What *are* gourmet foods? Exotic viands of far-off lands, touched with the mystery of strangeness? Ineffable delicacies, exciting to read about but beyond the capacities of the average homemaker or the facilities of her kitchen? We think that gourmet food is food with flair. It is sometimes a familiar food in a striking new dress with a retinue of unusual flavors. Or a beloved favorite dish in a new role in the drama of the dinner menu."[40] The editors perfectly summarized postwar attitudes about cooking and eating: an emphasis on "food with flair," on dramatic dinner menus, but, at the same time, attention to ease of preparation. Thus, an author could urge the reader to procure real Italian cheese for a pizza recipe but at the same time recommend using a "hot roll mix" for the crust. One author who urged women to learn about good wines and fresh green salads also recommended a startling "spaghetti curry" recipe calling for canned cream of mushroom soup, spaghetti, and real grated coconut. Even so staunch an advocate of fresh and unusual foods as James Beard did not scorn convenience foods. Along with his recipes for steak tartare, shrimp rémoulade, artichokes stuffed with crab meat, *vathoo vindaloo*, rabbit *agro dolce*, and dandelion salad, he included a chapter on using frozen foods for "quick meals" in his 1949 *Fireside Cookbook*.[41]

Increased travel to Europe contributed to the popularity of French and "continental" cuisine, but travel within the borders of the United States also broadened American palates. Of all the items that underwent mass production in the United States after the war, perhaps none so changed Americans' daily life as the automobile. By the mid 1950s, private families owned 67.4 million cars and more people than ever before hit the open road for weekend or summer vacations. As highways, freeways, and byways began to connect the states (in 1956, Congress passed the $76 billion National Defense Highway Act in order to ensure quick urban evacuation in the case of Russian nuclear attack), interest in regional cuisine rose. Numerous cookbooks with a regional focus appeared, and general cookbooks often included at least a few regional specialties. For instance, in 1946 the publishers of Shelia Hibben's extensive *American Regional Cookery* issued a substantially revised edition. Ruth Berolzheimer edited a large regional cookbook, tabbed like a dictionary. The tabs marked sections entitled "Pennsylvania Dutch," "Creole," "Southwest," and so on. Mary Margaret McBride, a popular author, wrote an enormous book of state-by-state recipes and essays on American regional cooking.[42]

The automobile helped create interest in regional cuisine, but it also played a major role in bringing about the kind of eating that fundamentally undermined regional differences: with the car came the fast food chain. In 1948, in San Bernardino, California, the first McDonald's restaurant introduced a limited menu featuring hamburgers, speedy service, and a sterile eating environment. It achieved almost instant success, and the concept of chain restaurants and fast food rapidly took shape. The novelty, and convenience of fast food soon posed a serious threat to regional cuisine, as thousands of Americans began to eat the exact same meal all over the country. The first motel chain also got its start in the 1950s and helped contribute to the decline of regional food eateries. The first Holiday Inn opened in 1952 and the Holiday Inn restaurants and dining rooms helped make a certain kind of homogenized "gourmet" dining mainstream. With cloth napkins, candlelight, and identical menus, Holiday Inns around the country helped create a more upscale version of fast food.[43]

The ascendancy of processed foods, more casual kinds of dining and entertaining, gourmet interest in foreign and novel dishes, and expanding automobile culture and growing mobility changed American eating habits and the recipes circulating in American society. These trends began before the war and grew slowly. In contrast, one uniquely postwar phenomenon managed to create a whole new kind of dining and inspire a whole new kind of convenience food in a matter of a few years: television. The number of families who owned television sets increased by the millions during the 1950s. In 1946, only 7,000 television sets existed in the United States. By 1950, 4.4 million families owned one, and by the end of the decade, that number reached 50 million. Television changed many aspects of the consumer's daily life. Advertising grew in sophistication by leaps and bounds, as did marketing research. The concept of leisure time and public space changed forever. Every other popular medium from newspapers to radio to the cinema felt the impact of television. It also radically altered the architecture of the middle-class home: the spatial arrangements of houses shifted when large sitting rooms became necessary for TV viewing, and the new suburbs all incorporated a TV or family room into their floor plans. And, of course, it changed how Americans ate.

Swanson's food company invented what became the most widely recognized symbol of how television changed American eating habits: the TV dinner. In 1953, Swanson introduced this new convenience food product at an October national meeting of food writers and editors. Created with the help of food-processing technology perfected during the war, this first TV dinner consisted of sliced turkey, gravy, dressing, whipped sweet potatoes, and peas presented in a partitioned foil tray. Swanson was not the first to offer consumers a complete frozen dinner, but it cornered the market by directly linking this product to television viewing. The company scored a direct hit with consumers who increasingly planned their meals around the television. Folding tray tables, soon known as "TV trays," first appeared in national advertising that year—and Americans learned that the president and his first lady enjoyed eating dinner on matching tray tables in front of the TV.[44]

When cookbook authors lauded new kinds of casual eating, they often mentioned the television. Dips, dunks, and nibbles all lent themselves to simultaneous eating and viewing. Part of the renewed popularity of the chafing dish lay with its portability: one could cook a Welsh rabbit and never miss a moment of the show. Cheese balls, Chex mix, pigs in a blanket, and miniature meatballs all worked well for TV-viewing snacks. They could be easily prepared at commercial breaks, required minimal silverware, and could be eaten while one's attention focused elsewhere. Clam dip, one of the most popular dips of the 1950s and perfect for TV snacking, made its first appearance on the *Kraft Music Hall* television show and immediately caused a run on canned clams in New York City. Kraft published the recipe (a mixture of canned clams, lemon juice, Worcestershire sauce, salt, pepper, and cream cheese) in its 1951 *Food Favorites from the Kraft Television Theater* cookbook. Each recipe in the book (all of which called for Kraft products) utilized step-by-step photographs, as if in a TV shot. Moreover, the cookbook could be folded open, propped up, and made to almost resemble one's own personal cookbook-television set. A 1957 cookbook, *Cooking at Home*, published in conjunction with a TV show by the same name, used a similar stand-up format to simulate television viewing.[45] Kraft and numerous other companies quickly utilized the new medium to sell their products and peddle their recipes. Just as radio provided an important medium for the spread of recipes, so cooking shows, both local and corporate, soon flooded TV airwaves.

Cooking shows and cooking on TV also provided processed-food corporations and appliance manufacturers with new marketing techniques. Fifteen- and thirty-minute advertisements for kitchen appliances and processed foods ran often, especially during the first few years of the television revolution.[46] For example, Westinghouse, maker of kitchen appliances, hired an appealing spokeswoman named Betty Furness for their "infomercials." Unlike many of her competitors, who usually came straight from radio work, Furness had on-camera experience from her days as a B-movie actress. Furness won substantial fame, considering that her only appearances on television took place standing by refrigerators, ovens, and electric fans.[47] Her 1954 cookbook, *The Betty Furness Westinghouse Cook Book*, did not achieve remarkable sales in the postwar cookbook-saturated market. But it did aptly demonstrate the growing interplay of television and food preparation. The cookbook, "prepared under the direction" of home economist Julia Kiene, did not mention Westinghouse appliances by name, but the strong association between Furness and the Westinghouse brand name must have assured the company that a cookbook simply authored by Furness could possibly boost appliance sales.

Although not directly associated with any one product, James Beard's television cookery career also received a great deal of commercial support. In 1946 he began making regular appearances on the Borden Dairy Company's variety show, spending fifteen minutes demonstrating recipes that utilized Borden products. He later endorsed a variety of kitchen utensils, food companies, and wines. But Beard's effusive and food-loving personality shaped his television cookery as much, perhaps more, than his commercial associations. His on-the-air cooking demonstrations helped create a new standard (and paved the way for Julia Child). Beard's lively, personality-based cookery instruction, and his emphasis on simple classic food far removed from the plastic-tasting convenience food popular during that time, showed the way of the future. Beard actively disliked his best-known competitor on the air: Dione Lucas. Lucas ran a cooking school and restaurant in New York, and her CBS program began shortly after Beard began his regular NBC appearances. In contrast to Beard, who developed his own American-based cooking style, Lucas adhered to the rules of the *Ecole du Cordon Bleu* in Paris, and she helped to popularize European-style cooking in the United States.[48] Their counterpart on ABC, Jessie DeBoth, wrote a syndicated newspaper column and published several cookbooks, including the brisk seller *It's Easy to Be a Good Cook*.

Cooking with the Experts, a 1955 cookbook edited by television writer and commentator William A. Kaufman, consisted entirely of recipes created by women from around the country (also one married couple and one male chef) who hosted their own cooking shows. Forty-five contributors, from both coasts, the South, the Midwest, and Hawaii, gave recipes for standard (shrimp puffs and lemon chicken) and more exotic fare (roast tongue with raisin sauce). At the end of the book, biographical and professional information about each contributor accompanied their photos. Most held home economics degrees and many worked in radio before making the move to television. "I doubt if there was ever a cooking school in the world that had as large an attendance as one cooking program seen on television in the smallest area in the United States," asserted Kaufman.[49]

Kaufman may have overestimated the impact of individual shows, but, cumulatively, cooking shows on television did indeed change the nature of cookery instruction (fig. 16). The publication of *Knox On-Camera Recipes* in 1962 demonstrated how Americans began to seek out visual cookery instruction: although no show by that title existed, each recipe had a set of step-by-step instructions photographed to resemble a television still shot.[50]

In many ways, detailed written cookery instruction naturally evolved into cooking on camera and other kinds of kitchen photography. Since the advent of the modern cookbook, manuals constantly strove for clearer and simpler direction—directions that any middle-class kitchen novice could follow. Photographic instruction seemed the next logical step. Still, television cooking shows could not replace more traditional written instruction, as the phenomenal increase in cookbook publication and sales indicated. But numerous authors felt compelled to at least

Figure 16 In the 1950s local and national televised cookery shows, building on the popularity of radio cooking shows in the 1930s, proliferated. Pictured here is Pearl Silverson, who hosted the *Kitchen Magic* cooking show out of Memphis, Tennessee. From William A. Kaufman, ed., *Cooking with the Experts* (New York: Random House, 1955).

acknowledge the way television changed eating in the home. Most seemed utterly resigned, like Ida Bailey Allen, who merely noted in her 1957 *Cook Book for Two* that television viewing often dictated when the family would eat meals. Or Gertrude Wilkinson, author of *The Standard Family Cook Book*, who sighed, "When the family's favorite show starts at the dinner hour, there is only one thing to do and this is to move the dinner in front of the TV set."[51] One author even embraced the idea of scheduling the family meals around television viewing. In her 1954 *The Queen Is in the Kitchen*, in a section entitled "Television—the Permanent Dinner Guest," Marguerite McCarthy claimed that both children and adults should be able to eat dinner in front of their favorite television shows: "As the clock strikes the hour, each child balances a tray and the procession moves into the realm of make-believe. You and Dad sink into comfortable chairs—far from the blare and blatt of the children's program—and enjoy a few minutes of peace and quiet as you sip your cocktails. Later, as you dine in front of your program, you realize that at last your goal has been reached—the family has found happiness under its own roof."[52] One cookbook reviewer, at least, agreed with McCarthy. In his 1955 review of McCarthy's book, Lawton Mackall wrote: "The monopolist by the name of Television who came to dinner and transformed the living-dining room into nomads' land can, it seems, be capitulated to on tolerable terms."[53]

Dining à la TV changed how many Americans ate in the postwar years, but in some ways home cooking in the United States did not change at all. Simply because television demanded new, more casual dining and because processed foods increasingly appeared at the dinner table did not mean that the basic composition—meat main dish, a starch side, a vegetable, and a dessert—of a home-cooked meal changed. Even TV dinners followed a similar composition. Moreover, we cannot assume that because certain types of recipes proliferated in the postwar period (especially those produced by processed food companies) Americans regularly followed those recipes. Some cookbook readers may have tried Betty Crocker's bologna soup, but many probably did not. Certainly, some food writers and columnists complained about the state of American cuisine in the 1950s. For example, caterer, columnist, and cookbook author Helen Evans Brown (who enjoyed a long correspondence with James Beard in the 1950s) scorned highly processed foods. She once described many of the salty snacks often served at postwar cocktail parties as "violently artificially colored, and not a few of them apparently flavored with soot, soap, or stale pepper."[54]

Those not directly involved in the food business also complained. In her 1954 memoir about family life on an island near Seattle, humorist Betty MacDonald wrote about having to choke down absurd combinations of food at feminine gatherings. She also criticized and satirized radio and domestic magazine food writers: "Another female house-hold hinter gave a recipe for a big hearty dish of elbow macaroni, mint jelly, lima beans, mayonnaise and cheese baked until 'hot and yummy.' Unless my taste buds are paralyzed, this dish could be baked until hell freezes over and it might get hot but never 'yummy.'" MacDonald surely did not speak for herself only when she complained about these recipe purveyors and about the kind of food served at "ladies only" social events. She scornfully described one such salad as "tuna fish and marshmallows and walnuts and pimento (just for the pretty color, our hostess explained later when she was giving us the recipe) and chunks of pure white lettuce and boiled dressing." "I almost gagged," MacDonald stated shortly.[55] The fact that Betty MacDonald encountered such food often enough to complain about it indicated its regular appearance at such gatherings. But on the other hand, her critical remarks about these kinds of recipes and the people who created them also showed that Americans did not uniformly accept strange and terrible combinations of processed foods.

Signs of use in cookbooks can reveal, in fragmentary ways, the many different ways individual Americans responded to recipes in the 1950s. For example, one woman who owned a copy of the strictly "home cooking" *Modern Family Cook Book* in the 1950s (a typical menu consisted of braised pork chops, gravy, mashed potatoes, buttered broccoli, head lettuce, Russian dressing, bread and butter, and pudding) seemed interested in cooking a novel vegetable: the artichoke. She stored a paper with handwritten instructions for cooking artichokes in salted water within the pages of her *Modern Family Cook Book*. Notes like these, made by anonymous owners of postwar cookbooks, are in many ways an incomplete information source, but they do indicate how people actually used cookbooks. First, cookbooks functioned as household repositories. In those I examined, owners placed recipes torn out of magazines, warranties and instructions for kitchen appliances, instructions for using canning jars, promotional pamphlets, and even family correspondence. In contrast to the handwritten "receipt books" of an earlier time, Americans in the twentieth century were likely to stuff recipe clippings and miscellaneous consumer information haphazardly into published, bound cookbooks. They would be more likely to sort through commercially published sources and clip recipes that caught their eye, rather than painstakingly recording recipes in long hand into blank books. They would also be far more likely to find recipes in promotional sources, in addition to or instead of from friends and family.

Some items offered even more information about how cookbook owners used recipe books for a variety of purposes. Just as cookbook owners did not uniformly accept strange and lurid casserole recipes, they did not uniformly embrace the growing emphasis on gourmet meals. A grocery list and a scribbled recipe found in James Beard's gourmet tome *The Fireside Cookbook* revealed an owner who still depended on simple American dishes far removed from Beard's steak tartare and vindaloo recipes. The grocery list included eggs, bacon, milk, lettuce, ground beef, a can of onion soup, noodles, and ice cream. The book also contained a recipe for a simple Jell-O salad that definitely would not have appeared on Beard's table. Like many practiced recipe recorders, the transcriber of this recipe did not include elaborate directions, but got right to the point:

Jello
Add 1 / 4 cup boiling H2O
Add ice cream (liquid), 1 pt fruit
Ice box 25–30 minutes.

The owner also included a recipe torn out of a domestic magazine that gave step-by-step instructions for perfect gravy, but she obviously found the instructions confusing. She added notes to herself in the margin: "Milk gravy use milk instead of potatoes," "1/4 cup flour and 1/4 cup fat + 2 cups cold water makes for 6–8 people." At the bottom of page she wrote "Use liquid cold then stir out lumps of flour in it. Then simmer five minutes." Though she owned Beard's book, and presumably used it enough to find it a handy place for recipe storage, this person did not strictly adhere to Beard's idea of fine food. She served bacon and eggs, noodle casseroles made with onion soup, ice cream for dessert, and Jell-O salad—and gravy seemed somewhat daunting to her.

Many authors simply made a check mark or some other kind of small mark next to recipes. Unless they added additional comments, we cannot know if these marks mean "tried once and liked," "tried," "want to try," or "don't try again." But sometimes owners included both a check and a comment. The woman who used *Cooking for Two*, a 1950s revision of an extremely popular early twentieth-century classic by Janet McKenzie Hill, checked a variety of beverages, cakes, and different sandwich fillings. She checked the cheese omelet recipe but noted that it "Needs a full hour"—she evidently meant to try it again. The baked apple dumpling recipe received a check mark but also the cryptic comment "poor." White sauce and potato recipes found more favor.[56] Individual likes and dislikes showed up in such markings. The owner of the *Woman's Day Collector's Cook Book* must have liked pecans, because she checked recipes for Southern pecan pie, chocolate pecan pie, butterscotch pecan roll, and Southern chicken with pecans.[57] Cookbook owners, though not given to lengthy comments, did feel free to employ some kind of reference system that made sense to them, and to change recipes to fit the needs of their own kitchen. For example, the person who owned a copy of the 1951 *Better Homes and Gardens Cook Book* pasted a pie recipe clipped from a newspaper into the cookbook—but wrote in the margin that this particular pie recipe required a different heat seating in her own oven.

In fact, the owner of this cookbook did not use it entirely as *Better Homes and Gardens* intended. The magazine's editors designed their cookbook to hold neatly the recipes they printed in a certain format every month, but the owner seems to have entirely ignored this intended function of the cookbook and simply pasted in her own clipped recipes in blank spaces and on chapter dividers. However, she did once refer to another *Better Homes and Gardens* publication. Beside a nut bread recipe she wrote "Glazed Lemon Nut Bread p. 275 BH&G Encyclopedia vol. 2." She used her cookbooks as a whole set of reference books, and cross-referenced them when necessary. A copy of the 1951 *Peggy Put the Kettle On* contained a similar cross-reference. This cookbook owner left especially thorough notes to herself, indicating the date she tried a certain recipe and often an additional comment on the recipe. Next to a recipe for Swiss steak, she wrote, "A much superior recipe for swiss [*sic*] steak is found in *The Joy of Cooking*." For many, as this comment suggests, Rombauer's kitchen bible remained the undisputed champ. But, this woman added, she found the Swiss steak recipe in *Peggy* "easy to make" and noted that it could be "prepared well ahead of time and reheating increases the flavor." She dated her entry 3 November 1953. This cookbook owner did not hesitate to improve on the book's recipes or to leave herself careful reminders. On the same page as the Swiss steak recipe, next to a recipe for roast beef, she wrote "3–10–53 Better when salt and pepper is rubbed into the meat. Cheaper grades need cloves of garlic stuck hither and yon."[58] A note next to the recipe title indicated that this recipe appeared often on her table. She characterized this recipe as, simply, the "Usual standby."

For the owner of this cookbook, some of the recipes seemed to function as checkpoints, where she could remind herself of a cooking time or an ingredient needed for "the usual standbys." Next to a recipe for soft-cooked eggs, she wrote "As always" and dated it 1 November 1953. And a chicken salad recipe received the note "Good. The old standby," dated 5 December 1953. A recipe for chocolate icing received what, in the 1950s, must have seemed like high praise: "12–14–61 Good. Tastes like a packaged frosting." Indeed, like many cookbook users, she paid particular attention to the recipes for cakes, cookies, and icing, and marked the mocha and orange icings as especially good. That section of the cookbook bears stains and traces of much use. But writing in her cookbook also served as a reminder of the recipes that didn't work. On 20 February 1953, she found the English peach pie recipe "Soggyish. A little too sweet. Fair." A recipe for spaghetti and meatballs (a simple combination of tomato paste, water, sugar, salt, pepper, onion, which required a cooking time of two hours) failed to make a good impression on the cookbook user: "Too time consuming rather ordinary," she wrote in an entry marked 2 December 1961. In an entry that demonstrated that not all housewives in the 1950s enjoyed making strange sticky salads, she expressed her distaste for a frozen fruit salad recipe comprised of heavy cream, mayonnaise, and one can of fruit cocktail: "We do not like frozen mayonnaise," she tersely commented on 21 January 1954. And she tried to improve (or perhaps kill) the flavor of a "Tutti-Frutti" frozen pudding dessert ("Good but not great") by crossing out "sherry wine" in the list of ingredients and writing in "Southern Comfort" on 13 March 1953.

Cookbooks functioned in practical ways for women in the 1950s. Cookbook owners sought out easy, reliable recipes, and if they discovered ways to improve those dishes, they might have made a note in the margin to remind themselves. Cookbooks also served in lieu of a recipe folder or box, providing a convenient place for owners to store recipes they gathered from the newspaper or magazines, or from friends. The owner of a 1958 copy of *Thoughts for Buffets* wrote numerous recipes in blank spaces in the book and credited them to other women: Iris's chicken salad, Phyllis's crab casserole, Frannie's cream puffs, and a brown rice recipe from Edna Mae, for example. The owner also used the book to store recipes clipped from the *San Francisco Examiner* and the *Oakland Tribune*, a typewritten recipe for applesauce cake from her friend Olivia, and a recipe for "Fiesta Rolls" from a newsletter for hospital volunteers. If a woman enjoyed collecting recipes or trying new recipes, she might very well have stored them within the pages of a handy cookbook. Cookbooks resided in an easily locatable place, although we cannot know how many recipes this cookbook owner actually used from *Thoughts for Buffets*, it does seem likely that the book had a permanent place in her kitchen and that it did play a role in her daily life.

Women left traces in their cookbooks of how they used and responded to the recipes. Many women may have skipped lengthy introductions, meal planning hints, and preachy nutritional sections, turning quickly to the actual recipes and searching for a reliable cookie recipe or an easily prepared main dish. But many must have read over the kitchen and cookery advice more carefully, or dreamily read through entire cookbooks searching for ideas, inspiration, and considering the many culinary possibilities found within every recipe book. If a woman enjoyed cooking, she might submit a recipe to the newspaper women's pages or the Pillsbury Bake-Off. The recipes found in those locations often emphasized simple foods, using name-brand products and premade ingredients, but they also showed the creativity and good taste of numerous amateur cooks from all over the United States. What remains more obscure, however, is how the ideology posited by postwar cookbooks entered or failed to enter into women's daily cooking tasks. Readers left little or no evidence about how they responded to the writing before, after, and between the recipes. And such writing proliferated in postwar cookbooks, as authors, editors, and corporations strove to make their book a unique addition to a bloated market. Whether their readers responded directly or not, many of these cookbook producers did not stop at merely printing recipes but imbued their cookery instruction with advice and messages on the larger meaning of home cooking. And they aimed their advice—as they had for decades—at middle-class female consumers.

Eating and cooking changed in the United States during the postwar years, with diets increasingly dominated by processed food, and food fashion dictating "fun" and "unusual" types of dishes. Cookbooks re-flected those trends and illustrated the way such changes seemed to require new instruction. A 1955 review pointed to a variety of practical reasons that cookbooks sold so well during the postwar era: "As the American standard of living moves farther above the fatback and hom-iny grits level, as pressure cookers, deep freezes, rotisseries, mixers, and barbecue pits multiply, as domestic servants get rarer, as interest in foreign culture increases, and as labor-saving devices allow the house-wife to devote herself more to the esthetically satisfying parts of house-work, cookbooks will be more and more in demand."[59] New appliances, fewer paid cooks, and growing interest in foreign food demanded new recipes. But cookbooks fulfilled another role as well: they instructed Americans on the proper social roles for men and women. Cookbooks persisted in emphasizing that men and women had to be understood as entirely different when it came to cooking and eating. Authors and editors persisted in layering ideology and rhetoric about gender on top of their recipes. They persisted in defining masculinity and femi-ninity via cooking and eating. Just as they had in 1920s and 1930s cookbooks, men in 1950s cookbooks preferred hearty meat-and-potato dishes, whereas women preferred to nibble on a dainty salad. Just as they had in 1920s and 1930s cookbooks, men in 1950s cookbooks en-joyed natural prowess and creativity at the stove, whereas women pro-duced stodgy, boring everyday meals.

9

"King of the Kitchen"

FOOD AND COOKERY

INSTRUCTION FOR MEN

Although they never sold quite as well as the dependable white models, kitchen appointments in aqua, light green, pale yellow, and hot pink represented the very latest in household fashion during the 1950s.[1] As Levittowns grew, as consumers rushed to buy the major household goods that had been unavailable during the war, and as all of America embraced the new push-button possibilities of the Space Age, decorators turned their attention to the food preparation area and kitchen colors bloomed. But even as an increasingly open floor plan made the kitchen a less isolated part of the middle-class home, pink refrigerators and stoves reinforced the gender boundaries around daily meal preparation. House planners and appliance manufacturers meant the brightly colored and sleekly modern look of the ideal 1950s kitchen to appeal to the woman of the family: a pink stove top clearly signaled a women-only space. But pastel kitchen appliances notwithstanding, cookery instruction for men expanded and proliferated during the postwar era. In the late 1940s and 1950s, cookbooks and recipes intended for men emphasized the same things as did earlier instruction: the differences in male and female food preferences and the creativity of the man at the stove (especially when compared with women's bland and uninspired cooking). Recipes for men, like similar recipes published in the 1920s and 1930s, employed pointedly masculine rhetoric. Authors compared cooking to sports, for example, and called for suitably masculine types of cooking, such as barbecuing. Authors and editors of cookbooks and recipes for men made sure to underscore the *manliness* of their cookery directions and of the man in the kitchen.

Consumers snapped up stoves and mixers in decidedly feminine colors, but in an ideal postwar suburban home, the man of the family had his food preparation space as well: the backyard barbecue.[2] No food fashion during the postwar years so clearly illustrated how gender continued to shape food preparation as backyard barbecuing. Barbecues combined the two central aspects of gendered rhetoric around food: both the *kinds of food* and the *type of cooking* that a man did over a barbecue differed markedly from the daily food prepared by women over sleek new aqua stoves. Barbecuing required, first and foremost, meat. That alone marked the territory as male. Postwar cookbooks constantly linked men and meat, as had prewar instruction, and home grills provided the perfect conduit for meat cooking. "Man's Job: Steak," began the section on outdoor cookery in *The Picture Cook Book* (fig. 17).

Figure 17 "Man's Job: Steak," declared the editors of the *Picture Cook Book*. Here, a man presided over a special indoor charcoal grill. *Picture Cook Book* (New York: Time, 1958).

The editors asserted that "Whenever the menu calls for a delicate dish or a fancy pie, most men are more than happy to let their wives take care of the cooking. When it's a matter of steak, this tolerant attitude is replaced by an unassailable belief in masculine know-how. Steak is a man's job."[3] Because "Men Like Meat" (as Beth McLean titled her chapter on meat cookery in *Modern Homemaker's Cookbook*), that made them natural meat cookers; it made steak "a man's job."[4]

Instruction aimed at backyard barbecuing assured the reader that men would excel at cooking meat over an open fire simply because of the innate male preference for meat. In a chapter on outdoor cookery, the editors of *The General Foods Kitchens Cook Book* established the primal connection between men and meat. They described a caveman, millions of years ago, enjoying a saber-tooth-tiger steak that accidentally fell into the fire. Amazed by how good the roasted meat tastes, he grunts for his wife, who comes running. But she criticizes his discovery, saying: "It tastes okay, but why didn't you put it on a forked stick, so it wouldn't get all over ashes?" Caveman replies: "All right, you're so smart—*you* do it next time." The editors concluded this little myth by commenting: "And it's been that way ever since: Men continue to be inspired and resourceful cooks—and women continue to do most of the cooking."[5] General Foods reminded women readers that since the dawn of time, since the beginning of cooking itself, women had been responsible for "most of the cooking," but men nonetheless belonged by the fire cooking meat.

Outdoor cookery demanded masculine prowess not simply because meat most often appeared on backyard menus, but because barbecuing required working over an open fire, reminiscent of hunting trips and Boy Scout campouts. Marguerite McCarthy included a chapter on outdoor cooking in her 1954 cookbook *The Queen Is in the Kitchen* that began with an assertion about man's place by the grill: "This chapter should be labeled 'For Men Only.' To my way of thinking, no member of the gentler sex can appear at her best lugging wood for a fire or stooping over it to give a final poke. This is strictly a man's department and should be turned over to him." The author of a 1958 cookbook agreed with McCarthy's assertion that men belonged by the barbecue: "Of course, when it comes to outdoor cooking, I think the women should withdraw to the sunny side of the porch, and let the men have carte blanche at the barbecue." The editors of *Good Housekeeping* also assigned men outdoor grilling activities. In a regular feature that had step-by-step instructional photographs of a different recipe each month, a man's hands made a guest appearance in its 1946 cooking lesson "The Man of the House Barbecues Chicken."[6]

"Cooking over charcoal is a man's job and should have no interference from the distaff side of the family," wrote Helen Evans Brown and James Beard in *The Cookout Book*, published in 1961. "If the man of the house *prefers* to have his wife do the cooking, just skip the whole idea of doing it outdoors. Nothing makes a man look—and we should think, feel—more henpecked than to have his wife officiate at the cookout. And if she happens to be wearing pants at the time, one reaches the obvious conclusion."[7] Beard and Brown did not mean their advice to be taken completely seriously—after all, Brown had an extremely successful career as the maven of California cooking and Beard's exuberant personality did not even approach macho. Still, the recipes in this cookbook came from male-only cookout contests. And when the authors humorously suggested that only a henpecked man allowed his wife to take over the backyard barbecue, they touched on a long-standing association between masculinity and cooking slabs of meat over a roaring fire. As the author of an essay on outdoor cookery in the 1953 edition of *Esquire's Handbook for Hosts* wrote: "A woman presiding over a barbecue grill looks as incongruous as a man engaged in doing a trifle of lacy tatting."[8] Cookery books implied that it seemed only *natural* that men presided over the backyard barbecue, even if the man of the house never did any other kind of cooking. And if a man ventured into the kitchen, he might insist that a built-in fireplace grill be added to the kitchen appointments—as did the subject of a 1958 article in *American Home* entitled "Why Can't a Woman Cook Like a Man?"[9]

The accoutrements to outdoor cookery reinforced its masculine nature. Barbecues required large aprons with cartoon pictures or witty sayings, very different from the practical plastic aprons the woman of the house tied around her waist.[10] Barbecuing also called for a whole different set of cooking implements not found in the kitchen: large tongs, pronged forks, and fire starters all marked outdoor cookery as a clearly different kind of cooking than the daily meal preparation done by females. Authors also reinforced the boundaries between male and female cookery by noting that at cookout time, the woman of the house should provide the salads, drinks, desserts, condiments, eating utensils, napkins, and any other accompaniments to the meat main dish that the man prepared over the fire—in short, that women should remain in charge of all other cooking. For example, in "He's an Outdoor Chef," published in *Parents' Magazine* in 1956, writer Loyce Hargrove asserted that in her marriage she assumed all domestic duties: "Part of our happily-married-life philosophy has been that the house is mine to see to. No floor-scrubbing husband mine!" That extended, she explained, to certain cooking duties when her husband Raymond barbecued. "So when Raymond becomes an outdoor chef I do whatever advance preparations is required," she wrote. Those preparations included marinating the meat, making raw vegetable appetizers, cutting up and assembling the vegetable kebabs, making a tossed green salad, preparing corn on the cob for roasting, and cooking a peach topping for the ice cream dessert.[11] Not exactly a "night off" for mother.

If some cookbooks intimated that men restrict their cooking adventures to the barbecue, others such as *That Man in the Kitchen* did not hesitate to praise the prowess of men at the stove. The 1950s saw a marked increase in the by-men-and-for-men cookbooks that began to appear in the 1920s and 1930s. This reflected, in part, the increase in the publication of all kinds of cookbooks after World War II—and the desire of publishers to hit upon a popular specialty cookbook. Like their predecessors, cookbooks for men published in the 1950s often included more prose and less instruction than cookbooks for women and usually skipped the step-by-step directions for marketing, stocking one's pantry, setting the table, and learning basic nutrition that general cookbooks offered. Instruction for men often appeared in an almost novel-like format, including travel anecdotes, personal reminiscences, and lengthy essays on cuisine and fine dining.

From 1946 to 1960 at least thirteen cookbooks intended for men appeared in the United States, including Brick Gordon's 1947 *The Groom Boils and Stews*, Fletcher Pratt and Robeson Bailey's *A Man and His Meals* also published in 1947, Glenn Quilty's 1954 *Food for Men*, and Robert Loeb's *Wolf in Chef's Clothing*, first published in 1950 and revised in 1958. A preeminent magazine for men, *Esquire*, published a cookbook in 1955 and the well-known restaurateur "Trader Vic" (Victor Bergeron) authored at least two cookbooks during this period: *Trader Vic's Book of Food and Drink* in 1946 and *Trader Vic's Kitchen Kibitzer* in 1952. Comedian Lew Lehr tried his hand at recipe writing in *Lew Lehr's Cook Book for Men* in 1949. Although not intended solely for male readers, "The Mystery Chef" published another cookbook in 1949 (after sales of his first cookbook topped 180,000) that shared many of the same characteristics as recipe books for men. A revised edition of Arthur H. Deute's *200 Dishes for Men*, originally published in 1944, was reissued in 1953 under the title *The Man's Cookbook*. Morrison Wood collected recipes from his travels in a 1949 cookbook entitled *With a Jug of Wine*. Another well-traveled man, Frank Dorn, assembled recipes and reminiscences in his 1953 *The Dorn Cookbook*. *Sunset* magazine compiled recipes from its long-running cooking-by-men column, "Chefs of the West," in a 1951 cookbook by the same name, and again in a 1957 cookbook entitled *Cooking Bold and Fearless*.[12] And at least two books intended specifically for the young male reader—Helen Evans and Philip S. Brown's 1959 *The Boys' Cookbook* and *The First Book of Boys' Cooking*, by Jerrold Biem, published in 1957—appeared as well.[13]

Did men really read or use these cookbooks? Such books did sell briskly. And the regular appearance of cookbooks for men on the new book list indicates that publishers believed that cookery instruction for men found a reliable market in the 1950s. Some bookstore owners also targeted men when promoting cookbooks during the 1950s.[14] Contests for men, such as the regular feature in *Sunset* magazine and the cook-outs described by Beard and Brown (and the undeniable popularity of backyard grills in the suburbs), suggest that men continued to try their hand at the kinds of cooking most frequently designated as masculine, such as grilling meat and tossing green salads. But of the cookbooks for men that I examined, only a few had check marks or any sign of use. The owner of a copy of *Wolf in Chef's Clothing*, dissatisfied with Loeb's vague cooking times, wrote in "20 minutes" next to a recipe for fried chicken. One page in a copy of Morrison Wood's cookbook that gives a recipe for roast pheasant with brandied orange stuffing bears signs of use. And an inscription dated 5 November 1956, in Glenn Quilty's *Food for Men* demonstrated one reader's belief in male culinary superiority: "Good Eating, my son," it reads. "The best cooks are men . . ." Because many of the cookbooks for men published in the 1950s offered humor, personal reminiscences, and life philosophy, perhaps Americans gave them as gifts or read them straight through as often or more often than they used them to cook. Cookbooks for men often did not function as manuals in everyday kitchens at the individual level: they did not hold clipped recipes or notes to the regular user as did more general cookbooks intended for women readers. Instead, cookbooks for men did share certain other qualities.

For example, several authors of recipe books for men mentioned that their wives' departure from the kitchen to seek employment during World War II necessitated cooking education for the man of the house. Gourmand Morrison Wood explained that while he made a hobby of cooking for the first eighteen years of his marriage, only when his wife and their cook left for the munitions factory did he feel compelled to cook on a daily basis: "Then World War II came along, and the Little Woman, burning with a desire to do her part, went into war work. She left the apartment each day at eight o'clock, and returned between five and six, completely frazzled. Our cook departed about the same time, correctly figuring that sixty dollars a week in a war plant was a hell of a lot more hay than slaving at the Maison Wood for fifteen dollars a week. Naturally, it doesn't take any I.Q. at all to guess who was left holding the bag!"[15] Wood's 1949 cookbook evidently meant to pass along the wisdom Wood had attained during this wartime emergency. Similarly, comedian Lew Lehr prefaced his cookbook with a remark on the relative newness of cookery instruction for men. He asserted that when women migrated from the kitchen during the war, men learned a great deal about cooking: "What progress Father has made in the kitchen since Mother hung up her skillet for a billet in the WACS!" Lehr also contrasted his own cooking knowledge with that of his father, who "could have starved to death right next to a pound of butter, a dozen eggs, and a frying pan."[16]

But, contrary to his belief that the war ushered in a whole new era of cookery by men, Lehr's assertions about his culinary ability strongly echoed prewar cooking instruction for men. In contrast to women's cooking, many authors and editors insisted, men approached the kitchen with creativity and natural flair. Men cooked unusual, tasty dishes, and favored hearty recipes with a minimum of "fuss." Men-only recipes also used quite a different tone—one that reinforced the masculinity of the intended audience. One product promotional cookbook, for example, contained a section entitled "Special Recipes" intended for the "amateur male cook." In this section, the recipes suddenly assumed a hearty "Just us guys" voice. A recipe called "Wieners Royale" (hot dogs stuffed with cheese and wrapped in bacon) gave especially macho instructions. The authors recommended that the male cook choose truly masculine hot dogs: "But let's start with husky, meat-filled Franks—none of the puny, anemic, cereal stuffed dogs will do." They offered equally testosterone-infused directions for slicing the hot dog and stuffing it with cheese: "With a sharp knife incise lengthwise about halfway through your Frankfurter, and press from both ends to make the gaping wound grin at you." They also offered manly serving suggestions: after broiling the wieners, they instructed, "pop a sizzling Frank into the bun. Pull out toothpicks, slosh with mustard to taste, clamp both pieces of the bun together, and fling your lips over as delicious a dish as Hebe ever served on Olympus."[17]

Adjectives such as "husky" and verbs such as "slosh," "clamp," and "fling," indicated that the fainthearted need not undertake this recipe. Men writing for other men used these kinds of adjectives freely throughout, imbuing cooking with a casual, fun-loving, and manly air not found in general commercial instruction. "Mix the ingredients in a jar, tighten the cap, and shake like hell," read Trader Vic's recipe for wine vinegar dressing.[18] Brick Gordon, the author of *The Groom Boils and Stews*, noted that one could easily roll out biscuits with a beer bottle rather than a wimpy rolling pin. He also called for a "man-sized lump of butter" to fry eggs. And no women's cookbook would have included recipes for "Spanked Baby Dressing" (a pink mixture of catsup and cream) or "Sweater Girl Salad" (chilled peach halves filled with cottage cheese, placed upside down on lettuce leaves and topped with a maraschino cherry).[19]

Recipes for men often gave vague measurements and cooking times, presumably because men simply did not need the more regimented instructions found in women's recipes. When Jack Bailey, emcee of *Queen for a Day*, included a recipe for pork roast in his 1949 *What's Cookin*,' he offered few explicit directions: "Cover it tightly and go sit down. Get up once in a while and turn it. When nice and brown and done, get up again and serve it. Then sit down again and eat it." Malcolm LaPrade suggested that baking a cake took approximately the same amount of time it took to wash a dog: begin washing a small dog when you put the cake in the oven, he counseled, and when the dog emerges clean, the cake will be done. The structure of the recipes themselves reiterated this casual approach, often forgoing a preliminary list of measured ingredients. Unlike the carefully composed complete menus and minute-by-minute instructions in general cookbooks, those for men often gave very casual suggestions for both serving and creating a dish. Lew Lehr directly contrasted what he perceived as the male and female approaches to recipes when he described a supposedly true incident in his kitchen. His daughter invited over a passel of her college friends and they gathered in the kitchen to watch Chef Lehr make a piecrust. As he attempted to explain the process, they vehemently protested his casual technique:

> "Wait a minute," said a bass-voiced platinum blonde, at my left shoulder. "What was that handful of flour and that extra squirt of water you just threw in? ...
>
> "Well," I fumbled sheepishly, "it didn't feel right, so I had to add—"
>
> "It didn't feel right?" they shrieked in unison. "How do you know when it 'feels right?' What kind of recipe is that?"[20]

Unable to comprehend the more spontaneous cooking of a masculine natural at the pastry board, the girls fled the kitchen, presumably in search of Fannie Farmer's inflexible piecrust recipe.

References to sports and hobbies provided the authors of cookbooks for men with another linguistic way to distinguish their type of recipes from those in general cookbooks aimed at female readers. Like cookery instruction for men in the 1920s and 1930s, 1950s cookbooks for men often drew on sports metaphors or made pointed comparisons between a man's culinary habit and other masculine hobbies. "Good cooking, like sailing a boat or building a house, takes a lot of attention," advised Fletcher Pratt and Robeson Bailey in the 1947 *A Man and His Meals*. Brick Gordon made a similar comparison: "Cooking, like building a bridge or shooting a game of pool, takes practice." And in a passage on cooking equipment, Gordon again drew the parallel: "A skilled carpenter or mechanic would not think of plying his trade without adequate tools. The same holds for a good cook."[21] Two cookbooks intended for the young male reader also emphasized how cookery should be viewed as a manly interest akin to sports. The Browns included a whole chapter on fish and game cookery in their 1959 cookbook for boys. Jerry Biem, author of *The First Book of Boys' Cooking*, characterized cooking as an entirely masculine hobby. "You know how enjoyable it is to use a hammer and other tools to build something out of wood. Or perhaps you enjoy making pictures, using brushes with paint, and, of course paper to draw on," he began. He then drew a parallel between these activities and cooking: "Cooking is very much like building or drawing. Instead of a hammer or brush your tools are pots, pans, spoons, bowls, and mixers. Instead of wood or paint the materials you put together are meats, vegetables, eggs, seasonings, and other food."

Biem also cautioned his reader to proceed through these recipes slowly, again drawing a parallel between cooking and other hobbies: "When a person learns how to do carpentry work he doesn't start by building a house. The same applies to cooking. Begin with a recipe that looks simple to you." He noted that "Like carpentry, painting, science, or sports, cooking has special language all its own," and he listed the ingredients in each recipe under the heading "Line-Up." Like the Browns, Biem included a chapter on "Cooking the Fish You Catch." And in a recipe for hamburgers, Biem instructed the reader to "Take some of the chopped beef in your hand, as if you were making a medium-sized snowball."[22] According to Biem, cooking was an extension of other hobbies a boy might wish to pursue.

Cookbooks of compiled man-created recipes (especially recipes collected or authored by famous men) continued to proliferate. Trader Vic, a celebrity himself, included a whole chapter of recipes attributed to other famous men in *Trader Vic's Kitchen Kibitzer*. Jack Bailey and Lew Lehr capitalized on their own fame when they authored cookbooks, and Lehr included fifty recipes from men like Fred Allen and Dale Carnegie. Domestic magazines followed suit and published recipes such as Broadway actor Walter Slezak's cherry ham.[23] But *Sunset* magazine provided perhaps the most widely read collection of men's recipes during the 1950s. Each month the magazine featured man-created recipes selected from reader entries. The "Chefs of West" column mailed a chef's hat to every man whose recipe the magazine printed. The popular feature generated two cookbooks in the 1950s, and a revised edition of *Cooking Bold and Fearless* in 1967. The long-standing popularity of the column indicated that a small but vocal percentage of American men (on the West Coast at least) possessed enough interest in cooking to keep *Sunset* supplied with a steady stream of recipes and to keep *Sunset*'s cookbooks for men selling briskly.

But not all recipes attributed to individual men in cookery books lauded male culinary accomplishment. Roy Ald edited a cookbook in 1949 composed entirely of recipes from male actors, popular singers, and celebrities, but many of the recipes in Ald's collection came from the favorite restaurants of the celebrity. Thus Cary Grant's recipe for oysters Rockefeller and Basil Rathbone's preparation instructions for Indian curry came not from their own kitchens but from those of their favorite professional chef. Numerous other contributors gave recipes credited to their wives, mothers, or cooks: Frank Sinatra praised Nancy's lasagna, Benny Goodman rhapsodized over his wife's fluffy omelet with smoked herring, and Jimmy Durante gave a recipe for his mother's custard. Roy Rogers made his own stew and John Wayne cooked his own hamburgers, but, of course, cowboy stew and meaty hamburgers constituted perfectly masculine dishes. Most of the celebrities in Ald's collection seemed unfamiliar with the kitchen.[24]

Even when cookbooks admitted that many men had little cooking experience, authors usually emphasized that men would take naturally to cooking—if only simple, tasty meals fit for male appetites. As Trader Vic counseled: "I maintain that it is just as important for a man to know how to cook as it is for a woman. I don't mean that he has to know how to bake a cake—although it wouldn't hurt him—but he should know how to roast meat, cook a steak, make a salad, and get a few good meals together."[25] He went on to urge his readers to buy cookbooks, read them, and learn from them. Naturally, his cookbook would address this information gap. So would Rob Loeb's *Wolf in Chef's Clothing*, published in 1950. Loeb, food and drinks editor for *Esquire* magazine, explained in the introduction to *Wolf in Chef's Clothing* that his cookbook could help fill a lamentable void in male culinary knowledge: "The purpose of this book is to enfranchise the male, to unshackle him from the role of refrigerator vulture, icebox scavenger, from being a parasitic gourmet forced to feed on the leftovers of female cookery. Instead, he can become a gustatory eagle, king of the kitchen and baron of the bar."[26]

Loeb's cookbook exemplified another trend in cookery instruction for men, one that had been less evident in earlier books. Post–World War II cookbooks for men regularly mentioned the seductive powers of a man in the kitchen. Indeed, Loeb's stated purpose in *Wolf in Chef's Clothing* was to provide recipes for bachelors interested in wooing women with the aid of home-cooked meals (fig. 18). Although satirical to a certain extent, the author also intended to provide practical cooking instruction to the amateur bachelor cook. To that end, his recipes

Figure 18 Cookbooks for men in the 1950s often pointed out how readers could employ cookery to seduce women. In this illustration from *Wolf in Chef's Clothing*, the wolf-chef contemplates which type of woman he plans to woo with a particular menu. Robert Loeb, *Wolf in Chef's Clothing* (Chicago: Wilcox and Follett, 1950).

consisted of simple drawings rather than lengthy written direction. Helmut Ripperger cattily remarked that *Wolf in Chef's Clothing* represented "an excellent example of how not to write or publish a cookery book," but the book sold enough copies to warrant a 1958 revision and to inspire a 1952 version for single females aiming to catch a man.[27] Loeb's book contained numerous cocktail recipes, appetizers ("Gastronomic Foreplay"), simple main dishes and salads, and breakfasts to appease either her conscience or one's own. He also suggested four different menus to woo four different types of females: steak and potatoes for the athletic girl, lamb chops and salad for the "round and fluffy" indoor type, spaghetti and coleslaw for the intellectual type, and fried chicken for "3 Bs" (brains, bonds, and beauty).[28]

Although Loeb made perhaps the most blatant connection between cooking and courtship, other authors also offered recipes for the culinary-minded bachelor. "There is an old saying, 'The way to a man's heart is through his stomach,'" began Eliot Elifson in his 1948 cookbook. But "ladies may also be won this way," he advised. After describing how a rich and eligible bachelor lost his chance with a gorgeous blonde because of culinary fumbling, Morrison Wood reminded the reader that "cooking offers a new and better approach than that time-worn gag, 'How would you like to come up and see my etchings?'" Malcolm LaPrade asserted that "the bachelor or widower who cultivates the culinary art is a potential Don Juan who will outstrip all competitors in the quest for popularity with the fair sex." He also described how a cozy home-cooked meal could impress a potential conquest: "How much better it is to entertain a lady in one's own home than in a crowded and noisy restaurant. A man looks his best in a long white apron, and he will so arrange the dinner hour that the lady will arrive while he is still at work in the kitchen. She will join him there and be impressed by his nonchalant manner of handling a broiler or porterhouse steak." Similarly, Ken Kling, a contributor to Lew Lehr's collection, confided that his pancake recipe had ensnared his wife-to-be. And Harry Botsford, in a 1947 article for *Woman's Home Companion* related an almost identical story about an artist who won over a woman with a goulash recipe. Botsford wrote that the artist's wife "insists that there were other factors involved in the final marriage agreement." But, he added, "all I can say is that his goulash has a quality, a memorable, rich and satisfying taste so distinctive that I can realize it might well break down the natural reserve of a career gal who had firmly decided not to marry." The seductive possibilities of goulash and pancakes also applied to teenage girls, according to the Browns in *The Boys' Cook Book:* "You know the old gag about 'the way to a man's heart is through his stomach?' Don't kid yourself that that doesn't go for the girls, too. Just try out one of your best dishes on the one who has been playing hard to get—you may be surprised!" Even the philosophical M. F. K. Fisher wrote on men, cooking, and courtship in the "B is for Bachelors" chapter of her 1949 *An Alphabet for Gourmets*.[29] In postwar cookbooks, men regularly swept women off their feet by romancing them with a little homemade supper or a superbly mixed cocktail.

But more than any other shared characteristic, cookery instruction for men in the 1950s consistently emphasized that men naturally possessed the ability to cook more creatively and with better results than women (fig. 19). As in the 1920s and 1930s, recipes by and for men made male cookery skills a central theme. The editors of *Chefs of the West*, for example, praised the male contributors for adventurous cooking spirit: "These men exercise the pioneering virtues of enterprise and ingenuity. They grate cheese in the meat grinder; barbecue over coals formed from grape shoots, orange or pure wood; broil salmon Indian fashion; make "orange" marmalade from Rangpur limes. They take on the listless zucchini, penetrate to its deeply hidden qualities, and elevate it to a place of honor at the table. To impart ginger flavor, they add ginger ale to a bubbling pot."[30] A man's ability to forgo recipes and exact measurements seemed worthy of high praise to Ralph Town as well. In his interview in *The American Home* article "Why Can't a Woman Cook Like a Man?" he stated: "I honestly think [men] have a greater feeling for food than women. Most women (my wife not

Figure 19 Recipes for men often featured exotic ingredients, such as the fresh coconut and chutney in this article from *American Home.* Aleks Bird, "There's a Man in the Kitchen," *American Home,* June 1949.

included) have reduced food to a science, measuring this, weighing that, afraid that if they let their imagination look up from a recipe they'll have nothing but a sorry mess on their hands. Men, on the other hand, are given to tasting things as they go along, letting their palate be their guide. As a rule they're adventurous, willing to take chances, like to live a little."[31] As in the 1920s and 1930s, 1950s cookery instruction for men constantly compared male free-handed adventures in the kitchen with women's hesitant, cookbook-bound culinary habits. Not for ladies Rangpur limes and rare herbs! No, women leaned on their cookbook crutches, whereas men took chances and "lived a little" in the kitchen.

When the editors of *Esquire,* an aggressively masculine magazine aimed at a middle- and upper-class audience, published a cookbook in 1955, they criticized "cooking by the book." They implied that their male readers could rely more on innate good taste than a formulaic (and feminine) recipe: "We don't want to take away from Fanny Farmer [*sic*] and the other pioneers who brought science into the kitchen, but we'd like to bet that you'll make out all right if you trust your taste buds— even when your measuring spoons are at half mast."[32] Such advice might well apply to *anyone* interested in learning how to be comfortable in the kitchen, but male cookery advice in the 1950s often asserted that women—either by nature or by habit—simply could not "trust their taste buds" in the kitchen. Indeed, the 1950s saw an increase in such cookbook rhetoric. Even more regularly than in the prewar period, cookbooks for and by men insisted not only that men made inspired and excellent cooks, but that women prepared dull and tasteless daily meals.

For example, the *Robertshaw Measured Heat Cook Book* utilized "cave man" imagery to describe man's natural superiority at the fire or the stove: "Although kitchens are women's realm by right of eminent domain, many men invade these sacred precincts, and by daring exploration, produce epicurean dishes. The first invasion probably occurred when Mister Stonehatchet growled about the way Madam Stonehatchet cooked the dinosaur steak and she replied, 'If you think you can do any better . . .' Like all his sex, Stonehatchet was a pushover for that line of chatter, and shoving her away from the fire, he probably doused the dinosaur steak with a handful of wild onions. Thus the first chef was created." The editors went on to caution that their recipes intended for the male reader "need not be followed slavishly. Toss tradition out the window, accelerate your imagination, and you'll create inspired masterpieces that will thrill your taste buds."[33] Again, women's taste buds simply could not cope with adventurous meals—and had been unable to cope since dinosaurs roamed the earth.

In cookbooks for men, authors often felt it necessary to point out women's shortcomings in the kitchen. Brick Gordon described his strawberry pie recipe as "Not the kind Mother used to make, but the kind Mother use to try to make and wonder why she couldn't."[34] Perhaps mother had relied too much on magazines or everyday cookbooks for her recipes. Several authors of cookery instruction for men in the 1950s insisted that recipes in domestic magazines, general cookbooks, and promotional booklets accounted for much of the drab and unappetizing food produced in women's kitchens. Malcolm LaPrade asserted that for men, "a contempt for routine recipes is second nature," and went on to criticize women's cookbooks for producing such "routine recipes: "Thousands of cook books have been written for women, and innumerable women's magazines regularly publish pages of recipes, elaborately illustrated in color. Women are especially susceptible to color and many of them, I regret to say, are more concerned with the appearance of a meal than with its taste. Nothing is so pleasing to the average housewife, when entertaining 'the girls' at a bridge luncheon, as to place something upon the table which defies recognition. No words of praise are so welcome as: 'My dear, it's perfectly stunning! But what on earth is it?' " LaPrade included two parodic recipes to illustrate his point: a casserole containing pimento, mayonnaise, salmon, avocado, green pepper, chili sauce, tarragon vinegar, sardines, cauliflower, and anchovies, and a Jell-O salad laboriously formed into a lobster shape.

In a chapter entitled "Teaching a Woman to Cook," LaPrade continued his criticism of women's recipes, this time making the connection between American consumption of processed foods and women's cookery instruction. Writing for the young groom "who sets out to teach his bride to cook," LaPrade cautioned that general cookbooks had already "handicapped" the bride: "She will have read magazine articles designed for the intending bride; she may have dipped into cook books which include special chapters aimed at the young married woman. Space does not permit a complete analysis of this phase of the problem, but in all cases these publications emphasize the use of canned and packaged foods, and instead of advocating sound cookery, suggest a compromise by means of pre-cooked and ready-mixed products." Authors and commentators often associated the growing gourmet movement with men, and here, conversely, LaPrade associated jiffy cooking with women. Specifically, he criticized recipes and cookbooks themselves for brainwashing women and turning women into bad cooks. Radio cookery instruction also evoked LaPrade's wrath: "While instructing his wife in cookery, a husband must be constantly on his guard to protect her against the pernicious influence of fantastic recipes which are sure to reach her via daytime radio programs. I would suggest that during the first few months of her apprenticeship, he make sure that the radio receiving set develops a short circuit and blows out a tube every time she turns it on." Finally, women's recipe exchanges (between friends, neighbors, and family members) could also result in inedible meals, according to LaPrade.[35] For LaPrade, virtually every recipe source that women consulted ensured inedible meals that did not remotely resemble good, wholesome food.

Other authors of cookbooks for men made the same link between women's allegedly unappetizing and uninspired home cooking and the instruction and recipes in popular magazines aimed at female readers. For example, Morrison Wood lamented the suggestions for unappealing meals found in cookery advice for the new bride. He described a typical menu in such cookbooks as "a sweet fruit-juice rickey, a melon and grape salad made with ginger ale and fruit juices, biscuits made with tomato and cheese, and a rather tricky chocolate cake for dessert!" This sweet, skimpy, ladylike lunch would completely fail to satisfy any hungry husband, Wood asserted. "Can you imagine Tall, Dark, and Handsome coming home from a hard day at the office, with only enough time off at noon for a sandwich and a glass of milk, and being confronted with a dinner such as that?" he asked. "If it wouldn't drive any self-respecting male to pack his grip and go home to mother, I'm a ring-tailed monkey!" he added.[36] Frank Dorn more generously acknowledged that women's recipes could occasionally produce a tasty dish. "All too often the Women's Pages of the newspapers are full of budget-saving recipes, inspired thoughts as to how you can make round steak taste like Chateaubriand, or reducing diets that don't reduce," he complained. But he added that he sometimes happened to find a good recipe "between Household Hints and the Baby Food column."[37] In an effort to distinguish its own kind of cookery advice as unique and better suited for male readers, cookery instruction for men did not hesitate to disparage the recipes and cookbooks on the market intended for women: recipes for *men* would never drive a man home to mother or suggest fussy, tasteless salad combinations in lurid, unattractive colors.

Authors did occasionally acknowledge that the tiresome task of preparing three meals a day while caring for children could easily make women uninspired cooks. Malcolm LaPrade urged the man of the house to take over the nightly dinner preparation—especially if that man worked a cushy white-collar job and needed exercise—thereby giving mother time to take a cool shower and fix her hair before dinner. Morrison Wood admitted that men had an advantage over women in the realm of cooking because men did not *have* to do it every day: "I do believe that it is true that most men approach cooking in an adventuresome spirit, simply because they are not obliged to cook day in and day out. It is to them first a game, then a pastime, and finally a hobby." "It's hard to find glamour or even fun," he admitted, "in cooking three meals a day, seven days a week, fifty-two weeks a year." The authors of a cookbook for teenagers put it even more bluntly: "Men can usually be much more relaxed about cooking than women. They don't run the risk of being stuck in a kitchen for the rest of their lives, even if it does have the latest fixings. They can remain happy amateurs and cook when and where it suits them."[38]

When women wrote on men's cooking, they often echoed such assertions about female cookery. Because of their daily food preparation responsibilities, noted authors in women's magazines and general cookbooks, a woman could not be as creative in the kitchen as the man in the house could. Some also asserted that men simply enjoyed a natural ability to excel at cookery, especially meat cookery. But in contrast to by-men-for-men cookery books, cookery instruction for women often advised wives on how to teach men the rudiments of cooking and gently to encourage men to enter the kitchen. Authors like LaPrade, Wood, Gordon, and the editors of *Esquire* depicted men who, in defense against their wives' bad cooking, drew on their natural abilities and taught themselves how to cook. Many general cookbooks aimed at female readers depicted men in the kitchen quite differently: they described women encouraging men to slowly learn the most basic cooking technique. An article called "Let Your Man Lend a Hand," published in a 1951 issue of *Good Housekeeping*, advised the woman of the house to do all the initial preparation of a recipe before the man entered the kitchen. Carol Brock, the author of the article, designated the gender-specific cooking tasks of each simple recipe. To make doughnut holes, for example, a man heated fat while the woman mixed all the doughnut ingredients and formed the doughnuts. The man took over again when it came to frying. Brock made it clear that the woman remained in charge of the kitchen, humoring the man along in his culinary explorations: "Read the recipes with him—and steel yourself for his inevitable remarks: 'Cooking's a cinch. Anyone who can read can cook. Why do women fuss so much?' Pretend it's for laughs—but do offer him an apron. (You don't want cleaning bills on your conscience.)"[39]

Unlike the strident LaPrade, who included a pompous chapter on teaching one's wife to cook, these authors assumed a gently placating tone, in which women quietly but efficiently led men to the stove (and worried about the cleaning bills that might result). The editors of the *General Foods Kitchens Cookbook*, in one of its numerous sections on different kinds of cooking situations, advised the reader on how to instruct a man in the kitchen. In this particular scenario, a neighbor has fallen ill and her husband "George" must cook a meal for the family. In a section entitled "But George Can't Boil Water!" the editors recommended supplying George with frozen dinners and very detailed preparation instructions. The suggested menu: quick-frozen chicken dinners, lettuce and tomato salad, rolls and butter, "Minted Pineapple Cup," milk and coffee. The sample note of instructions for George read:

Dear George:
Hail to the chef! Here's what to do, and when:
40 minutes before dinnertime, turn on oven to 425 degrees.
Take chicken dinners out of freezer. Package directions tell what
    to do.
Slice tomatoes and arrange on lettuce leaves (both are in the crisper
    drawer—bottom right-hand side—of refrigerator. Salad dressing's
    in the little cruet with oil-water-vinegar markings—top shelf of
    refrigerator. Shake well before pouring.
Open can of pineapple (refrigerator) and put in dessert dishes
    (kitchen table). Garnish each with mint sprig (it's the bouquet
    on the kitchen table).
Heat water for instant coffee, pour milk, put on rolls (bread box)
    and butter.

This note contained, according to the editors, "tactful guidance." George might be so inspired by his culinary adventures, they asserted, that "by the time George's wife is on her feet again, he will probably feel he's qualified as something of a cook; and, who knows?—next week he may want to try a steak!"[40] George's potential inability to locate the dinner rolls and the lettuce (has George never seen a breadbox or a crisper drawer?) could not have presented a more different picture than the confident epicure featured in most cookery instruction for men.

The author of a 1953 *House and Garden* article interviewed several newlywed couples to find out how real-life brides had lured their husbands into the kitchen. The article advised the young wife to first get her husband to come into the kitchen and taste a sauce. From there on out, the man's natural inclination toward cookery would take over, but the clever wife had to subtly direct his culinary energies: "Whether your sauce is good, bad, or indifferent, your tender husband will pronounce it superb, adding as an afterthought that perhaps it 'could stand something.' He'll promptly make an uninvited tour of the herb cabinet, sniff the spices and taste the condiments—all with the air of a connoisseur. This may be considered symptomatic behavior, a stage which requires quick and skillful action, because your husband can be put to work immediately. Thrust the recipe for salad dressing into his hand, firmly but not too eagerly."[41] Thus, a little gentle feminine trickery should be employed in capturing a man's interest in cooking.

Marguerite McCarthy recommended a similar approach in her 1947 *The Cook Is in the Parlor.* In a chapter entitled "The Husband Cooks" McCarthy explained how to ease a man into cookery: "Some evening suggest that he mix the salad. Perhaps, at first, it may be that all he can manage is to shred and arrange the greens, tossing them with the salad dressing that you have already prepared. Later show him how to make French dressing. Have him practice in the privacy of the family until he is so well drilled that he can make the dressing and complete the salad with the confidence of a professional. Then, but not until then, is he ready to make his first public appearance as a chef." McCarthy also suggested giving husbands a chance to cook egg dishes for breakfast. "Select a recipe that may used also as a supper dish," she wrote, "so that after a little practice he may preen himself in front of guests while making a tasty supper entrée." Again, in McCarthy's depiction of the man at the stove, a woman had to be sure to lead him by the hand through simple recipes, then build up his ego by allowing him to cook supper and "preen himself" in front of guests.

In McCarthy's cookbook, however, male culinary wizardry with salads and eggs did not extend to pastry. She poked gentle fun at a man who attempted to make piecrust: "One man told me quite seriously that he had 'spent hours' mixing the piecrust, and when the pie was baked it was so heavy he had difficulty in removing it from the oven."[42] In general cookbooks and in women's domestic magazines, when men entered the kitchen they sometimes became the objects of such mild humor, although they also received flattering attention and support from the woman of the house. Authors commented on what they perceived as a male aversion to a neat and tidy kitchen, for instance. Kate Smith praised men for the adventurousness culinary spirit, but added that men "do have one failing however! They seem to use every pot in the kitchen; and keep in mind that the clean-up, or K.P. part of the project, is rarely in their over-all plans."[43]

Some authors also took issue with male culinary egos. A cartoon in a 1956 *Ladies' Home Journal* illustrated how domestic magazines and general cookery instruction sometimes made a self-important cook-husband the object of fun. In this cartoon, a man stands over the stove with an apron tied around his waist. Wife and children hover around him as he asks, surgeonlike, for "Onions! Fork! Salt! Pepper! Bay leaves!"[44] This magazine also occasionally published cartoons poking fun at male cookery in general. In a 1957 edition, a frowning wife listens to her would-be-chef husband explain, "I just added a bay leaf, paprika, a touch of garlic salt, some capers, a tiny bit of chili powder . . . and threw it out." Similarly, in 1953 the magazine included a cartoon of a man bending over a flaming chafing dish, while his wife stood in the background brandishing a fire extinguisher. Like earlier examples of such cartoons, the humor in these drawings depended upon assumptions about which member of the family would be ultimately responsible for the family's meals. Because men cooked only occasionally, ruining a dish with too many spices could be a humorous subject. Male cookery incompetence did not present a really serious matter.

Cookbook authors occasionally complained about or poked fun at male egotism in the kitchen. H. Allen Smith, in his essay "Hambones in the Kitchen," originally published in *Esquire* and then in the *Esquire Cook-Book*, attributed his humorous remarks on the "hamminess" of male cooks to his wife. According to Smith, his wife entered the study as he tried to write this article, and vented her feelings about the topic at hand—men in the kitchen:

> I don't object to men trying to cook, if they'd just go in there and cook and keep their big mouths shut. Men are such *hams* in the kitchen. What hambones! First thing they do is start hollering about the knives. The knives are never sharp enough. Next they start rattling and banging around, and grousing because they can't find the right-size pan. *All* the equipment is wrong. They yell about wanting a garlic press, and where's

the saffron, and isn't there a so-and-so lid that'll fit this so-and-so pot, and how's a man gonna do anything without ramekins, and go get me some peanut oil, and so on and so on. Why can't they just grab a pan, turn on the stove and throw their stuff in and shut up about it?

She supposedly made similarly pointed remarks about men at the barbecue: "They wouldn't go near a kitchen stove, but the minute anyone suggests cooking outdoors, they go into their act; they slap on their ridiculous chef hats and their goofy aprons with wisecracks all over them and they start to work over a bed of smoky coals. What hambones! They've got to make a production out of it, in the cheapest theatrical sense. It's a wonder to me they don't hire a line of chorus girls to prance up and down in front of the barbecue while they're reducing the meat to cinders."[45] When Smith gave his wife credit for his own comic satire of the male cook, he joined the small group of cookbook authors and domestic magazine writers who protested male culinary egos and male attitudes toward the art of cooking in the 1950s.

"Men are dopes as cooks!" declared Eleanor Pollock in a 1949 *Good Housekeeping* article. She criticized the male penchant for claiming superiority at the stove, although men only sporadically cooked: "You've all met him. One-dish Harry, who, if the wind is right and everything else equal, can prepare an entrée, a salad, or a dessert quite well. He is the one who claims that men are better cooks than women, basing his argument on his solitary talent or a similar one possessed by some fellow amateur." Pollock compared men's occasional cooking with the real, practiced, everyday cookery skills of women: "The fact that most women prepare entire meals not only on grand occasions, but night after night he considers not at all. Or thinks it is not germane to his argument. The average amateur male cook, faced with the triple threat of marketing, preparing, and serving an entire meal, would make for the nearest hamburger heaven on the double-quick." Pollock lamented that popular periodicals only bolstered men's smugness in the kitchen: "It is abetted by such protagonists as Pierre de Rochan, who writes a cooking column for a New York newspaper. Recently he went all out to say that extra-special recipes are strictly for men cooks and not suitable for what he calls careless women cooks, who 'cut corners and end up in ignominious failure as women in the kitchen usually do.'" She added, despairingly: "Men editors are passionately interested in men who can cook, and vice versa. I have worked for any number of men who think that a picture of a prominent citizen stirring up his favorite concoction is worthy of page one."[46] Both Pollock's belief that magazines and newspapers applauded every male effort in the kitchen while denigrating women's cooking and her own views on this phenomenon revealed postwar trends in cookery instruction. Recipes for men proliferated, periodicals and cookbooks raved about male culinary ability, and a few humorists and cookery writers satirized the trend.

In a 1952 *House Beautiful* article entitled "Whose Kitchen Is It Anyway?" Evelyn Humphreys complained about her husband's self-satisfied salad-making technique. She described how he washed the lettuce, used up all her towels drying each leaf, took out every spice and condiment in the kitchen cabinet to dress the salad, and then left her to do the rest of the work: "[H]e knocks off to enjoy a gig of sherry, leaving me to juggle popovers, steak, hashed-brown potatoes, asparagus, and strawberries with cream around a mountainous pile of tangled vegetable matter on the kitchen drainboard. Then he is convinced that he prepared the dinner."[47] Humphreys's particular complaint about men and salads had some basis—cookbooks often urged men to exercise their natural flair for salad making. For example, in *Betty Crocker's Picture Cook Book*, the salad section began with a flattering drawing of a men in a chef's apron tossing an enormous salad, surrounded by his admiring wife, children, and elderly parents. Cookbook author Beth McLean noted that men "often pride themselves on their special prowess at the salad bowl. As *The First Book of Boys' Cooking* explained: "The day-to-day cooking for the family is usually done by a woman. But in many families the man is considered the expert when it comes to mixing a salad. . . . At dinner parties and in fine restaurants men will often call for the salad ingredients and mix them right at the table."[48] Cookery instruction, then, reinforced the idea that men belonged at the salad bowl, exercising their "special prowess" with mixed greens and blue cheese dressing. But Humphreys underscored what could have been a more pointed criticism about male ego and green salads with humor. Although her experiences with a husband convinced of his own "special prowess at the salad bowl" might have been truly annoying, she maintained a satirical tone.

And she did not question her own place in the kitchen—as the title of the article demonstrated. Neither did Lucille Britt in her 1958 article for *American Mercury* entitled "Husband, Stay Away from My (Kitchen) Door!" Like Humphreys, Britt protested the invasion of her domain by men convinced they could cook. She asserted that the growing numbers of cookbooks for men revealed how many husbands had taken up cooking as a hobby: "Witness the rise in popularity of the cookbook for men. *Esquire's* cookbook sells for $5.95 and some 15,000 copies have been sold. *Gourmet,* a magazine edited for the man who finds pleasure in good eating, has sold some 150,000 copies of their cookbook, priced at $12.50." Her reference to the *Gourmet Cookbook* illustrated how the rise of the food movement that bore this magazine's name often evoked images of the male epicure. Many Americans associated the growing popularity of fine dining, fresh ingredients, and foreign dishes with men. Britt lamented this trend, complaining that men left enormous messes when they cooked, used excessive amounts of everything, and could not locate the simplest items in the kitchen.[49] By 1960, according to Patricia K. Brooks in an article for *McCall's*, one's bridegroom might have the mistaken idea that his own cooking prowess exceeded his bride's. Brooks jokingly advised the reader, in the title and body of her article, to "Never Marry a Man Who Can Cook," and told of her struggle to retain the rights to her own kitchen.[50] As writers satirized the man at the stove, they reiterated the proper gender division of household labor: women, not blustering, pompous, inefficient men, belonged in the kitchen.

But virtually all cookbooks agreed on one thing: male appetites differed from those of women, and no matter who cooked the meal, the male preferences for hearty, meaty, uncomplicated dishes must be kept in mind. Most post–World War II cookbooks and recipes insisted that men could not be fed with the same kinds of fussy, delicate dishes favored by women. Authors and editors made this especially clear in directions for "Stag Night" meals. For instance, Jane, the fictional protagonist in the 1958 *1001 Ways to Please a Husband*, described the menu she prepared for her husband's men-only gathering: "I had to prepare a masculine style meal—that is, hearty, robust, and not even slightly dainty." Because "men like protein food," Jane chose roast beef as the main dish. For an appetizer, she decided upon shrimp cocktail, because "most men's favorite appetizer is shrimp." She also chose an appropriately masculine salad. "The salad should be virile, too" Jane pondered. "The virilest salad I know is one with Roquefort dressing," she concluded. Her husband Peter hovered nervously around the kitchen before the party began, asking his wife to be sure all doilies had been removed from the table and that the beer had been iced.[51] He did not, however, take charge of the meal. The preparation of the properly masculine meal remained the responsibility of the woman of the house.

Not surprisingly, most general cookbooks assumed that the reader, a woman, would be the one doing the real cooking for the men's stag dinner. In a section entitled "Strictly for the Boys," *The General Foods Kitchens Cook Book* gave a menu for those occasions "when the men return from a day's fishing, or the poker club meets at your house"—a meal that the woman of the house could cook ahead of time and leave for the "boys" to reheat. The editors suggested "a big, manly soup" and sandwiches. They advised that the wife could make the soup ahead and leave it on the stove "for Himself to heat up when he's ready." They offered similar directions for the sandwiches: "Set out a pan of rolls, and loaves of bread on a cutting board, with bread knife alongside; and put a tray of sandwich makings, ready to serve, in the refrigerator. Good makings: cold ham, tongue, meat loaf, Swiss and American cheese, cucumber slices, shrimp salad." The men would enjoy this meal, assured the editors, and it would free up the Mrs. for an evening out: "They will fare well; and so will you, as you go skipping off to your own evening of cards or a movie with the girls."[52] The reader might "go skipping off," but only after preparing and arranging the entire dinner.

The authors of *The Basic Cook Book*, a popular and encyclopedic cookbook, gave very similar directions for women catering a husband's stag party. Leave out a platter of assorted cold meats and cheeses, or "opened cans of sardines and sandwich spreads maybe set out conveniently near a loaf of bread and bowl of creamed butter. A jar of salad dressing, another of prepared mustard, and a dish of relishes might complete the list of ingredients." They advised that the wife should also make sure that the coffee is "measured and placed in the coffee-maker to be connected with the electric current at the appointed hour."[53] For Poker Night, suggested the author of a 1956 promotional cookbook published by General Motors, a wife should prepare an entire meal and leave it in the oven for the male revelers: "What better method to cook a meal for friend husband and his poker-playing pals than in the oven? All he has to do is to turn off the oven control, take the casseroles out of the oven, and place them on heat-resistant pads or in casserole holders arranged on the buffet or in the breakfast room." The menu included baked steak, string bean casserole, oven-browned potatoes, lettuce salad with celery and egg dressing, hot rolls, pecan pie, and coffee. Refreshments for all-male gatherings, whether prepared by indulgent wives or by the men themselves, demanded certain kinds of foods: hearty, filling, "man-sized" portions, and so on. In a section entitled "For Men Only," this same cookbook included a number of recipes to tempt a masculine appetite: clam dip, beef and vegetable stew, spareribs, whole stuffed pear salad, chocolate devil's food cake, and ice cream.[54]

When authors suggested that "friend husband" and his pals actually do some of the cooking at men-only gatherings, they limited the recipes to such masculine favorites as green salad, garlic bread, and steak. At a stag party, men might grill a steak or toss the salad, but their kitchen repertoire remained limited to strictly virile dishes. *Better Homes and Gardens* suggested hash and a green salad for men's night: "When father cooks, the 'boys' will like corned-beef hash, turned into a casserole, moistened with cream, and baked brown. To make salad bowl, cut fat chunks of tomatoes, cucumbers, radishes, celery in lettuce-lined bowl rubbed with cut clove of garlic."[55] The kinds of foods suggested for the male palate had remained unchanged from similar menu suggestions in the prewar period: crisp green salads with strongly flavored dressings, roasted meats, strong coffee, cakes, pies, and hot breads all passed muster for the male menu.

Again and again, in both general and male-oriented cookbooks, authors and editors insisted that men loved particular kinds of foods. "I daresay if you were planning a meal to please a man, and you did not know his tastes, you might make strawberry shortcake or an apple pie and not be wrong," asserted Jessie DeBoth in *It's Easy to Be a Good Cook*. "Man or boy, where is one who doesn't go for spareribs?" asked the Browns in their cookbook for boys. Although she cited no statistics, Julie Benell claimed in her 1961 cookbook that apple pie "is the most popular American dessert with men all over the country." In a chart describing different kinds of cheese, the editors of the *Better Homes and Gardens Cook Book* linked men and limburger: "Men like it on dark breads, with salty potato chips, pretzels, and coffee." Other cookbooks recommended dishes such as bean soup, endive salad with Roquefort dressing, hot biscuits with butter, rice pilaf, peach cobbler, chicken paprika, "Atomic Beets" (beets with a butter and horseradish sauce) and, for the fun-loving bachelors who read *Esquire*, "Drunk's Soup" (a combination of sauerkraut juice and frankfurters guaranteed to banish a hangover). In his cookbook for the single woman, *She Cooks to Conquer*, Robert Loeb gave detailed directions on the different types of food required to win over the hearts of different types of men. "Muscle-Men" should be served deviled eggs, steak, pan-fried potatoes, and asparagus. A jovial, chubby eater should receive something like chicken soup, veal, potatoes, and salad greens with onion, parsley, and hard boiled egg. If a girl wished to ensnare an intellectual "Lean-Man," counseled Loeb, she would do well to serve a clam juice cocktail, lamb, baked potatoes, and romaine and watercress salad. All men, according to Loeb, enjoyed a dessert of fresh fruit and cheese.[56] Loeb gave no explanation for these menu suggestions, but numerous other authors also asserted that men always liked certain kinds of food and that women should be sure to serve them to husbands and male guests.

Men and women simply liked different kinds of food, cookbook authors agreed (fig. 20). For example, although commercially published cookbooks had, for decades, tried to steer women away from serving marshmallow-encrusted salads to *anyone*, postwar cooking authorities asserted that women might sometimes enjoy sweet and jellied salads, but men never. "If you are aware that your husband has always regarded the jellied aspic (beautifully molded with gleaming fruits and served with a side bowl of sour-cream dressing) with a very jaundiced eye, don't serve it to him," explained Mildred Knopf. "Save it for the girl friends," she advised, and serve men their salad favorite: "mixed greens flecked through with crumbled bits of Danish Blue Cheese."[57] Male

Figure 20 These photographs from a 1956 article in *Woman's Home Companion* clearly illustrated gender-specific cooking activities for the whole family. Mother presided over a flaming peach dessert, Father concocted an exotic spaghetti sauce of clams and sherry, Sister fussed over a strawberry pie, and Brother skewered marinated frankfurters with a kabob stick. From Edalen Stohr, "120 Ways You Can Put Glamour into Just Plain Food," *Woman's Home Companion*, March 1956.

appetites always required such plain, hearty foods, served without fuss, and male gatherings required enormous amounts of such food. The editors of the *General Foods Kitchens Cookbook*, for instance, contained two entirely different menus for two gender-specific high school graduation parties: a tea party for a girl or a casual get-together for a boy. The menu and decorations for the girl's party included open-faced cucumber tea sandwiches, nut bread triangles with cream cheese, shrimp salad, cheese wafers, pink-frosted sugar cookies, apricot coconut balls, brownies, tea and coffee. For decorations, the editors urged daintiness: "For this party, a pretty table, by all means—a pastel tablecloth, and a basket of tiny, individual corsages—paper-lace backed, ribbon-trimmed, for each party-goer to take home with her. Sweetheart roses; phlox, stock, or delphinium florets with baby's breath; small-leaf ivy with pink geraniums—any would be lovely."

In contrast, the boy's party required simpler fare and decorations. The entire menu consisted of hero sandwiches, butterscotch pecan pie, cola, and chocolate milk. "For this party you need no decoration other than the grins of your guests when they see the most Heroic Hero Sandwich opportunity of all time. Do it up proud: Have the plainest possible table—an outdoor picnic one, or boards on sawhorses in the play room—and let the food be the show. Great six-to-eight-inch hunks of split and buttered French or Italian bread; and then, every kind of meat, fish salad, cheese, vegetable, pickle, relish you can possibly call to mind. . . . Set out the dessert and beverage—and then stand clear:

there are *men* at work here" (emphasis in original).[58] In postwar cookbooks, as in the 1920s and 1930, the male appetite demanded great "hunks" of food, served with a minimum of presentation. On the other hand, dainty, sweet, light refreshments appealed to women and girls. For decades, cookery instruction and recipes for men had emphasized male culinary prowess and masculine propensity for hearty, beefy, virile foods. But in the 1950s, it became even more important for men's food to be unquestionably male—and the increase in instruction by and for men showed it.

In an era when the man in the gray flannel suit threatened to displace a more rugged ideal of manhood, men in the kitchen boldly mixed flavors, slapped on sauces, and flexed their muscles wielding the potato masher. In the 1920s, anxiety about the role of women in the new, modern, post–World War I, postsuffrage world, as well as anxiety about women in higher education, rising divorce rates, and changing sexual mores helped shape the rhetoric about men's and women's social roles in cookery instruction. By the 1950s concerns about gender roles, specifically concerns about the masculinity of white middle-class men, had only intensified. The rise of white-collar work for middle-class men seemed to especially trouble a nation that had often equated masculinity with physical strength and stamina. Manhood in the era of suburban life seemed in need of redefinition. Sociologists worried about the "organization man." Could a corporate drone really foster his own inherent, rugged, manliness? Social scientists worried about the decreasing stamina, health, and power of middle-class men, as fewer and fewer of them took jobs that required physical activity.

Robert Loeb may have poked fun at the Cold War atmosphere in the United States when he included a recipe for "Un-American Activities Gastronomic" spaghetti and a "Salade Subversive" (made with Russian dressing) in his 1950 cookbook.[59] But for most authors and editors of cookery instruction for men, the importance of maintaining the rigid gender divisions of kitchen duties and taste buds only increased during the Cold War. During the 1920s and 1930s cookery instruction for men had helped to define better the increasingly important cooking tasks of white middle-class women. In the 1950s cookery instruction for men took on a new vehemence in an increasingly bitter Cold War—what would happen to men during this automated, sedentary age? Could they meet the challenges of the new nuclear era?

During the Cold War, cultural commentators frequently evoked the trope of "softness" to illustrate their fears about the vulnerability of the country. Politicians fretted about being perceived as "soft" on communism. Popular literature ranging from do-it-yourself guides to diet books urged men to shun "soft living."[60] The fear of subversion—and perversion—also marked American fears about masculinity. Inflamed rhetoric about a homosexual fifth column added another dimension to the concern about manly American men. The persecution of gay men and lesbians reached a fever pitch during the 1950s. Although the House Un-American Activities Committee primarily targeted communists, it also focused on "the homosexual menace." Cold War politicians argued that homosexuals were susceptible to blackmail and "moral turpitude" and created dangerous weaknesses in our national defense.[61] Alfred Kinsey's reports, which indicated that a significant percentage of American men had experienced sexual intimacy with another man, fed the furor. Thousands of military personnel, teachers, and federal employees lost their jobs in the frenzy to eliminate this supposed risk to national security. It should not be surprising that during the McCarthy era, when fear of homosexual "perversion" powerfully influenced federal policies, local police activity, and political commentary, authors and editors of recipe books for men took care to underscore the masculinity of "kitchen kings." In cookery, the virility of men remained unchallenged and obvious.

Cookery instruction for men that emphasized the differences between male and female appetites and recipes that depicted the powerful stomachs and taste buds of men reinforced the messages of other popular publications about masculinity. Men's cooking had to be depicted as an entirely different occupation than the womanly preparation of daily meals. Cookbooks had to portray men in the kitchen as epicures, as creative gastronomes, as hearty eaters with an appetite for the unusual. They had to show, as the author of "The Manly Art of Cooking" in *Holiday* magazine asserted in 1953, that "any male with a *normal* interest in fine food" could take up cookery as a hobby (emphasis added).[62] They had to show that the real he-man, at the stove or at table, required bold, hearty, aggressive food and that cookery by men could be as *normal* as golfing or making snowballs. In one striking example, the authors of *Simple Cooking for the Epicure* recommended sandwich loaves (made with ingredients such as rye or pumpernickel bread, Roquefort cheese spread, cheese creamed with sherry, deviled ham and cream cheese, canned chicken mixed with peanut butter and margarine, smoked salmon, dried beef, or chopped chicken liver) for luncheons at which men would be present. They asserted that these hearty loaves would satisfy masculine appetites and would also not threaten the heterosexuality of male guests: "Sandwich loaves are a decorative addition to any table. Here is a variation that will not leave your male guests feeling like characters in a play by Oscar Wilde."[63]

Precisely because masculinity seemed in question, cookbook authors and editors had to reinforce and reiterate the manliness of the man in the kitchen. Cookbooks implied that men "naturally" excelled at cooking over an open fire and men "naturally" craved hearty meals. But authors and editors felt it necessary to explain, over and over, the differences between masculine appetites and feminine appetites, differences between masculine cookery and ladylike recipes. Perhaps the differences were not as clear as they, and many Americans, wished. The constant and vehement differentiation between the sexes in the kitchen showed how Americans had reason to question those supposed differences. Now Cold War fears only added to the same kinds of anxieties provoked by changes in cookery and food technology, declining servant labor, and women's expanding social roles in the 1920s and 1930s.

Cookery instruction for men in the 1950s reiterated many of the same assertions about men in the kitchen that similar kinds of cookbooks and popular articles had in the 1920s and 1930s, but with increased vehemence. In the prewar era, recipes for men had helped to define better the cooking duties of middle-class, maidless white women. In the 1950s, it helped to define masculinity itself. But as the rhetoric about manly appetites and cookery ability increased in vehemence and in amount during the 1950s, so did prescriptions about women's cookery duties. And in the anxious days of the Cold War, women's home-cooked meals assumed a heavy mantle of symbolic responsibility not borne by men's cookery.

10

The Most Important Meal

WOMEN'S HOME COOKING,

DOMESTIC IDEOLOGY, AND COOKBOOKS

In her article "Prescriptions for Penelope: Literature on Women's Obligations to Returning World War II Veterans," historian Susan M. Hartmann asserts that in the late 1940s anxiety about how the war disrupted gender norms drove psychologists, magazine writers, movie makers, sociologists, and government officials to produce massive amounts of prescriptive literature for women. She argues that as the war wound to a close, these experts urged women to reassume their traditional place in society and in the family. They urged women to give up paid employment, to cater to the needs and wants of their husbands, and, in short, to embody femininity.[1]

In 1963 journalist Betty Friedan gave such postwar prescriptions for women a name: the feminine mystique. In her book by the same name, Friedan argued that the combined effects of the media, Freudian thought, functionalism, and advertising created an unobtainable and untenable feminine ideal, which trapped women into being identified solely as wives and mothers at great cost to their intellectual and emotional health.[2] *The Feminine Mystique* made sweeping generalizations about all women when in fact Friedan's data dealt exclusively with married, college-educated, middle-class women. But in the case of cookery instruction for women, Friedan's assessment remains persuasive precisely because *The Feminine Mystique* focused on the experiences of married, middle-class, white women—the same demographic that most interested the authors and editors of commercial cookery instruction. An examination of post–World War II cookery instruction for women plainly shows that this body of popular literature created a kind of feminine mystique of its own.

In the 1920s and 1930s the cookbook redefined cooking as a creative and artistic task for newly cookless white woman. In the 1950s cookbooks went further: they redefined the cooking tasks of middle-class women as an essential part of being a good wife and mother—and a good American. While general cookbooks ceased treating food as a weapon of war, they continued to represent food preparation and certain kinds of food as gendered: men and women cooked and ate in markedly different ways in postwar cookery instruction. In fact, the importance of a woman's home-cooked meal in the Cold War era assumed even more frantic levels of domestic symbolism in 1950s cookbooks than in prewar books. As they had for decades, editors, authors, newspaper columnists, and food manufacturers focused all their attention on how women cooked the daily meals and emphasized the centrality of food preparation to female social roles.

Like cookbooks in the 1920s and 1930s, those in the 1950s addressed their instructions to the middle-class mistress of a home who would be "doing her own cooking." Although post–World War I cookery instruction had paid far more attention to the newly cookless plight of its readers, instruction after World War II did sometimes mention the fact that middle-class households employed domestic servants or cooks in rapidly decreasing numbers. Cookbook reviewers linked the declining numbers of household servants after the war with the rise in cookbook publication in the late 1940s and early 1950s. Wrote one: "Since the last war, which created a scarcity of household help, there has been an increasing interest by housewives in cookery which has manifested itself in a steady demand for reliable recipes."[3] In a 1949 article for *Publishers' Weekly,* a bookseller in New England made the same link, writing that her store had chosen to hold a large cookbook sale because, "since the war, women who knew little more than how to boil water have been forced into the kitchen."[4]

Cookbook authors themselves also sometimes referred to how wartime employment had lured cooks away from private employment; they commented on how the war precipitated the end of servant labor in middle-class homes. The title of Marguerite McCarthy's 1954 cookbook—*The Queen Is in the Kitchen*—alluded directly to this phenomenon. In her introduction, McCarthy explained to the reader: "Once upon a time you sat in the parlor, like the queen, while someone else prepared the bread and honey. But now, you—the queen of your household—may find yourself in the kitchen." She asserted that for many of her readers,

World War II forced upper- and middle-class women's entry into the kitchen. She went on to argue that the virtual disappearance of home cooks after the war ensured that many white middle-class and upper-class women remained on K.P. even in peacetime:

> Perhaps you first stepped into these surroundings during World War II. If so, it was probably for patriotic reason or necessity and not for love of the daily grind within those four walls. Washing pots and pans, stretching rationed food, catering to the whims of the family was your response to the urge to "Do your bit."
>
> We all looked forward to the day when Sadie or Annie would return from the factory and we would again be free. But it didn't work out that way, did it? Cooks vanished with the war. We, the Queens, were trapped.[5]

Few authors or editors stated it so plainly or so clearly revealed the social status of the women they believed would be reading cookbooks. But a number of cookbooks did mention that servants had become quite scarce and that the "queens of the parlor" had indeed been "trapped" into regular kitchen duty.

As in the 1920s and 1930s, however, cookery books did not lament the fact that middle- and upper-class women would have to turn to cookery instruction rather than paid cooks in order produce their own delicious meals. Some, like *The General Foods Kitchens Cookbook*, implied that middle-class women needed to simply accept the fact that the heyday of cooks and servants had come to an end. Although the editors included a short section on maid service, most of the instruction for serving and dining focused on "When You're Alone," that is, without household help: "It's great fun to dream about the immaculately uniformed maid and her sure and silent service, or the wonderfully capable woman in the kitchen who's taking so much of the responsibility off your hands. But let's face it—most of us do the planning, preparation, and serving of our company dinners solo."[6] Others positively applauded the trend in maidless entertaining. The author of the *Cocktail-Supper Cookbook* heralded what she saw as a revolution in entertaining: "The era of the formal seated dinner party with numerous courses of rich dishes, served perhaps by butlers and party maids, is drawing to a close. Today you can serve *what* you want, *when* you want, *where* you want."[7] She apparently exulted in the new freedom servantless houses afforded the mistress—or at least encouraged her readers to do so.

A number of cookbooks also suggested that kitchen conveniences, such as appliances, had taken the place of servants. For example, the author of *Ann MacGregor's Cookbook for Frozen Foods* compared a freezer to a paid cook: "[O]wning a freezer is like having an excellent chef working for you, a chef who can come up with the most delicious dishes on those occasions when the best is needed and there is little time in which to prepare it."[8] *The Picture Cook Book* even credited postwar interest in kitchen decor and improved kitchen architecture to the exodus of paid cooks: " 'As cooks go,' a British wit once wrote of a cherished servant, 'she went.' And that about sums up the situation in the U.S. today. Now the disappearance of domestic help has sent most householders into their own kitchens—and some have been surprised by what they found. In the nineteenth century, when cooks were plentiful, the American kitchen was a remote, inefficient enclosure, totally lacking in charm. When the housewife went to work in it, she found herself in the position of a hostess who tries her own guest room and finds that the bed sags badly."[9] Cookbooks told their readers that better parties and better kitchens awaited the "queens" who had been summoned from the parlor. The departure of paid kitchen labor need not cause alarm, but should be a cause for remodeling and new appliances.

Although a few cookbooks in the 1950s still included sections on how to instruct a maid in the rules of dining service, virtually none assumed that the reader would employ somebody else to do the cooking. In a typical statement, the author of a Whirlpool appliance promotional cookbook advised the reader to hire kitchen help for dinner parties, but only for serving and cleaning: "[I]t is my suggestion that you do the cooking yourself and get your helper in to serve and clean up afterward. To my mind, the proper pride you can take in serving guests your own best cooking is something not to be missed." Serving meals and washing dishes retained the taint of menial labor, but by the 1950s authors consistently depicted cooking as a purely enjoyable and rewarding activity. The author of *High Adventure in the Kitchen* seemed confident that kitchen novices would enjoy their new cookery duties: "Since recently, we have been cookless, and most of us maidless as well, many women who have never before had anything to do with the actual preparation of food, have told me that they have found it great fun to cook, and a source of satisfaction to be able to turn out superlative meals." Or, as one author put it, a woman's own cookery provided something that even professional chefs could not provide. "Most of us cannot afford to hire an Escoffier to our own personal pleasure," she wrote. She asserted that people who lived in metropolitan areas could dine in restaurants every night of the week, but "this is not only expensive but never as delightful as a fine meal served in your own familiar surroundings and undisturbed by strangers."[10]

In fact, they had better make sure that they could produce such Epicurean and congenial meals. In 1959, at the American National Exhibition in Moscow, Vice-President Nixon and Soviet Premier Nikita Khrushchev engaged in what later became known as the "kitchen debates." Nixon, touring the trade exhibits of washing machines, living rooms, and kitchens (all outfitted with the latest in household technology) extolled the American way of life not through a discourse on the finer points of democracy but by lauding the domestic arrangements of an ideal suburban middle-class home. At a pivotal moment in the Cold War, an important U.S. leader evoked the image of an enormous streamlined kitchen as the most powerful tool in the American arsenal against the communist menace. As historian Elaine Tyler May has shown, widespread anticommunism sentiment, fears about social instability, and pervasive anxiety about nuclear war helped create intense domestic ideology during the Cold War. She asserts that the United States enacted a social policy of sexual and social "containment" of women during the late 1940s and 1950s.[11] In the 1950s psychiatrists and cultural commentators spent considerable energy attempting to convince women that only by being a wife and mother—and nothing else—could a woman achieve true feminine completion. Marital sex manuals insisted that only by embracing the notion of motherhood could a woman enjoy real orgasmic fulfillment. Home economics courses, long divested of their early emphasis on hard science and careers for women, instead emphasized homemaking, marriage, and care of children. Cookbooks added their own kind of domestic prescriptions to the popular literature that urged women to focus entirely on their family's welfare, for the good of their families and for the nation.

In particular, cookery instruction for women emphasized that dinner—the main meal of the day served in the evening—should be "the most important meal of the day."[12] Women should carefully and painstakingly prepare excellent dinners every day and, in addition, help to ensure a pleasant and relaxed atmosphere at the dinner table. At a time when many Americans shared a fear of nuclear holocaust, cookbooks upheld the family unit as the antithesis to a nerve-wracking world. In the postwar era, Americans turned to the familiar image of the family unit, safe and well fed, protected under the wing of the "angel of the house." But they asked much of their meatloaf and potatoes. Although Americans in the 1950s enjoyed greater financial stability than ever before and celebrated an end to wartime deprivations and fears, the 1950s could also be characterized as a time of widespread unease. Experts tried to assuage American misgivings about the atomic bomb by insisting that nuclear power could do everything from fuel jet-cars to cure cancer. But fearful Americans continued to stock their backyard bomb shelters—and housewives studied civil defense brochures on how to feed a family of four during a nuclear attack.[13] Cookbooks did not offer explicit advice on how to whip up comfort food in the aftermath of an atomic apocalypse, but they did stress the importance of women's home-cooked dinners to the health, happiness, and security of families.

"The times we live in are hurrying times, and we are a hurrying people. But it is still possible to provide the necessary islands of peaceful, enjoyable family living that are traditionally associated with the table," began *The General Foods Kitchens Cook Book*. According to the editors, "The family dinner should be the pleasantest, most unhurried time of day—a time for good conversation and good companionship, as well as good food."[14] In *The Standard Family Cook Book*, Gertrude Wilkinson explained that "Scientists have taught the tense, keyed-up businessmen of America that when the dinner hour arrives business worries must be set aside, mind and body must gradually relax." She described how family dinners could provide a refuge from the worries of the day: "The dinner table is the center of the family's leisure time together. At the end of the day when the tasks are done, every member of the family looks forward to this hour of congenial companionship, relaxation and rest. There is no more pleasant spot than a cheerfully lighted dining room, with a good table, appetizing fragrances, and the companionship of one's own family."[15] The 1951 edition of *Wonderful Ways to Cook*, by Edith Key Haines, assured readers that the recipes found in this cookbook could greatly ease life's burdens. Consider these uncertain times, she wrote, when "fear, upset, [and] headlines" knotted the stomach muscles. Haines asserted that her cookery instructions could easily combat the daily stress that preyed on American appetites: "These recipes restore good conversation, a zest for life, the relaxed digestive tract, and they will, if you tie on an apron and go to it, reward you with an avid, unashamed interest in three square meals a day."[16] In times like these, implied Haines and many other cookery book authors, a woman could not afford to provide her family with anything less than "appetite-whetting recipes."

Dinner meant more than an appetizing meal in a congenial atmosphere. Family dinners, prepared by the mistress of the home, kept the family strong. And strong families kept the nation strong. The 1947 edition of the *Home Institute Cookbook* made an especially pointed connection between a woman's home cooking and a strong, healthy country: "The world today needs people with stamina and courage. Good meals can help to supply them. Each homemaker has a part to play through seeing that her individual family is provided with the essentials for giving it health and vigor. *Family security, as well as national security, results from good management of meals*" (emphasis in original). The editors asserted that "one way to express good citizenship is through food," and suggested that during World War II, memories of good meals "did much to give strength and courage to our boys, as they spent difficult and lonely hours thousands of miles away from home. They may have fought a little harder because of them."[17] Now that the boys had come home, women had a responsibility to feed them the food for which soldiers had "fought a little harder." American men had quite literally fought for mom, apple pie, and family dinners, asserted these editors and numerous others. In peacetime women now had a responsibility to preserve these treasured American institutions.

In the postwar era the family dinner and the family itself received an enormous amount of attention in a wide variety of popular publications. Everywhere in the 1950s Americans read and heard advice about the family. By the mid 1950s the baby boom had reached its peak, and women married in increasing numbers and at younger ages than ever before. Everyone from politicians to women's magazine writers urged citizens to practice "family togetherness," and at the same time Americans worried more than ever about divorce and the newly termed "juvenile delinquency." While insisting that only by bearing and raising children could women truly feel fulfilled, psychiatrists also lambasted mothers for being overprotective and overbearing. "Momism" reached a crescendo in the 1950s, as assorted experts blamed poor mothering for what they perceived as a rise in juvenile crime and unruly teenage behavior. Cookbook authors and editors offered their own slant on family togetherness and linked it to mother's home cooking. For example, in the introduction to her 1958 *Foolproof Cook Book*, Fairy White explained how home cooking could help prevent broken homes, divorce, and teenage crime: "Louis Diet, famous chef at the Ritz Carleton, New York City, said, when the hotel opened in 1910, 'Good cooking would cut the divorce rate.' We wonder what he would say today! I, a housekeeper, wonder if teaching boys (and girls) to cook in our home kitchens might decrease delinquency, giving children something to do, a new interest." Or, as the editors of the *Home Institute Cookbook* pontificated, "One may, indeed, wonder how many of the cases which come up in juvenile courts might have been entirely avoided if the children had been trained to the habit of coming home to meals and if they could have enjoyed good food in an atmosphere of good will and contentment." The editors of the *Parents' Magazine Family Cookbook* remarked, more mildly, that "Good meals served in a pleasant atmosphere strengthen family ties and give children a feeling of security."[18]

Malcolm LaPrade forcefully connected the decline of women's down-home cooking abilities with the decline of society: "In my grandmother's time every American girl of marriageable age was capable of wringing a chicken's neck, of plucking its feathers, cleaning it, singeing it and cutting it up for fricassee. Those were the days of large and happy families, infrequent divorce, and few cases of stomach ulcers."[19] Ric Riccarodo, in an introduction to Morrison Wood's 1949 cookbook, also alluded to women's disinterest in cooking as a probable cause of divorce: "I am not one to insist that the wife be chained to a stove, but if the modern woman would give more thought to preparing delectable dishes and less to the bridge table, perhaps the divorce courts wouldn't be so busy." He went so far as to link lack of home cooking with world unrest: "The fact that cooking is often at such low ebb in this age may account largely for the dyspeptic, psychotic condition of this world. Bad food and brutality are more akin than many us are willing to recognize."[20] As Riccarodo's comment illustrated, cookbook authors—like many cultural commentators and politicians in the 1950s—routinely made the link between tasty dinners and democracy. They did not hesitate to connect family meals, prepared by mom, with a stable society. In cookbooks, a woman's home-cooked meal offered one more defense against a fifth column.

A cookie jar might not seem like a powerful Cold War weapon, but cookbooks in the late 1940s and 1950s frequently equated a well-filled cookie jar with national and family security. In a chapter of cookie recipes, the editors of *Betty Crocker's Picture Cook Book* implied that cookies represented everything good and dear about home. "A full cooky jar makes a home 'homey,'" began the chapter. "Some of the sweetest memories of Home are bound up with Mother's Cooky Jar. Long after the spicy fragrance of her ginger cookies baking has faded into the years . . . the thought of that ample cooky jar on the shelf will bring back vividly the old-time peace . . . and comfort . . . and security of Home. Every Home should have a cooky jar!" (capitalization and ellipses in original).[21] Of course, General Mills had a vested interest in ensuring that, despite mixes and premade cookies, women continued to buy flour and continued to do home baking. But other general cookbooks made similar comments about the family's cookie jar. The editors of the "Tested Recipe Institute," in *A Picture Treasury of Good Cooking*, chided the reader: "Is there a cookie jar in your kitchen? Or, in the rush of everyday living, have you forgotten what fun it is to have cookies (of your own making) ready to serve to an unexpected caller, for the kids and their friends, or to have as a bedtime snack, with a glass of cool milk and a tart, red apple?"[22] Even the author of *The Short Cut Cook Book*, who advocated many different types of quick meals and hurry-up dishes, also advocated for the cookie jar: "The old-fashioned cookie jar is kept filled with home-made cookies in many households, even in these days when such a variety of these sweet cakes can be purchased."[23]

Jessie DeBoth asserted that both husbands and children appreciated the family cookie jar: "A perennially filled cookie jar is a lifework, but almost a necessity in view of the infinite hollowness of children's stomachs. And since no cookie jar was ever out of bounds for grown men, make plenty. Nobody's cookies will ever taste so good as yours."[24] Mildred Knopf made a similar argument when she extolled women to perfect the art of baking. She guaranteed that baking skills would garner a husband's praises and a child's loyalty. Your husband will boast to his friends about your prowess as a cook, she wrote, and the children will flock to your kitchen: "They will bring friends to *your* kitchen, rather than rummage around another woman's cooky jar."[25] A plentiful supply of homemade cookies meant a woman doing her most important job—homemaking (and home cooking). Like Knopf, many authors asserted that *both* children and husbands required a plentiful supply of cookies baked by the woman of the house. *Betty Crocker's Picture Cook Book*, for example, included a section of cookie recipes entitled "Beau-Catchers and Husband-Keepers."[26] The security of the family, upon which rested the security of the nation, began with the security of the marriage. And postwar cookbooks constantly depicted home cooking—and cookie jars—as central to a happy marriage.

The Well-Fed Bridegroom, an aptly titled 1957 cookbook by Margaret Williams, placed cookery only second to love as the most important foundation of a marriage: "Aside from love, good food is the cornerstone of a happy household," asserted the author in her introduction.[27] Other cookbooks intended for the new bride often made such statements about the importance of good food to marital security. The author of *Cookbook for Brides*, published in 1947, assured the reader that a wonderful home-cooked meal would guarantee a husband's deep appreciation (and would, incidentally, be enormous fun): "It's fun to cook! It's a great thrill to produce a luscious spicy apple pie which is eaten to its last flaky crumb, or an old-fashioned strawberry shortcake tumbled with crimson berries and smothered under snowy whipped cream. It's an even greater thrill to watch the light of admiration that creeps into a husband's eyes when he realizes that he has snatched a very jewel from the matrimonial mart and that he will be well and delightfully fed all the days of his life!"[28] Nothing like that old masculine favorite, homemade apple pie, to prove one's worth as a wife. And nothing like home cooking to ensure smooth sailing throughout one's married life. Cookbooks aimed much of their advice and many of their recipes at the married reader. And they almost inevitably urged the reader to give home cooking careful attention, for the sake of her marriage. As Myra Waldo summarized in *1001 Ways to Please a Husband*, "Of course, good food is not all there is to marriage, but it is certainly a vital element that cannot be overlooked."[29]

Cookbook authors felt free to mingle marital advice and recipes. For instance, in *Cook, My Darling Daughter,* in a chapter on how to cook wild game, Mildred Knopf advised her daughter that producing a delicious meal from hubby's catch would help bolster his ego. "Watch his ego perk, his shoulders lift, his chest expand. Whether you realize it or not, this response will enrich your spiritual bank to a point that will pay dividends the rest of your days! A brace of wild duck, a haunch of venison, or a string of trout can do this for you? Take it from me, it can and it will. Make him *big* and the chances are you will never be left to feel little yourself. And whatever he brings, cook it with care. He will love you as never before" (emphasis in original).[30] Knopf, like other cookery experts in the 1950s, made it clear that cooking for one's husband constituted an essential part of the wife's duties. And if cooking a man's catch ensured that he would "love you like never before," so did cooking a man's favorite foods. Cookbook authors and domestic magazine writers often counseled that women should be sure to provide their husbands with the kinds of foods that men liked. As Eleanor Richey Johnston, the author of a 1948 article in *Better Homes and Gardens* entitled "Is Your Husband Hard to Cook For?" asserted: "Unless you are one wife in a thousand, you cook—and eat—to satisfy the food habits and prejudices of the *man* at your house" (emphasis in original).[31] Just as instruction for men reiterated that men enjoyed eating certain kinds of food, instruction for women urged readers to prepare and serve those kinds of foods.

According to many cookbooks, however, what a man liked best probably did not rank high on a woman's list of food preferences. Like cookbooks in the 1920s and 1930s, instruction in the 1950s contrasted women's more delicate appetites with the hearty foods supposedly preferred by men. Authors often prefaced their recipes for gelatin salads or crustless sandwiches with comments like "This is a ladies' dish" or "Teatime with the girls." In her cookbook for children, Irma Rombauer explained that boys and girls liked different kinds of sandwiches: "Girls usually like more delicate concoctions, either open or covered, but boys like good old double-deckers with plenty of heft in between." In *Betty Crocker's Good and Easy Cook Book* (one of the many cookbooks General Mills published under Betty Crocker's name after the success of the *Picture Cook Book*), the editors described their recipes for chicken a la king, scallop casserole, and asparagus ham rolls as "especially for the Girls." The author of *What Cooks in Suburbia,* published in 1961, gave two separate menus for social gatherings, arranged according to the gender of the guests: a gathering of "the Girls" called for dainty pastries and tea sandwiches, but stag parties demanded hot meat sandwiches, "hamburger pizzas," and sausage casserole.[32] Almost invariably, when authors mentioned luncheons or offered menus for such gather-

ings, they assumed that the guests would be female and would appreciate dainty, pretty food such as soufflés, aspics, or creamed meat dishes.
Recipes for the kind of "just us girls" food that gagged Betty Mac-
Donald routinely appeared in party cookbooks and entertaining guides
in the 1950s. Although most authors continued to insist that salads
should be crisp and green, not sweet or multicolored, when they did
offer recipes for gelatin salads and other such "pretty" dishes they
designated them as strictly feminine eating.

General cookbooks, however, paid far more attention to a woman's
cooking duties than to the types of foods she might enjoy eating. Like
other kinds of popular literature in the 1950s, cookbooks often emphasized that a happy, well-adjusted woman focused all her energies on
homemaking and raising children. Of course, in cookbooks the daily
cooking comprised an essential part of the homemaking role. Authors
and recipe purveyors indicated again and again that a woman's most
important job, as a woman, consisted of shopping for, preparing, and
serving the family's daily meals. Mildred Knopf's daughter Wendy,
who wrote the introduction to Knopf's *Cook, My Darling Daughter*,
offered a striking example of how recipe books depicted cooking as a
natural expression of femininity and an essential part of true womanhood. In the introduction, Wendy explained that her mother had always
exemplified homemaking and had inspired Wendy to dream of the day
when she too could run a household and prepare the daily meals: "Just
as I knew that someday I would wear lipstick and high heels, I knew
that I would learn to cook."[33] Learning how to cook seemed as much a
part of a woman's social role as the most marked signs of femininity.

Postwar cookbooks offered far more than simple directions for cooking. They infused their instruction with rhetoric about how preparing
the daily meals could provide deep fulfillment for women—rhetoric
about how cookery constituted one of the essential womanly characteristics and duties. "The love of a wife and mother tangibly expresses
itself in the care, variety, and imagination which she brings to cooking
her family's meals," wrote Carol Traux, editor of the *Ladies Home
Journal Cook Book*.[34] Women had a responsibility, according to these
cookbooks, to provide that tangible expression of love and motherly
care. Cookbook rhetoric in the 1920s and 1930s emphasized that cooking could be fun and creative. In the 1950s, the rhetoric took a more
serious turn and held up cookery for the family as the almost sacred
duty of a wife and mother. One cookbook even suggested a "creed,"
a solemn vow, for the woman of the house: "My family's enjoyment
of food is my responsibility therefore—I will increase their pleasure
by planning for variety, for flavorful dishes, for attractive color, for
appetizing combinations."[35] This duty included providing not simply

meals but the right attitude—the attitude of a woman wholly fulfilled and perfectly happy with preparing and serving three meals a day.

Nowhere did cookbooks so strongly drive home their messages about a woman's attitude toward cooking as in their recipes and instructions for breakfast foods. Believing, with good reason, that many women dreaded the breakfast hour, cookbooks rebuked women for not taking more care with the family's first meal of the day. And they regularly recommended that women set their minds to providing a cheerful atmosphere along with a tasty breakfast. Charlotte Adams, author of a promotional cookbook for Whirlpool appliances, depicted a woman creating such delectable morning treats that the family would hurry to the breakfast table: "Give your family something to look forward to each morning—for instance, the lovely scent which makes them dress faster because they can't wait to find out what kind of muffin it is today; or the appetizing aroma of bacon crisping, which makes them eager to see what's to go with it!" The editors of *Betty Crocker's Good and Easy Cook Book* instructed the reader that breakfast should not only be nutritionally sound but also "a happy family meeting place" and "the foundation for a happy day." They promised that a good breakfast helps "keep us more cheerful all day long."[36]

Authors lamented that the busy schedules of a nuclear family at midcentury often cut into the breakfast hour. The author of *The Groom Boils and Stews* bemoaned what he saw as the rise of hurried, unfulfilling breakfasts around America: "The good old-fashioned American breakfast, with the whole family gathered around the table for a solid meal, has become ancient history. Now it's hit, miss and grab the 8:13 to make the office at nine." He complained that "today, the average breakfast is built around the news headlines, toast and coffee, with the accent on coffee to start the day."[37] Cookery instruction for women, though, insisted that breakfast should be much more than toast and coffee. Bacon, eggs, hot breads, hot and cold cereals, fruits, juice, pancakes, waffles, and all other manner of breakfast dishes received plenty of attention in 1950s cookbooks. Cookbooks also offered a considerable amount of advice for the woman preparing and serving those foods. Your husband and your children, they scolded the reader, deserve your brightest, happiest morning face. The author of a cookbook for brides even suggested that a woman rise early, to ensure she had time to make up a happy morning face: "An intelligent and beautiful bride I once knew had an excellent plan of procedure. Setting her mind to it, she rose fifteen minutes before her husband and slipped noiselessly into her dressing room. There she tinted her complexion and put on a beguiling breakfast coat. When her husband's eye rested on her, a few minutes afterward, she looked as though she had just stepped from a freshly washed and rosy cloud. Breakfast proceeded happily and at the last check the marriage was proceeding securely." This author also explained that with the right attitude, a wife could easily encourage a husband to put down the newspaper at breakfast: "If you're bright and good company, and if breakfast is tasty and plentiful, your husband will never take defensively to the morning newspaper." "I have often wondered whether that paper blotted out the look of an unattractive table and monotonous food or was just better company than a wife too sleepy to be present in more than outline," she wrote. She summarized her advice on breakfast cookery by advising the reader to, simply, "Be pretty, be bright, be cheerful—and be a good cook!"[38]

A good number of authors gave almost identical advice concerning the preparation of breakfast. Ida Baily Allen, in her 1952 *Solving the High Cost of Eating*, described breakfast as a time for the woman of the house to "be pleasant and even-tempered." "The family will follow your example," she promised. She went on to detail how a woman might face the day smiling: "[I]f you will use your own good will and make up your mind to face the new day without the feeling that the burden of the whole world is on your shoulders, before you know it, there will be a smile on your face, a light in your eyes and cheer in your voice to glamorize the whole family." It's all in your attitude and your determination to "be pleasant and even-tempered," Allen wrote. By simply getting up fifteen minutes earlier, the reader could "take a moment to pretty up," "put together a good breakfast," and treat herself to that first cup of coffee.[39]

Many post–World War II cookery books bolstered the feminine mystique in this way. They insisted that preparing meals meant more than producing nutritious and tasty food on time—it meant devoting oneself wholly to caring for the home and the family and doing so with the right attitude. It meant preparing meals, of course, but moreover, preparing meals while remaining "pleasant and even-tempered." Good home cooking simply symbolized the care with which a woman fulfilled her domestic obligations as wife and mother. According to many authors and experts, a woman provided the daily meals not merely from a sense of duty but because she found deep personal fulfillment in their preparation. A good percentage of cookbooks in the late 1940s and 1950s failed to even consider the possibility that a woman might grow bored with providing the daily meals or find them truly difficult to organize and prepare. Women, many editors and authors seemed to assume, would always want to prepare three meals a day, to make innumerable TV snacks and "nibbles," and to keep the cookie jar filled. Because in doing so, authors asserted, women would experience the greatest feminine fulfillment: homemaking. By cooking every day, a woman could make a house a home. As the author of *The Busy Woman's Cook Book*, published in 1951, claimed when she urged women to prepare the daily meals: "It will no longer be just *a* home. It will become *your* home, your own castle, simply because you do your own cooking there."[40] In postwar cookery instruction for men, husbands and fathers reigned as "kings of the kitchen," but in instruction for women, wives and mothers had the responsibility of transforming the castle into a home by providing sunny breakfasts and keeping the cookie jar full.

But not all book authors and editors assumed that women would shoulder their meal duties without a murmur. Many acknowledged that women might feel bored or frustrated by the never-ending grind of shopping, cooking, and cleaning up after cooking. Some offered suggestions about how to beat "the homemaker blahs." Authors like Mary Dean Williams in her 1948 *Everyday Cooking with Introduction for Brides* wrote that the homemaker would do well to make time for half an hour of "complete relaxation." She advised that "the rest of the day will go more smoothly for taking a little time out to rest," and even described the most refreshing way of resting: "It is best to lie down if possible, close the eyes and make the mind a blank."[41] Few authors went so far as to insist that women make their minds go blank at regular intervals, but cookbooks often included sections on how to avoid everyday fatigue. General Foods recommended that the homemaker "Sit down in the most comfortable spot you can find, and relax—with a new magazine, with soft music from radio or phonograph, or with television— whichever carries you farthest away from routine. And when you go back to your job, you'll find yourself miraculously refreshed, and ready to tackle the rest of the day's assignments." And *Betty Crocker's Picture Cook Book* gave two pages of hints on how the homemaker could help her days pass more pleasantly: "While children are napping, do something refreshing. Write, knit, or listen to pleasant music." "If you have just a minute, sit down, put your feet up on a chair, close your eyes and just relax your muscles. Let your arms, hands, and head fall limp." "Harbor pleasant thoughts while working. It will make every task lighter and pleasanter." "Notice humorous and interesting incidents to relate at dinnertime."[42]

Cookery experts usually did not attempt to validate women's feelings of lethargy or weariness—rather, they exhorted women to overcome dullness and boredom and to "be pretty, be bright, and be a good cook." Many did not suggest other alternatives for producing good meals, such as relying upon frozen and precooked foods, hiring someone else to do the cooking, or enlisting other members of the family to help out in the kitchen. Marian Taylor, for example, warned that "modern psychiatrists tell us that happy is she who reaps satisfaction from the work she does. Including her cooking—of which she will average some 50,000 hours of her married life." Taylor did not suggest that women cook less but rather that they change their attitude about cooking to conform better to the modern psychiatrist's dictates.[43] She, and many other authors and editors, asserted that women did not need to cook less but to learn how to enjoy cooking. As the editors of the *Home Institute Cook Book* explained, "Homemakers sometimes become impatient with the 'mediocrity' of their lot. It is only 'mediocrity' as they make it so."[44]

Unlike 1920s and 1930s cookbooks, which emphasized that middle-class married women would take naturally to the creative joy of cookery, cookbooks in the late 1940s and 1950s often included advice on how to force oneself to delight in preparing the daily meals. They stressed the necessity of cooking—few mentioned the possibility of employing a paid cook—and the necessity of enjoying it. Ruth Stout, author of a 1960 domestic advice manual called *It's a Woman's World*, articulated the view of numerous cookbook authors when she asserted that if a woman did not particularly enjoy cooking, that woman simply needed a change of attitude: "I have heard a woman I know say often throughout forty years: 'I *hate* to cook.' She's actually a pleasant person, but when she says those words the expression on her face is far from attractive. If, during all that time, she had forced herself to think and to say aloud 'I like to cook,' or even 'I don't mind getting dinner,' my conviction is that by now she *wouldn't* mind it. If it had been impossible for her to say she enjoyed cooking, she could at least have tried never to think of her hatred; failing that, she certainly could have managed not to express it." Stout went on to remind the reader that "the majority of women are obliged to fix meals, however little they like the idea."[45] Authors and editors of cookbooks in the 1950s often made similar assertions about how to approach the task of daily cookery. They urged women to "force themselves" to start enjoying cooking. And what of the numerous women who already enjoyed cooking—women who did not need a cookbook to tell them how to get pleasure out of cooking the daily meals? Cookbooks, like other types of prescriptive literature, assumed their readerships needed instruction. They assumed their readers needed to learn the lessons they taught.

Cookbooks authors sometimes suggested that simply by learning new recipes and cooking techniques, women might be able to *learn* how to like cooking. Even more so than in prewar cookery instruction, general cookbooks in the late 1940s and 1950s assumed a complete lack of experience or knowledge on the part of their readers. Those assumptions had some truth to them. Building on a decades-long trend, fewer and fewer women learned cookery skills from friends or family members in the 1950s. Cookbooks became the most reliable daily guide for cooking, and authors and editors naturally capitalized on women's inexperience. As Dorothy Malone wrote in her 1947 *Cookbook for Brides*, "Moonlight and roses can make you a bride . . . but you can't become a cook without a cookbook."[46] Since the end of World War I, families were increasingly mobile, so generations of women gathered together less often in the kitchen. High school became a permanent part of American society and ensured that girls would spend most of their teen years in school and not at home learning homemaking skills. A few authors and magazine writers responded to these changes and berated women for not initiating daughters into the kitchen. In a 1956 article for *American Home*, Harry Botsford urged mothers to make sure their daughters knew basic cooking: "Show the gal how to make an honest stew, how to broil a slice of ham, how to prepare the steak before it goes under the broiler. Tell her how long it should remain there. Instead of giving her a printed recipe for pastry, sit down with her and show her how it is done."[47] Most authors and editors, like Botsford, assumed that a girl did not receive cooking instruction in the home, or that instant and processed foods ensured that girls never learned real culinary skills. Publishers sought to fill the gap and to make sure that cookbooks would be the way many women would learn how to cook.

They rushed to assure their readers that learning to cook could be a pleasant experience but cautioned that a woman must have the right attitude in order to learn how to cook well. With it, Ida Bailey Allen suggested, anyone could learn how to cook: "The person who cooks with love and good will is calm; rarely forgets an ingredient; seldom burns the food; has controlled energy to beat a batter when needed; gentleness to fold whipped egg whites into a cake. A person who loves to cook and feels kindly toward those for whom the food is being prepared, is not only a good cook, but literally 'does good' with the cooking."[48] To "do good" with one's cooking, Allen and other authors wrote, women had to cultivate love and devotion to their husbands and their families; use cookery as an expression of that love and devotion; and learn how to approach cooking as an act of unselfish and even delightful duty. A woman had to cook, they acknowledged, so why not do so with the best of intentions and with a heart full of love for the job? "A cake must be baked with love," wrote Poppy Canon in her 1954 *The Bride's Cookbook*. In a poem at the beginning of the book, she asked "How can I say I love you / as I do," and answered "just by the foods (seasoned with joy) that I cook for you."[49] The love, care, and attention that women showed their food would reflect and demonstrate the love they felt for their jobs as homemakers and for their families. Again, authors and editors seemed to ignore the innumerable women who already enjoyed expressing their love and care for their families with home-cooked meals. They seemed far more interested in convincing the woman who did not enjoy cooking about the importance of home cooking.

Cookery instruction increasingly emphasized the effort a woman had to make in the kitchen—even if that effort simply meant doctoring up canned or frozen ingredients. Everyone from cookbook authors and frozen food manufacturers to cake mix advertisers and domestic magazine writers applauded the arrival of quick and easy meals, but 1950s cookbooks imposed certain limitations on convenience and speedy meal preparation. Authors expected women to be creative with processed foods, because the food processors had done all the real work already. Serving your family food straight from the can or the package seemed to indicate an unwomanly interest in providing for your family, hence a proliferation of recipes that "doctored up" processed foods and required additional kitchen work in order to serve the very foods that were supposed to be more convenient. In one of the best examples of this phenomenon, the author of a cookbook for brides gave directions for how to pickle and can vegetables that had already been processed. She offered a chutney recipe made out of canned pears and canned tomatoes, for example, and a recipe for cherry preserves that called for one can of pitted red cherries, sugar, and lemon rind.[50] Karal Ann Marling, popular culture historian, asserts that during the 1950s, "even convenience foods [had to] be slaved over to show love."[51] Although recipe books relied on canned and packaged foods, authors also directed women toward elaborate ruses to cover up the fact that they used convenience food.

The emphasis on glazing, decorating, and fussing with food, in the face of increasingly popular and available instant and canned foods, indicated unease over the implications of such processed foods. By "doctoring" food, women retained their position as the only real cook of the family. Any member of the family could open a can, but only mom knew to add chopped watercress and milk to a can of potato soup and make "Watercress Vichyssoise." Even a cookbook devoted entirely to cooking foods out of cans emphasized that a woman's home cooking demanded much more than simply opening a can and heating the contents. In the introduction to the 1961 edition of Poppy Canon's *The Can-Opener Cook Book*, the author reminded the reader that "Gone are the days when anything quick was considered a triumph and concoctions of tuna fish, cream of mushroom soup, and potato chips flourished among the hurry-up menus."[52] Canon explained, in her 1954 cookbook for brides, that because food-processing companies and canners had already completed the drudgery of cooking, a young wife simply needed to add a woman's special touch to those foods: "No longer plagued by kitchen-maid chores, which have been taken over by the food manufacturer, she soon becomes an artist at her stove, adept in the realms of cookless cookery, where a dash of herbs, a splash of wine, an unusual garnish, may lift the ready soup, the frozen stew, the prepared cake mix, from just plain food to a social art." Freed from "kitchen-maid chores," women nonetheless still had an obligation to lift food into the realm of art, into the realm of "real" home cooking. The editors of *The General Foods Kitchens Cookbook* reminded their readers that processed foods and time-saving appliances simply meant more time to add special touches to a meal: "In place of household servants and unlimited time for preparing meals, we have time-and-labor-saving appliances, prepared or partially-prepared foods, and a greater variety of foods, more information about them, and more delightful ways of serving them, than anybody's ever had before. We can still make the most important meals, the family meals, memorable—not just once in a while, but most of the while." All the frozen dinners in the world did not negate the fact that a woman still needed to ensure that most of her family's meals be "memorable." The author of *The Well-Fred Bridegroom* summarized: "[Effort] is an essential part of any dish; without it I firmly believe that good cooking cannot be achieved." She scolded that "Love and care are ingredients as important as salt and pepper. What is your hurry, anyway? After all, feeding the master of the house is one of your major jobs."[53]

In these cookbooks, women retained sole responsibility for the preparation of the daily meals—even as cooking itself became an easier undertaking. Many recipes demanded a minimal amount of cooking knowledge, but they also took on a symbolic burden that only a *woman's* cooking could fulfill. As historian Erika Endrijonas argues in her examination of post–World War II cookbooks, cookery instruction insisted that women act as a "perpetual hostess" to both guests and to the members of the family, even at short notice.[54] Only a most devoted wife could provide those essential "emergency" meals when a husband or child brought home guests unexpectedly. In many cookbooks, this situation separated the dependable, competent homemakers from the careless, inattentive wives. Nothing, they asserted, gives a man such a sense of well-being and marital joy or "Junior" a sense of confidence in his mother than being able to bring home unexpected guests for dinner.[55] Even though that meal might consist solely of combined and tweaked canned foods, the meal clearly remained a woman's duty—whatever and whenever the meal, even under trying circumstances.

Anecdotal evidence suggests that many women felt intense pressure during the 1950s to conform to a feminine (and cooking) mystique, to provide home-cooked meals to every member of the family and to all guests, and to create a pleasant eating atmosphere in the home. Certainly the hundreds of letters received by Friedan after the publication of her book, and its wild success in terms of sales, shows that her analysis of domestic ideology struck a nerve.[56] Individual women writing in memoirs about the 1950s also sometimes refer to cooking as part of an overall normative gender ideology. Food historian Laura Shapiro bitterly describes her 1950s home economics course as an exercise in domestic ideology indoctrination: "Perhaps those classes, known by 1958 as 'Homemaking,' had a grip on us that we hardly suspected at the time, codifying as they did a grim and witless set of expectations that loomed across the future like a ten commandments for girls"—a view that hundreds of cookbooks published in the late 1940s and 1950s seemed to bolster.[57]

Culinary historian Nicole Humble, in an article on cookbooks in England, asserts that post–World War II cookery instruction played an important role in perpetuating a discourse that limited a woman's life to the domestic sphere. "The idea of cooking as a fulfilling activity had firmed by the 1950s into an ideology of domesticity that saw the home as the centre of a woman's existence," she writes.[58] Cookbooks, like other prescriptive literature in the postwar era, preached that women needed to embrace the domestic sphere. Convenience foods might ease some of the drudgery of cooking, so wrote authors and editors, but that just meant women would have more time to give food preparation that extra special touch. The anxieties and questions about gender roles that had been brewing in the United States, and reflected in cookery instruction, since at least 1920 were coming to a head. With ready-made food so widely available, with more women working outside the home, with so few paid cooks in the home, and in the aftermath of war, cookery instructors felt compelled to reiterate and emphasize that the modern woman would still gladly limit her existence to the domestic sphere. They felt it necessary to repeat, again and again, that women could, should, and would embrace traditional domestic duties, including food preparation. In fact, by the mid twentieth century food preparation itself had taken on an incredible burden of symbolic meaning in the modern world. By the 1950s food preparation was an entirely different activity than in the previous century. But the modern woman, comforted authors and editors, would still be in her place at the stove. The stove itself, and the home itself, had changed dramatically since the beginning of the century. But women would still provide the home cooking so many Americans seemed to crave.

By the late 1950s, however, two salient aspects of general cookery instruction contradicted that soothing image of mom's home cooking.

First, cookbooks began to increasingly note and provide recipes for women working outside the home. Second, a few authors began to acknowledge that the daily meals presented an unmitigated burden for many housewives. By 1960, as the numbers of middle-class white women employed outside the home increased, more and more cookery instruction addressed recipes and hints to the "woman who worked." Some recipe writers and cookbook editors knew that they could no longer insist that a woman make daily home-cooked meals her absolute first priority or assert that she should learn to enjoy cooking if she did not already. One author in particular—Peg Bracken—capitalized on the fact that many women simply did not enjoy any part of providing the daily meals. In 1960, the same year Ruth Stout advised women never even to say "I hate to cook," Bracken authored a successful commercial cookbook that encouraged women to embrace that very sentiment. By the early 1960s contradictions and cracks in the cooking mystique appeared throughout general cookery instruction.

11

"A Necessary Bore"

CONTRADICTIONS IN
THE COOKING MYSTIQUE

Today, the television sitcom families of the 1950s remain one of the most widely circulated images from the post–World War II period. *Leave it to Beaver, Father Knows Best,* and *Ozzie and Harriet* make regular appearances as late-night reruns around the country. And too often, Americans view the Cleaver and Nelson families as an accurate representation of life in the United States during the 1950s.[1] These highly idealized Hollywood versions of an utterly stable nuclear family life revealed more about an American mythology of family than the reality. Of course white, suburban, middle-class families with two children, a father who worked full time, and a mother who kept house full time did exist in the 1950s. But they represented, as always, a distinct minority. Sitcom families offered a reassuring image of a model family, untouched by the social changes and political unease of the postwar years. Families on TV did not worry about nuclear holocaust. The children did not learn "duck and cover" in school, nor did they go crazy at rock and roll concerts or become juvenile delinquents. The parents never received a summons from HUAC or found themselves hounded by other virulent anticommunist organizations. Nobody faced persecution for being "a sexual deviant" and nobody suffered from poverty. Everybody was white and the African American civil rights movement—which by the early 1950s began to reshape American society and politics radically—was nowhere to be seen.[2]

In a study of American cookbooks, however, one thing in particular about our popular, nostalgic, sitcom-influenced misrepresentation of the 1950s stands out: we have confused a domestic ideal, and powerful gender ideology, for the reality of women's experiences in the home, the world, and the kitchen. In recent years, social historians and feminist scholars have considerably complicated the Donna Reed image of women in the postwar years. Some have focused on uncovering the civic life and activism of middle-class white women working in political or religious organizations and community groups, as well as the way African American women played a central role in the civil rights movement. Other historians have extrapolated on the obvious fact that the political and social experiences of women of color, women in rural and urban areas, poor women, and lesbians during the 1950s differed dramatically from those of white, married, middle-class, suburban women. Others argue that a careful reading of excavated cultural artifacts supports the idea that gender and domestic ideology were not as omnipresent as Friedan suggested. Postwar popular culture, they assert, illustrated anxieties and uncertainties about domestic ideology and gender roles—uncertainties often overlooked by historians. They argue that films, television programs, and rock and roll from the 1950s presented contradictory messages about a woman's proper role in society.[3] Even as cookbooks published in the 1950s helped to disseminate and reinforce the "cooking mystique," they also revealed uncertainties about gender and domestic ideology. By the early 1960s cooking instruction often assumed that many American women did not devote themselves full time to homemaking and, moreover, that some of these women found cooking a dull and overwhelming chore.

At the same time that authors, editors, and test kitchens urged women to assume sole responsibility for family meals, they began to admit that cooking could be a tiresome task. Since the emergence of the modern cookbook in the 1920s, recipe rhetoric unceasingly urged women to enjoy the adventure, the creativity, the art of cooking; to take up gleefully the burden (cast off by departing servants) of preparing daily meals; to find new ways to spend time in the kitchen even as processed foods cut down on meal prep time. Although cookbooks did not stop insisting that women would find deep satisfaction and enjoyment in cooking, by 1960 cracks in the "cooking mystique" appeared regularly in cookery instruction. The emphasis on convenience and ready-made food, and the inclusion of very simple recipes in cookbooks reflected more than the power of food-processing companies to influence the American diet. It reflected a growing awareness on the part of marketers, publishers, and cookbook authors that many women simply did not enjoy lengthy sessions at the stove and would seek other means of personal fulfillment. Years before Betty Friedan articulated "the problem with no name," recipe purveyors knew that middle-class white women sometimes chafed at domestic duties and that these women would eagerly embrace recipes that demanded a minimum of time and effort.

One of the most important ways that cookbooks acknowledged women's nondomestic roles was to give new attention to how women with jobs outside the home might cope with cooking duties. Since at least 1920 cookbooks acknowledged the existence of "the working woman." Indeed, in the 1920s and 1930s some authors devoted considerable energy to denouncing women's outside employment and to chastising women for taking away men's jobs. During World War II cookery instruction practically ignored the fact that many married, middle-class, white women took on wartime employment. Instead, wartime cookery instruction reinforced traditional gender roles (i.e., women not working for pay outside the home) via heated rhetoric about women's patriotic responsibility in the kitchen. By the mid 1950s, however, cookbook authors and editors began to acknowledge more freely that their reader might hold a job outside the home—especially if the reader had recently married and had not yet had children. They also acknowledged that their readers might be active in community and volunteer organizations. The vast majority of cookbook authors and editors assumed that despite these outside responsibilities, a woman would remain solely accountable for the family's daily meals. But unlike earlier cookbooks, they regularly and consistently attempted to provide cooking solutions for the married woman who worked outside the home.

In doing so, authors and editors demonstrated their awareness of a changing reality: during the 1950s more married women with children took jobs outside the home than at any previous time in United States history. In 1950 women made up 29 percent of the total work force, and that number slowly grew to 35 percent by 1960. The number of women, with children, who maintained some kind of outside employment rose 400 percent during that time.[4] Middle-class Americans enjoyed unprecedented consumer power in the postwar years, but as the standard of living rose, so did the need for income. Numerous middle-class families living in comfortable suburbs needed a second income to secure the trappings of the good life, and women's salaries often went toward family vacations, a second car, new appliances, and new furniture. Although in some ways supplementary, a middle-class woman's income, even from a part-time job, often covered more than "pin money": it helped families attain the consumer paradise deferred during decades of economic depression and war. Traditional "feminine" employment such as secretarial work accounted for many of these women's new jobs. But during the postwar years, women working in female-dominated fields such as telecommunications and food service organized and agitated for better union representation. In the mid 1950s, at least two major studies done by a coalition of government, industry, and educational organizations recommended expanding employment opportunities for women.[5] Even when cookbooks began with the premise that the woman of the house must always prepare the family's meals, by 1960 they also offered much advice on how to incorporate kitchen duties into a life shaped by outside employment and activities.

Cookery instruction that advised "the working wife" emphasized the same kinds of things that all general cookbooks recommended: simple menus, advance planning, and a judicious use of packaged and processed foods. As the author of a 1950 *Good Housekeeping* article summarized: "If you work all day and run a home on the side, as I do, you know it's difficult to get dinner ready fast. I know I couldn't prepare the kind of dinner my husband and I like—well-balanced, satisfying, and attractively served—if I didn't plan ahead, keep menus simple, and use lots of canned, packaged, and frozen foods."[6] Simple menus, built around processed foods, had been in vogue for decades, but they became even simpler in the postwar era, and authors touted them as particularly helpful for the working woman. When authors offered casserole recipes, for example, they often emphasized the convenience of a one-dish meal for the wife and mother who worked outside the home. They lauded the "plate dinner"—all the courses served together on one plate—for the busy woman in the 1920s. Similarly, in the 1950s the casserole received a good deal of attention from authors, editors, and writers who produced recipes intended for women busy with outside employment or volunteer activities.

Cookbooks had been recommending advance planning—writing a shopping list, making weekly menus, cooking things ahead—since middle-class white women had begun "doing their own cooking." But in the 1950s and early 1960s, instruction constantly underscored the necessity of planning and cooking ahead for the busy woman with career, household, children, and volunteer work. In her 1954 advice for brides, Poppy Canon recommended careful meal planning to both the new bride and the "working woman." When Houghton-Mifflin published Elinore Marvel's *Cooking It Ahead* cookbook it 1951, reviewers noted its usefulness for the "working girl who also manages a home." The authors of a 1945 cookbook explained that "Women who hurry home from a job to prepare and serve a good hot dinner to the family need to be masters of making the head save the heels. Careful planning is a must."[7] During the 1950s quite a number of such cookbooks appeared, declaring that their recipes could save a reader time and effort, and often mentioning that their quick and easy meals would be a boon for married women working outside the home.

One cookbook designated for both women working outside the home and busy full-time homemakers outlined a method for preparing dinners the night before. In *The Working Wives' (Salaried or Otherwise) Cookbook*, Theodora Zavin and Freda Stuart gave extensive advice on how to prepare every dinner ahead of time, so that the working woman need not rush to make the nightly meal. They painted a pretty picture of their system in action: "When the Working Wife comes home in the evenings she spends only a few minutes in the kitchen. All of the time-consuming preparation was taken care of the day before! Dinner then cooks itself while she relaxes, or plays with the children, or talks to her husband." Zavin and Stuart offered numerous strategies for saving time in the kitchen, including using appliances such as electric teacarts and automatic dishwashers. They asserted that the wife who worked outside the home actually had more of a need for an automatic dishwasher, because a woman's employment could be threatening to her husband's masculinity. Hence, a working woman could not ask her husband to help around the house too often: "The nonworking wife may be able to send her husband to the supermarket or give him the job of doing the dishes without repercussions. But the working wife must, of necessity, always be aware that the mere fact of her working may to some degree impinge on her husband's feeling of masculinity. She must be doubly cautious about not heaping 'women's work' on at home." If even drying a few dishes might undermine a man's confidence, meal planning and preparation remained strictly out of bounds. In fact, Zavin and Stuart based their book's entire premise on not asking one's husband to do any of the cooking. Their complicated cook-it-ahead system depended entirely upon the wife's planning, shopping, and cooking for every dinner. Even as they admitted that many employed women needed to cut down on kitchen prep time, Zavin and Stuart emphasized that a woman should make sure she produced delectable daily meals: "We have never known a man who waxed nostalgic over his mother's ability to mop floors or one who boasted that his wife could wash socks better than anyone on the block," they warned the reader. "But oh, the lovely pedestal that waits the woman who cooks!"[8]

Almost no cookbook author dared to disturb women's cooking pedestal. Only a very few suggested that a husband might assume some of the daily cooking chores if a wife engaged in employment outside the home. They assumed that even if a woman worked full time outside the home, she would keep her job as family cook. Even cookbooks intended specifically for the married "working girl" took female cooking responsibilities for granted. When Hazel Young followed up her popular 1938 cookbook *The Working Girl Must Eat* with *The Working Girl's Own Cook Book* in 1948, she dedicated the book to "the girl who puts in a full day's work at the office, then dashes home to get a dinner." She pointedly noted the success of her first book in helping working girls maintain happy marriages:

> Nine years ago, *The Working Girl Must Eat* was first offered to the public. Since that time it has gone into many printings and has, we hope, made the lives of thousands of working girls much easier. Not to mention the homes that it has kept from "cracking up!" At least, one young man wrote as follows: "We have been married six months. My wife knew absolutely nothing about cooking. In desperation, I visited a bookstore and came home with a copy of *The Working Girl Must Eat*. My wife devoured the book—and soon I devoured her cooking. I really believe that without your book, our marriage might have gone on the rocks."[9]

The author of the 1963 revised edition of *Glamour Magazine's After Five Cookbook*, a book with much the same aim as Young's work, made a similar assertion about the book's ability to help a working wife keep her husband well fed: "On Capri, a woman rushed up and kissed me, saying I had saved her marriage. Startled, I heard her explain: 'My husband and I began eating at home again, and discovered we were still in love.'"[10] Neither of the husbands, assumed the authors of these cookbooks for working women, would have dreamed of taking over even a few of the cooking duties themselves. The answer to a working wife's cooking problems lay with better, more streamlined cookbooks, not a possible disruption of gender norms.

Cookbooks often conflated a working wife's cooking problems with those of a woman busy with volunteer activities and again, in both cases, assumed that women would be shouldering the dinner duties regardless. General Foods Kitchens offered last-minute menu suggestions, noting that "It can happen—you're held up at the office, or the committee meeting ran late, or you had trouble with the car."[11] But whether secretary or Red Cross volunteer, a woman faced the problem of dinner every day. The Culinary Arts Institute published a recipe booklet in 1954 entitled *Quick Dishes for the Woman in a Hurry* that began with a reassurance that all active women—whether "the working woman, busy with career and apartment or the homemaker whose day is filled with community, club, home and family activities"—would find the recipes helpful.[12] The drawing on the title page illustrated the busy woman's kitchen chores: a woman still wearing her hat, with her purse and coat on a nearby chair, leans into the oven preparing the family's meal.

In *1001 Ways to Please a Husband,* Myra Waldo gave a particularly vivid fictional account of how a working wife must not expect her husband to assume any of the dinner duties. In one of Jane's (the fictional character who introduces the recipes in Waldo's book) "diary entries," she describes how dinner nearly ended in disaster the day she came home late from work. Jane knew her boss needed her to stay until 6:30 that evening, so she precooked dinner—a main course casserole and a lemon layer pudding for dessert—and left it for her husband Peter to reheat. When Jane returned home that evening at 7:30, she found Peter at work in the kitchen: "Peter, that sweet boy, was in the kitchen getting dinner ready. But wait! What was he doing? Putting the lemon cream mixture on top of the casserole! I practically snatched it out of his hands and saved our dinner from destruction. . . . It seemed that Peter had arrived home quite early that evening and having an hour or so with nothing to do, decided to take a short nap. He had awakened with a start a few moments before I came up the walk, and dashed madly (and three-quarters asleep) into the kitchen and that was how he almost put the lemon cream on top of the casserole."[13] Even a willing husband, suggested Waldo, could not be depended upon to make dinner on even an occasional basis.

When *Time* magazine solicited recipes from their readers, quite a few contributors to the 1949 cookbook emphasized that even though duties outside the home impinged on their time, cooking remained a priority. The editor described how the female readers of *Time* made a concerted effort to do the daily cooking despite their busy schedules: "Among other things—including child-rearing, club-managing, gardening, writing, enjoying *some* leisure, and quite often holding down jobs or building them up to careers—they cook!" And the recipe writers themselves often remarked upon their own careers or busy schedules. Mrs. Marie G. Crockett, of Valdosta, Georgia, wrote: "The most successful women I know do a swell job in the world of business, run their homes beautifully, are charming hostesses and can apply the same tactics in the kitchen that they use in the business world to turn out a well-done dish. I am a career woman too, the mother of two sons, and a good cook." Mrs. Meade Summers from St. Louis complained that "One of my pet peeves is that so many people think wives who have interests outside the home neglect that all-important job of making the fireside scene a happy one. Quite the contrary!" And Mrs. Frank J. Lausche, wife of the governor of Ohio, asserted that "Interests outside your home do not lessen your interests *in* it," but admitted "you do develop short cuts."[14] None wrote in with recipes created by husbands or children, and all the contributors, no matter how busy, found time to cook for their families.

At the same time, they did imply that nothing could be more natural than a woman working outside the home or developing interests in volunteer or community work. Many, like Mrs. Lausche, suggested short cuts in order to cut down on actual kitchen work time. During the 1950s some cookbook authors lamented America's increasing reliance on canned and packaged foods, but others sang their praises and asserted that processed foods offered the working woman an invaluable time-saver. "Canned soups are a boon to the cook who works all day," proclaimed the authors of *You Can Cook If You Can Read*, published in 1946. In the introduction to the 1961 edition of her *Can-Opener Cook Book*, Poppy Canon explained that as more women worked outside the home, more women relied on canned foods: "At one time a badge of shame, hallmark of the lazy lady and the careless wife, today the can opener is fast becoming a magic wand, especially in the hands of those brave, young women, nine million of them, who are engaged in frying as well as bringing home the bacon." One author of a 1959 general cookbook even ascribed the growing availability of processed foods to divine intervention acting in the interest of working women: "A special Providence looks out for the modern woman who combines homemaking and business or a profession. Not for her the long, leisurely hours of cooking foods that require elaborate advance preparation. [She] takes advantage of modern food processing, packaging, freezing, canning and drying."[15] In statements like these, cookbooks authors showed that along with the rigorous domestic ideology, postwar cookery instruction also reflected a change in attitudes toward working women. Far fewer cookbooks in the 1950s condemned the women who brought home as well as fried the bacon. True, the cooking duties of that bacon-earner remained unchanged. But when they offered tips and shortcuts for the working wife—especially when they praised packaged, canned, and processed foods—authors seemed to accept the notion of women working outside the home.

Cookbooks that declared the necessity of packaged and processed foods for the busy women illustrated another change in postwar cookery instruction. Cookbook authors, editors, and recipes writers paid more and more attention during the 1950s to ease of preparation and to foods that required a minimum of cooking time. Much instruction urged women to pour even more effort into cookery, now that corporate food processors had eliminated the kitchen-maid tasks. Thus, hundreds of cookbooks perpetuated the "cooking mystique." But quite a few others acknowledged the drudgery of daily cooking and actually urged women to spend less time preparing meals. In marked contrast to general cookbooks published in the 1920s and 1930s, in the 1950s cookbooks increasingly gave credence to the belief that cooking meals every day for one's family could be a tedious task. Food historian Harvey Levenstein notes how advertisements in the 1950s for certain labor-saving products portrayed cooking as an important part of nurturing one's family and, paradoxically, claimed that "new products, technology, and packaging would free women from this boring, unpleasant task." Levenstein quotes an especially revealing statement from a Campbell's Soup executive, who in 1958 gave the following response to a question about postwar demand for "highly packaged" foodstuffs: "The average housewife isn't interested in making a slave of herself. When you do it day after day, [cooking] tends to get a little tiresome and that young housewife is really less interested in her reputation as a home cook today." The executive concluded that the average women "doesn't regard slaving in the kitchen as an essential [part] of [being] a good wife and mother."[16]

In the 1920s and 1930s, cookery books depicted cooking as an artistic, highly enjoyable activity. Although many post–World War II cookbooks did the same, and although numerous authors urged women who found cooking tiresome to simply *learn* how to overcome the tedium of planning and cooking the daily meals, cookery instructors also acknowledged that providing the daily meals could be wearisome. Even cookbooks that recommended a daily rest period so that the woman of the house could arise refreshed and better able to handle the chores of the day acknowledged the fact that homemaking—and cooking every day—could take a lot out of a woman. In the post–World War II era, cookbooks regularly asserted that recipes could free the woman of the home from laborious food preparation. *Simple Cooking for the Epicure* began with a description of the old-fashioned, time-consuming, and boring kind of cooking that modern women wished to avoid: "Gone are the days of yesteryear, and the daily grind of soups, stews, and suet pudding that bogged down the family board and bored the family. The up-to-date woman . . . doesn't want to slave all day preparing meals. She has other things to do, perhaps a full-time job."[17] Numerous cookbooks scoffed at the notion of doggedly pursuing the "daily grind," and offered shortcut recipes utilizing processed foods and simpler menus for the woman who did not wish to "slave all day preparing meals."

As one author wrote, "The busy homemaker of today has no time to dally in the kitchen." Even a woman who had time to spend in the kitchen could, very conceivably, wish to avoid long and laborious cooking sessions, noted many authors. The title of Alice Richardson's 1952 cookbook epitomized the shift in post–World War II cookery instruction toward depicting cooking as a chore and not necessarily a creative pursuit: *The Just a Minute Cookbook.* Richardson made it clear in her introduction that the modern woman got her cooking duties out of the way as soon as possible so as to have more time for *fun:* "Kitchens can and should be attractive, convenient and comfortable, but if you are the type who likes to spend hours on end in them, this book is not for you. It's not for drudges, putterers or anti-social people. It's for people who like to serve food with a flair and like to sip a cocktail and be gay with their guests meanwhile." Similarly, the authors of *The 60 Minute Chef* explained in the introduction that "Life is too short to spend much of it over stove. There is no recipe in this book which you cannot prepare in the single hour which you are able or willing to spend in the kitchen."[18]

Cookbooks that emphasized quickly prepared food calling for a minimum of complicated kitchen work proliferated in the 1950s. *Be Your Own Guest,* proclaimed the title of Hale MacLaren's 1952 cookbook. "Freedom from kitchen drudgery is certainly a freedom which should be included in the life of every woman," wrote MacLaren. "With the present trend of making the kitchen the core of the house, old-fashioned slaving over a hot stove is more than ever distasteful."[19] Although many authors asserted that women should always spend a great deal of time and care on the family's daily meals, some, like Richardson's and like MacLaren's, emphasized that cooking (especially for company) should not be time-consuming. The editors of *Best Recipes of 1954* took "for granted the fact that every woman, whether she is running a large household or doing simple entertaining, wants to serve not only nourishing, attractive meals, but meals which do not tie her to the stove for hours."[20] Of course, the move toward depicting cookery as a daily nuisance that women should attempt to finish as quickly as possible owed a great deal to the ever increasing power of food-processing companies and gigantic corporations. These companies poured advertising dollars into convincing consumers that they needed to buy more packaged, prebaked, and canned foods. Manufacturers wielded the best tools their marketers could create and set out to persuade all of America that only piecrust mix and frozen chicken dinners could relieve housewives of unmitigated kitchen boredom.

But it also constituted what women's historian Eva Moskowitz has termed "a discourse of discontent." In her article " 'It's Good to Blow Your Top': Women's Magazines and a Discourse of Discontent, 1945–1965," Moskowitz argues that during the 1950s women's domestic magazines regularly published features describing the unhappiness and unease of suburban housewives. They regularly reported on the tedium of housekeeping, on marital problems, and on the frustrations of suburban life. But they urged women to overcome these problems by more fully accepting the feminine role.[21] Like cookbooks, these magazines had begun to describe "the problem with no name," that is, the lack of personal fulfillment and sense of individual frustration experienced by middle-class white homemakers during the post–World War II era. In the case of cookery instruction, authors and editors began to acknowledge the tedium of daily cooking. But, like the magazines examined by Moskowitz, most cookbooks did not suggest dramatic changes in the social structure but rather urged their readers to overcome their discontent.

In "Beyond the Feminine Mystique: A Reassessment of Postwar Mass Culture, 1946–1958," historian Joanne Meyerowitz makes a similar argument about domestic magazines published during the 1950s. She asserts that while these popular publications helped uphold the cult of domesticity, they also consistently portrayed women working outside the home and working in volunteer and community organizations in a positive light.[22] Cookbooks in the 1950s demonstrated a very similar tension: even as they counseled women on the importance of home cooking, they acknowledged that women did not wish to be slaves to the stove. Even as they depicted home cooking as a necessary tool in creating family and national security, they depicted women's activities outside the home in a positive light and tried to offer cooking solutions to the kitchen problems faced by the working woman. Even as some cookbooks suggested that no responsible mother would just open a can of soup, heat it up, and serve it to her family, others paid homage to the ease and convenience of premade foods, and strongly recommended them to the busy modern woman.

No cookbook so eloquently articulated women's post–World War II "discourse of discontent" about food preparation as Peg Bracken's enormously successful *The I Hate to Cook Book*. Published in 1960, this book remains one of the few privately authored cookbooks (not sponsored by a magazine or corporation) to achieve substantial sales: 1977 figures listed it as one of the top ten best-selling cookbooks ever, at 2,929,782 copies sold. Today, consumers have purchased well over 3 million copies of this cookbook. Moreover, the 1960 book enjoyed enough success to spawn two sequels and a collected, revised edition published in 1986 that is still in print today.[23] Given its 1960 publication date, *The I Hate to Cook Book* enjoys a remarkably large number of reader reviews (all of which praise Bracken's work effusively) on the World Wide Web site of Amazon.com. Interviews with Bracken, along with her recipes, still occasionally appear in newspapers, and she made regular personal appearances throughout the 1980s.[24] Like *The Joy of Cooking*, the best selling privately authored cookbook in the United States, Peg Bracken's book generated considerable consumer loyalty and popularity for its author.

But the contrast between the titles of these two popular cookbooks revealed the authors' entirely different approach to cookery. Irma Rombauer, in keeping with the post–World War I emphasis on creativity and artistry in cooking, titled her work *The Joy of Cooking*. Peg Bracken epitomized the sentiment expressed by a growing number of cookbook authors during the 1950s when she titled her book *The I Hate to Cook Book*. In fact, the title won Bracken her first book contract, while she was working as a freelance magazine writer. Jean Hopkins, the editor who acquired Bracken's book, explained in a 1998 *Washington Post* article the importance of Bracken's title. Even though Bracken had not completed a manuscript, Hopkins sold the idea to Harcourt Brace on the strength of the title alone. "It was," Hopkins remarked, "an absolutely original, marvelous title."[25]

Bracken's writing ability also set her apart from Rombauer and, indeed, most other cookery instruction authors. Bracken earned her B.A. in English at Antioch College, and since the publication of *The I Hate to Cook Book*, she has authored several other humor books, as well as her memoirs, a book of reflections on growing old, and numerous newspaper and magazine columns. *The I Hate to Cook Book* offered a great deal of humorous discussion about food preparation, along with the recipes. In many ways, Bracken's text presents a good example of what American studies scholar Nancy Walker has termed "domestic humor literature." In her article "Humor and Gender Roles: The 'Funny' Feminism of the Post–World War II Suburbs," Walker argues that domestic humor, by authors such as Shirley Jackson and Betty MacDonald, voiced a refusal to be fooled by the domestic ideology of the postwar years. Walker asserts that women writing about their experiences as 1950s suburban housewives targeted themselves as the object of their humor, but "a sensitive reading of these works makes it clear that there are specific causes for these women's feelings of inferiority and uneasiness, located in social norms and attitudes that decreed woman's separate sphere." By describing their own ineptitude in the housewife role and resulting domestic chaos, these authors reassured the reader about her own possible failures to live up to the perfect wife and mother images circulating in the 1950s. This kind of writing, Walker summarizes, "expressed a hostility toward rigid role definition that prefigures the issues of the women's movement."[26]

Bracken's text, like the ones examined by Walker, did not fundamentally call into question gender norms. Even if you hate to cook, Bracken implied, as a woman it will be your job to cook. But while Bracken never

asserted that women should rebel outright against the inequitable division of cooking duties, she certainly expressed "a hostility toward rigid
role definition." For example, she asserted that if you hate to cook, you
rely on already prepared foods "as often as you can." But, she added, a
woman could use premade foods only so often, because "right here you
usually run into a problem with the basic male." She wrote that a
husband "wants to see you knead that bread and tote that bale before
you go down cellar to make soap. This is known as Woman's Burden."
Still, she urged women to give ready-made foods a try, without extensive alterations. In direct contrast to many other cookbooks in the
1950s, she stated that many premade foods tasted just fine straight
from the can or the box. Convenience food should be convenient, she
wrote: "[I]f you add seven different herbs and grated cheese to everything this is supposed to be all ready, you might as well have started
from scratch in the first place."[27] Bracken made it clear that for women
who hated to cook, convenience food offered plenty of shortcuts, but
unlike other cookery books, she did not suggest doctoring that food.
Nor did she suggest that women used these products simply because
their busy schedule did not allow them to cook "from scratch."

But Bracken did accept the fact that her readers had to do the daily
cooking: she called for making very simple dishes, avoiding elaborate
entertaining, and relying on canned and packaged foods, but she never
suggested that another member of the household might do some of the
cooking. Culinary historian Nicole Humble (who notes that *The I Hate
to Cook Book* achieved strong sales in England) asserts that such strategies illustrate how middle-class white women in the 1950s felt utterly
trapped in their domestic roles. She characterizes Bracken's generation
(Bracken was in her late thirties in 1960), and books such as *The I Hate
to Cook Book*, as "marked by a pervasive sense of discontent with the
gender role established for them in the 1950s, but without a political
analysis that would enable them to formulate a response." Humble
summarizes: "Thus Bracken's solution to the fact that many women
hate to cook is not to question whether they should have to do so, but to
suggest ways in which they can deceive and cheat and get other women
to do it for them."[28]

Humble does not take into account how *The I Hate to Cook Book* fit
into the history of cookbooks in the United States. Read in this light,
Peg Bracken's work marked quite a serious departure from some of the
major trends in modern cookery instruction, namely the emphasis on
how modern women needed to take their place in America's kitchens
joyfully. *The I Hate to Cook Book* also signaled the beginning of the end
for widely published cookery advice laden with rhetoric about women's
domestic duties. Bracken did not ask her readers to try to like cooking if

Figure 21 Distinctive drawings by Hilary Knight helped reinforce Peg Bracken's assurances that women need not enjoy cooking. From *The I Hate to Cook Book* (Greenwich, CT: Fawcett, 1960).

they simply did not. In fact, she urged women not to feel guilty about disliking to cook (fig. 21). Bracken did not pretend that only the reader's busy schedule prevented more elaborate meals. Her readers did not want to spend a lot of time cooking because they did not like to cook, and Bracken sympathized:

> Some women, it is said, like to cook.
> This book is not for them.
> This book is for those of us who hate to, who have learned, through hard experience, that some activities become no less painful through repetition: childbearing, paying taxes, cooking. This book is for those of us who want to fold our big dishwater hands around a dry martini instead of a wet flounder, come the end of a long day.[29]

Bracken's recipes for "Stayabed Stew" and "Idiot Onions" did not claim gourmet status. In her introduction, Bracken explained that although she promised "no Escoffier creations you can build in five minutes," her book contained simple, reliable recipes that women who hated cooking might find helpful. "At the very least," she concluded, "you should find a hands-across-the-pantry feeling, coming right through the ink. It is always nice to know you are not alone."[30] Peg Bracken sought to establish the same kind of personal communication—a "hands-across-the-pantry feeling"—with her readers that Irma Rombauer successfully achieved and numerous other cookbook authors attempted. And, to a great extent, Bracken did just that.[31]

Bracken received (and continues to receive) hundreds of letters from fans writing to express their appreciation for *The I Hate to Cook Book*, and this correspondence demonstrates that Bracken's cookbook spoke to the food preparation needs of many women around the country. In 1977 a woman from Utah, summarized how many readers saw, and valued, Bracken's book as a novel approach to cookery: "You exploded the myth that cooking is a creative joy for Womankind and labeled it as the necessary bore it often is. You then proceeded to make it almost painless. I have used the recipes in the *I Hate to Cook Book* [*sic*] for years. I especially like the ones that call for five ingredients or less (so now you see where *my* head is when it comes to cooking)."[32] Over the years, some people have written to the publishers of Bracken's work and inquired as to the existence of Peg Bracken, wondering if she was a real woman or a Betty Crocker–like fictional character. But most of Bracken's fan mail, like the letter from Utah, shows that readers felt a personal connection to Bracken—and that they regularly used Bracken's recipes in daily life.

A letter from California, written in 1998, told Bracken about the reader's well-used copy of *The I Hate to Cook Book:* "[O]ur kids grew up on 'Stay Abed Stew.' *The I Hate to Cook Book* falls open at the Cockeyed Cake recipe (which has dribbles on it)." One woman wrote in 1999: "In my many moves, I lost the book. *I wept.*" In 1973 another fan described how she had bought numerous copies of the book: "I have given at least one copy of each to everyone I know for some birthday, Christmas, Mother's Day or Father's Day. I say *at least* one, because they *do* wear out and if borrowed they're gone for good! Thank goodness for 'paper back'!" Fans often mentioned giving *The I Hate to Cook Book* as gifts, as did this Oregonian in 1998, who also described her own battered copy of the cookbook: "I don't remember how your book entered my household, but you have felt like a friend for years. You should see the pages of our favorite recipes, now brown and splattered with years of use. . . . Have been many times to the Powell Bookstore on Burnside [a large bookstore in Portland which sells new and used books], buying all the *I Hate to Cook* [*sic*] books that I could find. Using them for bridal shower gifts and of course one for our daughter when she married, so she could make all 'our favorites.' " Another fan, divorced with two small children, wrote a letter in 1973 that revealed how Bracken's book helped her deal, on a day-to-day basis, with meal preparation: "When company comes for dinner I even let them in! I'll never *like* to cook, but let's face it, how many peanut butter and jelly sandwiches can you *eat?* And at least now I can get it over with and enjoy life. Thank you, thank you, thank you!" One woman who wrote from Virginia in 1970 praised the recipes in Bracken's book—"Your *I Hate to Cook Book* saw me through my first year of marriage"—as well as Bracken's humor. The fan even suggested that Bracken's advice could help smooth out domestic and international conflict: "If the world could inherit your wit and good humor, we'd never have another war—from husband and wife type to Viet Nam." Letters to Peg Bracken suggest that she did indeed establish a "hands-across-the-pantry" feeling with her readers. Her fans seem to have avidly followed Bracken's recipes and also seemed to appreciate Bracken's witty remarks on her frustration with cooking.

A married bookstore owner, self-identified as a member of Bracken's generation, wrote to Bracken in 1999 to express her appreciation for *The I Hate to Cook Book.* "I was married in '39 and in 1950 opened a Children's Book Shop," she wrote, adding that "my husband was a publisher's representative—so I had first hand information to go by." She went on to describe how *The I Hate to Cook Book* practically flew off her shelves in 1960 when the book was first published: "My shop and *The Hate to Cook Book* [*sic*] helped put our five kids through college," she quipped. She also related a story about how Bracken's humor cheered a particularly hard-to-please customer: "One day a rather down elderly lady came in with her daughter—and planted herself in a soft chair next to the fireplace. The expression on her face one of annoyance and boredom. My first shipment of *The Hate to Cook Book* [*sic*] was unpacked and on display—so I decided to try it out on old sourpuss—In no time she was howling with laughter—I had to re-order immediately—she'd cleaned me out—It was like that for years—I don't know how many I sold—but they kept coming back for more!" As a bookstore owner, with ties to the publishing world, this fan offered credible first-hand evidence about the popularity of *The I Hate to Cook Book.* She also noted that she often used her own copy of the cookbook, although "its condition from constant use is totally unsanitary!"

Significantly, a number of fans noted that *The I Hate to Cook Book* assumed a place of importance on their cookbook shelves—next to more extensive general cookbooks (Bracken's book contained only 180 recipes). "Since June of 1961, your cookbook, *I Hate to Cook* [*sic*] has been my all time favorite, along with a nineteen fifty something, Betty Crocker. Have a lot of cookbooks, but if could only keep two, the above would be the ones," wrote another Oregonian. Some readers, like a woman from Illinois who wrote to Bracken in 1980, explained that Bracken's book offered a welcome change from complicated recipes and overwhelming cookbooks:

> Not only had I never cooked in my life, but when I looked at cooking books I was terrified. There were three pages of spices for each recipe. There was no way I was going to take the plunge into a recipe that requires 5 hours to do.
>
> Then your book caught my eye—it was the title that was the real grabber. Ms. Bracken you're a genius. Your book not only taught me to cook, it kept me from being afraid and it even gave me the courage to try other, more complex cookbooks.

Other letters, from less inexperienced cooks, praised Bracken's book by describing it as a necessary addition to their "kitchen bibles." As a Wyoming woman wrote in 1969 "Your charming verse was all I knew of you till my sister sent me the cookbook and you went right up with Irma Rombauer among the kitchen angels."

In that woman's Wyoming kitchen, *The Joy of Cooking* and *The I Hate to Cook Book* sat comfortably side by side. The apparent contradiction, articulated by the titles of these books, did not seem to trouble the letter writer. And, indeed, Peg Bracken herself explained in the introduction to *The I Hate to Cook Book* that her recipes would not replace the big kitchen bibles that gave recipes for everything under the sun. Bracken did not hesitate to point out the numerous flaws in such cookbooks, asserting that "they contain too many recipes. Just look at all the things you can do with a chop, and aren't about to! What you want is just one little old dependable thing you can do with a chop besides broil it, that's all." She also criticized the overly explicit directions in such cookbooks, complaining that "they're also telling you what any chucklehead would know. 'Place dough in pan to rise and cover with a clean cloth,' they say. What did they *think* you'd cover it with?" But she noted that every kitchen required one of these massive cookbooks: "But perhaps the most depressing thing about those big fat cookbooks is that you have to have one. Maybe your mother-in-law gives you a bushel of peppers or a pumpkin, and you must make piccalilli or a pumpkin pie. Well, there's nothing to do but look it up in your big fat cookbook, that's all. But you can certainly train yourself not to look at anything else."[33]

While admitting the need for a big kitchen bible for occasional reference, Bracken also criticized much of the advice on cookery offered to American women in the 1950s. "We live in a cooking-happy age," she griped. "You watch your friends redoing their kitchens and hoarding their pennies for glamorous cooking equipment and new cookbooks called *Eggplant Comes To The Party* or *Let's Waltz into the Kitchen*, and presently you begin to feel un-American." She critiqued the writers of such cookbooks as well, for their impractical recipes and their overly cheerful rhetoric about cooking and food. For example, she took cookbook writers to task for giving extensive and unrealistic advice on how to use up leftovers and for chivying readers to learn to like vegetables, which, Bracken asserted, simply do not taste as good as other kinds of things. "Actually, the food experts know this, too, way down deep," she wrote. "You can tell they do from the reliance they put on adjectives whenever they bump into a vegetable. 'And with it serve a big bowl of tiny, buttery, fresh-from-the-garden beets!' they'll cry. But they're still only beets, and there's no need to get so excited about it." She even actively demythologized the photographs often accompanying cookery instruction. "But I'd like to mention here that it is unwise to expect your company meals to look precisely like the company meals you see in the full-color food spreads everywhere," she began and then described witnessing a major food photographer lacquering lobsters, dying gravy, and propping food up with toothpicks. "[F]ood photographers do not play fair and square," she informed the reader.

"Oh, you keep on buying cookbooks, the way a homely woman buys hat after hat in the vain hope that this one will do it," she admitted. "And, heaven knows, the choice is wide, from the haute cuisine cookbook that is so haute it requires a pressurized kitchen, through *Aunt Em's Down-on-the-Farm Book of Cornmeal Cookery*, all the way to the exotic little foreign recipe book, which is the last thing you want when you hate to cook. Not only are there pleasanter ways to shorten your life, but, more important, your husband won't take you out for enchiladas if he knows he can get good enchiladas at home."[34] For Bracken, the wide selection of cookbooks on the market in the 1950s presented daunting obstacles for the woman who hated to cook. They also contained some bad advice. Why learn how to cook complex foreign dishes when restaurants offered that kind of fare? Her commentary on the cookery instruction available to women in the 1950s showed her frustration with the outpouring of recipes, food suggestions, and cookbooks.

Bracken herself owns a substantial cookbook collection. In her memoirs, she mentions that she owns a large number of cookbooks, including some inherited from her mother, such as the *Boston Cooking School Cook Book* and a recipe book published by the Ladies Guild of the Ganister (Kansas) Presbyterian Church. Her collection also includes "a first-edition *The Joy of Cooking* that is nicely counterbalanced, I'm glad to say, by a first-edition *I Hate to Cook Book*."[35] Indeed, *The I Hate to Cook Book* counterbalanced *The Joy of Cooking* for millions of women around the country. Bracken's cookbook shelf (and her mother's) illustrated how American women, during the first half of the twentieth century, relied on a kitchen bible like Betty Crocker's or *The Joy of Cooking*, or perhaps a community cookbook full of recipes from friends, PTA members, or members of a church congregation. But as the 1950s progressed, their collections expanded to include foreign cookbooks, cookery instruction for new kinds of appliances, and cookbooks that emphasized convenience foods. Many added Peg Bracken's acerbic recipes to their cookbook collections. Middle-class women had been turning to cookery experts since the end of the nineteenth century and had relied on massive general cookbooks to guide them through their "first days in the kitchen"—and they continued to do so in the 1950s. Even a woman who disliked cooking gathered an arsenal of cookbooks around her and found herself turning to a "big fat cookbook" at Thanksgiving or when confronted with cucumbers that needed canning. But for everyday dinners, she may well have turned to the simple, speedy recipes in *The I Hate to Cook Book.*

Women collected recipes from each other, from popular magazines, local and national newspaper columns, and from appliance and food product promotions. And they relied on cookbooks to teach them how to cook, especially how to cook pies, cookies, and other baked goods.[36] During the 1950s, when publishers churned out cookbooks on every imaginable topic, women accumulated more cookery books and more recipes—even as authors and editors admitted that their readers did not wish to be "slaves to the stove." Somewhat paradoxically, Americans bought more and more cookbooks during the postwar era, but at the same time, fewer and fewer of them enjoyed home-cooked meals "from scratch." And, again somewhat paradoxically, as many cookbooks in the 1950s reinforced the "cookery mystique" that began with patriotic fervor during World War II, other cookery instruction began to lure buyers with the promise that their recipes could free a woman from kitchen enslavement.

Cooking school instructors in the late 1800s had depicted cookery as a perfectible science taught by trained experts. After World War I, as fewer middle-class households employed paid cooks, and canned and packaged foods became more available, cookery instruction took on a new tone, one that emphasized the "joy of cooking" and the art of cooking. After World War II, during which time cookery books emphasized the importance of women's home cooking to national defense, cookbook publishers and recipe purveyors continued to invest women's home cooking with domestic and social importance. And the definition of middle-class women's home cooking shifted again—from science to art to patriotic necessity to part of the feminine mystique and, finally, to tiresome chore best relieved by very simple recipes and by convenience foods. Throughout World War II, cookery instruction advised women to put their family's mealtime needs first, and by the late 1940s and 1950s authors and editors added to the chorus of postwar prescriptive literature that urged women out of the factory and back to the kitchen.

But by 1960, as middle-class white women's employment outside the home gained acceptance and women laid the groundwork for the second-wave feminist movement in the United States, general cookery instruction also revealed the instability of the domestic ideal. Although Peg Bracken did not suggest that husbands take over the family meals, she certainly did not urge women to "be pretty, be cheerful and be a good cook." Instead she satirized and openly scoffed at that ideal, perpetuated in other cookbooks. She, and an increasing number of other cookbook authors, spoke to the modern woman who found domesticity confining and preparing the daily meals to be necessary, but a bore. They spoke to women who wanted to get on with life and not spend endless hours cooking meals for their husbands and their children.

Gender and domestic ideology maintained a tight hold over United States society in the years following World War II. Cookery instruction aimed at male readers made it clear that men, as they had in prewar cookbooks, reigned as kings of the kitchen when they cooked a pot of spaghetti or a steak or some other suitably masculine dish. In the 1950s, according to the creators of cookery instruction for men, father cooked best. Both male and female authors lamented women's poor cooking habits and virtually all general cookbooks persisted in depicting the woman of the house as bearing sole responsibility for the family's daily meals—even if she engaged in outside activities or employment. Cookery instruction reiterated rigid gender norms at the site of food preparation throughout the 1950s. But contradictions in the cooking mystique also shaped post–World War II cookbooks, and cookbook readers did not always swallow recipes for domestic and gender roles. As the grateful letters to Peg Bracken suggest, women utilized basic and general cookbooks in practical, everyday ways, but readers also longed for a cookbook that assured them that they need not learn to love cooking. During the 1950s the cooking mystique shaped many magazine articles and cookbooks, and the vast majority of cooking instruction placed responsibility for daily cooking squarely on the shoulders of the woman of the house. But the success of *The I Hate to Cook Book,* and the numbers of general cookbooks that offered tips and hints on how to spend less time and effort cooking, indicated that the cooking mystique did not exercise omnipresent power.

By the end of the 1950s women sought new cooking strategies along with cookery instruction that did not constantly tell them that they must make a full cookie jar their life's work. Even those women who did, on the whole, enjoy cookery might have searched cookbooks for quick and easy recipes. Middle-class women, often well educated and with the privilege of financial security, embraced the new convenience foods and more streamlined cookery instruction in hopes of meeting the demands of their role as homemaker while also creating more time for their individual pursuits. Cookbook publishers, ever attuned to a changing market, scrambled to get out cookery instruction with easy, hurry-up recipes. The makers of canned and frozen foods emphasized the ease with which a woman might put together a delicious family dinner, and the free time that processed foods afforded the woman of the house. In these subtle but important ways, cookery instruction reflected the fact that, despite the reemergence of a powerful domestic ideology after World War II, gender norms had indeed been shaken during the early 1940s. Although most Americans strongly desired to "get back to normal" after the war, many of the women who enjoyed having a paycheck for the first time wished to continue working outside the home. Women ran homes, businesses, families, and heavy machinery while their husbands, fathers, and sweethearts fought in the war. And despite the onslaught of prescriptive literature at the end of the war that urged Rosie out of the factory and back to her real job, dramatic changes in women's social roles (changes that began the previous century) were imminent.

Cookery instruction for men and cookbooks that emphasized the importance of a woman's home cooking to her feminine identity showed that gender norms still marked food preparation in the United States after the war. But when authors began to promise women freedom from kitchen drudgery and to sing the praises of convenience food, and when women began to pass around *The I Hate to Cook Book*, cookery instruction also showed cracks in the cooking mystique. Women might have bought Betty Crocker's cookbook, but that did not mean that they bought into Betty Crocker's claims about the importance of the family cookie jar. Women purchased more cookbooks during the 1950s than at any other previous time, but as the numbers of cookbooks proliferated, the domestic and gender ideologies found in cookery instruction became more diffuse and contradictory. By the early 1960s, cookbook authors and editors readily admitted that cooking the daily meals need not be a critical part of a woman's domestic duties.

Since 1920 cookery instruction advised women that, while cooking led to a man's heart, it also lay at the heart of being a married woman. In the 1940s and early 1950s cookery instruction depicted food preparations as critical to domestic and national security. In the 1950s, as the feminine mystique flourished, many cookbooks advised married women and mothers to pay more attention to cooking the daily meals than ever before—because a woman's home-cooked meals kept the family secure and best expressed a woman's essential feminine nature. By the early 1960s, however, cookbooks began to instruct women on how to get out of the kitchen faster and how to fit their cooking duties into their busy schedules. Cookery instruction from the 1920s through the 1950s often tried to convince white, middle-class, educated readers that cooking constituted an essential part of homemaking—a woman's most important job. As the 1950s progressed, that task became markedly more difficult.

Conclusion

FROM JULIA CHILD TO COOKING.COM

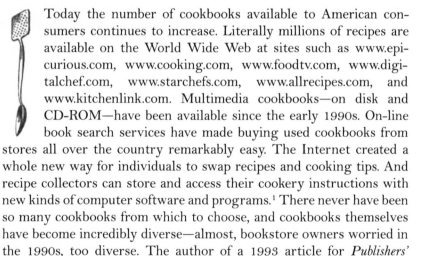 Today the number of cookbooks available to American con-
sumers continues to increase. Literally millions of recipes are
available on the World Wide Web at sites such as www.epi-
curious.com, www.cooking.com, www.foodtv.com, www.digi-
talchef.com, www.starchefs.com, www.allrecipes.com, and
www.kitchenlink.com. Multimedia cookbooks—on disk and
CD-ROM—have been available since the early 1990s. On-line
book search services have made buying used cookbooks from
stores all over the country remarkably easy. The Internet created a
whole new way for individuals to swap recipes and cooking tips. And
recipe collectors can store and access their cookery instructions with
new kinds of computer software and programs.[1] There never have been
so many cookbooks from which to choose, and cookbooks themselves
have become incredibly diverse—almost, bookstore owners worried in
the 1990s, too diverse. The author of a 1993 article for *Publishers'
Weekly* asserted, "Cookbook diversity is stretching the market to the
breaking point." Another *Publishers' Weekly* article, published in 2000,
pointed out that cookbook publishers face an "almost desperately competitive cookbook marketplace."[2]

Although Americans currently eat more fast food, more premade
food, and more meals in restaurants than at any other time in American
history, cookbooks and recipes continue to circulate in vast numbers.
New food-related magazines, packed with vivid color photographs of

gourmet meals, appear regularly on the newsstand. Star chefs such as Wolfgang Puck and Emeril Lagasse enjoy enormous popularity, and cookbooks featuring their recipes sell briskly. The Food Network airs cooking shows and food-related shows all day, every day of the week. Moreover, the food featured in these magazines and new cookbooks often requires lengthy preparations and expensive kitchen gadgets. Ingredients must be top-quality, fresh, organic, and authentic. Even though statistics show that barely half of American dinners feature one or more homemade dishes, the market for gourmet cookery instruction and equipment has increased exponentially in the past few decades. Increasingly, home buyers seek colossal kitchens with stainless steel appliances, prep sinks, and restaurant quality stoves. In 1996 gourmet cooking utensils and related housewares alone constituted a $25 billion dollar business.[3]

Of course, gourmet cookbooks are not unique to the twenty-first century. But the elaborate pastry and authentic Thai curry recipes found in magazines, on television, and on line do create a popular climate of gourmet sensibilities never before experienced by such a large number of Americans. One easily could argue that this is a change for the better, especially in terms of culinary diversity, taste quality, and healthfulness. Certainly many middle-class Americans eagerly embraced the changes in home cooking heralded by Julia Child in the late 1960s. No one did more than she, with her matter-of-fact approach to the intricacies of French cooking and her appreciation for all delicious food, to inspire home cooks to try gourmet cooking. Child's 1961 *Mastering the Art of French Cooking* has sold more than a million copies. But Child enjoyed her greatest fame via her public television cooking show, *The French Chef.* It debuted in 1963 to immediate success, and Child virtually single-handedly fostered new widespread appreciation for fresh ingredients and classic French cuisine—and ushered in the age of celebrity chefs.[4] Bolstered in large part by Child, the 1960s saw the rapid "gourmetization" of United States food culture. When the Kennedys hired a French chef at the White House, famous food critic Craig Claiborne applauded the decision as a reflection of the growing appreciation for fine foods. "Cookbook of the month" clubs flourished, and suburban ladies perfected sophisticated gourmet dishes.[5]

An even more far-reaching food revolution occurred in the 1970s: the natural foods movement and medical research on the effects of cholesterol created new popular awareness about diet and health. The 1962 publication of Rachel Carson's *Silent Spring* alerted many Americans to the dangers of insecticides and pollution, while Frances Moore Lappé's 1971 *Diet for a Small Planet* demonstrated how "eating low on the food chain" had important political ramifications. By the early

1970s numerous Americans cooked and consumed natural foods for both its health benefits and for its contribution to the good of the world.[6] Whole-food stores and health food restaurants flourished, and juicers, Crockpots, and food processors began to appear in more and more kitchens. The small but active subculture of American communes embraced vegetarian and organic cookery, and suspicion about artificial sweeteners and preservatives grew among Americans in general.[7] In 1972 the publication of a popular cookbook called *The Vegetarian Epicure* reflected the changing needs of home cooks. But only a few years later, Americans would turn with renewed interest toward culinary excesses: the 1980s saw a dramatic rise in gourmet magazines, pricey restaurants, and indulgent food treats such as high-fat ice cream. The phenomenal rise in restaurant dining also demonstrated Americans' willingness to spend ever increasing amounts of money on meals. As historian Mary Drake McFeely writes, "The language of the whole earth gave way to that of self-help and self-interest, and conspicuous consumption achieved heights that would have astonished Thorstein Veblen, the man who, in 1899, coined the phrase."[8]

Cookbooks reflected this shift. In 1986 culinary historian Laura Shapiro characterized contemporary American cookery books and magazines as an "expression of unashamed hedonism on the part of a middle class that's pleased with itself."[9] That "hedonism," and the accompanying proliferation of recipes, magazines, and cookbooks, continues today. The immense popularity of "ethnic" and fusion cuisine in the 1990s created new fields of cookery knowledge, requiring new kinds of cookery instruction.[10] Gourmet restaurants and celebrity chefs churn out new volumes of recipes on a regular basis. And even though cookbooks are an oversaturated market, with innumerable specialty books, General Mills, *Better Homes and Gardens*, and *Good Housekeeping* still sell a great deal of general cookery instruction. *Betty Crocker's Picture Cook Book* remains one of the most sought-after used cookbooks, and *Joy of Cooking* remains a steady best seller. And Peg Bracken continues to get grateful letters from fans.[11]

The simplicity of her recipes was one reason so many women found Peg Bracken's cookbook appealing. From 1920 through the 1950s, cookbooks promised perfection, if the reader carefully followed the recipe. And general cookbooks with simple home recipes could often guarantee that promise. But with the rapid spread of gourmet food standards in the 1960s, the growing health concerns in the 1970s, and the quest for culinary authenticity in the 1990s, providing the daily meals for one's family became more and more demanding. One could argue, as McFeely does, that cookbook authors of the past offered a great deal of advice aimed at the truly inexperienced home cook, whereas cookbooks in the 1990s seemed to require much more of their readers:

> Fannie Farmer was a teacher. Irma Rombauer was the surrogate mother (or perhaps the skilled and good-humored neighbor) who shared her cooking secrets and knew absolutely everything. Even "The French Chef," Julia Child, who had learned classic French cooking from experts so she could practice it at home, saw herself as a home-kitchen teacher. But now cookbook authors were professional cooks. For the cook at home, a recent cookbook or the latest issue of *Gourmet, Saveur, Bon Appétit*, or some newer food magazine in hand, these chef-instructors have given cooking a very different look, placing a high value on sophistication and the novelty of imaginative cooking.[12]

Today, our cookbooks demand fresh lemon grass and fish sauce, and a food processor with three different types of blades. No aspiring middle-class gourmet today would dream of using canned soup in *anything*. Cookbooks are, in large part, aimed more than ever at a financially secure audience, with the leisure and the money to pursue upwardly mobile eating and cooking. Martha Stewart's cookbooks and domestic advice, for instance, helped to create a whole new ideal of home cooking and entertaining, one even more impossible to attain than Betty Crocker's admonition to keep the cookie jar full.[13] A powerful domestic cooking ideal, aimed primarily at those with the disposable income necessary to pursue it, continues to shape cookery instruction.

Marjorie DeVault, in her sociological study of families and food preparation, describes the way food and cookery continue to play an important role in defining middle-class domesticity: "The nineteenth-century 'cult of domesticity' emphasized the construction of 'home' life in opposition to the larger society, and depended on the association of women with home and men with public activity outside the home. Now, women at home, producing an orderly haven for men and children, is no longer a central symbol of middle-class status. Middle-class husbands have begun to participate in family activities in new ways. But these changes have been accompanied by a renewed emphasis on the pleasures of eating, which seems to be one strand in a reconstruction of domesticity."[14] Cookbooks are an important part of this "reconstruction of domesticity." Cookbooks continue, in the new millennium, to reinforce our ideas about gender and domesticity. We have not escaped assumptions about what men eat and cook and what women eat and cook (fig. 22). The link between gender and certain kinds of food preparation remains strong.

As folklorist Thomas A. Adler points out in his well-known article,

Figure 22 A recent "Stone Soup" cartoon strip shows how Americans still make assumptions about what men cook. This cartoon appeared on 29 April 2001, in the *Oregonian*.

"Making Pancakes on Sunday: The Male Cook in Family Tradition," many Americans still see male cookery as special-occasion cuisine, as a markedly different kind of activity than day-to-day cooking. "Dad's cooking exists in evident contradistinction to Mom's on every level . . . his is socially and gastronomically experimental, hers mundane; his is dish-specific and temporally-marked, hers diversified and quotidian; his is play, hers is work," Adler writes.[15] A 1999 survey by the Barbecue Industry Association showed that men are still much more likely to grill food outdoors than women are: 73 percent of men, versus 33 percent of women.[16] As recently as 1992, the executive vice-president of Thermador, maker of high-end stoves and ranges, equated the kitchen with women: "A woman's kitchen is like a man's office or a child's bedroom. In the kitchen, she makes the decisions."[17]

Columnist Steven Bauer asserts that even though more American men cook, we still "think of the kitchen as a woman's space, one that's too risky for people of the male persuasion, even those who don't flinch at bungee jumping, hang gliding or facing a frothy set of class VI rapids." As Bauer explains, the risk, of course, is perceived feminization: "What can be worse for a boy than to be 'tied to mommy's apron strings'? The message is clear: overexposure to pots and pans can seriously affect a man's ability to make his way in the world."[18] More than six decades ago, authors began to make a concerted effort to differentiate men's cooking and women's cooking, and to carefully reiterate that cooking need not undermine a man's masculinity. Today Americans still express concern about a man's "overexposure to pots and pans." Cookbook authors and magazine writers still characterize the man in the kitchen the same way their counterparts did eighty years ago. They still use images of a caveman, cooking a haunch of wooly mammoth over an open fire, to explain the male propensity for barbecuing. They still suggest that men enjoy cooking a few specialty dishes, but that men do not take responsibility for the daily cooking. They compare cooking to other kinds of masculine activities, like woodworking or golf.[19] Even if, statistically, more men frequent the kitchen than they did fifty years ago, our ideas about *how* and *what* men cook have not changed much.

At least four cookbooks by and for men published in the last few years demonstrate this: *A Man, A Can, A Plan: 50 Great Guy Meals Even You Can Make!*, by David Joachim, published in 2002; Bob Sloan's 1993 *Dad's Own Cook Book; Bake It Like a Man* by David and Sharon Bowers, published in 1999; and Don Mauer's *A Guy's Guide to Great Eating: Big-Flavored Fat-Reduced Recipes for Men Who Love to Eat*, also published in 1999. Although health concerns prevent these authors from recommending thick steaks and fried foods to their male readers, and although second-wave feminism wrought enough changes in American society to ensure that these cookbooks do not dwell on the superiority of men in the kitchen, these authors make it clear that men engage in certain kinds of cooking and eat certain kinds of food. Author David Joachim's recipe for "BBQ Beer Ribs," for example, utilized the same kind of hearty ingredients and vigorous directions found in recipes for men eighty years earlier: "Dump all the ingredients [1/2 can beer, 1 1/2 cups spicy tomato juice cocktail, 1 cup honey barbecue sauce, and 8 pork ribs] into a ziplock bag. Down the leftover 1/2 can beer. Stick the bag in the fridge for two hours or overnight. Throw the ribs on the grill for 15 minutes."[20] Don Mauer explained that his low-fat recipes could satisfy a man-sized appetite. "I want to meet the man who eats a half cup of macaroni and cheese and can't eat another bite because he's so stuffed. *Puh-leeze*," he wrote. He continued: "A single four-inch buttermilk pancake doesn't fill me up in the mornings. A wussy little half sandwich for lunch doesn't keep my furnace fired up all afternoon. And anyone who thinks a three-ounce serving of chicken breast, a half cup of steamed green beans and a small boiled potato will keep me—or most men—from raiding the refrigerator an hour later should think again."[21] Cookery instruction for men no longer brags about the king of the kitchen nor does it advocate excessive amounts of red meat, butter, and fried foods. But in 1999 Don Mauer could generalize about the appetites of "most men" because our notions of what men and women eat—and cook—remain firmly entrenched. He could characterize a small sandwich as "wussy" and unfit for male consumption. A recent cover story on American eating habits in a popular Sunday newspaper magazine demonstrated this point. It depicted a man and woman, the woman about to tuck into a leafy salad, the man grinning over a triple cheeseburger.[22] The publication of the kitsch-conscious, graphic-heavy *Dude*

Food by pop culture fans Karen Brooks, Gideon Buskin, and Reed Darmon and the 2000 rerelease of Robert Loeb's *A Wolf in Chef's Clothing* show how cookery instruction for men is still a novelty item.

General cookbooks no longer aim their instructions solely at middle-class white women. Yet many of us still look to the woman of the home to provide the daily meals. In a recent article published in *Gourmet* magazine, A. Manette Ansay commented on this phenomenon, describing the astonishment of friends who learn that Ansay's husband, and not herself, prepares the couples' daily meals: "Why do people find my husband's cooking so remarkable, so baffling, so unexpected?" she asks. "Why do women friends sidle up to me, cooing, 'You're sooo lucky!' This is, after all, the '90s, the Era of Emeril." "The women I know who cook, which is to say most of the women I know, don't get this kind of attention," points out Ansay. "Nobody . . . would enter my parents' house and exclaim to my mother, 'You did all this yourself?' Nobody turns to my father and says, 'You mean you don't cook, ever?' "[23] Ansay's article offers an example of the way Americans continue to view home cooking as the sole province of women. The late twentieth and early twenty-first centuries may be the "Era of Emeril," but most of us still consider a man who cooks the family's meals a rarity.

Americans know that most married women and women with children will obtain employment outside the home, and that the majority of women in the United States hold jobs. Yet in some ways our expectations remain unchanged. We still expect men and women to eat different things, and many of us still expect women to do most of the cooking. Of course, a great many women and men truly enjoy cooking meals for their families and experimenting with new recipes. Some couples enjoy cooking together, or exploring their local farmers' market. And many find cooking, out of all the household chores required to keep a home running, the most pleasurable and fulfilling task. Cookery clearly offers innumerable Americans the opportunity for creative expression, for demonstrating care and affection, and for sensual, satisfying pleasures. But we should be aware that the cookbook we casually consult for a favorite recipe has a history. We should remember that, since at least the end of the nineteenth century, food manufacturers, cookbook authors, editors, and publishers used this medium to sell their products and their magazines. In the process, they helped establish links between gender and food preparation that remain strong to this day.

When the cookery schools of the late 1800s turned their attention away from the culinary education of immigrant and poor women and toward the kitchen habits of white, educated, middle-class, married women, they laid the groundwork for the emergence of the modern commercial cookbook. After World War I, cookery instruction in a variety of guises—food product advertisements, radio shows, domestic magazines, and cookbooks—increasingly offered advice and instruction on how women should learn to cook and assured these women that cooking could be an artistic and creative joy. Popular household magazines paid considerable attention to male culinary adventures, but emphasized that although men possessed natural cooking skills, they cooked for fun only. By depicting male food preferences and feminine appetites as diametrically opposed, cookery instruction reiterated the differences between how men cooked and ate and how women cooked and ate—and underscored the expectation that the woman of the middle-class home would prepare the family's daily meals.

During this period, the changing nature of servant labor ensured that fewer middle-income families would or could employ a paid cook. Although authors rarely overtly mentioned the race of their intended audience, cookbooks in the post–World War I era often characterized readers as newly "cookless" women—that is, white middle- and upper-class women bereft of the kitchen labor most often performed by women of color and immigrant women. During World War II, when employment opportunities opened up for women who previously had been limited to domestic labor in private homes, many cookbook authors and editors continued to speak most directly to middle-class white women. Cookbooks continued to urge their readers that the family's daily meals constituted an essential part of a woman's domestic duties. Authors and editors infused those duties with new patriotic import. Many married white women took jobs outside the home for the first time during the war, and that only fueled worry and anxiety about women's roles in society. As always in times of social change and upheaval, prescriptions for women's domestic behavior abounded, and cookery instruction often insisted that women must make food preparation their primary wartime task. Maude Reid's cookbook-scrapbook, "Ways and Means for War Days," shows how women took their task seriously but also felt disgruntled about food shortages and the difficulties of the rationing system. At war's end, middle-class Americans rushed to embrace an era of prosperity and consumer abundance—especially food abundance.

Cookery instruction in the late 1940s and 1950s reflected our nation's eagerness to enjoy the fruits of our labor after decades of economic depression and war. According to many promotional and privately authored cookbooks, a myriad of new household appliances and new canned, packaged, and frozen foods had ushered in an age of push-button ease. Suburban backyard grills offered the middle-class man another site for exercising his culinary skills, and, as in the 1920s and 1930s, cookery instruction for men during the 1950s emphasized hearty male appetites and creative male cooking. But the rhetoric about the "manliness" of the man in the kitchen increased, as concerns about masculinity in the gray flannel suit era grew. At the same time, the rhetoric about a woman's place at the stove that had been building since the early part of the century reached a crescendo. Adding their voices to a chorus of writers, psychiatrists, politicians, and child-rearing experts, cookbook authors and editors asserted that only in domesticity could a woman achieve true feminine fulfillment. Cookery instruction created its own version of the feminine mystique and depicted daily meal preparation as the almost sacred duty of a wife and mother. At the same time, Cold War fears helped sustain the notion of home cooking as family defense: good meals prepared by a loving and cheerful mother strengthened the family, which, in turn, strengthened the nation.

The cooking mystique continued mostly unabated throughout the 1950s. But as cookbooks deluged the nation, a faint but persistent "discourse of discontent" appeared in cookery instruction. Authors and editors began to assert less often that women would find cooking the daily meals an utterly rewarding pleasure and instead started to offer quick-fix recipes for readers who did not want to be a "slave to the stove." They began to acknowledge that women sought nondomestic activities and outside employment, and they even admitted that some women found cooking a tiresome chore. Peg Bracken struck a nerve with her 1960 *The I Hate to Cook Book*, and many women wrote to tell Bracken that they agreed with her wholeheartedly. Although practically all cookery instruction for both men and for women continued to assume that the woman of the house would remain solely responsible for daily food preparation, cookbook authors and editors no longer universally attempted to convince their readers that cookery always offered "a most enchanting occupation." In the cookery instruction published in the late 1950s and the early 1960s we can see, then, the beginnings of widespread resistance to the cult of domesticity—and, as always, the desire of cookbook publishers to tap into a changing market.

Cookbooks do not offer the historian a clear picture of how Americans cooked and ate at different points in time, although cookery instruction can give us some clues about food and cookery trends. They cannot tell us how many American women gladly embraced daily cookery duties as a creative, fulfilling task, and how many dreaded the dinner hour. Although the popularity of certain books and signs of use in individual cookbooks offer us some insights, a study of cookbooks themselves cannot give us extensive information about how women and men used cookbooks. But cookbooks do reveal what kinds of ideals we as a nation of consumers, producers, and marketers assigned to food preparation. They tell us how cooking instructors, magazine editors, food manufacturers, and individual authors helped create a new image of home cooking at the beginning of the century to reflect better the changing nature of middle-class domestic life. They tell us, specifically, how these experts charged middle-class women with the preparation of the daily meals when it became clear that the twentieth-century middle-class home would most likely not employ a paid cook and that changing food-processing technologies would remove much of the hard labor of cooking. And they show how these experts did so with increased vehemence after the social changes wrought by World War II. They tell a story of how our notions about cooking became entangled with our definitions of middle-class masculinity and femininity. Cookbooks tell us what kinds of expectations the lady and man of the house faced in the modern kitchen. And they show us that in the kitchens of the middle class, from 1920 through the 1950s and early 1960s, cookbooks did not serve simply as guides to food preparation. These cookbooks played no small role in shaping our ideas about masculine appetites and mom's home cooking—ideas that remain powerful today. Cookbooks in modern America helped create and reinforce links between gender and food preparation that still influence how we think about men, women, and cooking.

Notes

Introduction: *"The Purpose of a Cookery Book"*

1. On today's images of women's home cooking, see, for example, an advertisement for Domino brown sugar in a recent issue of *Woman's Day.* The ad featured, in the upper left-hand corner, a photograph of a blonde woman on a retro-style motorcycle, a dog in the side car, and, in the center of the ad, a huge, latticed apple pie. The text read, in part: "Nicole Kay. Switched careers in her mid 40's. Now corresponds with her college kids by E-mail. Changed the way she drives to work. *Won't ever change* the way she makes her irresistible apple pie" (emphasis in original). See *Woman's Day*, November 1999, 47. For citations on gender and housework, and cooking specifically, see Essay on Sources.

2. As culinary historian Nicola Humble asserts, the cookbook in its twentieth-century form "has invariably spoken to the middle-classes; in fact, its rise to cultural prominence is intimately tied up with the changing pattern of middle-class life and identity." Nicola Humble, "A Touch of *Bohème*," *Times Literary Supplement*, 14 June 1996, 15.

3. See Lynn Ireland, "The Compiled Cookbook as Foodways Autobiography," *Western Folklore* 40, no. 1 (January 1981): 111; Anne L. Bower, ed., *Recipes for Reading: Community Cookbooks, Stories, Histories* (Amherst: University of Massachusetts Press, 1997), and Marialisa Calta, "Hooray for Tuna Wiggle," *Eating Well*, May–June 1994, 24–25.

4. On such evidence, see Charles Camp, *American Foodways: What, When, Why and How We Eat in America* (Little Rock, AK: August House, 1989), 98–100. After examining an anonymous recipe collection found in a thrift store, Camp writes: "Looking through the notebook, which offers numerous clues but never names its

owner, is an enlightening but unsettling experience. The enlightening part is the wholeness of the thing—the overlap of holiday recipes and souvenirs, recipes gathered from people and from the local newspaper, and household information. The book is unsettling because it juxtaposes privacy and openness—obviously never intended to be read by others, yet most likely kept in an easy-to-reach place in a Baltimore kitchen for years. . . . [A] cook's records are the records of how regularly social world, special occasions, friends, family, and the world of food, recipes, instructions, mementos, converge, and how much the records of one world stand for the other." See also Stephen Mennell, Anne Murcott, and Anneke H. van Otterloo, *The Sociology of Food: Eating, Diet, and Culture* (London: Sage, 1992), 90. They point out that "the sociology of quite how people (children and men as well as women) learn to cook, and quite what use they make of printed materials in the process, is as yet seriously under-researched."

5. For a feminist critique of the study of prescription literature, see Anne D. Gordon, Merti Jo Buhle, and Nancy Schrom Dye, "The Problem of Women's History," in Bernice A. Carroll, ed., *Liberating Women's History* (Urbana: University of Illinois Press, 1976), 75–92. On the term "history of social ideas," see Connie Miller with Cornna Treitel, *Feminist Research Methods: An Annotated Bibliography* (New York: Greenwood Press, 1991), 112, 121. On studying social norms by interpreting prescriptive literature, see especially John Kasson, *Rudeness and Civility: Manners in Nineteenth Century Urban America* (New York: Hill and Wang, 1990), 3. For a clear and concise articulation of the benefits of studying the prescriptive rhetoric in cookbooks, see Erika Endrijonas, "No Experience Required: American Middle-Class Families and Their Cookbooks, 1945–1960" (Ph.D. diss., University of Southern California, 1996). For citations on scholarly investigation of specific types of prescriptive literature, see Essay on Sources.

6. As historian Mary Drake McFeely writes, "Most cookbooks project mainstream expectations and assume a middle-class lifestyle, but they are not labeled 'for the middle class only.' As agents of our consumer culture, they speak also to American ethnic groups: Italian Americans, Asian Americans, African Americans, Hispanic Americans, and indeed to all working-class Americans, saying, "This is what you ought to aspire to. . . . [I]t has been in the kitchen that a great deal of middle-class culture has been and is powerfully asserted as the American norm." See Mary Drake McFeely, *Can She Bake a Cherry Pie? American Women and the Kitchen in the Twentieth Century* (Amherst: University of Massachusetts Press, 2000), 3–4. Marjorie DeVault's research suggests that in contemporary America, working-class and white-collar women consult cookbooks less frequently than do professional women. See Marjorie L. DeVault, *Feeding the Family: The Social Organization of Caring as Gendered Work* (Chicago: University of Chicago Press, 1991), 206–14. See also Peggy Steiner Ratcheson, "Food and Fashion in United States Society: The Mass-Culturization of Gourmet-Cookery" (Ph.D. diss., Washington University, 1986), 131–34. In Ratcheson's sample, lower-income women owned far fewer specialty and gourmet cookbooks than professional and wealthy women did.

Chapter 1.
From Family Receipts to Fannie Farmer:
Cookbooks in the United States, 1796–1920

1. Patricia Storace, "Repasts Past: Delicious Memories from Antique Cookbooks," *House and Garden*, June 1986, 62. For further citations on studying cookbooks as historical documents, see Essay on Sources.

2. On the West's first cookbook, see Patrick L. Coyle, *Cooks' Books: An Affectionate Guide to the Literature of Food* (New York: Facts on File, 1985), 2. On *Forme of Curry*, see Karen Hess, ed., *Martha Washington's Booke of Cookery* (New York: Columbia University Press, 1995), 450; and Thomas H. Wolf, "Once upon a Time a Cookbook Was a Recipe for Excess," *Smithsonian*, November 1991, 118.

3. Stephen Mennell, *All Manners of Food: Eating and Taste in England and France from the Middle Ages to the Present*, 2nd ed. (Urbana: University of Illinois Press, 1996), 83–89.

4. Eleanor T. Fordyce, "Cookbooks of the 1800s," in *Dining in America, 1850–1900*, ed. Kathryn Grover (Amherst: University of Massachusetts Press, 1987), 85, 88.

5. Waldo Lincoln, *American Cookery Books, 1742–1860* (rev. and exp. Eleanor Lowenstein, Worcester, MA: American Antiquarian Society, 1954).

6. Waverly Root and Richard de Rochement, *Eating in America: A History* (New York: Eco Press, 1976), 74–75. See also Steven M. Tobias, "Early American Cookbooks as Cultural Artifacts," *Papers on Language and Literature* 34, no. 1 (1998): 3. On the shared duties of food preparation between men and women in colonial America, see Ruth Schwartz Cowan, *More Work for Mother: The Ironies of Household Technology from the Open Hearth to the Microwave* (New York: Basic Books, 1983), 23–25.

7. Hess, *Martha Washington's Book of Cookery*, 20–22. On delicacies advertised for sale in the *American Weekly Mercury*, see William Weaver, "From Fraise to Fricassee: Seventeenth Century Cooking in Commonwealth Kitchens," *Pennsylvania Heritage* 10, no. 2 (1984): 12.

8. Jeanne Boydtson, *Home and Work: Housework, Wages, and the Ideology of the Early Republic* (New York: Oxford University Press, 1990), 80.

9. On eighteenth-century English cookbooks for upper-class ladies, see Mennell, *All Manners of Food*, 95. On *La cuisinière bourgeoise*, see Coyle, *Cook's Books*, 12. On handwritten English recipe collections, see Hess, *Martha Washington's Book of Cookery*, 451.

10. On Eliza Smith, see Jan Longone, "History of American Cookbooks," in *Proceedings of Special Clemson University Symposium, Food and Society*, ed. C. Alan Grubb and M. Elizabeth Kunkel (Clemson, SC: Clemson University Press, 1986), 1. On Americanized recipes, see Richard J. Hooker, *Food and Drink in America: A History* (New York: Bobbs-Merrill, 1981), 67. On Hannah Glasse, see Annegret S. Ogden, *The Great American Housewife: From Helpmate to Wage Earner, 1775–1986* (Westport, CT: Greenwood Press, 1986), 17. On *The Frugal Housewife*, see Jan Longone, *American Cookery: The Bicentennial, 1776–1996: An Exhibition of 200 Years of American Cookbooks at the Clements Library* (Ann Arbor: Clements Library and University of Michigan Press, 1996), 2. On medicine and household hints in

cookbooks, see Fordyce, "Cookbooks of the 1800s," 96. See also Mildred Jailer, "Bible for the Happy Housewife," *Antiques & Collecting*, February 1993, 18–20.

11. As quoted by Glynis Ridley, "The First American Cookbook," *Eighteenth Century Life* 23, no. 2 (1999): 115.

12. On surviving copies, see Longone, *American Cookery*, ii. On lack of information on Simmons, see Jan Longone and Daniel Longone, *American Cookbooks and Wine Books, 1797–1950* (Ann Arbor, MI: Clements Library and University of Michigan Press, 1984), 1. On later editions, see Ridley, "The First American Cookbook," and Root and Rochemont, *Eating in America*, 107. See also Mary Tolford Wilson, "Amelia Simmons Fills a Need: *American Cookery*, 1796," *William and Mary Quarterly* 14, no. 1 (January 1957): 16–30; Claire Hopley, "American Cookery," *American History* 31, no. 2 (1996): 16–19; Victoria von Biel, "Amelia Simmons: The Author of the Country's First Cookbook Remains a Mystery," *Bon Appetite*, October 1998, 73–76; Irene Sax, "Amelia Simmons, Orphan," *Cuisine*, February 1984, 30; Martha Brown, "Of Pearl Ash, Emptins, and Tree Sweetin'," *American Heritage* 32, no. 5 (1981): 104–7.

13. Ridley, "The First American Cookbook," 114–23. Jan Longone describes *American Cookery* as "a second American declaration of independence"; Roy Meador, "The Joy of Cookbooks," *Biblio*, February 1999, 46.

14. Amelia Simmons, *American Cookery, or The Art of Dressing Viands, Fish, Poultry and Vegetables, and the Best Modes of Making Pastes, Puffs, Pies, Tarts, Pudding, Custards and Preserves, and All Kinds of Cakes Adapted to this Country and All Grades of Life* (1796; reprint, New York: Oxford University Press, n.d.), 26. In the original text, the typography makes each "s" appear as an "f." For purposes of easy reading, I have made the substitution here.

15. Boydtson, *Home and Work*, 107. On stoves, see Joan Priscilla Brewer, "Home Fires: Cultural Responses to the Introduction of the Cookstove, 1815–1900" (Ph.D. diss., Brown University, 1987), and " 'We Have Got a Very Good Cooking Stove': Advertising, Design, and Consumer Response to the Cookstove, 1815–1880," *Winterthur Portfolio* 25, no. 1 (1990): 35–54. See also Elaine N. McIntosh, *American Food Habits in Historical Perspective* (Westport, CT: Praeger, 1995), 79; Fordyce, "Cookbooks of the 1800s," 91–92. For an in-depth look at how the advent of the cookstove changed the social and cultural significance of one type of food (gravy), see William Woys Weaver, "White Gravies in American Popular Diet," in *Food in Change: Eating Habits from the Middle Ages to the Present Day, Fifth International Conference on Ethnological Food Research, October 1983*, ed. Alexander Fenton and Eszter Kisbán (Edinburgh: John Donald, 1986), 41–52. On the increase of cooking work with the advent of the stove, see Cowan, *More Work for Mother*, 62.

16. On kitchen appliances, see Hooker, *Food and Drink in America*, 212. On vegetarian and diet cookbooks, see Longone, "History of American Cookbooks," 4.

17. Nancy Woloch, *Women and the American Experience* (New York: Alfred A. Knopf, 1984), 115. See also Jean Gordon and Jan McArthur, "American Women and Domestic Consumption, 1800–1920: Four Interpretive Themes," in *Making the American Home: Middle Class Women and Domestic Material Culture, 1840–1940*, ed. Marilyn Ferris Motz and Pat Browne (Bowling Green, OH: Bowling Green State University Popular Press, 1988); Stuart M. Blumin, *The Emergence of the*

Middle Class: Social Experience in the American City, 1760–1900 (New York: Cambridge University Press, 1989), 191.

18. Simmons, *American Cookery*, 5.

19. Ogden, *The Great American Housewife*, 4. See also Glenda Riley, *Inventing the American Woman: A Perspective on Women's History* (Arlington Heights, IL: Harlan Davidson, 1987), 66; and Faye E. Dudden, *Serving Women: Household Service in Nineteenth-Century America* (Middletown, CT: Wesleyan University Press, 1983), 155.

20. Judith Rollins, *Between Women: Domestics and Their Employer* (Philadelphia: Temple University Press, 1985), 50; Dudden, *Serving Women*, 10, 44.

21. Daniel E. Sutherland, *Americans and Their Servants: Domestic Service in the United States from 1800–1920* (Baton Rouge: Louisiana State University Press, 1981), 14. On Chinese immigrants, see Jones, *American Food*, 129.

22. Peter Berg, " 'The Dignity of Our Character as Rational Beings': Images of Women in American Cookbooks, 1820–1860" (master's thesis, Michigan State University, 1982), 11.

23. Longone, "Cookbooks in American History," 3.

24. Dudden, *Serving Women*, 134.

25. On the kitchen duties of a middle-class housekeeper, see Anne Mendelson, *Stand Facing the Stove: The Story of the Women Who Gave America "The Joy of Cooking"* (New York: Henry Holt, 1996), 108. On instructions in early and mid nineteenth-century cookbooks to new female members of the middle class, see Tobias, "Early American Cookbooks as Cultural Artifacts," 4. On the new elaborateness of meals, see Ray Tannahill, *Food in History* (1973; reprint, New York: Crown, 1988), 322. For examples of nineteenth-century recipes, see Sandra Oddo, *Home Made: Recipes from the Nineteenth Century* (New York: Atheneum, 1972). See also Susan Williams, *Savory Suppers and Fashionable Feasts: Dining in Victoria America* (Knoxville: University of Tennessee Press, 1996), and Lila Perl, *Junk Food, Fast Food, Health Food: What America Eats and Why* (New York: Clarion Books, 1980), 11. On the popularity of French cuisine and French cookery manuals, see Dudden, *Serving Women*, 134; Evan Jones, *American Food: The Gastronomic Story* (New York: E. P. Dutton, 1975), 34; Harvey Levenstein, "The 'Servant Problem' and American Cookery," *Revue Française d'Etudes Américaines* 11, nos. 27–28 (1986): 128.

26. Laura Shapiro, *Perfection Salad: Women and Cooking at the Turn of the Century* (New York: Farrar, Straus and Giroux, 1986), 13. See also Fordyce, "Cookbooks of the 1800s," 95; Glenna Matthews, *"Just a Housewife": The Rise and Fall of Domesticity in America* (New York: Oxford University Press, 1987), 11–12.

27. Susan Strasser, *Never Done: A History of American Housework* (New York: Pantheon Books, 1982), 185.

28. Woloch, *Women and the American Experience*, 131. See also Kathleen Anne McHugh, *American Domesticity: From How-to-Manual to Hollywood Melodrama* (New York: Oxford University Press, 1999), 15.

29. As quoted by Root and Rochemont, *Eating in America*, 107.

30. As quoted by Berg, " 'The Dignity of Our Character as Rational Beings,' "
30. On Child, see Hildegard Hoeller, "A Quilt for Life: Lydia Maria Child's *The American Frugal Housewife*," *ATQ* 13, no. 2 (1999): 89–104.

31. See, for example, Eliza Leslie, *Miss Leslie's New Receipts for Cooking*, 2nd ed. (Philadelphia: T. B. Peterson and Brothers, 1874); Sarah Josepha Hale, *Mrs. Hale's New Cook Book* (Philadelphia: T. B. Peterson, 1857); Elizabeth Putnam, *Mrs. Putnam's Receipt Book and Young Housekeeper's Assistant* (Boston: Ticknor, Reed and Fields, 1849), Mrs. A. L. Webster, *The Improved Housewife* (1843; reprint, with a foreword by Louis Szathmáry, New York: Arno Press, 1973); and Mrs. T. J. Crowen, *Every Lady's Cook Book* (Auborn, NJ: Derby and Miller, 1847).

32. Eliza Leslie, *Miss Leslie's Directions for Cooking: An Unabridged Reprint of the 1851 Classic with a New Introduction by Jan Longone* (Mineola, NY: Dover, 1999), ix–x.

33. McHugh, *American Domesticity*, 28.

34. As quoted by Berg, " 'The Dignity of Our Character as Rational Beings,' " 31.

35. Janet Theophano, "A Life's Work: Women Writing from the Kitchen," in *Fields of Folklore: Essays in Honor of Kenneth S. Goldstein*, ed. Roger D. Abrahams (Bloomington, IN: Trickster Press, 1995), 293. See also John G. Wuchenich, "The Social and Educational Advancement of the American Woman as Reflected in the Cookbook, 1776–1899" (Ph.D. diss., University of Pittsburgh, 1978).

36. Charlsie E. Berly, "Early American Cookbooks (1783–1861): Windows on Household Life and a Developing Culture," *Lamar Journal of the Humanities* 14, nos. 1–2 (1988): 15, 17; Berg, " 'The Dignity of Our Character as Rational Beings,' " 26.

37. Ogden, *The Great American Housewife*, 58.

38. Strasser, *Never Done*, 167.

39. On the increase in cookbook publication, see Coyle, *Cooks' Books*, 18. On cooking columns in newspapers, see Hooker, *Food and Drink in America*, 215. On women's periodicals, see Fordyce, "Cookbooks in the 1800s," 112. On community cookbooks, see Bob Brown and Eleanor Brown, *Culinary Americana: Cookbooks Published in the Cities and Towns of the United States of America during the Years from 1860 through 1960* (New York: Roving Eye Press, 1961), vii. For an in-depth reading of one woman's recipe collection, see Alice Ross, "Ella Smith's Unfinished Community Cookbook: A Social History of Women and Work in Smithtown, New York, 1884–1922," in *Recipes for Reading: Community Cookbooks, Stories, Histories*, ed. Anne L. Bower (Amherst: University of Massachusetts Press, 1997). On recipe booklets promoting manufacturers, see Longone, "Cookbooks in American History," 5; Bunny Crumpacker, *The Old-Time Brand-Name Cookbook: Recipes, Illustrations, and Advice from the Early Kitchens of America's Most Trusted Food Makers* (New York: Smithmark, 1998); Ellen M. Plante, "Little Recipe Books," *Antiques and Collecting*, April 1992, 51, 67. On the impact of the Civil War on canning, see McIntosh, *American Food Habits in Historical Perspective*, 89. On home canning, see Hooker, *Food and Drink in America*, 215. On refined sugar and new recipes, see Mendelson, *Stand Facing the Stove*, 116. On railways, cattle ranching, and restaurants, see Tannahill, *Food in History*, 306–28.

40. Strasser, *Never Done*, 245, 204. On Corson's cookbooks, see Hooker, *Food and Drink in America*, 216.

41. Shapiro, *Perfection Salad*, 134–39. See also Alan M. Kraut, "Ethnic Foodways: The Significance of Food in the Designation of Cultural Boundaries be-

tween Immigrant Groups in the U.S., 1840–1921," *Journal of American Culture* 2 (fall 1979): 409–20. On the New England kitchen, see Sarah Stage, "Ellen Richards and the Social Significance of the Home Economics Movement," in *Rethinking Home Economics: Women and the History of a Profession*, ed. Sarah Stage and Virginia B. Vincenti (Ithaca, NY: Cornell University Press, 1997), 23–24. See also Virginia Bramble Vincenti, "A History of the Philosophy of Home Economics" (Ph.D. diss., Pennsylvania State University, 1981), 82–83, and Alice Ross, "Health and Diet in 19th Century America: A Food Historian's Point of View," *Historical Archaeology* 27, no. 2 (1993): 47. On cookery as antidote for alcoholism, see also Stephen Mennell, Anne Murcott, and Anneke H. van Otterloo, *The Sociology of Food: Eating, Diet, and Culture* (London: Sage, 1992), 89.

42. Levenstein, "The 'Servant Problem' and American Cookery," 129; Sutherland, *Americans and Their Servants*, 14.

43. Harvey Levenstein, *Revolution at the Table: The Transformation of the American Diet* (New York: Oxford University Press, 1988), 62–63. On the growth of women's paid employment after the Civil War, see William Chafe, *The Paradox of Change: American Women in the 20th Century* (New York: Oxford University Press, 1991), 13. On household servants, see Allyson Sherman Grossman, "Women in Domestic Work: Yesterday and Today," *Monthly Labor Review* 8, no. 103 (1980): 17–18.

44. On Sarah Tyson Rorer, see Emma Seifrit Weigly, "Mrs. Rorer and New York Foodways," *New York Folklore* 6, nos. 3–4 (1980): 195–207, and *Sarah Tyson Rorer: The Nation's Instructress in Dietetics and Cookery* (Philadelphia: American Philosophical Society, 1977). On the National Household Economics Association and other such organizations, see Levenstein, "The 'Servant Problem' and American Cookery," 130.

45. Shapiro, *Perfection Salad*, 50–62.

46. As quoted by Jan Longone, in Mary J. Lincoln, *Boston Cooking School Cook Book: A Reprint of the 1884 Classic* (1884; reprint, with an introduction by Jan Longone, New York: Dover Publications, 1996), iv–v. Cookbook authors and the general population used the hyphenated term "cook-book," along with the more common use of two separate words ("cook book") well into the twentieth century.

47. Mary J. Lincoln, *Boston Cooking School Cook Book*, xv–xvi.

48. Ibid., 272.

49. Ibid., xv.

50. Levenstein, *Revolution at the Table*, 55–56.

51. *Definitive Themes in Home Economics and Their Impact on Families, 1909–1984* (Washington, DC: American Home Economics Association, 1984), 4. On land-grant colleges, see also David W. Miller, "Technology and the Ideal: Production Quality and Kitchen Reform in Nineteenth-Century America," in Grover, *Dining in America, 1850–1900*, 76; Virginia Railsback Gunn, "Industrialists Not Butterflies: Women's Higher Education at Kansas State Agricultural College, 1873–1882," *Kansas History* 17, no. 1 (spring 1994): 2–17.

52. Shapiro, *Perfection Salad*, 44.

53. Longone and Longone, *American Cookbooks and Wine Books*, 9.

54. As quoted by Fordyce, "Cookbooks in the 1800s," 109. On Fannie Farmer, see Joseph Gustaitis, "Fannie Farmer: Recipe for Perennial Success," *American*

History Illustrated, December 1986, 46–47; Mary Drake McFeely, "You've Come a Long Way, Fannie," *Yankee,* April 1996, 78–88.

55. On the trend toward smaller meals, see McIntosh, *American Food Habits in Historical Perspective,* 106. On convenience food, see Mendelson, *Stand Facing the Stove,* 118. On cookbook advice about purchasing food, see Strasser, *Never Done,* 243. On grocery stores and new kinds of appliances, see Hooker, *Food and Drink in America,* 306–7. On the popularity of the gelatin mold, see Miller, "Technology and the Ideal," 59. On the links between manufacturers and recipes, see Shapiro, *Perfection Salad,* 192, and Miller, "Technology and the Ideal," 82.

56. Brander Matthews, "Concerning Cook-Books," *Munsey's Magazine,* July 1913, 575. See also Calvin Winter, "What a Good Cook Book Should Be," *Book-man,* February 1914, 663–65.

57. On the food pledges, see Levenstein, *Revolution at the Table,* 137–38. On the slogan "Food Will Win the War," see Hooker, *Food and Drink in America,* 300.

58. Woloch, *Women and the American Experience,* 295.

59. Elizabeth MacDonald, "The Homemaker's Open Forum," *House Beautiful,* March 1927, 344.

60. Mary Drake McFeely, *Can She Bake a Cherry Pie? American Women and the Kitchen in the Twentieth Century* (Amherst: University of Massachusetts Press, 2000), 40.

Chapter 2.
Recipes for a New Era: Food Trends, Consumerism, Cooks, and Cookbooks

1. On consumerism, see Frank Freidel and Alan Brinkley, *America in the Twentieth Century* (New York: Alfred A. Knopf, 1982), 171; James T. Patterson, *America in the Twentieth Century: A History* (New York: Harcourt Brace, 1994), 143–45. On women in the 1920s, see Dorothy M. Brown, *Setting a Course: American Women in the 1920s* (Boston: Twayne, 1987). On the A&P, see Lila Perl, *Junk Food, Fast Food, Health Food: What America Eats and Why* (New York: Clarion Books, 1980), 16.

2. On the rise in electricity usage, see Heidi Hartmann, "Capitalism and Women's Work in the Home, 1900–1930" (Ph.D. diss., Yale University, 1974), 90. On the battle among the ice, gas, and electric industries, see Lisa Mae Robinson, "Safeguarded by Your Refrigerator: Mary Engle Pennington's Struggle with the National Association of Ice Industries," in *Rethinking Home Economics: Women and the History of a Profession,* ed. Sarah Stage and Virginia B. Vincenti (Ithaca, NY: Cornell University Press, 1997), 253. For the *Good Housekeeping* article, see "Let Your Refrigerator Do the Work," *Good Housekeeping,* May 1932, 84. On the Alice Bradley refrigerator cookbook, see Sylvia Lovegren, *Fashionable Food: Seven Decades of Food Fads* (New York: Macmillan, 1995), 9–11. For an example of a cookbook that continued to offer advice on using an ice box, see Margaret Pratt Allen and Ida Oram Hutton, *Man-Sized Meals from the Kitchenette* (New York: Vanguard Press, 1928), 22–23. For Alasker's comments, see Alasker Ramus, *Adventures in Cooking* (New York: Grant Publications, 1927), 9.

3. On home economists working at utility companies, see Carolyn M. Goldstein, "Part of the Package: Home Economists in the Consumer Product Indus-

tries, 1920–1940," in Stage and Vincenti, *Rethinking Home Economics*, 287. On gender norms and the popularity of the chafing dish before 1920, see Lauar Naus, "'The Most Social Utensil in the World': Chafing Dish Recipes for Popularity, 1880–1920" (master's thesis, University of Delaware, 1991).

4. On advertising, see Glenna Matthews, *"Just a Housewife": The Rise and Fall of Domesticity in America* (New York: Oxford University Press, 198:7), 179–80. See also Susan Strasser, *Satisfaction Guaranteed: The Making of the American Mass Market* (Washington, DC: Smithsonian Institute Press, 1995). On food-processing industries, see Hartmann, "Capitalism and Women's Work in the Home, 1900–1930," 89. See also Elaine N. McIntosh, *American Food Habits in Historical Perspective* (Westport, CT: Praeger, 1995), 112. On the growing employment of home economists by food corporations, see Regina Lee Blaszezyk, "'Where Mrs. Homemaker Is Never Forgotten': Lucy Maltby and Home Economics and Corning Glass Works, 1929–1965," in Stage and Vincenti, *Rethinking Home Economics*, 194, and Robinson, "Safeguarded by Your Refrigerator," 253. See also Harvey Levenstein, *Revolution at the Table: The Transforming of the American Diet* (New York: Oxford University Press, 1988), 156, and Laura Shapiro, *Perfection Salad: Women and Cooking at the Turn of the Century* (New York: Farrar, Straus and Giroux, 1986), 206. On promotional recipe booklets, see Bunny Crumpacker, *The Old-Time Brand-Name Cookbook: Recipes, Illustrations, and Advice from the Early Kitchens of America's Most Trusted Food Makers* (New York: Smithmark, 1998).

5. Levenstein, *Revolution at the Table*, 156. See also Anne Mendelson, *Stand Facing the Stove: The Story of the Women Who Gave America "The Joy of Cooking"* (New York: Henry Holt, 1996), 119.

6. As quoted by Levenstein, *Revolution at the Table*, 156.

7. Liora Gvion-Rosenberg, "Telling the Story of Ethnicity: American Cookbooks, 1850–1990" (master's thesis, State University of New York at Stony Brook, 1996), 214.

8. See Ellye Howell Gover, *Atlas Flour Cook book* (Milwaukee: Atlas Flour Mills, 1923).

9. *Cupid's Book* (Oakland, CA: Kiessling & Son, 1921), 48.

10. See Evelyn Birkby, *Neighboring on the Air: Cooking with the KMA Radio Homemakers* (Iowa City: University of Iowa Press, 1991), and Nelljean M. Rice, "A Tale of Three Cakes: On the Air and in the Books," in *Recipes for Reading: Community Cookbooks, Stories, Histories*, ed. Anne L. Bower (Amherst: University of Massachusetts Press, 1997).

11. *General Foods Cook Book* (New York: General Foods Corporation, 1932), 64.

12. Harvey Levenstein, *Paradox of Plenty: A Social History of Eating in Modern America* (New York: Oxford University Press, 1993), 33.

13. Mary Drake McFeely, *Can She Bake a Cherry Pie? American Women and the Kitchen in the Twentieth Century* (Amherst: University of Massachusetts Press, 2000), 56–57.

14. Ida Bailey Allen, *Ida Bailey Allen's Modern Cook Book* (Garden City, NY: Garden City Publishing, 1932).

15. Lovegren, *Fashionable Food*, 51, and John MacPherson, *The Mystery Chef's Own Cook Book* (New York: Longman, Green, 1934), 98.

16. Jan Longone, phone conversation with author, 4 June 1999.

17. Dan Nelson, nephew of Edna Nelson Jackson, phone conversation with author, 21 September 1999.

18. Mary Stevens, *A Primer of Modern Cooking: New Methods and New Dishes for Experienced Cooks and For Beginners* (New York: Home Institute, 1934), 3.

19. Mary Chambers, *One-Piece Dinners* (Boston: Little, Brown, 1924), 60. Chambers's title referred to the growing popularity of "plate dinners," that is, the entire meal served on one plate rather than in courses.

20. See Lillian Gunn, *What to Serve at Parties* (New York: *McCall's* Magazine, 1922).

21. Mary Grosvenor Ellsworth, *Much Depends on Dinner* (New York: Alfred A. Knopf, 1939), 163–64; Lucy G. Allen, *Modern Menus and Recipes* (Boston: Little, Brown, 1935), 5.

22. On Aunt Jemima, see Kimberly Wallace Sanders, "Dishing Up Dixie: Recycling the Old South in the Early-Twentieth Century Domestic Ideal," in *Burning Down the House: Recycling Domesticity*, ed. Rosemary Marangoly George (Boulder, CO: Westview Press, 1998).

23. See Harvey Levenstein, "The American Response to Italian Food, 1880–1930," *Food and Foodways* 1 (1985): 1–23.

24. See Edith Key Haines, *Edith Key Haines' Cook Book* (New York: Farrar & Rinehart, 1937).

25. The Home Institute of the *New York Herald Tribune, American's Cookbook* (New York: Charles Scribner's Sons, 1938), 878. On smaller breakfasts, see Stephen Mennell, Anne Murcott, and Anneke H. van Otterloo, *The Sociology of Food: Eating, Diet, and Culture* (London: Sage, 1992), 70.

26. Bernarr Macfadden, *Physical Culture Cook Book* (New York: Macfadden Publication, 1924). On Macfadden's career, see William R. Hunt, *Body Love: The Amazing Career of Bernarr Macfadden* (Bowling Green, OH: Bowling Green State University Popular Press, 1989). On Macfadden as health food advocate, see McFeely, *Can She Bake a Cherry Pie*, 131–32.

27. George Conforth, *Good Food: How to Prepare It* (Washington, DC: Review and Herald, 1920), and *Better Meals for Less* (Washington, DC: Review and Herald, 1930).

28. Levenstein, *Paradox of Plenty*, 37.

29. Ibid., 45.

30. Lovegren, *Fashionable Food*, 29–30.

31. See Mary L. Perrie Kuhlmann, *The White Ribbon Recipe Book* (Washington, DC: Griffith Brothers, 1923).

32. Mac C. Sheridan, *The Stag Cookbook: Written for Men by Men* (New York: George H. Dornan, 1922), 37.

33. Levenstein, *Paradox of Plenty*, 34.

34. Elizabeth MacDonald, "The Homemaker's Open Forum," *House Beautiful,* March 1927, 344.

35. Daisy Maryles and Dick Donahue, "Who's Minding the Stove?" *Publishers' Weekly*, 26 July 1999, 36.

36. "Customer's Choice," *Publishers' Weekly*, 6 May 1933, 1465. Catherine Manton, *Fed Up: Women and Food in America* (Westport, CT: Bergin and Garvey,

1999), 53. See also Perl, *Junk Food, Fast Food, Health Food*, 12.

37. "Customer's Choice," 1465.

38. Helmut Ripperger, "Cookery Books for Gourmet," *Publishers' Weekly*, 13 October 1934, 1371–73.

39. Helmut Ripperger, "More of the World's Fare," *Publishers' Weekly*, 29 July 1939, 292; Helmut Ripperger, "And Still More Cookbooks," *Publishers' Weekly*, 12 April 1938, 1448–51.

40. On Ripperger, see Mendelson, *Stand Facing the Stove*, 284–85.

41. On home economists and home demonstration agents during the Depression, see Kathleen R. Babbitt, "Legitimizing Nutrition Education: The Impact of the Great Depression," in Stage and Vincenti, *Rethinking Home Economics*, 145–61, and Virginia Bramble Vincenti, "A History of the Philosophy of Home Economics" (Ph.D. diss., Pennsylvania State University, 1981), 144. The lack of practical, economical advice in many cookbooks also stands in contrast to the housewife activists who protested high food prices and organized cooperative gardens. See Annelise Orleck, " 'We Are That Mythical Thing Called The Public': Militant Housewives during the Great Depression," *Feminist Studies* 10, no. 1 (spring 1993): 147–73.

42. Helmut Ripperger, "More Cookery Books," *Publishers' Weekly*, 21 September 1935, 990.

43. Helmut Ripperger, "To Sell Like Hot Cakes," *Publishers' Weekly*, 12 June 12 1937, 2404; The Home Institute of the *New York Herald Tribune, America's Cookbook*, v.

44. *Pictorial Review*, July 1935, 56–57; Jean Simpson, "A Cookery Clinic," *Ladies' Home Journal*, February 1932, 91.

45. Mendelson, *Stand Facing the Stove*, 153, 233–35. The 1962–63 copyright applications dropped "The" from the title, but previous editions bore the title *The Joy of Cooking* and most people still refer to it that way. For purposes of clarity, I will use the earlier title whenever I refer to this cookbook. For Marion Rombauer Becker's account of her mother's and her own work on *The Joy of Cooking*, see Marion Rombauer Becker, *Little Acorn: The Story behind The Joy of Cooking, 1931–1966* (Indianapolis: Bobbs-Merrill, 1966). When Bobbs-Merrill issued a new edition of *The Joy of Cooking* in 1997, a totally revised edition containing recipes from over 100 prominent chefs, numerous book critics and food writers lamented the loss of Rombauer's personal style. See, for example, Molly O'Neill, "It's a New 'Joy,' But Is It the Old Love?" *New York Times*, 5 November 1997, sec. B, p. 1, 8; Paul Gray, "Ode to Joy: A classic cookbook gets a total facelift; purists worry; some contributors simmer; will the pot boil over?" *Time*, 5 November 1997 92–96; Russ Parsons, "A Heaping Cupful of Conflict," *Los Angeles Times*, 5 November 1997, sec. A, p. 1, 24.

46. "One World, One Cookbook," *Time*, 16 August 1943, 102–3.

47. "Customer's Choice," 1468.

48. Mendelson, *Stand Facing the Stove*, 117.

49. Jane Abbott and Henrietta Wilcox Penny, *Polly Put the Kettle On: A Story for Girls* (Philadelphia: J. B. Lippincott, 1925); Constance Wagner, *Kitchen Magic* (New York: Farrar and Rinehart, 1932); Louise Bennet Weaver and Helen Cowless LeCron; *When Sue Began to Cook with Bettina's Best Recipes: A Beginning Cook-*

book for Girls from Eight to Fifteen (New York: Alburt Company, 1924); Inez Mcfee, *Young People's Cook Book or How the Daytons Cooked at Home and in Camp* (New York: Thomas Y. Crowell, 1925). Popular magazines also encouraged children to cook. See Caroline B. King, "Children Find Cooking Good Fun," *Ladies' Home Journal*, November 1935, 138–40; Bob Davis, "Come into the Kitchen, Boys," *Delineator*, July 1936, 20–21; Alice Bradley, "When the Children Cook," *Woman's Home Companion*, August 1926, 98. For an example of an early twentieth-century children's cookbook, see the Pillsbury Company's very first promotional cookbook, L. P. Hummard, *A Little Book for a Little Cook* (1905; reprint, Bedford, MA: Applewood Books, 1995). In the 1920s and 1930s cookbooks for children also included Louise Price Bell, *Jane-Louise's Cook Book: A Cook Book for Children* (New York: Coward-McCann, 1930); Marie P. Hill and Frances H. Gained, eds., *Fun in the Kitchen: A Record Cook Book of Easy Recipes for Little Girls* (Chicago: Reilly & Lee, 1927); Clara Ingram Judson, *Cooking without Mother's Help: A Story Cook Book for Beginners* (New York: Nourse, 1920); Lucy Mary Maltby, *It's Fun to Cook* (Philadelphia: Winston, 1938); Elizabeth Robins and Octavia Wilberforce, *Prudence and Peter and Their Adventures with Pots and Pans* (New York: Morrow, 1928). On the history of gendered cookery instruction for children, and gender ideology, see Sherrie A. Inness, " 'The Enchantment of Mixing-Spoons': Cooking Lessons for Boys and Girls, 1900–1960," in *Kitchen Culture: Representations of Food, Gender, and Race*, ed. Sherrie A. Inness (Philadelphia: University of Pennsylvania Press, 2000).

50. Abbott and Penny, *Polly Put the Kettle On*, 15, 24–26, 32, 234–37.

51. Ibid., 14.

52. "Pyrex Ovenware 39% to 50% Lower in Price," *Woman's Home Companion*, February 1939, 95.

53. Alice A. Deck, " 'Now Then—Who Said Biscuits?' The Black Woman Cook as Fetish in American Advertising, 1905–1953," in Inness, *Kitchen Culture*, 70.

54. Daniel E. Sutherland, *Americans and Their Servants: Domestic Service in the United States from 1800–1920* (Baton Rouge: Louisiana State University Press, 1981), 185.

55. Hartmann, "Capitalism and Women's Work in the Home," 171, 253; Judith Rollins, *Between Women: Domestics and Their Employers* (Philadelphia: Temple University Press, 1985), 53–54. See also Ruth Schwartz Cowan, *More Work for Mother: The Ironies of Household Technology from the Open Hearth to the Microwave* (New York: Basic Books, 1983), 175.

56. Henry H. Curran, "The Cooks Are Coming," *Ladies' Home Journal*, November 1924, 174.

57. Eleanor Roosevelt, "Woman's Work is Never Done," *Woman's Home Companion*, April 1935, 4.

58. Douglas Bowers, "Cooking Trends Echo Changing Roles of Women," *Food Review*, January–April 2000, 5. See also McFeely, *Can She Bake a Cherry Pie*, 42.

59. Joanne Vanke, "Time Spent in Housework," in *A Heritage of Her Own: Toward a New Social History of American Women*, ed. Nancy F. Cott and Elizabeth H. Pleck (New York: Simon and Schuster, 1979), 499; Marjorie L. DeVault, *Feeding the Family: The Social Organization of Caring as Gendered Work* (Chicago: University of Chicago Press, 1991), 36.

60. Jean Aaberg, *Don't Phone Mother* (Philadelphia: Penn Publishing, 1940), 38.

61. June Platt, "No Cook and a Kitchenette," *House and Garden*, October 1935, 60–61, 101.

62. June Platt, "How to Cook without a Cook," *House and Garden*, August 1939, 37.

63. Helen Hilles, *To the Queen's Taste: A Cook Book for Moderns* (New York: Random House, 1937), 4.

64. Mabel Claire, *Macy's Cook Book for the Busy Woman* (New York: Greenberg, 1932), 69; Dorothy Meyerson, *Homemaker's Handbook* (1935; reprint, New York: Garden City Publishing, 1939), 29.

65. Alice Foote MacDougall, *Alice Foote MacDougall's Cook Book* (Boston: Lothrop, Lee and Shephard, 1935), 78–79.

66. Betty Thornley Stuart, "The Cook's Day In," *Collier's*, 17 June 1933, 18, 38. It is unclear to me if the liqueurs utilized by these girls contained alcohol or not.

67. Mendelson points out one of the reasons for *The Joy of Cooking*'s success was Rombauer's own experiences as a well-to-do woman with little practical cooking experience. Rombauer supplied easy, stylish dishes for entertaining and simple home recipes for the family, and suggested an overall approach to cooking as something of "a lark," to use June Platt's phrase, but not a serious undertaking to which one should devote much of one's time.

68. Stuart, "The Cook's Day In," 38.

Chapter 3.
"Cooking Is Fun": Women's Home Cookery as Art, Science, and Necessity

1. Nancy Woloch, *Women and the American Experience* (New York: Alfred Knopf, 1984), 282, 284–85, 291; William H. Chafe, *The Paradox of Change: American Women in the Twentieth Century* (New York: Oxford University Press, 1981), 66.

2. Woloch, *Women and the American Experience*, 389, 408.

3. Rosalyn Baxandall, Linda Gordon, and Susan Reverby, eds., *America's Working Women: A Documentary History—1600 to the Present* (New York: Vintage Books, 1976), 245.

4. Chafe, *Paradox of Change*, 100–101, 113.

5. Katherine Parkin, "Campbell's Soup and Long Shelf Life of Traditional Gender Roles," in *Kitchen Culture in America: Representations of Food, Gender, and Race*, ed. Sherrie A. Inness (Philadelphia: University of Pennsylvania Press, 2000), 52.

6. Faye E. Dudden, *Serving Women: Household Service in Nineteenth-Century America* (Middletown, CT: Wesleyan University Press, 1983), 187.

7. See Dolores Hayden, "Two Utopian Feminists and Their Campaign for Kitchenless Houses," *Signs: Journal of Women and Culture in Society* 4, no. 2 (1978): 274–90, and Dolores Hayden, *The Grand Domestic Revolution: A History of Feminist Designs for American Homes, Neighborhoods, and Cities* (Cambridge, MA: MIT Press, 1981).

8. Charlotte Perkins Gilman, "A Modest Proposal for Freeing Women from Housework," in *The Female Experience: An American Documentary*, ed. Gerda Lerner (Indianapolis: Bobbs-Merrill, 1977), 145.

9. Mary Borden, *The Technique of Marriage* (Garden City, NY: Doubleday,

Doran, 1933), 88–92, 97–100. For a more detailed discussion, see Jessamyn Neuhaus, "The Joy of Sex Instruction: Women and Cooking in Marital Sex Manuals, 1920–1963," in Inness, *Kitchen Culture in America.*

10. Cammille Dooven, *The Modern Cook Book* (Boston: Colonial Press, 1928), v.

11. Ida Bailey Allen, *Ida Bailey Allen's Modern Cook Book* (Garden City, NY: Garden City Publishing, 1932), viii.

12. George Frederick, *Cooking as Men Like It* (New York: Business Bourse, 1930), 2–5, 52.

13. Alice Foote MacDougall, *Alice Foote MacDougall's Cook Book* (Boston: Lothrop, Lee and Shephard, 1935), 267–68.

14. Hazel Young, *The Working Girl Must Eat* (Boston: Little, Brown, 1938), 60.

15. Iris Prouty, *Feeding Peter* (Philadelphia: J. B. Lippincott, 1924), 7.

16. *Cupid's Book* (Oakland, CA: Kiessling & Son, 1921), 39.

17. Ida Bailey Allen, *Modern Menus and Recipes* (Boston: Little, Brown, 1935), 4.

18. Jessie Marie DeBoth, *The Home Maker's Cooking School Cook Book* (Chicago, 1925), 5.

19. *General Foods Cook Book* (New York: General Foods Corporation, 1932), 89.

20. Mary Stevens, *A Primer of Modern Cooking: New Methods and New Dishes for Experienced Cooks and for Beginners* (New York: Home Institute, 1934), 3.

21. Mabel Claire, *Macy's Cook Book for the Busy Woman* (New York: Greenberg, 1932), 12.

22. Jean Aaberg, *Don't Phone Mother* (Philadelphia: Penn Publishing, 1940), 9.

23. I want to emphasize that the idea of cooking as an art did not begin in the 1920s. For example, a handwritten cookbook by Maude Reid of Lake Charles, Louisiana, included a short essay by Kate Douglas Wiggins entitled "The Art of Cookery," apparently clipped from a fundraising cookbook published in 1911. Wiggins made a comparison between cooking and artistic pursuits similar to the kinds of comparisons that proliferated in 1920s and 1930s cookbooks: "Who would not rather make a delicious strawberry shortcake than play 'The Maiden's Prayer' on the piano? Where is the painted tablescarf that can compare with an honest loaf of milk white bread? Is a bunch of wax or paper flowers any more artistic than a ball of perfect butter stamped with a garland of daisies? No." Authors in the 1920s and 1930s went even further than Wiggins, however, and argued that the art of cookery surpassed symphonies and oil paintings. And cookbooks in the post–World War I era depicted cooking as art with such persistent regularity that we should understand this aspect of cookery instruction as a unique feature of cookbooks published in the 1920s and 1930s.

24. Alasker Ramus, *Adventures in Cooking* (New York: Grant Publications, 1927), 18.

25. Margaret Pratt Allen and Ida Oram Hutton, *Man-Sized Meals from the Kitchenette* (New York: Vanguard Press, 1928), 19.

26. Hannah Dutaud, *The Glorious Art of Home Cooking* (Chicago: Associate Authors, 1935), ix.

27. Claire Sugden, *The Romantic and Practical Side of Cookery* (New York: Louis S. Siegfried, 1931), n.p.; Allen, *Ida Bailey Allen's New Modern Cook Book,* 564.

28. Claire, *Macy's Cook Book for the Busy Woman,* 11.

29. *Anyone Can Bake* (New York: Royal Baking Powder Company, 1927), 3.

30. Ann Batchelder, "Still Life, by Mother," *Ladies' Home Journal,* September 1936, 28.

31. John MacPherson, *The Mystery Chef's Own Cook Book* (New York: Longman, Green, 1934), xiii.

32. Phoebe Dane, *333 New Ways to a Man's Heart* (New York: True Story Magazine, 1931), 3.

33. Constance Wagner, *Kitchen Magic* (New York: Farrar and Rinehart, 1932), 5–6.

34. Jane Abbott and Henrietta Wilcox Penny, *Polly Put the Kettle On: A Story for Girls* (Philadelphia: J. B. Lippincott, 1925), 22.

35. Mary Grosvenor Ellsworth, *Much Depends on Dinner* (New York: Alfred A. Knopf, 1939), n.p.; William Rhode, *Of Cabbages and Kings* (New York: Stackpole Sons, 1938), 8; Hazel Young, *Better Meals for Less Money* (Boston: Little, Brown, 1940), v.

36. George Conforth, *Good Food: How to Prepare It* (Washington, DC: Review and Herald, 1920), 7.

37. Young, *The Working Girl Must Eat,* 6.

38. Dane, *333 New Ways to a Man's Heart,* 5–6.

Chapter 4.
Ladylike Lunches and Manly Meals: The Gendering of Food and Cooking

1. Byron MacFadyen, "When a Man Goes Culinary," *Good Housekeeping,* January 1930, 90–91, 104; "Courses—Course—Courses," *Good Housekeeping,* June 1930, 90–91, 164; "A Man Cooks with French Dressing," *Good Housekeeping,* April 1930, 94, 226; "Dishes Fit for Gods—And Men!" *Good Housekeeping,* March 1933, 81, 112, 114; "Picnics for Men Who Hate to Leave Home," *Good Housekeeping,* June 1937, 86–87, 211–12; "Sweets to the Meat," *Good Housekeeping,* October 1935, 88–89, 112–13; and "A Man Cooks in Ramekins," *Good Housekeeping,* September 1931, 90–91, 104.

2. For an insightful look at how candy companies during the late nineteenth and early twentieth century marketed certain kinds of candy as a suitably masculine snack, see Jane Dusselier, "Bonbons, Lemon Drops, and Oh Henry! Bars: Candy, Consumer Culture, and the Construction of Gender, 1895–1920," in *Kitchen Culture in America: Popular Representations of Food, Gender, and Race,* ed. Sherrie A. Inness (Philadelphia: University of Pennsylvania Press, 2000).

3. See, for example, Bettina Berch, "The Development of Housework," *International Journal of Women's Studies* 1, no. 4 (July–August 1978): 336–48; Nona Glazer, "Servants to Capital: Unpaid Domestic Labor and Paid Work," *Review of Radical Political Economics* 16, no. 1 (1987): 61–87; Eileen Boris, "The Home as Workplace: Deconstructing Dichotomies," *International Review of Social History* 39, no. 3 (1994): 415–28. For a close look at how housework and wage work played out in working-class women's lives during the 1930s, see Kari Boyd McBride, "A (Boarding) House is Not a Home: Women's Work and Women's Worth," *Frontiers* 17, no. 1 (May 1996): 90–112.

4. Writer and philosopher Sallie Tisdale argues that the advent of gas and electric stoves and the phasing out of wood stoves marked the final demise of

male and female shared kitchen duties. See Sallie Tisdale, *The Best Thing I Ever Tasted* (New York: Putnam, 2000). See also Jeanne Boydtson, *Home and Work: Housework, Wages, and the Ideology of the Early Republic* (New York: Oxford University Press, 1990), 41.

5. Fannie Merritt Farmer, *The Boston Cooking-School Cook Book* (Boston: Little, Brown, 1933), n.p.

6. Eleanor Howe, *Feeding Father* (New York: Treasure Chest Publications, 1939), 4.

7. Leone B. Moats, "Meals for Men," *House and Garden*, February 1934, 33, 65–66.

8. Mary Stevens, *A Primer of Modern Cooking: New Methods and New Dishes for Experienced Cooks and For Beginners* (New York: Home Institute, 1934), 16; Coral Smith, *New Dishes from Left-overs* (New York: Frederick A. Stokes, 1934), 54; Edith Key Haines, *Edith Key Haines' Cook Book* (New York: Farrar and Rinehart, 1937), 608; Julia Pain Gooding, *Formal Dinners* (Boston: Houghton Mifflin, 1940), 61; Helen Kroeger Muhs, *Sunset's Host and Hostess Book* (San Francisco: Lane Publishing, 1940), 162–75.

9. Hazel Young, *The Working Girl Must Eat* (Boston: Little, Brown, 1938), 38, 86, 156.

10. Marjorie Hillis and Bertina Foltz, *Corned Beef and Caviar: For the Live-Aloner* (Indianapolis: Bobbs-Merrill, 1937), 122, 134–35, 148, 184–85. For other descriptions of male food preferences, see Edna Sibley Tipton, "What the Men Like," *Pictorial Review*, January 1926, 32; "Food for Husbands: Reader Recipes for a Man's Appetite," *Delineator*, October 1935, 53; "Dishes to Tempt the Hard-to-Please Husband," *Delineator*, March 1928, 49; Shirley Warner, "Why Men Hate Spinach," *American Home*, March 1940, 55, 89; Louella G. Shouer, "They Know What They Like," *Ladies' Home Journal*, August 1937, 40–43; Ann Batchelder, "A Meal for Men," *Ladies' Home Journal*, October 1934, 20–21; Betty Thornley Stuart, "Men Eat It Up," *Collier's*, 2 January 1932, 18, 39; Ann Batchelder, "Why Men Like to Eat Out," *Ladies' Home Journal*, March 1936, 36; Gaynor Maddox, "Men Eat Chicken," *Woman's Home Companion*, May 1933, 59; Edna Sibley Tipton, "When Men Entertain," *Better Homes and Gardens*, March 1931, 25.

11. Louise Bennet Weaver and Helen Cowless LeCron; *When Sue Began to Cook with Bettina's Best Recipes: A Beginning Cookbook for Girls from Eight to Fifteen* (New York: Alburt Company, 1924), 92, 149, 155.

12. Howe, *Feeding Father*, 27, 5, 4, 41, 6.

13. Hazel Young, *Better Meals for Less Money* (Boston: Little, Brown, 1940), 46; Marjorie Swift and Christine Terhune Herrick, *Feed the Brute* (New York: Frederick Stokes Company, 1926), ix.

14. Kenon Breazelea, "In Spite of Women: *Esquire* Magazine and the Construction of the Male Consumer," *Signs: Journal of Women in Culture and Society* 20, no. 1 (1994): 6.

15. George Frederick, *Cooking as Men Like It* (New York: Business Bourse, 1930), 37, 29–30, 1–2, 11.

16. "It doesn't look much like the picture, does it?" in *Delineator*, September 1935, 64; "Very well. If this is the ice cream, what did you do with the meat?" in *Delineator*, October 1935, 64; "And the way he said 'gobble, gobble!' " in *Delineator*,

November 1935, 64; "You would light the plum-pudding!" in *Delineator*, December 1935, 63.

17. Bozeman Bulger, "What to Cook When the Wife Is Away," *Ladies' Home Journal*, July 1921, 75.

18. George Rector, "When the Wife's Away," *Saturday Evening Post*, 1 December 1934, 14–15, 53–56.

19. Byron MacFadyen, "Teach Your Boys to Cook," *Good Housekeeping*, August 1929, 101.

20. "Men, Meet the Kitchen!" *American Home*, May 1933, 288–89.

21. "And We Learned about Cooking From Men!" *American Home*, September 1933, 241–42; Jean Guthrie, "Mere Men . . . but Can They Cook!" *Better Homes and Gardens*, June 1937, 70–71, 92–93.

22. Mac Sheridan, *The Stag Cookbook: Written for Men by Men* (New York: George H. Dornan, 1922), n.p., vii, 32.

23. Montague Glass, "Amateur Cooking for Husbands," *Good Housekeeping*, July 1931, 44.

24. Sheridan, *The Stag Cookbook*, 78.

25. Nell B. Nichols, "When He Cooks," *Woman's Home Companion*, February 1934, 25.

26. Mary Grosvenor Ellsworth, *Much Depends on Dinner* (New York: Alfred A. Knopf, 1939), 313.

27. "Men, Meet the Kitchen!" 288.

28. Sheridan, *The Stag Cookbook*, 69, 41, 51.

29. Ted Shane, "Women Can't Cook," *Collier's*, 18 March 1939, 16, 42, 43.

30. Mary Dunham, "Men Can't Cook," *Collier's*, 18 March 1939, 17, 73.

31. See, for example, Elmer T. Peterson, "A New Kind of Man Cook," *Better Homes and Gardens*, April 1939, 43, 52, 72; Frazier Hunt, "Give Me a Man Cook Every Time!" *Better Homes and Gardens*, February 1935, 24–25, 58–59; "Come into the Kitchen, Gentlemen!" *The Literary Digest*, December 28, 1929, 39; "Beefsteak as William Allen White Prepares It," *Better Homes and Gardens*, April 1934, 97.

32. Louise Bennet Weaver and Helen Cowless LeCron, *A Thousand Ways to Please a Husband with Bettina's Best Recipes*, 2nd ed., rev. and exp. (New York: Alburt Company 1932), 25, 55, 380.

33. Sheridan, *The Stag Cookbook*, 53.

34. As culinary historian Stephen Mennell points out, a printed recipe collection firmly fixes the boundaries of certain kinds of dishes. With the advent of printed recipes, "the identity of a dish and its ingredients consequently became more firmly fixed, and the scope for idiosyncratic improvisation diminished." See Stephen Mennell, *All Manners of Food: Eating and Taste in England and France from the Middle Ages to the Present*, 2nd ed. (Urbana: University of Illinois Press, 1996), 345. A printed recipe, also, according to literary and film scholar Anne McHugh, "fosters solitary learning, it facilitates the privatization of housework, the isolation of housewives from one another. The written recipe obviates the need for interpersonal demonstration or instruction." See Kathleen Anne McHugh, *American Domesticity: From How-to-Manual to Hollywood Melodrama* (New York: Oxford University Press, 1999), 29. On the structure of recipes, see also Emma Kafalenos,

"Reading to Cook / Cooking to Read: Structure in the Kitchen," *Southwest Review* 73, no. 2 (spring 1988): 210–19.

35. Ida Migliaro et al., *The Household Searchlight Recipe Book* (Topeka, KS: *Household Magazine*, 1939), 5.

36. Lisa Buchinger Aldrich (granddaughter of Sadie Lenore Winterstein), phone conversation with author, 22 September 1999. This recipe collection is currently in my possession, and I am very much indebted to Lisa Buchinger Aldrich for sharing this recipe collection and memories of her grandmother with me.

Chapter 5.
Lima Loaf and Butter Stretchers

1. See, for example, John W. Jeffries, *Wartime America: The World War II Home Front* (Chicago: Ivan R. Dee, 1996); John Morton Blum, *V Was for Victory* (New York: Harcourt Brace Javonovich, 1976); Daniel Kryder, *Divided Arsenal: Race and the American State during World War II* (New York: Cambridge University Press, 2000); Phillip McGuire, *Taps for a Jim Crow Army* (Lexington: University Press of Kentucky, 1993); David S. Wyman, *The Abandonment of the Jews* (New York: Pantheon Books, 1984); Studs Terkel, *The "Good War"* (New York: Pantheon Books, 1984).

2. Polly Patterson, *Victory Vittles* (Los Angeles: Warren F. Lewis, 1942). On Billie Burke, see Mary Drake McFeely, *Can She Bake a Cherry Pie? American Women and the Kitchen in the Twentieth Century* (Amherst: University of Massachusetts Press, 2000), 80. For a nostalgic look at wartime cookery, see Joanne Lamb Hayes, *Grandma's Wartime Kitchen: World War II and the Way We Cooked* (New York: St. Martins, 2000).

3. Helmut Ripperger, "The Aids to Noble Life," *Publishers' Weekly*, 14 March 1942, 1100.

4. Gwendolyn Starr, "Lady, Do You Need a Cookbook?" *Consumers' Research Bulletin*, August 1943, 18.

5. Harvey Levenstein, *Paradox of Plenty: A Social History of Eating in Modern America* (New York: Oxford University Press, 1993), 124.

6. Anne Mendelson, *Stand Facing the Stove: The Story of the Women Who Gave America "The Joy of Cooking"* (New York: Henry Holt, 1996), 246–48, 178.

7. M. F. K. Fisher, "How to Cook a Wolf," in *The Art of Eating* (New York: Macmillan, 1990), 240–43.

8. Mendelson, *Stand Facing the Stove*, 254–55.

9. As quoted by Jane Stern and Michael Stern, *American Gourmet* (New York: Harper Collins, 1991), 10. The gourmet movement did not, however, remain untouched by the war. A 4 May 1942 article from the *American Press* (pasted into Maude Reid's wartime scrapbook) described how a group of gourmets had vowed to adhere to wartime rationing: "With brave heart but faltering stomach, the Gourmet Society of Brooklyn in convention assembled today formulated and adopted the following 'ten commandments for victory,'" wrote the reporter. The gourmets vowed to drink only one cup of coffee a day and to refrain from experimenting with new food concoctions, among other resolutions.

10. On restaurant growth, see Levenstein, *Paradox of Plenty*, 127. On refugee chefs, see Stern and Stern, *American Gourmet*, 9.

11. James Beard, "The Favorite Cookbooks of Four Famous Gourmets," *House Beautiful*, October 1942, 65, 107; "Seven Cooks in Search of a Gourmet," *House and Garden*, February 1942, 28, 78–79.

12. *How to Prepare Appetizing, Healthful Meals with Food Available Today* (Minneapolis: General Mills, 1943), 24. This piecrust recipe is from a 1943 General Foods booklet entitled *How to Bake by Ration Book*, as quoted by Jane Stern and Michael Stern, *Square Meals* (New York: Alfred Knopf, 1984), 205.

13. Harriet Anderson, "What's Cooking?" *Woman's Home Companion*, April 1943, 37. For general cookbooks, Anderson recommended Alice Winn-Smith's *Thrifty Cooking for Wartime*, Margot Murphy's *Wartime Meals*, and *What Do We Eat Now?* by Helen Robertson, Sarah MacLeod, and Frances Preston.

14. Helmut Ripperger, "Too Much Pudding," *Publishers' Weekly*, 19 July 1941, 161; Helmut Ripperger, "Cookery Books Go to War," *Publishers' Weekly*, 6 June 1942, 2113–14.

15. Helmut Ripperger, "The Cookery Books of 1942," *Publishers' Weekly*, 2 January 1943, 23–24. See also Helmut Ripperger, "Christmas Cheer with Cookery Books," *Publishers' Weekly*, 6 December 1941, 2164.

16. Amy Bentley, *Eating for Victory: Food Rationing and the Politics of Domesticity* (Urbana: University of Illinois Press, 1998), 103.

17. On the rationing system, see Gerry Schremp, *Kitchen Culture: Fifty Years of Food Fads* (New York: Pharos Books, 1991), 9. For an example of the advice found in women's magazines about planning meals around rationing, see Katherine Fisher, "Rationing Won't Get You Down If You Plan Your Meals This Way," *Good Housekeeping*, June 1943, 89–91.

18. As quoted by Stern and Stern, *Square Meals*, 199.

19. Bentley, *Eating for Victory*, 18.

20. Prudence Penny (Florence Richardson), *Coupon Cookery: A Guide to Good Meals under Wartime Conditions of Rationing and Food Shortages* (Los Angeles: Hearst Publications, 1943), 45.

21. See Ann Robbins, *100 Meat-Saving Recipes* (New York: Thomas Y. Crowell, 1943).

22. Ruth Berolzheimer, ed., *The American Woman's Meals without Meat Cook Book* (Chicago: Consolidated Books, 1943), 40, 46.

23. *Mrs. Knox's Meatless Main Dishes and Leftover Hints* (Johnstown, NY: Charles B. Knox Gelatin Company, 1942). For examples of "escalloped" and hash recipes, see Clare Newman and Bell Wiley, *A Cookbook of Leftovers* (Boston: Little, Brown, 1941).

24. Arthur H. Deute, *200 Dishes for Men to Cook* (New York: M. Barrow, 1944), 175, 145.

25. Betty Watson, *Cooking without Cans* (Philadelphia: Ruttle, Shaw & Wetherwill, 1943), 17; Marjorie Mills, *Cooking on a Ration: Food Is Still Fun* (Boston: Houghton Mifflin, 1943), 23.

26. Levenstein, *Paradox of Plenty*, 65.

27. Margot Murphy, *Wartime Meals: How to Plan Them, How to Buy Them, How to Cook Them* (New York: Greenberg, 1942), 89.

28. Sylvia Lovegren, *Fashionable Food: Seven Decades of Food Fads* (New York: Macmillan, 1995), 116.

29. Levenstein, *Paradox of Plenty*, 75.

30. As quoted by Stern and Stern, *Square Meals*, 222. The 1942 edition of *The Joy of Cooking* went to press too soon to take shortages and substitutions into account.

31. Leona M. Bayer and Edith S. Green, *Kitchen Strategy: Vitamin Values Made Easy* (San Francisco: Lithotype Process, 1943); Katherine Fisher, "Main Dishes for These Times," *Good Housekeeping*, September 1943, 89.

32. Ida Bailey Allen, *Double-Quick Cooking for Part-Time Homemakers* (New York: M. Barrows, 1943); *Your Share* (Minneapolis: General Mills, 1943), 21; Elizabeth Case and Martha Wyman, *Cook's Away: A Collection of Simple Rules, Helpful Facts, and Choice Recipes Designed to Make Cooking Easy* (New York: Longmans, Green, 1943), 55.

33. Bentley, *Eating for Victory*, 85–113.

34. Case and Wyman, *Cook's Away*, 92–101; Harriet H. Hester, *300 Sugar Saving Recipes* (New York: M. Barrows, 1942), n.p.; Ruth Berolzheimer, ed., *The Wartime Cook Book: 500 Recipes, Victory Substitutes, and Economical Suggestions for Wartime Needs* (Chicago: Consolidated Books, 1942), 56; Ruth Odell, *Sugarless Recipes: Aids for Housewives in Solving Sugar Rationing Problems for Beverages, Cakes, Cookies, Frostings, Fruit Dishes, Frozen Desserts, Puddings, and Pies* (Washington, DC: Newspaper Information Service, 1942), 5.

35. *Your Share*, 14–15; Allen, *Double-Quick Recipes*, 188; Mary Patterson, *Coupon Cookery* (Hollywood, CA: Murray and Gee, 1943), 98. On the rise in margarine consumption, see Schremp, *Kitchen Culture*, 12.

36. Watson, *Cooking without Cans*, iii, 177. Watson was also the only cookbook author I read who directly mentioned the famine conditions in much of the rest of the world, and chastised Americans for believing that their own limited amounts of cooking fats (which were enormous compared to Europe's) constituted a real crisis.

37. Hester, *300 Sugar Saving Recipes*, 125.

38. Mills, *Cooking on a Ration*, 40. Similar advice on the importance of fresh and well-cooked vegetables had appeared during the First World War, as well. See, for example, Anna Barrows, "The War Bride's New Work: If He 'Won't Eat Vegetables,' the Reason May Lie in the Cooking," *Ladies' Home Journal*, May 1919, 85.

39. Bentley, *Eating for Victory*, 117.

40. Alice B. Winn-Smith, *Thrifty Cooking for Wartime* (New York: Macmillan, 1942), 90.

41. Marjorie Dean and Eleanor Lynch, ed., *The Modern Hostess Cook Book* (New York: Dell, September 1942), 84.

42. Marion White, *Mother Hubbard's Cookbook* (New York: M. S. Mill, 1944).

43. Frank Shay, *The Best Men Are Cooks* (New York: Coward-McCann, 1941).

Chapter 6.
"Ways and Means for War Days":
The Cookbook-Scrapbook Compiled by Maude Reid

1. I am indebted to Jennie Germann, who currently owns this document, for sharing it with me, as well as her friend Mary Clark who originally bought it at

the estate sale. Ms. Germann gave me leave to use her extensive notes on the volume and loaned me the document itself for my research. Her generosity allowed me access to a unique original source and I am very grateful. The original document has no page numbers; therefore all future references will not include citation information.

2. This document also comes from Jennie Germann's collection, acquired through the same estate sale.

3. I would like to offer a special thanks to Kathie Bordelon, the archivist at McNeese State University, who helped me locate this document, stored in the Maude Reid Collection. Her assistance greatly deepened my analysis of Reid's wartime cookbook-diary. I also wish to thank the anonymous member of Reid's extended family who first directed me to the collection at McNeese State.

4. Reid also mentioned how she had trouble obtaining shoes, which were rationed. In addition, she complained about the difficulty of finding and purchasing pepper and cleaning powder.

5. Fats continued to be saved and recycled in the year following the war, according to Reid. In July 1946, she wrote: "We are still being urged to save fats which if brought to your grocer will pay you four cents a pound. Later, this discarded fat will be sold to manufacturers of soap and other products."

Chapter 7.
"The Hand That Cuts the Ration Coupon May Win the War":
Women's Home-Cooked Patriotism

1. See "Yes Sir, we men baked 38 cakes—and did the ladies' eyes pop!" *Ladies' Home Journal*, April 1942, 41; "Meal Props That Whip Shortages," *Better Homes and Gardens*, February 1943, 34–35; Harry Botsford, "Just a Man with a Pan," *Woman's Home Companion*, November 1941, 82–83; Harry Day, "Picnics I Like," *American Home*, August 1941, 57; Corey Ford, "You Say We Can't Cook?" *Better Homes and Gardens*, June 1941, 64, 94–95, 97; Carl Malmberg, "Dad and Daughter Cook," *Parents' Magazine*, February 1941, 44, 63–64.

2. On African American domestic workers leaving the employment of private white households, see Amy Bentley, *Eating for Victory: Food Rationing and the Politics of Domesticity* (Urbana: University of Illinois Press, 1998), 47–49. On African American women's employment during the war, see Karen Anderson, "Last Hired, First Fired: Black Women during World War II," *Journal of American History* 69, no. 1 (June 1982): 82–97. See also Richard R. Jefferson, "Negro Employment in St. Louis War Production," in *America's Working Women: A Documentary History 1600 to the Present*, ed. Rosalyn Baxandall, Linda Gordon, and Susan Reverby (New York: Vintage Books, 1976). On how domestic employment agencies attempted to woo back African American women, see Phyllis Palmer, *Domesticity and Dirt: Housewives and Domestic Servants in the United States, 1920–1945* (Philadelphia: Temple University Press, 1989), 154; Bentley, *Eating for Victory*, 10; Sylvia Lovegren, *Fashionable Food: Seven Decades of Food Fads* (New York: Macmillan, 1995), 117; Glenda Riley, *Inventing the American Woman: A Perspective on Women's History* (Arlington Heights, IL: Harlan Davidson, 1987), 230.

3. See William Chafe, *The Paradox of Change: American Women in the 20th Cen-*

tury (New York: Oxford University Press, 1991), 144, 151; Nancy Woloch, *Women and the American Experience* (New York: Alfred A. Knopf, 1984), 465. On day care during and after the war, see Emilie Stoltzfus, "Working Mothers vs. City Hall: The Post-WWII Battle for Publicly Funded Day Care in Cleveland, Ohio" (paper presented at the annual meeting of the American Historical Association-Pacific Coast Branch, Portland, Oregon, August 1997). For further citations on women's roles during World War II, see my Essay on Sources.

4. See Barbara Whitmore Henry, "6 O'Clock Steak Dinner for an Office Wife," *American Home*, March 1941, 114–15.

5. Hazel Young, *The Working Girl Must Eat* (Boston: Little, Brown, 1944), v.

6. See Susan B. Anthony, *Out of the Kitchen—Into the War* (New York: Stephen Day, 1943).

7. Bentley, *Eating for Victory*, 42–44.

8. Florence Brobeck, *Serve It Buffet* (New York: M. Barrows, 1944), vii.

9. Mary L. R. Taylor, *Economy for Epicures: A Practical Menu and Recipe Book* (New York: Oxford University Press, 1943), n.p.

10. Demetria Taylor, *Ration Cookbook* (New York: Recklam Press, 1943), 11.

11. Helen Robertson, Sarah MacLeod, and Frances Preston, *What Do We Eat Now?* (Philadelphia: Lippincott, 1942), v.

12. Alice Winn-Smith, *Thrifty Cooking for Wartime* (New York: Macmillan, 1942), n.p.

13. *Your Share* (Minneapolis: General Mills, 1943), n.p.

14. The Home Institute of the *New York Herald Tribune, America's Cook Book* (New York: Charles Scribner's Sons, 1943).

15. Winn-Smith, *Thrifty Cooking for Wartime*, vii.

16. *The Authentic Victory Cook Book* (New York: Authentic Publications, 1942), 3.

17. Ruth Berolzheimer, ed., *The Wartime Cook Book: 500 Recipes, Victory Substitutes, and Economical Suggestions for Wartime Needs* (Chicago: Consolidated Books, 1942), 64.

18. *What's New in Foods and Nutrition* (Beloit, WI: Harvey and Howe, 1942–43), 1.

19. Demetria Taylor, *Square Meals on Short Rations* (New York: Home Guide Publications, 1943), iv.

20. Quite a few cookbooks noted that a woman could save time and guarantee higher-quality groceries by doing her own marketing, rather than phoning in an order. Interestingly, very few grocery stores provide phone-in marketing services today, but consumers have started to purchase food sight unseen via the Internet.

21. *The Good Housekeeping Cook Book*, 7th ed. (New York: Farrar and Rinehart, 1944), vi.

22. *The Authentic Victory Cook Book: Tested Recipes of Delicious, Point-Saving Dishes and a Guide to Home Canning* (New York: Authentic Publications, 1943), 28.

23. Mary Drake McFeely, *Can She Bake a Cherry Pie? American Women and the Kitchen in the Twentieth Century* (Amherst: University of Massachusetts Press, 2000), 69.

24. Ruth Berolzheimer, ed., *Military Meals at Home* (Chicago: Consolidated Books, 1943), 16–46. For similar rhetoric, see, for example, Louella G. Shouer, "Take Some Tips from the Army," *Ladies' Home Journal*, March 1942, 116–17.

25. Mary Patterson, *Coupon Cookery* (Hollywood, CA: Murray and Gee, 1943), 97.

26. McFeely, *Can She Bake a Cherry Pie*, 84–85.

27. Ida Bailey Allen, *Ida Bailey Allen's Money-Saving Cook Book: Eating for Victory* (Garden City, NY: Garden City Publishing, 1942), 184; Margot Murphy, *Wartime Meals: How to Plan Them, How to Buy Them, How to Cook Them*, (New York: Greenberg, 1942), 313.

28. Marjorie Mills, *Cooking on a Ration: Food Is Still Fun* (Boston: Houghton Mifflin, 1943), 110.

29. Taylor, *Ration Cook Book*, 29.

30. Robertson, MacLeod, and Preston, *What Do We Eat Now?*, xi.

31. Ann Robbins, *100 Meat-Saving Recipes* (New York: Thomas Y. Crowell, 1943), viii.

32. Mills, *Cooking on a Ration*, 40.

33. Patterson, *Coupon Cookery*, 21–22.

34. Berolzhimer, *The Wartime Cook Book*, 3.

35. Dorothy Mars, "I've Got My First Job—And I Still Get the Meals," *Good Housekeeping*, February 1943, 84. For examples of popular magazine articles that depicted husbands helping in the kitchen, see "How to Have a Husband and a Job Too," *House Beautiful*, June 1943, 74–75; Ted Hatch, "What Every Bridegroom Should Know!" *American Home*, August 1941, 52–53. For a prewar example, see Louella G. Shouer, "Two Cooks Are Better Than One," *Ladies' Home Journal*, March 1941, 106–7.

36. "Meet the Berkmans: The Story of a Mother Working on Two Fronts," *Ladies' Home Journal*, October 1942, 99.

37. Helmut Ripperger, "The Aids to Noble Life," *Publishers' Weekly*, 14 March 1942, 1101.

38. Frank Shay, *The Best Men Are Cooks* (New York: Coward-McCann, 1941), 107, 131, 185, 240, 268–69, 239.

39. Lawrence Keating, *Men in Aprons: "If He Could Only Cook"* (New York: M. S. Mill, 1944), xv, 17–20, 82, x–xi, 22–23, 80, 119–20, 21. George Rector was a well-known restaurateur in the post–World War I period.

40. George Martin, *Come and Get It! The Compleat Outdoor Chef* (New York: A. S. Barnes, 1942), vii.

41. Arthur H. Deute, *200 Dishes for Men to Cook* (New York: M. Barrow, 1944), 60.

42. See also Byron MacFadyen, "Give a Man Man's Food," *Good Housekeeping*, March 1941, 106; Herman Smith, "A Golf Dinner That Will Go Down in History!" *American Home*, August 1941, 60–61.

43. "On Leave!" *American Home*, April 1942, 82–83.

44. Marion White, *Mother Hubbard's Cookbook* (New York: M. S. Mill, 1944), v.

45. Ethel McCall Head, "For Men?" *American Home*, February 1941, 65.

46. Florence Harris, *Victory Vitamin Cook Book for Wartime Meals* (New York: W. M. Penn Publishing, 1943), 34–35.

47. I think the vast numbers of baked good recipes—virtually always the most plentiful kind of recipe in general cookbooks—attest to their popularity among women. Many of the cookbooks I examined had checkmarks or other signs of use next to baking recipes and no other kinds of recipe.

Chapter 8.
The Betty Crocker Era

1. See, for example, "Using the New Emergency Type-Flour," *Good House-keeping*, June 1946, 103–4. On polls indicating willingness to comply with voluntary restrictions, see Harvey Levenstein, *Paradox of Plenty: A Social History of Eating in Modern America* (New York: Oxford University Press, 1993), 97, and Amy Bentley, *Eating for Victory: Food Rationing and the Politics of Domesticity* (Urbana: University of Illinois Press, 1998), 146, 155.

2. Levenstein, *Paradox of Plenty*, 98–99.

3. "Sell Cook Books Stressing Inexpensive and Meatless Meals," *Publishers' Weekly*, 29 November 1947, 2462.

4. Not that all cookbook readers, even by the mid 1950s, considered *The Joy of Cooking* a unique classic. A cookbook reviewer for *Vogue* magazine dismissed *The Joy of Cooking* as "A variation on *The Boston Cookbook*, but with slightly less material." See "Presents for a Literary Cook," *Vogue*, November 1956, 146. On the other hand, Helmut Ripperger (a personal friend of Rombauer's) greeted the 1951 edition of *The Joy of Cooking* with effusive praise: "One of the most sensible and illuminating writers in her field, Mrs. Rombauer has done an even better job with the new than the old, which was almost perfect when issued twenty years ago." See Helmut Ripperger, "A Sport without a Season," *Publishers' Weekly*, 11 August 1951, 553.

5. Thomas E. Cooney, "The Trade in Taste," *American Review*, 12 February 1955, 40.

6. See, for example, Arthur Williams, "Fannie Farmer's New Dress," *Publishers' Weekly*, 6 October 1951, 1518–22. On cookbooks in bookstores, see "Shop Talk," *Publishers' Weekly*, 5 July 1952, 34–36; Morton Levin, "Kroch's Two-Fold Plan Applied to Cookbook Selling," *Publishers' Weekly*, 24 December 1949, 2490–91; Caroline Rollins, "A Plan to Promote Cookbooks When There Is a Late Winter Lull," *Publishers' Weekly*, 24 December 1949, 2492–94; "Cookery Books, New and Perennial," *Publishers' Weekly*, 17 August 1946, 685; Harriet Anderson, "Cookbooks Go On Forever," *Publishers' Weekly*, 11 August 1951, 555–56.

7. Elinor Parker, "Too Many Cooks: Cook Books to Be Published This Spring," *Publishers' Weekly*, 3 May 1952, 1836; "Too Many Cookbooks," *Newsweek*, 19 May 1952, 112–14; A. I. M. S. Street, "The Gastronomical Year," *Saturday Review*, 13 February 1954, 35.

8. Sydney Flynn, "My Mother's Cookbook," *McCall's*, May 1987, 52.

9. Juanita Wittenborn, "Cook Books Make Good Gifts," *Parents' Magazine*, December 1947, 62.

10. Margaret Cusser and Mary L. De Give, *Twixt the Cup and the Lip: Psychology and Sociological Cultural Factors Affecting Food Habits* (New York: Twayne, 1952), 168.

11. Blanche C. Firman, *Peggy Put the Kettle On* (New York: Exposition Press, 1951), 99.

12. The Pillsbury Bake-Off remains popular today. See, for example, Shawn Humbler, "You Can Have Your Cake and Eat It Too," *Los Angeles Times*, 11 February 1996, sec. A, p. 1. A man won the contest for the first time in 1996. See Karola Saekel, "Local Cake Makes Good: Single Dad Wins Pillsbury Bake-Off," *San Francisco Chronicle*, 28 February 1996, sec. F, p. 1.

13. For example, cookbook author Margaret Potter described promotional cooking pamphlets as biased but often containing "nuggets of real value." See Margaret Yardley Potter, *At Home on the Range or How to Make Friends with Your Stove* (Philadelphia: J. B. Lippinoctt, 1947), 209.

14. Mary Anna DuSablon, *America's Collectible Cookbooks: The History, the Politics, the Recipes* (Athens: Ohio University Press, 1994), 110–12. On the history of General Mills, see also Reagan Walker, "General Mills and Pillsbury Compete for Our Palates," *Oregonian*, 22 February 2000, sec. OP, p. 1. For a summary of Adelaide Hawley Cumming's career as Betty Crocker, see her obituary in the *New York Times*, 25 December 1998, sec. B, p. 11.

15. For reproduction and discussion of Betty Crocker's portraits, see Gerry Schremp, *Kitchen Culture: Fifty Years of Food Fads from Spam to Spa Cuisine* (New York: Pharos Books, 1991), 133. For a discussion of the 1998 reissue of the original 1950 *Betty Crocker's Picture Cook Book*, see Laura Shapiro, "Betty Goes Back to the Future," *Newsweek*, 19 October 1998, 68–69. On the composite Betty Crocker of the late 1990s, see "Melting Pot Betty Crocker: 75 Faces to Be Blended into New Look," *Palm Beach Post*, 12 September 1995, sec. A, p. 1. For web site, see www.bettycrocker.com. Today, Betty's portrait appears far less often than her signifier: a red spoon with her "signature" currently appears on more than 200 General Mills products. According to General Mills, *Betty Crocker's New Cook Book*, has sold 27 million copies.

16. On the nickname "Big Red," see Rosyln Siegel, "After 65 Years on the Kitchen Betty Crocker Is Still Strong," *Publishers' Weekly*, 19 July 1991, 23–24. For an in-depth discussion on the photographic method in the cookbook, see Karal Ann Marling's chapter "Betty Crocker's Picture Cook Book: The Aesthetics of Food in the 1950s," in *As Seen on TV: The Visual Culture and Everyday Life in the 1950s* (Cambridge, MA: Harvard University Press, 1994), 202–40.

17. Ripperger, "A Sport without a Season," 549.

18. For sales figures of *Betty Crocker's Picture Cook Book*, see Jim Achmutey, "200 Years of Cookbooks," *Atlanta Constitution*, 17 October 1996, sec. H., p. 1. For sales figures of *The Better Homes and Gardens Cook Book*, see Bridget Kinsella, "The Checkered Career of a Kitchen Classic," *Publishers' Weekly*, 2 September 1996, 34–36.

19. Roland Barthes, *Mythologies*, trans. Annette Lavers (1957; reprint, New York: Hill and Wang, 1972), 78.

20. See, for example, Joshua Gitelson, "Populox: The Suburban Cuisine of the 1950s," *Journal of American Culture* 15, no. 3 (fall 1992): 73–78.

21. Beth Bailey McLean, *Modern Homemaker's Cookbook* (New York: M. Barrows, 1950), 300.

22. Ruth Berolzheimer, ed., *The Body Building Dishes for Children Cook Book* (Chicago: Consolidated Book Publishers, 1949); *Better Homes and Gardens Junior Cook Book* (Des Moines, IA: Meredith Publishing, 1955), 450–51, 166–67; Blanche M. Stover, ed., *Parents' Magazine Family Cookbook* (New York: *Parents' Magazine* Publications, 1953), 251.

23. Margaret Gossett and Mary Elting, *Now You're Cookin'* (Philadelphia: Westminster Press, 1948), 14.

24. See *Betty Crocker's Cookbook for Boys and Girls* (New York: Golden Press, 1957).

25. *The General Foods Kitchens Cook Book* (New York: Random House, 1959), 81. In a cookbook review, Street wrote despairingly of certain kinds of recipes found in juvenile cookbooks: "It was rather disheartening to see that bridge-club pest of yesteryear turning up again—a fantasy consisting of lettuce leaf, one slice of canned pineapple with a half banana standing upright at its center, the whole dripping with mayonnaise. But perhaps—pity the poor young palates!—it has found its niche, a birthday party attended by befrilled small girls." See Street, "The Gastronomical Year," 35.

26. Dorothy Malone, *Cookbook for Brides* (New York: A. A. Wyn, 1947), 38.

27. Mary Scot Welch, *Your First Hundred Meals* (New York: Charles Scribner's Sons, 1948), 180. For examples of step-by-step cookbooks or entertaining guides, see Betty Watson, *Dinners That Wait* (New York: Doubleday, 1954), and Mildred O. Knopf, *The Perfect Hostess Cook Book* (New York: Alfred A. Knopf, 1950).

28. *The Parents' Magazine Cook Book*, 263.

29. McLean, *Modern Homemaker's Cookbook*, 280. For a cookbook in which all the soup recipes called for combining canned soups, see Marion Taylor Young, *Martha Dean's Cooking for Compliments* (New York: M. Barrows, 1954).

30. Mildred O. Knopf, *Cook, My Darling Daughter* (New York: Alfred A. Knopf, 1959), 33.

31. Jane Stern and Michael Stern, *Square Meals* (New York: Alfred A. Knopf, 1984), 264.

32. James Gilbert, email to author, 25 September 1999. On suburbia, see also Kenneth Jackson, *The Crabgrass Frontier* (New York: Oxford University Press, 1985), and Philip C. Dolce, *Suburbia: The American Dream and Dilemma* (Garden City, NY: Doubleday, 1976). For commentary written during the postwar period, see, for example, Robert Wood, *Suburbia: Its People and Their Politics* (Boston: Houghton Mifflin, 1959).

33. Ida Bailey Allen, *Ida Bailey Allen's Cook Book for Two* (1947; reprint, Garden City, NY: Garden City Books, 1957), 1.

34. *The General Foods Kitchens Cookbook*, 121–54.

35. Marion Flexner, *Cocktail-Supper Cookbook* (New York: M. Barrows, 1955); Stella Standard, *Complete American Cookbook* (Cleveland: World Publishing, 1957).

36. Jean Hamilton Campbell and Gloria Kameran, *Simple Cooking for the Epicure* (New York: Viking Press, 1949), 3.

37. *The General Foods Kitchens Cookbook*, 141, 154.

38. *The Gourmet Cookbook* (New York: Gourmet Distributing Corporation, 1950), 7.

39. *Picture Cook Book* (New York: Time, 1958), 1, 203.

40. Culinary Arts Institute, Staff Home Economists, *The Gourmet Foods Cookbook* (Chicago: Book Production Industries, 1955), n.p.

41. Myra Waldo, *1001 Ways to Please a Husband* (New York: D. Van Nostrand, 1958), 212, 207; see James Beard, *The Fireside Cook Book* (New York: Simon and Schuster, 1949). See also Potter, *At Home on the Range*, 46.

42. Ruth Berolzheimer, ed., *The United States Regional Cookbook* (Chicago: Consolidated Book Publishers, 1956), and Mary Margaret McBride, *Harvest of American Cooking with Recipes for 1,000 of America's Favorite Dishes* (New York: G. P. Putnam's Sons, 1957).

43. See David Halberstam, *The Fifties* (New York: Fawcett Columbine, 1993), 155–79, for a discussion of the inception and growth of McDonald's and Holiday Inn. On dining at the Holiday Inn, see Jane and Michael Stern, *American Gourmet* (New York: Harper Collins, 1991), 146.

44. Marling, *As Seen on TV*, 232, 188.

45. On snacks for television viewing, see Stern and Stern, *Square Meals*, 253–63. On canned clam dip, see Sylvia Lovegren, *Fashionable Food: Seven Decades of Food Fads* (New York: Macmillan, 1995), 208. For clam dip recipe, see *Food Favorites from the Kraft Television Theatre* (Chicago: Kraft Foods Company, 1951), 3. See also *Cooking At Home* (New York: Dell Publishing, 1957).

46. Stern and Stern, *American Gourmet*, 100.

47. Halberstam, *The Fifties*, 496–500.

48. Stern and Stern, *American Gourmet*, 101–4. See also James Beard, *Love and Kisses and a Halo of Truffles: Letters to Helen Evans Brown*, ed. John Ferrone (New York: Arcade Publishing, 1994), 13–14, 30, 112, 244, 283, 299–300, for descriptions of Beard's dislike of Lucas and her cooking.

49. William I. Kaufman, *Cooking with the Experts: Over 400 Simple, Easy-to-Follow Taste-Tempting Recipes Selected by Television's Best Cooks* (New York: Random House, 1955), vii. For a discussion of how one television cook's popularity seemed to be rooted in her cheerful inability to cook and her unfamiliarity with domestic matters, see Mark Williams, "Considering Monty Margetts's *Cook's Corner:* Oral History and Television History," in *Television, History, and American Culture: Feminist Critical Essays*, ed. Mary Beth Haralovich and Laura Rabinovitz (Durham: Duke University Press, 1999). For a summary of one woman's on-camera cooking career, see Wayne S. Wooden, "Edith Green: TV Pioneer and Seventh Generation Shepherd," *Western State Jewish History* 3, no. 28 (1996): 119–27.

50. See *Knox On-Camera Recipes* (Johnstown, NY: Knox Gelatin, 1962).

51. Allen, *Cook Book for Two*, v; Gertrude Wilkinson, *The Standard Family Cook Book* (New York: World Scope Encyclopedia, 1959), 503.

52. Marguerite Gilbert McCarthy, *The Queen Is in the Kitchen* (New York: Charles Scribner's Sons, 1954), 3, 5.

53. Lawton Mackall, "Jesse, Casseroles, and the Virgins," *American Review*, 12 February 1955, 57.

54. Helen Evans Brown, *Helen Brown's Holiday Cook Book* (Boston: Little, Brown, 1952), 26. For Brown's correspondence with James Beard, see Beard, *Love and Kisses and a Halo of Truffles*.

55. Betty MacDonald, *Onions in the Stew* (Philadelphia: J. B. Lippincott, 1954), 179, 177. See also Delmer Davis, "From Eggs to Stew: The Importance of Food in Two Popular Narratives of Betty MacDonald," in *Cooking by the Book: Food in Literature and Culture*, ed. Mary Anne Schofield (Bowling Green, OH: Bowling Green State University Popular Press, 1989).

56. See Janet McKenzie Hill, *Cooking for Two: Completely Revised by Sally Larkin* (Boston: Little, Brown, 1951).

57. See *Woman's Day Collector's Cook Book* (Greenwich, CT: Fawcett, 1960).

58. Thanks to Bill and Irene Butdorf, John and Lori Neuhaus, Alison and Jason Rash, Phil and Alison Payne, and Dana Payne for helping decipher this note.

59. Cooney, "The Taste in Trade," 40.

Chapter 9.
"King of the Kitchen": Food and Cookery Instruction for Men

1. Karal Ann Marling, *As Seen on TV: The Visual Culture and Everyday Life in the 1950s* (Cambridge, MA: Harvard University Press, 1994), 264. See also Thomas Hine, *Populuxe* (New York: Knopf, 1986), 22.

2. I use the term "barbecue" because most cookery instruction used that term. I am aware that "barbecue" meant something else entirely for most of the southern United States (long-cooked meat, usually pork, in a spicy sauce). For an interesting contemporary cookbook that combines nostalgia for and ironic commentary on the backyard barbecue craze, see Gideon Bosker, Karen Brooks, Leland Payton, and Crystal Payton, *Patio-Daddy-O* (San Francisco: Chronicle Books, 1996). Suburban houses also marked men-only space at the site of the basement workshop.

3. *Picture Cook Book* (New York: Time, 1958), 8.

4. Beth Bailey McLean, *Modern Homemaker's Cookbook* (New York: M. Barrows, 1950), 29.

5. *The General Foods Kitchens Cook Book* (New York: Random House, 1959), 295.

6. Marguerite Gilbert McCarthy, *The Queen Is in the Kitchen* (New York: Charles Scribner's Sons, 1954), 203; Kate Smith, *The Kate Smith's Company's Coming Cook Book* (Englewood, NJ: Prentice-Hall, 1958), 272; "The Man of the House Barbecues Chicken," *Good Housekeeping*, July 1946, 91. *Better Homes and Gardens* published a similar photo essay of manly cookery tips in 1950. See "Cooking Secrets from the Man of the House," *Better Homes and Gardens*, February 1950, 82–84. On male culinary prowess at the backyard barbecue, see also Jean Austin, "Good Victuals," *American Home*, June 1956, 53–55. An article in *Sunset* magazine suggested that given the choice, a male teenage cook would rather grill hamburgers than cook any other kind of dish. See "Why Don't You Cook Dinner," *Sunset*, February 1956, 131. When *Parents' Magazine* published a review of cookbooks suitable for masculine cooks, they emphasized outdoor and appliance cookery. See "Cookbooks for Fathers," *Parents' Magazine*, March 1950, 92. An annotated cookbook bibliography in the *Saturday Review* included several outdoor cookery books. See Lita Bane, "Victual du Jour," *Saturday Review*, 22 April 1950, 43–47.

7. Helen Evans Brown and James Beard, *The Cookout Book: Selected Recipes from America's Cookout Championships* (Los Angeles: Ward Ritchie Press, 1961), 17.

8. As quoted in Harvey Levenstein, *Paradox of Plenty: A Social History of Eating in Modern America* (New York: Oxford University Press, 1993), 132.

9. "Why Can't a Woman Cook Like a Man?" *American Home*, March 1958, 60. See also Nancy Crawford Wood, "Papa Does the Cooking," *Ladies' Home Journal*, February 1959, 166–67, and Richard Blake, "Pop's in the Kitchen," *Parents' Magazine*, June 1947, 50–68.

10. On the history of the apron, see Joyce Corbett, "Fashion Domesticated: The Apron," *Journal of Unconventional History* 4, no. 1 (1992): 31–38, and Joyce Cheney, *Aprons: Icons of the American Home* (Philadelphia: Running Press, 2000).

11. Loyce Hargrove, "He's an Outdoor Chef," *Parents' Magazine,* June 1956, 61–62.

12. *Sunset* had also published an outdoor cookery book for men in 1934. See Charles M. Mugler, *Sunset's Grubstake Cook Book* (San Francisco: Sunset Magazine, 1934).

13. *McCall's* published a photo essay on a cooking school for young boys (all of whom wore tall white chef's hats) in 1955. See Katherine Best and Katharine Hillyer, "We Visit a Boys' Cooking School," *McCall's,* March 1955, 24–26.

14. See Caroline Rollins, "A Plan to Promote Cookbooks When There Is a Late Winter Lull," *Publishers' Weekly,* 24 December 1949, 2492–93.

15. Morrison Wood, *With a Jug of Wine* (New York: Farrar, Straus, 1949), xix.

16. Lew Lehr, *Lew Lehr's Cook Book for Men* (New York: Didier, 1949), 5–6.

17. *Robertshaw Measured Heat Cook Book* (Youngwood, PA: Robertshaw Fulton Controls Company, 1951), 71–74.

18. Victor Bergeron, *Trader Vic's Kitchen Kibitzer* (New York: Doubleday, 1952), 75. *House Beautiful* published an excerpt from this book in 1952. See Victor Bergeron, "Advice to Kitchen Kibitzers—Culinary and Otherwise," *House Beautiful,* September 1952, 136, 172, 175.

19. Brick Gordon, *The Groom Boils and Stews: A Man's Cook Book for Men* (San Antonio: Naylor Company, 1947), 6, 19.

20. Jack Bailey, *What's Cookin'* (Cleveland: World Publishing, 1949), 41; Malcolm LaPrade, *That Man in the Kitchen* (Boston: Houghton Mifflin, 1946), 172; Lehr, *Lew Lehr's Cook Book for Men,* 203.

21. Fletcher Pratt and Robeson Bailey, *A Man and His Meals* (New York: Henry Holt, 1947), 35; Gordon, *The Groom Boils and Stews,* 39–40.

22. Jerry Biem, *The First Book of Boys' Cooking* (New York: Franklin Watts, 1957), 1, 4, 7, 77, 27.

23. "Dinner by Male," *American Home,* July 1957, 9.

24. See Roy Ald, *Favorite Recipes of Famous Men* (Chicago: Ziff-Davis, 1949).

25. Beregon, *Trader Vic's Kitchen Kibitzer,* 7–8.

26. Rob Loeb, *Wolf in Chef's Clothing* (Chicago: Wilcox & Follett, 1950), 9–10.

27. Helmut Ripperger, "A Sport without a Season," *Publisher' Weekly,* 11 August 1951, 550. Loeb's other two cookbooks (one for the female reader and one for teenagers) made similar links between cooking and courtship. See Rob Loeb, *Date Bait: The Younger Set's Picture Cook Book* (Chicago: Wilcox and Follett, 1952), and *She Cooks to Conquer* (New York: Wilfred Funk, 1952).

28. Loeb, *Wolf in Chef's Clothing,* 33–35.

29. Eliot Elifson, *Food Is a Four Letter Word* (New York: Rinehart, 1948), 12; Wood, *With a Jug of Wine,* xx; LaPrade, *That Man in the Kitchen,* 22–23; Lehr, *Lew Lehr's Cook Book for Men,* 159; Harry Botsford, "Super Chefs," *Woman's Home Companion,* August 1947, 66; Helen Evans Brown and Philip Brown, *The Boys' Cook Book* (Garden City, NY: Doubleday, 1959), 9; M. F. K. Fisher, "An Alphabet for Gourmets," in *The Art of Eating* (New York: Collier Books, 1990), 584–88.

30. *Chefs of the West* (Menlo Park, CA: Lane, 1951), n.p.

31. "Why Can't a Woman Cook Like a Man," 58. See also Robert Fontaine, "Lady, You Can Cook, but You Just Haven't Enough Imagination," *Better Homes*

and Gardens, February 1946, 82; Thomas L. O'Brien, "Father's in the Kitchen," *House and Garden,* February 1949, 90, 125–28; Alfred Tooms, "Man over a Hot Stove," *Collier's,* 27 August 1949, 22–23, 72–73; Jean A. Kacer, "When a Man Cooks," *American Home,* May 1950, 57–58, 73; Donald Hough, "My Stews Are My Pride," *Saturday Evening Post,* 20 January 1951, 25, 121–22; Austin, "Good Victuals"; Sarah Shields Pfeiffer, "He Might Like Cooking," *Parents' Magazine,* February 1946, 47, 55–56. See especially the three-month series *Ladies' Home Journal* ran of articles authored by well-known male cookery experts: Harry Botsford, "Meals by Men," *Ladies' Home Journal,* March 1948, 148–49; Malcolm LaPrade, "Meals by Men," *Ladies' Home Journal,* April 1948, 286–87; Leslie Hohman, "Meals by Men," *Ladies' Home Journal,* May 1948, 196–97, 228.

    32. Editors of *Esquire, Esquire Cook-Book* (New York: McGraw-Hill, 1955), 17.

    33. *Robertshaw Measured Heat Cook Book,* 71.

    34. Gordon, *The Groom Boils and Stews,* 171.

    35. LaPrade, *That Man in the Kitchen,* 26, 216, 225.

    36. Wood, *With a Jug of Wine,* 240.

    37. Frank Dorn, *The Dorn Cookbook* (Chicago: Henry Regnery, 1953), 13. A cookbook reviewer in 1954 described Dorn's book as particularly macho: "[Dorn] has done a robust he-man book, full of highly-seasoned manfare, with not a hesitating or questioning note from one cover to the next." See A. I. M. S. Street, "The Gastronomical Year," *Saturday Review,* 13 February 1954, 37.

    38. LaPrade, *That Man in the Kitchen,* 16–17; Wood, *With a Jug of Wine,* xx; Margaret Gossett and Mary Elting, *Now You're Cookin'* (Philadelphia: Westminster Press, 1948), 9.

    39. Carol Brock, "Let Your Man Lend a Hand," *Good Housekeeping,* March 1951, 160–62, 184. See also Leonore Freeman, "The Husband Helps Out," *Good Housekeeping,* March 1949, 186–87; Genevieve Callahan, "Good Meals and Thrifty," *Good Housekeeping,* February 1949, 136–39; "Husband-and-Wife Cookery," *Sunset,* April 1955, 201–2.

    40. *General Foods Kitchens Cook Book,* 363–64.

    41. "The Groom Is in the Kitchen," *House and Garden,* May 1953, 134. See also Aleck Bird, "There's a Man in the Kitchen!" *American Home,* June 1949, 70–71.

    42. Marguerite Gilbert McCarthy, *The Cook Is in the Parlor* (Boston: Little, Brown, 1947), 94.

    43. Smith, *Kate Smith's Company's Coming Cook Book,* 372.

    44. *Ladies' Home Journal,* February 1956, 46; Martha Blanchard, "I just added . . . ," *Ladies' Home Journal,* August 1957, 28; *Ladies' Home Journal,* June 1953, 50.

    45. *Esquire Cook-Book,* 292–93.

    46. Eleanor Pollock, "Men Are Dopes as Cooks," *Good Housekeeping,* February 1949, 32, 38, 118.

    47. Evelyn Humphreys, "Whose Kitchen Is It Anyway?" *House Beautiful,* April 1952, 190.

    48. *Betty Crocker's Picture Cook Book* (Minneapolis: McGraw-Hill and General Mills, 1950), 331; Biem, *The First Book of Boys' Cooking,* 45; McLean, *Modern Homemaker's Cookbook,* 132, 180.

49. Lucille Britt, "Husband, Stay Away from My (Kitchen) Door!" *American Mercury*, December 1958, 89–90.

50. See Patricia K. Brooks, "Never Marry a Man Who Can Cook," *McCall's*, February 1960, 161.

51. Myra Waldo, *1001 Ways to Please a Husband* (New York: D. Van Nostrand, 1958), 223.

52. *General Foods Kitchens Cook Book*, 228.

53. Marjorie Heseltine and Ula M. Dow, *The Basic Cook Book* (Boston: Houghton Mifflin, 1947), 726.

54. Mary Louise Bohn, *Menu Magic: A Fine Selection of Proven Taste-Tempting Recipes Courtesy of Your Chevrolet Dealer* (Detroit: General Motors, 1956), 180–87.

55. *Better Homes and Gardens Cook Book* (Des Moines, IA: Meredith Publishing, 1951), 7.

56. Jessie DeBoth, *It's Easy to Be a Good Cook* (Garden City, NY: Garden City Books, 1951), 78; Brown and Brown, *The Boys' Cook Book*, 154; Julie Benell, *Let's Eat at Home* (New York: Thomas Y. Crowell, 1961), 169; *Better Homes and Gardens Cook Book*, 2; *Esquire Cookbook*, 79; Loeb, *She Cooks to Conquer*, 31–59.

57. Mildred O. Knopf, *Cook, My Darling Daughter* (New York: Alfred A. Knopf, 1959), 331. For a discussion of the links between gelatin and femininity, masculinity and meat, see Jessamyn Neuhaus, "The Way to a Man's Heart: Gender Roles, Domestic Ideology, and Cookbooks in the 1950s," *Journal of Social History* 32, no. 2 (spring 1999): 529–55.

58. *General Foods Kitchens Cookbook*, 271–73.

59. Loeb, *Wolf in Chef's Clothing*, 46, 57.

60. On do-it-yourself guides, see Steven M. Gelber, "Do-It-Yourself: Constructing, Repairing and Maintaining Domestic Masculinity," *American Quarterly* 49, no. 1 (March 1997): 66–111. On dieting, see Jesse Berrett, "Feeding the Organization Man: Diet and Masculinity in Postwar America," *Journal of Social History* 30, no. 4 (summer 1997): 805–25.

61. See John D'Emilio, "The Homosexual Menace: The Politics of Sexuality in Cold War America," in *Passion and Power: Sexuality in History*, ed. Kathy Peiss and Christina Simmons (Philadelphia: Temple University Press, 1989); Robert Corber, *Homosexuality in Cold War America: Resistance and the Crisis of Masculinity* (Durham: Duke University Press, 1997).

62. Herbert Asbury, "The Manly Art of Cooking," *Holiday*, October 1953, 65.

63. Jean Hamilton Campbell and Gloria Kameran, *Simple Cooking for the Epicure* (New York: Viking Press, 1949), 180.

Chapter 10.
The Most Important Meal:
Women's Home Cooking, Domestic Ideology, and Cookbooks

1. Susan M. Hartmann, "Prescriptions for Penelope: Literature on Women's Obligations to Returning World War II Veterans," *Women's Studies* 5 (1978): 223–39.

2. Betty Friedan, *The Feminine Mystique*, 2nd ed. (New York: W. W. Norton, 1974).

3. Mackall Lawton, "Gustatory Stimuli for Gastronomes," *Saturday Review of Literature*, 10 March 1951, 48.

4. Caroline Rollins, "A Plan to Promote Cookbooks When There Is a Late Winter Lull," *Publishers' Weekly*, 24 December 1949, 2492.

5. Marguerite Gilbert McCarthy, *The Queen Is in the Kitchen* (New York: Charles Scribner's Sons, 1954), 1.

6. *The General Foods Kitchens Cook Book* (New York: Random House, 1959), 87.

7. Marion Flexner, *Cocktail-Supper Cookbook* (New York: M. Barrows, 1955), 8. Several cookbooks explained that appetizers served casually allowed the "cook-hostess" to put the finishing touches on her dinner in the kitchen while her guests enjoyed cocktails and snacks out in the living room. See, for example, Myra Waldo, *1001 Ways to Please a Husband* (New York: D. Van Nostrand, 1958), 13, and Lila Perl, *What Cooks in Suburbia* (New York: E. P. Dutton, 1961), 135.

8. Charlotte Adams, *Anne MacGregor's Cookbook for Frozen Foods* (New York: MACO Magazine Corporation, 1957), 5.

9. *Picture Cook Book* (New York: Time, 1958), 202.

10. Charlotte Adams, *The Whirlpool Menu Cook Book* (New York: Popular Library, 1962), 110; Jean Whitaker, *High Adventure in the Kitchen: A Collection of Unusual Recipes for the Discerning Hostess* (Los Angeles: Wetzel, 1949), 8; Eliot Elifson, *Food Is a Four Letter Word* (New York: Rinehart, 1948), 3.

11. See Elaine Tyler May, *Homeward Bound: American Families in the Cold War Era* (New York: Basic Books, 1988). Interestingly, a cookbook reviewer in 1940 had specially warned Americans away from cookery instruction authored by the avowed socialists Cora Rose and Bob Brown. See M. C. Phillips, "Are There Reds in the Kitchen?" *Consumers' Digest*, September 1940, 47–52.

12. Other kinds of prescriptive texts also assigned importance to the family dinner hour. See, for example, the 1950 "mental hygiene" film intended for high school social studies students, "A Date with Your Family," in *Ephemeral Films 1931–1960*, comp. Rick Prelinger (New York: Voyager, 1994), CD-ROM.

13. May, *Homeward Bound*, 105.

14. *General Foods Kitchens Cook Book*, 1, 11.

15. Gertrude Wilkinson, *The Standard Family Cook Book* (New York: World Scope Encyclopedia, 1959), 13.

16. Edith Key Haines, *Wonderful Ways to Cook* (New York: Rinehart, 1927, 1951), vii.

17. *Home Institute Cookbook* (New York: Charles Scribner's Sons, 1947), 1–2, 4.

18. Fairy Mapp White, *Foolproof Cook Book* (Baltimore: Monumental Press, 1958), 14; *Home Institute Cookbook*, 4; *Parents' Magazine Family Cookbook* (New York: *Parents' Magazine* Publications, 1953), vi.

19. Malcolm LaPrade, *That Man in the Kitchen* (New York: Houghton Mifflin, 1946), 216.

20. Morrison Wood, *With a Jug of Wine* (New York: Farrar, Straus, 1949), xi–xii.

21. *Betty Crocker's Picture Cook Book* (New York: McGraw-Hill and General Mills, 1950), 173. On cookie jars as symbols of motherly affection, see Erika Endrijonas, "Processed Foods from Scratch: Cooking for a Family in the 1950s," in

Kitchen Culture in America: Popular Representations of Food, Gender, and Race, ed. Sherrie A. Inness (Philadelphia: University of Pennsylvania Press, 2000), 163.

22. Lilian Zeigfeld and Demetria M. Taylor, *A Picture Treasure of Good Cooking: A Tested Recipe Institute Cook Book* (New York: Tested Recipe Institute, 1953), 105.

23. Edith Barber, *The Short Cut Cook Book* (New York: Sterling, 1952), 128.

24. Jessie DeBoth, *It's Easy to Be a Good Cook* (Garden City, NY: Garden City Books, 1951, 97.

25. Mildred O. Knopf, *Cook, My Darling Daughter* (New York: Alfred A. Knopf, 1959), 385.

26. *Betty Crocker's Picture Cook Book*, 174.

27. Margaret Williams, *The Well-Fed Bridegroom* (Garden City, NY: Doubleday, 1957), 7.

28. Dorothy Malone, *Cookbook for Brides* (New York: A. A. Wyn, 1947), n.p.

29. Waldo, *1001 Ways to Please a Husband*, vi.

30. Knopf, *Cook, My Darling Daughter*, 225–26.

31. Eleanor Richey Johnston, "Is Your Husband Hard to Cook For?" *Better Homes and Gardens*, March 1948, 260. See also Edith M. Barber, "Consider Me Too, Says Father," *Parents' Magazine*, February 1947, 58. See also Julia Bliss Joyner, "Cooking His Favorite Meat," *American Home*, January 1946, 72–74; Ann Batchelder, "Here's to Father!" *Ladies' Home Journal*, June 1948, 72–73, 210; Charles Archer Gates, "The Man Who Hurries Home to Dinner," *Better Homes and Gardens*, April 1950, 172, 193.

32. Stella Standard, *More Than Cooking* (New York: Vanguard, 1946), 146, Waldo, *1001 Ways to Please a Husband*, 199; Irma Rombauer, *A Cookbook for Girls and Boys* (New York: Bobbs-Merrill, 1946), 22; *Betty Crocker's Good and Easy Cook Book* (New York: Simon and Schuster and General Mills, 1954), 55; Perl, *What Cooks in Suburbia*, 65, 77.

33. Knopf, *Cook, My Darling Daughter*, xi.

34. Carol Traux, ed., *Ladies' Home Journal Cook Book* (Garden City, NY: Doubleday, 1960), n.p.

35. Meta Givens, *The Modern Family Cook Book*, rev. ed. (Chicago: J. G. Ferguson Publishing, 1942, 1958), 22.

36. Adams, *The Whirlpool Menu Cook Book*, 13; *Betty Crocker's Good and Easy Cook Book*, 4.

37. Brick Gordon, *The Groom Boils and Stews: A Man's Cook Book for Men* (San Antonio: Naylor Company, 1947), 41.

38. Malone, *Cookbook for Brides*, 34–36.

39. Ida Bailey Allen, *Solving the High Cost of Eating: A Cook Book to Live By* (New York: Farrar, Strauss and Young, 1952), 44.

40. Anne Williams-Heller, *The Busy Woman's Cook Book* (New York: Stephen Days, 1951), 11.

41. Mary Dean William, *Everyday Cooking with Introduction for Brides* (Huntington, IN: Indiana Farmer's Guide, 1948), 8.

42. *General Foods Kitchens Cook Book*, 49; *Betty Crocker's Picture Cook Book*, 431.

43. Marion Taylor Young, *Martha Dean's Cooking for Compliments* (New York: M. Barrows, 1954), 9–10.

44. *Home Institute Cook Book,* 4.

45. Ruth Stout, *It's a Woman's World* (New York: Doubleday, 1960), 35–36, 39.

46. Malone, *Cookbook for Brides,* 27.

47. Harry Botsford, "Is Your Daughter a Cook or a Kitchen Mechanic?" *American Home,* February 1956, 90.

48. Allen, *Solving the High Cost of Eating,* 56.

49. Poppy Canon, *The Bride's Cookbook* (New York: Henry Holt, 1954), 64, 376.

50. Malone, *Cookbook for Brides,* 272–73.

51. Karal Ann Marling, *As Seen on TV: The Visual Culture and Everyday Life in the 1950s* (Cambridge, MA: Harvard University Press, 1994), 222. See also Laura Shapiro, "Do Women Like to Cook?" *Granta* 52 (winter 1995): 155–62.

52. Poppy Canon, *The Can-Opener Cook Book* (New York: MacFadden Books, 1951, 1961), 7.

53. Canon, *The Bride's Cookbook,* x; *The General Foods Kitchens Cook Book,* 1; Williams, *The Well-Fed Bridegroom,* 7.

54. Erika Endrijonas, "No Experience Required: American Middle-Class Families and Their Cookbooks, 1945–1960" (Ph.D. diss., University of Southern California, 1996), 159.

55. I have to note, however, that cookbooks and advertisers had given women advice on the "emergency meal" since at least the late 1800s. Louisa May Alcott made gentle fun of homemakers' "emergency meals" in her 1869 novel *Little Women,* when new bride Meg has a miserable day making jelly and utterly fails to rise to the occasion when her husband brings home an unexpected guest for dinner. See Louisa May Alcott, *Little Women* (1869; reprint, New York: Macmillan, 1962), 306–20. And in the first half of the twentieth century, cookbook authors and advertising copywriters often pointed out the importance of a wife's ability to create a good meal when her husband brought home guests unexpectedly, or how a good dinner for "the boss" could assist her husband's career. *American Home* published an infamous example of such rhetoric in 1939, when one of their advertisements in a food industry magazine read "Hitler Threatens Europe—but Betty Havens' Husband's Boss Is Coming to Dinner and *That's* What *Really* Counts." As quoted by Harvey Levenstein, *Paradox of Plenty: A Social History of Eating in Modern America* (New York: Oxford University Press, 1993), 32.

56. On letters to Friedan, see May, *Homeward Bound,* 209–17. See also Betty Friedan, *It Changed My Life: Writings on the Women's Movement* (New York: Random House, 1976).

57. Laura Shapiro, *Perfection Salad: Women and Cooking at the Turn of the Century* (New York: Farrar, Straus and Giroux, 1986), 217. For further citation on social histories of the 1950s, see Essay on Sources.

58. Nicola Humble, "A Touch of Bohème," *Times Literary Supplement,* 14 June 1996, 15.

Chapter 11.
"A Necessary Bore": Contradictions in the Cooking Mystique

1. See Stephanie Coontz, *The Way We Never Were: American Families and the Nostalgia Trap* (New York: Harper Collins, 1992). For feminist analysis of 1950s

sitcoms, see Mary Beth Haralovich, "Sit-Coms and Suburbs: Positioning the 1950s Homemaker," in *Private Screenings: Television and the Female Consumer*, ed. Lynn Spigel (Minneapolis: University of Minnesota Press, 1992); Lynn Spigel, "Installing the Television Set: Popular Discourse on Television and Domestic Space, 1948–1955," in Spigel, *Private Screenings;* Margaret Finnegan, "From Spurs to Silk Stockings: Women in Prime-Time Television, 1950–1965," *UCLA Historical Journal* 11 (spring 1991): 1–30; Lynn Spigel, *Make Room for TV: Television and the Family Ideal in Postwar America* (Chicago: University of Chicago Press, 1992).

2. For citations on McCarthyism, teenagers, homosexuality, and the civil rights movement in the 1950s, see Essay on Sources.

3. On women's political involvement, see "They Make Their Voices Heard" and "Victory from Defeat," *Ladies' Home Journal June*, March 1953, 54–55. These two articles discussed housewives' involvement in political activities, drawing on interviews with average women. Significantly, the latter article described how a mother of three did not let her volunteer duties interfere with feeding her family: "Fortunately, it [the phone] is at the end of the counter where I give the family breakfast and lunch, so I could stir the soup with one hand, knead the bread with the other, and still talk or listen with the phone propped on my shoulder!" See "Victory from Defeat," 55. For further citations on women in the 1950s, see Essay on Sources.

4. Glenda Riley, *Inventing the American Woman: A Perspective on Women's History* (Arlington Heights, IL: Harlan Davidson, 1987), 240. Historian William Chafe points out that although "a job for a wife over thirty-five became normal—at least by statistical standards," many Americans "continued to subscribe to the belief that women were (and should remain) primarily homemakers." William H. Chafe, *The Paradox of Change: American Women in the 20th Century* (New York: Oxford University Press, 1991), 166.

5. On unions, see Dorothy Sue Cobble, "Recapturing Working-Class Feminism: Union Women in the Postwar Era," in *Not June Cleaver*, ed. Joanne Meyerowitz (Philadelphia: Temple University Press, 1994); Nancy Gabin, *Feminism in the Labor Movement: Women and the United Auto Workers, 1935–1975* (Ithaca, NY: Cornell University Press, 1990); Daniel Horowitz, "Rethinking Betty Friedan and The Feminine Mystique: Labor Union Radicalism and Feminism in Cold War America," *American Quarterly* 48 (spring 1996): 1–42. On the work of NMC (National Manpower Council) and CEW (Commission on the Education of Women), see Susan M. Hartmann, "Women's Employment and the Domestic Ideal," in Meyerowitz, *Not June Cleaver.*

6. Lee Chapman, "Three Quick Meals that Taste So Good," *Good Housekeeping*, February 1950, 137.

7. Poppy Canon, *The Bride's Cookbook* (New York: Henry Holt, 1954), 220; "General and Specialized Cook Books to Appear This Season," *Publishers' Weekly*, 15 September 1951, 1134; Maxine Erikson and Joan M. Rock, *The Book of Good Neighbor Recipes: A Hand-Picked Collection of Favorite Recipes* (New York: Bond Whellwright, 1945), 375.

8. Theodora Zavin and Freda Stuart, *The Working Wives' (Salaried or Otherwise) Cook Book* (New York: Crown, 1963), n.p., 10, n.p.

9. Hazel Young, *The Working Girl's Own Cook Book* (Boston: Little, Brown, 1948), viii.

10. Beverly Pepper, *Glamour Magazine's New After Five Cookbook* (1952; reprint, Garden City, NY: Doubleday, 1963), v. A good recipe book could also help the single working girl capture a man's affections, at least according to one cookbook author: "These dishes are rather simple, many can be made from canned goods, and almost every dish can be prepared in less than two hours. The working girl can still get home from the office and trap her man with taste-tingling, sense-exciting dinner at eight." See Eliot Elifson, *Food Is a Four Letter Word* (New York: Rinehart, 1948), 5.

11. *The General Foods Kitchens Cook Book* (New York: Random House, 1959), 47.

12. Culinary Arts Institute, Staff Home Economists, *Quick Dishes for the Woman in a Hurry* (Chicago: Culinary Arts Institute, 1955), 3.

13. Myra Waldo, *1001 Ways to Please a Husband* (New York: D. Van Nostrand, 1958), 116–17.

14. Florence Arfman, *The Time Reader's Book of Recipes: Two Hundred and Thirty Favorite Recipes of the Women Who Read Time* (New York: E. P. Dutton, 1949), 4, 84, 14, 37. Helmut Ripperger found few redeeming qualities in this cookbook: "Why the readers of *Time* magazine were given a book of their own is hard to see unless the publisher hoped that each and every reader might buy a copy. The collection is uneven and its editing even more so." See Helmut Ripperger, "A Sport without a Season," *Publishers' Weekly,* 11 August 1951, 550.

15. Muriel Fitzimmons and Cortland Fitzsimmons, *You Can Cook If You Can Read* (New York: Vicking Press, 1946), 336; Poppy Canon, *The Can-Opener Cook Book* (New York: MacFadden Books, 1951, 1961), 7; Gertrude Wilkinson, *The Standard Family Cook Book* (New York: World Scope Encyclopedia, 1959), 356.

16. Harvey Levenstein, *Paradox of Plenty: A Social History of Eating in Modern America* (New York: Oxford University Press, 1993), 108–9.

17. Jean Hamilton Campbell and Gloria Kameran, *Simple Cooking for the Epicure* (New York: Viking Press, 1949), 1.

18. Julie Benell, *Let's Eat at Home* (New York: Thomas Y. Crowell, 1961), 285; Alice Wilson Richardson, *The Just a Minute Cookbook* (New York: Prentice-Hall, 1952), 1; Carol Truax and Lillian McCue, *The 60 Minute Chef* (New York: Macmillan, 1947), xi.

19. Hale MacLaren, *Be Your Own Guest* (Boston: Houghton Mifflin, 1952), vii.

20. *Best Recipes of 1954: A New Collection of Family-Style Recipes from the Private Files of Experienced Household Cooks* (New York: Toby Press, 1954), iii.

21. Eva Moskowitz, " 'It's Good to Blow Your Top': Women's Magazines and a Discourse of Discontent, 1945–1965," *Journal of Women's History* 18, no. 3 (fall 1996): 66–98.

22. Joanne Meyerowitz, "Beyond the Feminine Mystique: A Reassessment of Postwar Mass Culture, 1946–1958," in Meyerowitz, *Not June Cleaver.*

23. Peg Bracken, *The I Hate to Cook Book* (New York: Harcourt, Brace and World, 1960); *Peg Bracken's Appendix to The I Hate to Cook Book* (Greenwich, CT: Fawcett, 1966); *The I Hate to Cook Almanack* (Greenwich, CT: Fawcett, 1976); and

The Complete I Hate to Cook Book (New York: Bantam Books, 1986). Bracken also authored a book of housekeeping tips and an etiquette manual on the same theme. See *The I Hate to Housekeep Book* (Greenwich, CT: Fawcett, 1963) and *I Try to Behave Myself* (Greenwich, CT: Fawcett, 1964).

24. See, for example, Sara Perry, "Peg Bracken's Simple Ways Turn Strangers into Friends," *Oregonian*, 31 October 1999, sec. L, p. 18.

25. Donna Florio, "She's Still Cooking," *Washington Post*, 2 December 1998, sec. E, p. 2. I am grateful to Alison Payne for bringing this article to my attention.

26. Nancy Walker, "Humor and Gender Roles: The 'Funny' Feminism of the Post–World War II Suburbs," *American Quarterly* 37, no. 1 (spring 1985): 101, 113.

27. Bracken, *The I Hate to Cook Book*, 24, 137–38.

28. Nicola Humble, "A Touch of Bohème," *Times Literary Supplement*, 14 June 1996, 16.

29. Bracken, *The I Hate to Cook Book*, ix. Bracken also challenged another aspect of gender and cookery instruction. She asserted that women did not truly enjoy the kind of fussy, fancy food often found at a "ladies luncheon," arguing that the only way to really enjoy a ladies lunch was to hold it at a local restaurant: "There they may relax and swap tatting patterns, serene in the knowledge that they needn't eat anything molded unless they order it." See Bracken, *The I Hate to Cook Book*, 84.

30. Ibid., 3–4, xi.

31. In her interview with Peg Bracken for the *Washington Post*, Donna Florio related a story that illustrated how clearly Bracken spoke to many women's frustration with cooking and housekeeping. One day Bracken was studying the meat counter in a supermarket and an obviously harried shopper and a stranger to Bracken, turned to her and said "You know, some days I feel just like Peg Bracken!" See Florio, "She's Still Cooking," sec. E, p. 2.

32. For reasons of privacy, I do not give the names of individuals who wrote unpublished letters to Peg Bracken. These letters are currently in Ms. Bracken's possession, and she graciously allowed me access to them during a visit to her home in Portland, Oregon, on 22 September 1999. I am sincerely grateful for her generosity.

33. Bracken, *The I Hate to Cook Book*, x–xi.

34. Ibid., 41, 754, ix–x.

35. Peg Bracken, *A Window over the Sink* (New York: Harcourt Brace, 1981), 62. She also notes that her mother had a copy of the 1917 edition of *A Thousand Ways to Please a Husband* by Louise Bennett and Helen Cowless LeCron.

36. For a discussion of how individual women utilized cookbooks such as *Betty Crocker's Picture Cook Book* and *Better Homes and Gardens Cook Book*, see "Recalling Books That Inspired Us to Cook," *Oregonian*, 30 November 1999, sec. F, p. 6.

Conclusion: *From Julia Child to Cooking.com*

1. See Ellen Dunkle, "Care for a Byte to Eat?" *Publishers' Weekly*, 11 July 1994, 42–43; Barbara Durbin, "www.do.you.cook?com" *Oregonian*, 3 August 1999, sec.

FD, p. 1; Susan Gilbert, "What's Cooking: Culinary CD-ROMS," *Computer Shopper* 17, no. 2 (1997): 282–344. For further citation on cookbooks and computers, see my Essay on Sources. On locating used cookbooks via the Internet, see S. A. Belzer, "Finding Lost Cookbooks on the Internet," *New York Times*, 7 April 1999, sec. B, p. 14; Amy Martinez Starke, "Internet Brings the World of Used Cookbook Right to Your Home," *Oregonian*, 30 November 1999, sec. FD, p. 7. On sharing recipes on line, see Carole Sugarman, "Cooking Up Some Brand New Recipes via Computer: Online Subscribers Swap Healthy Suggestions and Helpful Hints," *Washington Post*, 17 May 1994, sec. Z, p. 16. For additional citations, see Essay on Sources.

2. Natalie Dandford, "Surfeit at the Stores," *Publishers' Weekly*, 12 July 1993, 44; Robert Dahlin, "Stirring the Sales Post," *Publishers' Weekly*, July 24, 2000, 36–50. On the variety of available cookbooks, see Dulcy Brainard, "From Apple Pie to Pad Thai," *Publishers' Weekly*, 24 July, 1995, 28–29. For a discussion of how recipes circulated in promotional literature in the late 1980s, see Jeff Makos, Libby Morse, and Dulcy Brainard, "Cookbook Sales beyond the Bookstore," *Publishers' Weekly*, 8 September, 1989, 30–33.

3. On the growing number of food-related magazines and gourmet cookbooks, see Peggy Steiner Ratcheson, "Food and Fashion in United States Society: The Mass-Culturization of Gourmet-Cookery" (Ph.D. diss., Washington University, 1986). On television cooking shows, see Judith Crist, "The Joy of Looking," *Gourmet*, June 2000, 98–105. For statistics on home-cooked food and on the popularity of gourmet kitchens, see Douglas Bowers, "Cooking Trends Echo Changing Roles of Women," *Food Review*, January–April 2000, 1–23; Jennifer Lach, "Home on the Range Top," *American Demographics*, October 1999, n.p. On the popularity of gourmet kitchens, see Susan Krafft, "The Heart of the Home," *American Demographics* 14, no. 6 (June 1992): 46–50. See also David Brooks, *Bobos in Paradise* (New York: Simon and Schuster, 2000). On the sale of gourmet cooking utensils, see Rana Dogar and Damon Darlin, "Recipes That Grandma Never Used," *Forbes*, 21 October 1996, 25.

4. Jane Stern and Michael Stern, *American Gourmet* (New York: Harper Collins, 1991), 108. See also Evan Jones, *American Food: The Gastronomic Story* (New York: E. P. Dutton, 1975), 138, and Julia Child, "Slice of History," *People*, 7 June 1999, 169–73.

5. Mary Drake McFeely, *Can She Bake a Cherry Pie? American Women and the Kitchen in the Twentieth Century* (Amherst: University of Massachusetts Press, 2000), 115–19.

6. Ibid., 137–38. For a definitive history, see Warren J. Belasco, *Appetite for Change: How the Counterculture Took on the Food Industry* (Ithaca, NY: Cornell University Press, 1993). See also Mahadev Apte and Judit Katona-Apte, "Diet and Social Movements in American Society: The Last Two Decades," in *Food in Change: Eating Habits from the Middle Ages to the Present Day*, Fifth International Conference on Ethnological Food Research, October 1983, ed. Alexander Fenton and Eszter Kisbán (Edinburgh: John Donald, 1986): 26–33.

7. Jones, *American Food*, 141.

8. McFeely, *Can She Bake a Cherry Pie*, 148.

9. Laura Shapiro, *Perfection Salad: Women and Cooking at the Turn of the Century* (New York: Farrar, Straus and Giroux, 1986), 232.

10. Catherine Manton, *Fed Up: Women and Food in America* (Westport, CT: Bergin and Garvey, 1999), 75.

11. On the long-standing popularity of these books, see "The Case of the Missing Cookbooks," *Cooking Light*, April 1999, 86. As one bookstore owner said about *Joy of Cooking*, "People always buy it. It's the title they know." See Danford, "Surfeit at the Stores," 44.

12. McFeely, *Can She Bake a Cherry Pie*, 152.

13. I am grateful to Barbara Coleman, who drew this particular comparison to my attention. See "Betty Crocker and Martha Stewart as Icons of Domesticity" (paper presented at the annual symposium of the American Heritage Center on The Fifties Turn Fifty: The "Nuclear Family" and Postwar American Culture, University of Wyoming, September 1999).

14. Marjorie L. DeVault, *Feeding the Family: The Social Organization of Caring as Gendered Work* (Chicago: University of Chicago Press, 1991), 226.

15. Thomas A. Adler, "Making Pancakes on Sunday: The Male Cook in Family Tradition," *Western Folklore* 40, no. 1 (1981): 45–54. See also Charles Camp, *American Foodways: What, When, Why and How We Eat in America* (Little Rock, AK: August House, 1989), 97; Nickie Charles and Marion Kerr, *Women, Food and Families* (Manchester: Manchester University Press, 1988), 1; Jim Henderson, "An Alpha Male Recipe Tale," *Bon Appétit*, July 2000, 40.

16. William R. Wood, "It's a Man's World: Gender Equality Hasn't Reached Grilling, Studies Find," *Kalamazoo Gazette*, 2 July 2001, sec. D, p. 1. Thanks to A. Lori Neuhaus for bringing this article to my attention.

17. As quoted by Krafft, "The Heart of the Home," 49.

18. Steven Bauer, "A Man Who Cooks," *Glamour*, June 1995, 93.

19. See Lolis Eric Elie, "The Tao of Barbecue," *Forbes*, May 5, 1997, 125–28; Adam Sachs, "Kitchens without Women," *GQ*, March 1999, 98; Jim Shahin, "Kings of the Kitchen," *Parents*, December 1995, 125–27; Stephen Perrine, "Cookbooks for Men," *Men's Health*, November 1994, 122–24; "Musings from the Mud Porch," *Successful Farming*, November 1997, 72.

20. David Joachim and the Editors of *Men's Health, A Man, A Can, A Plan: 50 Great Guy Meals Even You Can Make!* (Emmaus, PA: Rodale, 2002), 40. Thanks to John Neuhaus for bringing this cookbook to my attention. In the early 1970s, in the heyday of a feminist backlash, some authors still felt they could make assertions about male superiority in the kitchen. See Cory Kilvert, *The Male Chauvinist's Cookbook* (New York: Winchester Press, 1974).

21. Don Mauer, *A Guy's Guide to Great Eating: Big-Flavored Fat-Reduced Recipes for Men Who Love to Eat* (Boston: Houghton Mifflin, 1999), ix. A recipe published recently in *Details* magazine, a periodical aimed at male readers, used the same kind of brusque directions found in cookbooks for men published decades earlier. The recipe instructed the reader, for example, to "Take your skillet, throw in a 14 1/2 ounce can of tomatoes . . ." and to "Let simmer for five minutes, stirring to break up the tomatoes and alleviate boredom." See "Guy Food," *Details*, April 1999, 128. For a sociological examination of men and cooking in England, see

Tony Coxon, "Men in the Kitchen: Notes from a Cookery Class," in *The Sociology of Food and Eating: Essays on the Sociological Significance of Food*, ed. Ann Murcott (Aldershot: Gower Publishing, 1983).

22. *Parade*, 14 November 1999, cover. Interestingly, the actor and actress on this cover play television sitcom characters who do not conform to typical gender norms. Kelsey Grammer plays Fraiser, an opera buff, psychiatrist, and sherry connoisseur, and Peri Gilpin plays his producer Roz, a tough-talking, sexually aggressive single mother. Yet on the cover, their gender dictates their meal.

23. Manette A. Ansay, "And He Cooks, Too," *Gourmet*, December 1999, 238.

Essay on Sources

A history of twentieth century cookbooks must take into account the history of food and eating in the United States. And a study of food in America should begin with Harvey Levenstein's seminal works, *Revolution at the Table: The Transformation of the American Diet* (New York: Oxford University Press, 1988), and *Paradox of Plenty: A Social History of Eating in Modern America* (New York: Oxford University Press, 1993). Other helpful general monographs include Richard J. Hooker's *Food and Drink in America: A History* (New York: Bobbs-Merrill, 1981), Elaine McIntosh's *American Food Habits in Historical Perspective* (Westport, CT: Praeger, 1995), and Carole Counihan and Penny Van Esterick, eds., *Food and Culture: A Reader* (New York: Routledge, 1997). Although not academic in tone, Jane and Michael Stern's books on eating in the United States contain a wealth of detailed information about twentieth-century food trends. See especially *Square Meals* (New York: Alfred A. Knopf, 1984) and *American Gourmet* (New York: Harper Collins, 1991).

Laura Shapiro's *Perfection Salad: Women and Cooking at the Turn of the Century* (New York: Farrar, Straus and Giroux, 1986) offers the perfect starting place for a study of gender and cookery in the United States. Her discussion of the cooking school movement and scientific cookery in the United States in the late 1800s and early 1900s remains unparalleled. On food preparation and gender during World War II, see Amy Bentley's perceptive analysis in *Eating for Victory: Food Rationing and the Politics of Domesticity* (Urbana: University of Illinois Press, 1998). On women and cooking in the twentieth century, see Mary Drake McFeely, *Can She Bake a Cherry Pie? American Women and the Kitchen in the Twentieth Century* (Amherst: University of Massachusetts Press, 2000). For an excellent discussion of gender and food preparation in the United States, see Sherrie Inness, *Dinner Roles: American Women and Culinary Culture* (Iowa City: University of Iowa Press, 2001).

There are very few book-length works on cookbooks themselves. Janet Theophano's *Eat My Words: Reading Women's Lives through the Cookbooks They Wrote* (Hampshire: Palgrave Macmillan, 2002), offers the most in-depth look to date on the way cookbooks reflect and shape women's history. Journalist Anne Mendelson's outstanding history of *The Joy of Cooking*, entitled *Stand Facing the Stove: The Story of the Women Who Gave America "The Joy of Cooking"* (New York: Henry Holt, 1996), provides an in-depth history of one particular cookbook as well as an overview of the publishing history of cookbooks in the United States. An anthology on community cookbooks offers a fascinating range of articles on the history and function of noncommercial cookbooks. See Anne L. Bower, ed., *Recipes for Reading: Community Cookbooks, Stories, Histories* (Amherst: University of Massachusetts Press, 1997). Several unpublished doctoral and masters theses examine the history of cookbooks. See, in particular, Liora Gvion-Rosenberg, "Telling the Story of Ethnicity: American Cookbooks, 1850–1990" (master's thesis, State University of New York at Stony Brook, 1996), and Erika Endrijonas, "No Experience Required: American Middle-Class Families and Their Cookbooks, 1945–1960" (Ph.D. diss., University of Southern California, 1996). Sherrie A. Inness's recent work on juvenile cookery books demonstrates how cookery instruction for young people contained the same kinds of messages about gender ideology as cookbooks for men and women. See Sherrie A. Inness, "'The Enchantment of Mixing-Spoons': Cooking Lessons for Boys and Girls, 1900–1960," in *Kitchen Culture in America: Representations of Food, Gender, and Race*, ed. Sherrie A. Inness (Philadelphia: University of Pennsylvania Press, 2000). Jan Longone, curator of American culinary history at the University of Michigan's Clement Library, has published two concise and informative exhibition catalogs, complete with illustrations. See Jan Longone and Daniel Longone, *American Cookbooks and Wine Books, 1796–1950* (Ann Arbor, MI: Clements Library, 1984), and Jan Longone, *American Cookery: The Bicentennial, 1796–1996: An Exhibition of 200 Years of American Cookbooks at the Clements Library* (Ann Arbor, MI: Clements Library and University of Michigan Press, 1996).

For my own publications on the history of cookery, cookbooks, and gender in the United States, please see "Is Meatloaf for Men? Gender and Meatloaf Recipes, 1920–1960," in *Cooking Lessons: The Politics of Gender and Food*, ed. Sherrie A. Inness (Lanham, MD: Rowman and Littlefield, 2001); "The Joy of Sex Instruction: Women and Cooking in Marital Sex Manuals, 1920–1963," in Inness, *Kitchen Culture;* "The Way to a Man's Heart: Gender Roles, Domestic Ideology, and Cookbooks in the 1950s," *Journal of Social History* 32, no. 3 (spring 1999): 529–55.

Several significant articles on eighteenth- and nineteenth-century cookbooks helped me understand the long history of cookbooks in the United States: Charlsie E. Berly, "Early American Cookbooks (1783–1861): Windows on Household Life and a Developing Culture," *Lamar Journal of the Humanities* 14, nos. 1–2 (1988): 5–18; Eleanor Fordyce, "Cookbooks of the 1800s," in *Dining in America, 1850–1900*, ed. Kathyrn Grover (Amherst: University of Massachusetts Press, 1987); Glynis Ridley, "The First American Cookbook," *Eighteenth Century Life* 23, no. 2 (1999): 114–23, and Janet Theopano, "A Life's Work: Women Writing from the Kitchen," in *Fields of Folklore: Essays in Honor of Kenneth S. Goldstein*, ed. Roger D. Abrahams (Bloomington, IN: Trickster Press, 1995). See also Peter Berg, "'The Dignity of Our Character as Rational Beings': Images of Women in American Cookbooks, 1820–1860" (master's thesis, Michigan State University, 1982).

For a discussion of cookbooks as historical documents, see especially Edith Horander, "The Recipe Book as a Cultural and Socio-Historical Document," in *Food in Perspective: Proceedings from the Third International Conference in Ethnological Food Research*, ed. Alexander Fenton and Frefor M. Owen (Edinburgh: John Donald, 1981). See also Mitchell Owns, "Antique Cookbooks Return as Time Machines," *New York Times*, 7 August 1997, sec. C, p. 3; Ron Gasbarro, "Chapters from the Past," *Washington Post*, 26 February 1992, sec. E, p. 1; Barbara Carton, "Cooking by the Book," *Boston Globe*, 9 December 1992, sec. F., p. 69; William Logan, "Teaspoons and Tattered Pages," *House Beautiful*, September 1993, 32; Kathy Seal, "Life's Little Rewards: The Tales Old Cookbooks Tell," *Family Circle*, February 2000, 20; Royster Alexander, "They Did Things Martha Stewart Can Only Dream About: Antique Recipes," *New York Times*, 25 June 1995, sec. E, p. 7; Mary Cantwell, "Cookbooks with a Past," *Food and Wine*, October 1995, 48; Anita Diamant, "Cookbook Archive: Measuring History in Tablespoons," *Ms.*, February 1986, 38; Steven M. Tobias, "Early American Cookbooks as Cultural Artifacts," *Papers on Language and Literature* 34, no. 1 (1998): 3–19. On collecting old cookbooks, see, for example, Robert J. Hughes, "Cooking into the Past: Vintage Cookbooks Soar as Hot Relics of the Past," *Wall Street Journal*, 31 December 1999, sec. E, p. 12; Carol McCabe, "Collecting Cookbooks," *Early American Life*, February 1994, 10–11, 75.

A surprising number of articles published in the late 1990s address the issue of cookbooks on computer. See, for example, "Mac Can Cook: Cookbooks, Cook Forums and Culinary Tips," *Mac User* 11, no. 9 (1995): 130; Eric Asimov, "Out of the Frying Pan and Onto the Desktop," *New York Times*, 18 March 1994, sec. D, p. 10; Bart Ziegler, "Let Your PC Dish Up a Cornucopia of Tips on Cooking, Recipes," *Wall Street Journal*, 8 January 1998, sec. B, p. 1; Amy Martinez Starke, "Recipes Go PC," *Oregonian*, 14 September 1999, sec. FD, p. 1; "Cooking Goes PC: Cookbooks Makes the Transition from Kitchen to PC," *PC Magazine* 18, no. 3 (1999): 273–78; Andrew Baker, "Cookbooks Byte by Byte," *Sunset*, March 1997, 116; Jeffrey Steingarten, "Cuisine by Computer," *Vogue*, October 1996, 238; "Best Bytes for Cooks," *Consumer Reports*, December 1996, 24–27.

Race appeared as a subtext in many cookbooks during the early twentieth century. The twentieth-century cookbook genre began, in some ways, by setting up a dichotomy between the newly "helpless" middle-class white woman and the culinary abilities of African American, immigrant, and other women of color working as cooks. Authors and editors never stated outright that they meant these instructional texts for white readers, but their constant references to the newly cookless woman implied as much, because household cooks had, for decades, been mainly women of color or European immigrants employed by white women. In the early to mid twentieth century, many commercial cookbook publishers seemed to assume that white women, and only white women, actually required cookery instruction—which in turn gives us some insight into mainstream stereotypes of women of color. Paradoxically, commercial cookbooks also emphasized that only the (white) mistress of the home, and not a paid servant, had the intelligence and artistic ability to produce truly appetizing, healthful food. Thus, general commercial cookbooks offer far more solid historical information about the construction of white middle-class identity than about food and cooking in immigrant communities or among ethnic groups such as Mexican Americans and African Americans.

We must keep in mind that economic inequities ensured that the poorest people in the United States, including a disproportionately high number of immigrants and people of color, would not have had access to general cookbook publishing, and that cookbooks reflect the interests of their producers. Furthermore, food traditions arguably play a very different role among systematically oppressed groups than among those with the most financial, cultural, and material resources. Sharing food and culinary traditions may reinforce a sense of community and identity in a world where that identity is not honored. And the exchange of recipes in this setting operates under a very different power system. It may be a way for African Americans to uphold their culinary heritage, which had been regularly co-opted by white cookbook authors who routinely stole recipes from black servants and published them as their own. Evidence also suggests that fund-raising cookbooks, oral traditions, and other means of recipe exchanges, rather than general commercial cookbooks, provide a more reliable way to study the connections between food preparation, gender, and identity among those who had an interest in maintaining a cultural or ethnic heritage. Harvey Levenstein speculates that working-class people and immigrants do not rely on cookbooks the way that middle-class Americans in recent history have. He points out that his mother, a Jewish immigrant from Poland, never owned a cookbook, but her middle-class children use them regularly (Harvey Levenstein, e-mail exchange with author, 23 September 1999).

Scholars interested in the intersection of cookbooks, food, culinary traditions, and ethnicity may consult a wide range of excellent secondary sources. On African American cookbooks and culinary culture, see Doris Witt, *Black Hunger: Food and the Politics of U.S. Identity* (New York: Oxford University Press, 1999); Doris Smith, "In Search of Our Mother's Cookbooks: Gathering African American Culinary Traditions," *Iris: A Journal about Women* 26 (fall 1991): 23–43; Jennifer Lyn Grady, "Get 'em While They're Hot: African American Cookbooks as References to Black Culture," *North Carolina Libraries* 50, no. 4 (winter 1992): 215; J. Schinto, "Dinner Roles," *Women's Review of Books* 10, no. 1 (October 1992): 16; Quandra Prettyman, "Come Eat at My Table: Lives with Recipes," *Southern Quarterly* 30, nos. 1–2 (1992): 131–40; Curtia James, "A Century of Traditional Black Cookery," *Essence*, May 1985, 164–65; Jualynne E. Dodson and Cheryl Townsend Gilkes, " 'There's Nothing Like Church Food': Food and the U.S. Afro-Christian Tradition: Re-Membering Community and Feeding the Embodied Spirit (s)," *Journal of the American Academy of Religion* 63, no. 3 (1995): 519–38; Jonell Nash, "Mama's Table: Our Food Legacy," *Essence*, February 1994, 91–92; Sally Bishop Shigley, "Empathy, Energy, and Eating: Politics and Power in *The Black Family Dinner Quilt Cookbook*," in Bower, *Recipes for Reading*; Rafia Zafar, "The Signifying Dish: Autobiography and History in Two Black Women's Cookbooks," *Feminist Studies* 25, no. 2 (1999): 449–69; Gary Puckrein, "Beyond Soul Food," *American Visions* 13, no. 4 (August–September 1998), 39; Carolyn Jung, "Books Explore Roots of American Soul Food and African Cuisines," *Knight-Ridder/Tribune News Service*, 21 December 1998. On the oldest known cookbook by an African American, see Abby Fisher, *What*

Mrs. Fisher Knows about Old Southern Cooking (1881, reprint with historical notes by Karen Hess, Bedford, MA: Applewood Books, 1995).

On Jewish cookery and identity, see, for example, Barbara Kirshenblatt-Gimblett, "The Kosher Gourmet in the 19th Century Kitchen: Three Jewish Cookbooks in Historical Perspective," *Journal of Gastronomy* 2, no. 4 (winter 1986–87): 1–22; Diana Cole, "Fin-de-Siècle Feminist Food Culture," *Lilith* 22, no. 4 (January 1998): 31; Judith Friedlander, "Jewish Cooking in the American Melting Pot," *Revue Française d'Etudes Américaines* 11, no. 27 (1986): 87–98; Nicole Dyann Rousso, " 'People of the (Cook)Book': The Enculturation of American Jewish Women" (master's thesis, University of Southern California, 1998). On cooking in Mexican American communities, see Florence Fabricant, "Memories of Mexico: Seasoned by Time," *New York Times*, 2 December 1998, sec. F, p. 3; Brett Williams, "Why Migrant Women Feed Their Husbands Tamales: Foodways as a Basis for a Revisionist View of Tejano Family Life," in Linda Keller Brown and Kay Mussell, eds., *Ethnic and Regional Foodways in the U.S.: The Performance of Group Identity* (Knoxville: University of Tennessee Press, 1984). On cookbooks in Italian American communities, see Donna R. Gabaccia, "Italian American Cookbooks: From Oral to Print Culture," *Italian Americana* 16, no. 1 (1998): 15–23. On culinary traditions and identity in an Indian American community, see Krishendu Ray, "Meals, Migration and Modernity: Domestic Cooking and Bengali Indian Identity in the United States," *Amerasia Journal* 24, no. 1 (spring 1998): 105–27. See also Uma Narayan, "Eating Cultures: Incorporation, Identity and Indian Food," *Social Identities* 1, no. 1 (1995): 63–87. For a discussion of food traditions in a Japanese American community, see Valerie Matsumoto, "Rice and Reflections," in *Farming the Home Place: A Japanese American Community in California, 1919–1982* (Ithaca, NY: Cornell University Press, 1993). On cookbooks and Cajun culture, see Michael James Forêt, "A Cookbook View of Cajun Culture," *Journal of Popular Culture* 23, no. 1 (1989): 23–26; C. Paige Gutierrez, *Cajun Foodways* (Jackson: University Press of Mississippi, 1992); Patricia Perrine, "Louisiana French Foodways: The Perpetuation of Ethnicity in the Lafourche Area," *North American Culture* 2 (1985): 3–9; Bethany Ewald Bultman. "A True and Delectable History of Creole Cooking," *American Heritage* 38, no. 1 (1986): 66–73.

On gender, food, and cultural identity, see, for example, Josephine A. Beoku-Bettes, "We Got Our Own Way of Doing Things: Women, Food and Preservation of Cultural Identity among the Gullah," *Gender and Society* 9, no. 5 (October 1995): 535–55. On recipes and imperialism, see S. Zlotnick, "Domesticating Imperialism: Curry and Cookbooks in Victorian England," *Frontiers* 16, no. 213 (1996): 51–68. For an example of how recipes and food traditions sustained individuals under the most extreme conditions of oppression, that is, a Nazi concentration camp during World War II, see Cara Desilva, ed., *In Memory's Kitchen: A Legacy from the Women of Terezin* (Northvale, NJ: J. Aronson, 1996). See also Janet Fletcher, "Tattered Cookbook Sustains Life in a POW Camp," *San Francisco Chronicle*, 11 November 1998, sec. F, p. 1. On cookbooks, ethnicity, and identity, see Janet Theophano, "Home Cooking: Boston Baked Beans and Sizzling Rice Soup as Recipes for Pride and Prejudice," in Inness, *Kitchen Culture*. For a collection of essays dealing with women, ethnicity, race, sexual identity, oppression, class, food, and cooking, see Arlen Voski Avakian, ed., *Through the Kitchen Window: Women Writers Explore the*

Intimate Meanings of Food and Culture (Boston: Beacon Press, 1997), and Sherrie A. Inness, ed., *Pilaf, Pozole, and Pad Thais: American Women and Ethnic Food* (Amherst: University of Massachusetts Press, 2001).

The history of domesticity plays a central role in the history of American cookbooks. On the early history of domesticity, see Faye E. Dudden, *Serving Women: Household Service in Nineteenth-Century America* (Middletown, CT: Wesleyan University Press, 1983), Daniel E. Sutherland, *Americans and Their Servants: Domestic Service in the United States from 1800–1920* (Baton Rouge: Louisiana State University Press, 1981), Jeanne Boydston, *Home and Work: Housework, Wages, and the Ideology of Labor in the Early Republic* (New York: Oxford University Press, 1990). For good general monographs on domesticity, see Ruth Schwartz Cowan, *More Work for Mother: The Ironies of Household Technology from the Open Hearth to the Microwave* (New York: Basic Books, 1983); Glenna Matthews, *"Just a Housewife": The Rise and Fall of Domesticity in America* (New York: Oxford University Press, 1987); Hannah Glasse, *The Great American Housewife: From Helpmate to Wage Earner, 1775–1986* (Westport, CT: Greenwood Press, 1986), and Phyllis Palmer, *Domesticity and Dirt: Housewives and Domestic Servants in the United State, 1920–1945* (Philadelphia: Temple University Press, 1989). On the issue of gender, class, domesticity, and food preparation in particular, see especially Marjorie L. DeVault, *Feeding the Family: The Social Organization of Caring as Gendered Work* (Chicago: University of Chicago Press, 1991). For a study conducted in England, see Nickie Charles and Marion Kerr, *Women, Food and Families* (Manchester: Manchester University Press, 1988). For a limited, but interesting, survey of women's attitudes toward cooking, see Nancy Kate, "They Love to Cook," *American Demographics*, March 1989, 62.

For a feminist analysis of contemporary domestic ideology and its connection to cookbook publication, see Norma Allen Lesser, "Nothin' Says Lovin' Like Something from the Oven," *Off Our Backs*, May 1970, 10, and Susan J. Berkson, "Food for Thought," *Iris: A Journal about Women* 31 (summer 1994): 47. See also sociologist Beth A. Rubin's comments about a 1963 copy of *McCall's Cookbook* she received as a gift in 1973. Beth A. Rubin, *Shifts in the Social Contract: Understanding Change in American Society* (Thousand Oaks, CA: Fine Forge Press, 1996), 12. On the continued importance of cookery to defining women's social roles, see Elisabeth L'Orange Furst, "Cooking and Femininity," *Women's Studies International Forum* 20, no. 3 (1997): 441–58. See also Laura Shapiro, "Mmm, mmm, good," *Newsweek*, 25 September 1995, 64–67. On the *reality* of home cooking, that is, the rapidly decreasing number of families who actually eat "home-made" meals on a regular basis, see Margaret McKenzie, "Is the Family Meal Disappearing?" *Journal of Gastronomy* 7, no. 1 (winter–spring 1993): 34–45; Marilyn Gardner, "Is Anyone in the Kitchen with Dinah?" *Christian Science Monitor*, 25 February 1992, 14; and Elizabeth Larsen, "What's Not Cooking," *Utne Reader*, November–December 1992, 18–19. On the historical question of "family dinners," see Anne Murcott, "Family Meals: A Thing of the Past?" in *Food, Health, and Identity*, ed. Pat Caplan (New York: Routledge, 1997). For statistics on and discussion about women's responsibility for meal preparation, see Robert B. Schafer and Elisabeth Schafer, "Relationships between Gender and Food Roles in the Family," *Journal of Nutrition Education* 21, no. 3 (June 1989): 119–27; Lisa Harnack et al., "Guess Who's Cooking? The Role of Men in Meal Planning, Shopping, and Preparation in U.S. Families," *Journal of the American Dietetic Association* 98, no. 9 (September 1998): 995–1001; William McIntosh and Mary Zey, "Women as Gatekeepers of Food Consumption: A Sociological Critique," *Food and Foodways* 3, no. 4 (1989): 317–32.

For discussions about the time women and men spend on all domestic labor, see Susan Krafft, "The Heart of the Home," *American Demographics* 14, no. 6 (June 1992): 46–50; Beth Anne Shelton, *Women, Men, and Time: Gender Differences in Paid Work, Housework, and Leisure* (New York: Greenwood Press, 1992); Scott Coltrane, *Family Man: Fatherhood, Housework, and Gender Equity* (New York: Oxford University Press, 1996); Sarah Fenstermaker Berk, *The Gender Factory: The Apportionment of Work in American Households* (New York: Plenum Press, 1985); Julia A. Heath and David W. Bourne, "Husbands and Housework: Parity or Parody?" *Social Science Quarterly* 76, no. 1 (March 1995): 195–204; Judith Lorber, *Paradoxes of Gender* (New Haven: Yale University Press, 1994); Suzanne M. Bianchi, Melissa A. Milkie, Liana C. Sayer, and John P. Robinson, "Is Anyone Doing the Housework? Trends in the Gender Division of Household Labor," *Social Forces* 79, no. 1 (September 2000): 191–229.

A number of significant works on women and World War II address the issue of domesticity and women's social roles. See Susan M. Hartmann, *The Home Front and Beyond: American Women in the 1940s* (Boston: Twayne Publishers, 1982); Karen Anderson, *Wartime Women: Sex Roles, Family Relations, and the Status of Women during World War II* (Westport, CT: Greenwood Press, 1983); Lelia J. Rupp, *Mobilizing Women for War: German and American Propaganda* (Princeton: Princeton University Press, 1978); Elaine Tyler May, *Pushing the Limits: American Women, 1940–1961* (New York: Oxford University Press, 1994); Sharon Gluck, *Rosie the Riveter Revisited: Women, the War and Social Change* (Boston: Twayne Publishers, 1987); Maureen Honey, *Creating Rosie the Riveter: Class, Gender and Propaganda during World War II* (Amherst: University of Massachusetts Press, 1984).

Three important articles on women in the 1950s markedly influenced my analysis of post–WWII cookbooks: Joanne Meyerowitz, "Beyond the Feminine Mystique: A Reassessment of Postwar Mass Culture, 1946–1958," in *Not June Cleaver*, ed. Joanne Meyerowitz (Philadelphia: Temple University Press, 1994); Eva Moskowitz, " 'It's Good to Blow Your Top': Women's Magazines and a Discourse of Discontent, 1945–1965," *Journal of Women's History* 18, no. 3 (fall 1996): 66–98; and Nancy Walker, "Humor and Gender Roles: The 'Funny' Feminism of the Post–World War Suburbs," *American Quarterly* 37, no. 1 (spring 1985): 98–113.

Other secondary sources on women's experiences in the 1950s that shaped my work on the post–World War II era include Joyce Antler, "Between Culture and Politics: The Emma Lazarus Federation of Jewish Women's Clubs and the Promulgation of Women's History, 1944–1989," in *U.S. History as Women's History: New Feminist Essays*, ed. Linda K. Kerber, Alice Kessler-Harris, and Kathryn Kish Sklar (Chapel Hill: University of North Carolina Press, 1995); Xiaolan Bao, "When Women Arrived: The Transformation of New York's Chinatown," in Meyerowitz, *Not June Cleaver*; Ruth Feldstein, " 'I Wanted the Whole World to See': Race, Gender, and Constructions of Motherhood in the Death of Emmett Till," in Meyerowitz, *Not June Cleaver*; Margaret Rose, "Gender and Civic Activism in Mexican American Barrios in California: The Community Service Organization, 1947–

1962," in Meyerowitz, *Not June Cleaver;* Ricki Solinger, *Wake Up Little Susie: Single Pregnancy and Race before Roe v. Wade* (New York: Routledge, 1992).

On lesbian experiences during the 1950s, see John D'Emilio, *Sexual Politics, Sexual Communities: The Making of a Homosexual Minority in the United States, 1940– 1970* (Chicago: University of Chicago Press, 1983); Donna Penn, "The Sexualized Woman: The Lesbian, the Prostitute, and the Containment of Female Sexuality in Postwar America," in Meyerowitz, *Not June Cleaver;* Lillian Faderman, *Odd Girls and Twilight Lovers: A History of Lesbian Life in Twentieth Century America* (New York: Columbia University Press, 1991). For a detailed discussion of the lesbian bar subculture that flourished in the post–World War II era, see Elizabeth Lapovsky Kennedy and Madeline D. Davis, *Boots of Leather, Slippers of Gold: The History of a Lesbian Community* (New York: Routledge, 1993). On gay and lesbian life in the 1940s and 1950s, see Allan Bérubé, *Coming Out under Fire: The History of Gay Men and Women in World War II* (New York: Plume, 1990). See especially John D'Emilio, "The Homosexual Menace: The Politics of Sexuality in Cold War America," in *Passion and Power: Sexuality in History,* ed. Kathy Peiss and Christina Simmons (Philadelphia: Temple University Press, 1989).

On women and politics in the 1950s, see Harriet Hyman Alonso, "Mayhem and Moderation: Women Peace Activists during the McCarthy Era," in Meyerowitz, *Not June Cleaver;* Birmingham Feminist History Group, "Feminism as Femininity in the Nineteen Fifties?" *Feminist Review* 3 (1979): 48–65; Cynthia Harrison, *On Account of Sex: The Politics of Women's Issues, 1950–1968* (Berkeley: University of California Press, 1988); Susan Lynn, *Progressive Women in Conservative Times: Racial Justice, Peace, and Feminism, 1945 to the 1960s* (New Brunswick, NJ: Rutgers University Press, 1992); Leila J. Rupp and Verta Taylor, *Survival in the Doldrums: The American Women's Rights Movement, 1945 to the 1960s* (New York: Oxford University Press, 1987); Amy Swerdlow, "The Congress of American Women: Left-Feminist Peace Politics in the Cold War," in Kerber, Kessler-Harris, and Sklar, *U.S. History as Women's History;* Lynn Weiner, "Motherhood and the PTA: Bridging the Spheres of Private and Public Life in the Postwar Era" (paper presented at the annual symposium of the American Heritage Center on The Fifties Turn Fifty: The "Nuclear Family" and Postwar American Culture, University of Wyoming, September 1999).

For women's individual memories of domestic ideology in the 1950s, see Marge Piercy, *Parti-Colored Blocks for a Quilt* (Ann Arbor: University of Michigan Press, 1982); Caryl Rivers, *Aphrodite at Mid-Century: Growing Up Catholic and Female in Post-War America* (New York: Doubleday, 1973); Brett Harvey, *The Fifties: A Women's Oral History* (New York: Harper Collins, 1993); Benita Eisler, *Private Lives: Men and Women of the Fifties* (New York: Franklin Watts, 1986).

On popular culture and gender in the 1950s, see Wini Breines, *Young, White, and Miserable: Growing Up Female in the Fifties* (Boston: Beacon Press, 1992); Susan J. Douglas, *Where the Girls Are: Growing Up Female with the Mass Media* (New York: Times Books, 1994); Brandon French, *On the Verge of Revolt: Women in American Films of the Fifties* (New York: Frederick Ungar, 1978); Andrea Press, *Women Watching Television: Gender, Class, and Generation in the American Television Experience* (Philadelphia: University of Pennsylvania Press, 1991); Marion Nowak,

"'How to Be a Woman': Theories of Female Education in the 1950s," *Journal of Popular Culture* 9 (summer 1975): 77–83.

Social, political, and cultural histories of the 1950s abound. On McCarthyism and Cold War fears, see Paul Boyer, *By the Bomb's Early Light: American Thought and Culture at the Dawn of the Atomic Age* (Chapel Hill: University of North Carolina Press, 1994); Douglas Miller and Marion Nowak, *The Fifties: The Way We Really Were* (Garden City, NY: Doubleday, 1977); Mary Jeezer, *The Dark Ages: Life in the United States, 1945–1960* (Boston: South End Press, 1982); David M. Oshinsky, *A Conspiracy So Immense: The World of Joe McCarthy* (New York: Free Press, 1983); and Ellen Schrecker, *Many Are the Crimes: McCarthyisms in America* (Boston: Little, Brown, 1998). See also *Duck and Cover* (Washington, DC: Office of Civil Defense, 1983), video recording. On teenagers, see William Gaebner, *Coming of Age in Buffalo: Youth and Authority in the Postwar Era* (Philadelphia: Temple University Press, 1990); Beth Bailey, "Rebels without a Cause? Teenagers in the 1950s," *History Today* 40 (February 1990): 25–31; James Gilbert, *A Cycle of Outrage: America's Reaction to the Juvenile Delinquent in the 1950s* (New York: Oxford University Press, 1986).

On the civil rights movement, see Harvard Sitkoff, *A New Deal for Blacks* (New York: Oxford University Press, 1978); David J. Garrow, ed., *The Montgomery Bus Boycott and the Women Who Started It: The Memoir of Jo Ann Gibson Robinson* (Knoxville: University of Tennessee, 1987); Ann Moody, *Coming of Age in Mississippi* (New York: Dell, 1968); Thomas R. Brooks, *Walls Come Tumbling Down* (Englewood Cliffs, NJ: Prentice-Hall, 1974); Taylor Branch, *Parting the Waters: America in the King Years, 1954–1963* (New York: Simon and Schuster, 1988); Robert Wiesbrot, *Freedom Bound: A History of America's Civil Rights Movement* (New York: Norton, 1990); Juan Williams, ed., *Eyes on the Prize: America's Civil Rights Years, 1954–1965* (New York: Viking Press, 1987). On how television coverage of the civil rights movement affected viewers around the country, see David Halberstam, *The Fifties* (New York: Fawcett Columbine, 1993), 677–81.

To help frame my study of the prescriptive rhetoric in cookbooks, I consulted several secondary sources on others kinds of prescriptive literature. On etiquette manuals, see A. M. Schlesinger, *Learning How to Behave: A Historical Study of American Etiquette Books* (New York: Cooper Square, 1968); E. B. Aresty, *The Best Behavior* (New York: Simon and Schuster, 1970); Cas Wouters, "Etiquette Books and Emotion Management in the Twentieth Century," *Journal of Social History* 29, no. 2 (1995): 325–39. On parenting advice, see, for example, Nancy Weiss, "Mother, the Invention of Necessity: Dr. Benjamin Spock's Baby and Child Care," *American Quarterly* 18 (1977): 151–74. On sex advice and sex manuals, see Ronald Walters, *Primers for Prudery: Sexual Advice to Victorian America* (Baltimore: Johns Hopkins University Press, 2000); Peter Laipson, "'Kiss without Shame, for She Desires It': Sexual Foreplay in American Marital Advice Literature, 1900–1925," *Journal of Social History* 29, no. 3 (1996): 507–25. On medical advice, see, for example, Anita Fellman and Gordon Fellman, *Making Sense of Self: Medical Advice Literature in Late 19th-Century America* (Philadelphia: University of Pennsylvania Press, 1981). On gender, repression, and prescriptive literature, see Barbara Ehrenreich and Deirdre English, *For Her Own Good: 150 Years of Experts' Advice to*

Women (Garden City, NY: Anchor Press, 1978). On prescriptive literature and gender norms during the post–World War II period, see Susan Hartmann, "Prescriptions for Penelope: Literature on Women's Obligations to Returning World War II Veterans," *Women's Studies* 5 (1978): 223–39. On women's magazines as agents of both gender normalization and resistance, see Jacquelin Bix, "A Place to Resist: Reevaluating Women's Magazine," *Journal of Communication Inquiry* 16, no. 1 (1992): 56–71; Janice Winship, *Inside Women's Magazines* (New York: Pandora, 1987); Francesa Cancian and Steven Gordon, "Changing Emotion Norms in Marriage: Love and Anger in Women's Magazines Since 1900," *Gender and Society* 2, no. 3 (1988): 308–42; Cristanne Miller, "Who Talks Like a Women's Magazine? Language and Gender in Popular Women's and Men's Magazines," *Journal of American Culture* vol. 10, no. 3 (1987): 1–9; Jennifer Scanlon, *Inarticulate Longings: The Ladies' Home Journal, Gender, and the Promises of Consumer Culture* (New York: Routledge, 1995).

Scholars who study prescriptive literature offer a range of frameworks for investigating this aspect of popular culture. For an examination of prescriptive literature that argues that such advice has a direct and repressive influence on readers, see M.E. Melody and Linda M. Peterson, *Teaching America about Sex: Marriage Guides and Sex Manuals from the Late Victorians to Dr. Ruth* (New York: New York University Press, 1999). See also Meryl Altman, "Everything They Always Wanted You to Know: The Ideology of Popular Sex Literature," in *Pleasure and Danger: Exploring Female Sexuality,* ed. Carole S. Vance (New York: Routledge, 1984). For an analysis of the problems in using prescriptive literature in historical study, see Carl N. Degler, "What Ought to Be and What Was: Women's Sexuality in the Nineteenth Century," *American Historical Review* 5 (1974): 1476–90.

I took my sample of original sources from the cookbook collection at the Library of Congress (LOC) in Washington, DC. I chose to conduct my research at the Library of Congress for a number of reasons. The LOC maintains a high-quality World Wide Web site, which allows for a good deal of reliable long-distance on-line research. In addition, the LOC is the only library in the world that attempts to obtain a copy of every book published in the United States. Although this may be an impossible goal, and although books that are ostensibly housed in the LOC are sometimes lost or unavailable to the researcher, the LOC remains the most likely place to obtain a truly representative and systematically arranged sample of mainstream twentieth-century popular literature.

I also compared the LOC cookbook collection catalog information with the catalog information of the two other preeminent cookbook collections housed in research libraries—the Schlesinger Library at Radcliffe College and the New York City Public Library. I found the LOC collection had markedly more cookbooks available for the years 1920 to 1963. The Schlesinger owns a wonderfully diverse collection of charity and fund-raising cookbooks and cookery ephemera, as well as a good number of rare early American cookery texts, but has far fewer commercial cookbooks published from 1920 to 1963 (about 104 published from 1920 to 1941, as compared with 226 at the LOC; about 29 published from 1941 to 1945, as compared with 89 at the LOC; and about 102 published from 1946 to 1963, as compared with 215 at the LOC). Moreover, out of the 235 cookbooks listed at the Schlesinger, published from 1920 to 1963, I was able to examine 99 of those books at the LOC or about 42 percent. The New York City Public Library owns a more extensive commercial cookbook collection, but it is significantly smaller than the LOC's (about 199 published from 1920 to 1941, as compared with 226 at the LOC; about 59 published from 1941 to 1945, as compared with 89 at the LOC; and about 156 published from 1946 to 1963, as compared with 215 at the LOC). At least half of the books in the NYCPL collection (about 50 percent) are also listed in the LOC catalog.

Using the on-line Experimental Search System (ESS) at the Library of Congress web site, I found all entries listed under "cookery, American," and limited my search to books published during three time periods: the years 1920 to 1940, 1941 to 1945, and 1946 to 1963. The ESS provided an especially effective search tool because, unlike the other tools available at the time, the ESS allowed me to limit my search by date. It was a reliable system to the extent that over the course of two years, these particular searches yielded the same lists of books. However, the LOC categorized the ESS as an interim on-line catalog information retrieval system and has now phased out the ESS.

I disqualified a book for one or more of the following reasons: the book was a home economics or domestic science text not intended for home use but for school instruction; the book was permanently missing from the library's collection; the book was published by a community organization for fund-raising purposes; the book was limited to regional recipes only; the book was a repeated entry or a later edition of an earlier book that had not been substantially revised; the book disqualified for miscellaneous reasons (it was not a cookbook, it was published in England, it was self-published or no publisher was listed, recipes in book were intended for business and not personal use, date of publication was missing or unclear, recipes were for historical interest only and not for personal use). Most of the books that I disqualified I personally examined. The ESS entry sometimes provided enough information to disqualify a book without my examining it, especially in the case of fund-raising cookbooks.

Out of the 763 books listed for the years 1920 to 1941, 226 qualified for my sample. I disqualified 65 books as home economics texts, 38 books as missing, 122 books as fund-raising books, 43 books as regional books, 71 books as repeated entries, and 198 books for miscellaneous reasons. Of the remaining 226 books, I closely examined 111 books, or about half of the sample (49 percent). This 49 percent was chosen randomly from the overall sample. In addition, I examined seven books in the Library of Congress collection that were not listed under "cookery, American" but under "cookery" or "cookery, juvenile literature." I included these seven as examples of important trends in cookbook publishing—cookbooks for children, cookbooks for small kitchens, and cookbooks written by men—that were not adequately represented in the original sample. I chose them randomly from available books.

Out of the 182 books listed for the years 1941 to 1945, 89 qualified for my sample. I disqualified 7 books as home economics texts, 4 books as missing, 19 books as fundraising books, 12 books as regional books, 15 books as repeated entries, and 36 books for miscellaneous reasons. Of the remaining 89 books, I closely examined 58 or a little over half (53 percent). This 53 percent was chosen randomly from the overall sample.

Out of the 538 books listed for the years 1946 to 1963, under "cookery, American," 215 qualified for my sample. I disqualified 17 books as home economics texts, 16 books as missing, 81 books as fundraising books, 67 books as regional books, 54 books as repeated entries, and 88 books for miscellaneous reasons. Of the remaining 215 books, I closely examined 115 or a little over half (53 percent). This 53 percent was chosen randomly from the overall sample. The fact that this sample was smaller than the sample of books published from 1920 to 1940 does not reflect a decrease in cookbook publication after World War II. In fact, it shows the opposite. Because the Library of Congress holds significantly more cookbooks published from 1946 to 1963, it has created more detailed categories for these cookbooks. For instance, the LOC does not list a cookbook of casserole recipes published in the postwar period under "cookery, American," but under "cookery, casseroles." Although experts in the field of cookbook history note that we cannot know exactly how many cookbooks are in circulation at any one time, primary sources such as *Publishers' Weekly* offer evidence that publication of cookbooks increased after World War II.

With this variable in mind, I examined 44 additional books in the Library of Congress collection not listed under "cookery, American" but under "cookery" or "cookery, juvenile literature." I included these books as examples of important trends in cookbook publishing—cookbooks for children, cookbooks for small kitchens, cookbooks written by men, "gourmet" cookbooks, outdoor cookery, cooking in the suburbs, cookbooks written for use with electric appliances, and additional examples of widely published authors whose other work appeared in the original sample but were not adequately represented in the original sample. I chose these randomly from available books.

Only a few cookbooks in the LOC collection offer the researcher any information beyond the printed text. In other words, the majority of cookbooks owned by the library contain no markings inside the book or in the margins, and certainly no additional clippings or notes stuck in the pages. Few of the cookbooks owned by the LOC have been used for cooking in private homes. They lack, therefore, some of these important historical clues about how people actually utilized cookbooks. In fact, Jan Longone, in her capacity as proprietor and archivist at the Wine and Food Library in Ann Arbor, Michigan, has seen only a small percentage of cookbooks with written expressions of use out of the literally thousands of cookbooks that have passed through her store. The information cited about margin notes and recipe clippings that owners left in cookbooks came from additional, outside copies of the same books that I examined at the LOC. I was only able to obtain a small percentage of additional copies. I or friends and family purchased most of these second copies, owned and used by individual consumers, at secondhand bookstores in Michigan, Ohio, California, Oregon, Virginia, or Washington, DC, or I received them as gifts. This evidence is obviously fragmentary, but nonetheless compelling, and I have utilized it as much as possible while freely acknowledging its limitations.

My sample also included recipes and cooking tips in domestic magazines published from 1920 to 1963. Such evidence can, at a minimum, give us some information about what other kinds of gender-specific recipes and rhetoric existed during this time. Furthermore, it reveals some of the ways that advertisers promoted food products and kitchen appliances to a large, mainstream audience.

I chose to limit my close study of cookbooks to the years 1920 to 1963 for three important reasons. First, most historians concur that 1920—a year that saw the end of World War I, the suffrage of American women, and the concerted beginnings of a truly consumerist society—ushered in what we know now as the modern era in the United States. Second, the year 1963 stands as a significant turning point in the American political and cultural landscape. The publication of Betty Friedan's *The Feminine Mystique* (New York: Norton, 1963) created important changes in popular discussions of gender, and the assassination of President John F. Kennedy effectively marked the ending of an idealistic postwar period in the United States. Finally, cookbook publication itself changed significantly in the early 1960s. Most notably, the number of cookbooks published in the United States increased dramatically. Cookbook publication has increased every year since the end of World War I, but in the mid-1960s general commercial cookbooks became, in my opinion, simply too numerous and too diverse for the historian to obtain a truly representative sample. Instead, I limited my discussion about post-1963 cookbooks to broad observations and comments.

Finally, a note on the theoretical framework of this book. Like feminist historian Joan Wallach Scott, I believe that scholars interested in gender issues must not limit their research by reiterating "man" and "woman" as natural givens. Rather, we should attempt "to understand the operations of the complex and changing discursive processes by which identities are ascribed, resisted, or embraced, and which processes themselves are unremarked, indeed, achieve their effect because they are not noticed." See Joan Wallach Scott, "Experience," in *Feminists Theorize the Political*, ed. Judith Butler and Joan W. Scott (New York: Routledge, 1992), 33. As mass-produced texts, often created to promote a particular food or appliance, cookbooks in the 1920s through the 1950s usually remained "unnoticed" by consumers and by cultural critics. But as instructional texts, they gave detailed accounts of the "correct," often gender-specific way to undertake the activity of cooking. They ascribed gender, as well as class and race, onto the activity of cooking, and often did so in subtle ways. In particular, cookbook authors reiterated and emphasized the differences between male and female appetites, food preferences, and cookery techniques. They implied the "naturalness" of these differences, but a natural, obvious difference does not require constant definition and explanation. Cookbooks constantly and uniformly linked certain kinds of food preparation and gender; authors and editors clearly felt that these links needed to be articulated and explained. For a detailed discussion of the way such rhetoric reveals the unnaturalness of gender categories, see Judith Butler, "Imitation and Gender Insubordination," in *The Lesbian and Gay Studies Reader*, ed. Henry Abelove, Michele Aina Barale, and David M. Halpern (New York: Routledge, 1993).

Index